TOWNS IN A RURAL WORLD

Ashgate Economic Geography Series

Series Editors:

Michael Taylor, University of Birmingham, UK
Peter Nijkamp, VU University Amsterdam, The Netherlands
Jessie Poon, University at Buffalo-SUNY, USA

Innovative and stimulating, this series enlivens the field of economic geography and regional development, providing key volumes for academic use across a variety of disciplines. Exploring a broad range of interrelated topics, the series enhances our understanding of the dynamics of modern economies in developed and developing countries, as well as the dynamics of transition economies. It embraces both cutting edge research monographs and strongly themed edited volumes, thus offering significant added value to the field and to the individual topics addressed.

Other titles in the series include:

Global Companies, Local Innovations
Why the Engineering Aspects of Innovation Making Require Co-location
Yasuyuki Motoyama

Economic Spaces of Pastoral Production and Commodity Systems
Markets and Livelihoods
Edited by Jörg Gertel and Richard Le Heron

Towns in a Rural World

Edited by

TERESA DE NORONHA VAZ
Universidade do Algarve, Portugal

EVELINE VAN LEEUWEN
VU University Amsterdam, The Netherlands

PETER NIJKAMP
VU University Amsterdam, The Netherlands

Routledge
Taylor & Francis Group

LONDON AND NEW YORK

First published 2013 by Ashgate Publishing

Published 2016 by Routledge
2 Park Square, Milton Park, Abingdon, Oxfordshire OX14 4RN
711 Third Avenue, New York, NY 10017, USA

First issued in paperback 2016

Routledge is an imprint of the Taylor & Francis Group, an informa business

British Library Cataloguing in Publication Data
Towns in a Rural World. – (Ashgate Economic Geography Series)
    1. Rural development. 2. Rural-urban relations. I. Series II. Vaz, Teresa de Noronha.
    III. Leeuwen, Eveline S. van. IV. Nijkamp, Peter.
    307.1'412–dc23

The Library of Congress has cataloged the printed edition as follows:
Towns in a Rural World / [edited] by Teresa de Noronha Vaz, Eveline van Leeuwen
    and Peter Nijkamp.
    pages cm. – (Ashgate Economic Geography Series)
    Includes bibliographical references and index.
    1. Rural development. 2. Small cities. 3. Rural-urban relations. I. Vaz, Teresa de
    Noronha. II. Leeuwen, Eveline S. van. III. Nijkamp, Peter.
    HN49.C6T69 2013
    307.1'412–dc23   2012047422

ISBN 13: 978-1-138-24603-4 (pbk)
ISBN 13: 978-1-4094-0692-1 (hbk)

Contents

List of Figures

List of Tables

List of Contributors

Aliye Ahu Akgün, Department of Urban and Regional Planning, Istanbul Technical University, Turkey.

José Antonio Camacho Ballesta, International and Spanish Economics Department, Regional Development Institute, University of Granada, Spain.

Ana Paula Barreira, Faculty of Economics, University of Algarve, Faro, Portugal.

Tüzin Baycan, Department of Urban and Regional Planning, Istanbul Technical University, Turkey.

Claudia Chlebek, North Central College, Ireland.

Rita D. Coelho, Catholic University, Lisbon, Portugal.

J. Dias Coelho, Faculty of Economics, New University of Lisbon, Portugal.

Daniela L. Constantin, Department of Statistics and Econometrics, Academy of Economic Studies, Bucharest, Romania.

Anca Dachin, Department of Economics and Economic Policies, Academy of Economic Studies, Bucharest, Romania.

Ségolène Darly, Department of Geography, University Paris 8 Vincennes Saint-Denis.

Tomaz Dentinho, University of the Azores, Portugal.

John Dodd, EUROCITIES Network, Brussels, Belgium.

José Luis Navarro Espigares, International and Spanish Economics Department, Regional Development Institute, University of Granada, Spain.

Zbigniew Florianczyk, Institute of Agricultural and Food Economics - National Research Institute, Poland.

Fernando P. Fonseca, University of Minho, Portugal.

John Glasson, Oxford Brookes University, United Kingdom.

Jenny Grek, Department of Economics, Jönköping International Business School, Jönköping University, Sweden.

Zizi Goschin, Department of Statistics and Econometrics, Academy of Economic Studies, Bucharest, Romania.

Keith Harrison, Economic Development Officer, Gateshead City Council.

Charlie Karlsson, Department of Economics, Jönköping International Business School, Jönköping University, Sweden.

Johan Klaesson, Department of Economics, Jönköping International Business School, Jönköping University, Sweden.

Helen Lawton-Smith, Department of Management, Birkbeck, University of London, United Kingdom.

Eveline van Leeuwen, Faculty of Economics and Business Administration, VU University, Amsterdam, the Netherlands.

Peter Nijkamp, Faculty of Economics and Business Administration, VU University, Amsterdam, the Netherlands.

Teresa de Noronha Vaz, Faculty of Economics, University of Algarve, Faro, Portugal.

José António Porfírio, Department of Social Sciences and Management, Universidade Aberta, Portugal.

Rui A. R. Ramos, Department of Civil Engineering, University of Minho, Portugal.

Waldemar Ratajczak, Institute of Socio-Economic Geography and Spatial Management, Adam Mickiewicz University, Poznań, Poland.

Emília Malcata Rebelo, Faculty of Engineering, Oporto University, Portugal.

André Torre, National Institute for Agronomic Research, Paris, France.

Adam Wasilewski, Institute of Agricultural and Food Economics – National Research Institute, Poland.

Clive Winters, Institute of Applied Entrepreneurship, Coventry University, United Kingdom.

Preface

The dichotomy of urban versus rural areas is increasingly losing its relevance. Urban lifestyles, industrial high-tech development, advanced service production, access to higher education, use of modern ICT facilities, they can all be found in rural areas. These areas are increasingly seen as ecological landmarks, characterized by a healthy life, a high environmental quality and a highly respected local identity. Nevertheless, rural areas are not uniform. On the contrary, they exhibit a rich variety of socio-economic, cultural, ecological and physical-geographical appearances. In addition, they also have a great diversity of settlement patterns in which normally towns play a key role of carriers and poles of socio-economic, cultural and political activity. Towns form the links between rural tradition and modern life.

Nowadays, it is almost impossible to write on such a topic like the future of small towns without taking into account societal views on the values of rural heritage and tradition, as a counterbalance for urban cultural and technical progress. In general, people are divided on what concerns the advantages and disadvantages of the historical rural exodus. During recent decades, this exodus has gradually emptied small rural towns to enlarge big towns all over the world. Such global movements have raised several social concerns such as whether high quality of life in big agglomerations is possible, and how the social tensions may be manageable in the future.

Rural towns are not just players in a protected and quiet rural area, but also are subjected to the forces of internationalization, social networks, and modern ICT and technology. Their economic vitality is not undisputed, and in various cases it is even threatened. Although a resort to the old traditional 'village model' is not feasible, it is important to explore pathways that link the historical position of rural towns to the challenges of a high-tech society. Can we combine rurality with modernity?

Solutions for such concerns require a broad social consensus, and through informed democratic channels citizens have to be made aware of actions that are needed in times of change. Hence, policy makers and planners are no longer totally free to act independently from deep-rooted public opinion. It is important to find out what the citizens really want before taking final decisions on rurality and urbanity. Taking this into consideration, for citizens, local living conditions belong to those sets of amenities that mean much to them. In general, the population is reluctant to let small towns vanish, as they are part of a poetic and romantic imagery of childhood and enchantment – a historic past view of hope and expectation of glory. It is painful to abandon the best memories and forget the poetry of past lifestyles. So, is it really necessary to let such memories fade away?

This volume contains a set of original research contributions on the position of towns in rural areas. They are the result of a research programme at the University of the Algarve in Faro, Portugal on rural-urban developments. After a careful review procedure they were selected for publication in the present book. The editors wish to thank Patricia Ellman, who took care of the editorial check of this volume, and Ellen Woudstra, who did the finishing touch. And of course, all authors have to be thanked for their willingness to torture their brains in order to produce a high-quality contribution to this volume on 'Towns in a Rural World'

Faro and Amsterdam

TERESA DE NORONHA VAZ,
EVELINE VAN LEEUWEN and PETER NIJKAMP

PART I
Introduction

Chapter 1

Small Towns of Hope and Glory

Teresa de Noronha Vaz and Peter Nijkamp

Our world has undergone drastic changes in settlement patterns over the past few centuries, moving from a mainly rural world to a predominantly urban world. This spatial transformation has made cities – and, more in general, urban areas – focal points of economics, cultural and political power. This urbanization trend has exerted significant impacts on the position of rural areas, which are nowadays often associated with peripheral areas, less favoured areas or low-potential areas.

It should be noted, however, that rural regions are nowadays striking back, for three main reasons: their potential as a resource area for advanced, high-tech agriculture; their increasingly important role as a playground for creative and innovative small business activities; and their sustainability function in ecologically-protected areas. Against this background, it is interesting to address the socio-economic potential of towns in rural areas, as they are often the anchor points for new developments. They also form a bridge between social community capital and ecological cultural heritage, on the one hand, and the new growth and creativity trends, on the other.

Free market forces will most likely erode the socio-economic and cultural position of rural areas and their historically-grown settlement patterns. But strict governmental intervention to safeguard towns in rural areas will most likely fail as well. So, is there a 'third way' in which the self-reliance and self-organization of these towns can be enhanced through smart policies?

These and other concerns have been expressed at the level of the free blogsphere where civil society shows increasing interest in sharing the responsibility of participating together with policy makers in those decision-taking processes related to urban planning and landscape shaping.

Notwithstanding this, sociologists, economists and architects seem to be in favour of a general trend to concentrate assets in and around the large cities. Now that new technologies are available, it seems possible to manage agglomerations so efficiently that cost reductions become unbeatable and tempting. But, does the rural world have to stay apart from technological innovation and knowledge sharing? Why should not new information and communication technologies or other innovative inputs be available outside the big agglomerations and thus allow old localities to undertake other, novel, functions?

Most probably many citizens are ready to be open-minded in order to construct a different world in the rural environments. As argued in Vaz et al. (2006, 2008), multitasking is possible in the rural word, indicating that small and medium-sized towns have a very specific role in promoting economic activities outside big urban agglomerations. Simultaneously reflecting the past and envisioning the future, policy makers should in any case act to consider the potential major role of small towns. Were they to remain inactive, the future trends would not leave much for new generations to recall nostalgically about the small towns.

But, how is it possible to argue in favour of such small urban structures if, at a first sight, they generate less agglomeration or scale economies, and neither, so far, do they produce economic efficiencies or opportunities?

The strength of supportive arguments for rural areas lies in the pro-active functions that such towns may display: they are able to define a local networking system that provides a framework for sustaining knowledge, agent relationships, tourism and environmental responsibilities, thereby contributing to the concept of new rurality (Vaz and Nijkamp, 2009).

The present book focuses on the strategic position of towns in rural development. By acting as hotspots for knowledge creation and diffusion so essential for vital business life and innovativeness, and for social networks and community bonds, towns – even the smallest – can cope with the processes of socio-economic decline and promote a geographically-balanced income distribution and sustainable production structure. How to take advantage of the great potential offered by urban areas in the rural world in order to stimulate competitiveness and encourage economic activity is extensively discussed in the 17 chapters included in this volume "*Towns in a Rural World*".

The authors of the various contributions have tried to identify the main socio-economic advantages generated by the urbanized population settlements that small and medium-sized rural towns can provide – seen from a European perspective. And, notwithstanding the current attention to the efficient use of scarce natural resources and land, they argue for the increasingly important economic and social role of towns in rural areas. To that end, a rich set of empirical observations from different small towns across many European countries – Sweden, Portugal, France, the Netherlands, Romania, the United Kingdom, the Netherlands and Poland – is presented.

The book is subdivided into five parts. Part I, the Introduction, is composed of two different chapters. Chapter 1, *Small Towns of Hope and Glory*, co-authored by Teresa de Noronha Vaz and Peter Nijkamp, focuses on those restrictions and responsibilities expected from modern urban systems when sustainable development is on the agenda. Chapter 2, *Towns Today and their Multifunctional Activities*, by Eveline van Leeuwen, describes those advantages that are emerging in today's multifunctional rural world. Indeed, they can help to meet the strict ecological requirements by promoting social inclusion and economic performance – the dual perspective which reflects the reality of European rurality today.

In order to discuss how small and medium-sized towns are becoming prepared for the new challenges of the future, Parts II – IV of the book are devoted to the analysis of networking, knowledge transfers and the consequently-created urban-rural interdependencies, and attempts to define new models of land-use management. It may be considered that this book supplies information and methods that shift from the meso-economic approaches to a micro-understanding of the agents' attitudes.

Part II, Rural Networks and Partnerships, is composed of five chapters which analyse the macroeconomic conditions for efficient networking in rural contexts.

In Chapter 3, *The Role of Small and Medium-sized Towns in Local and Regional Economies* by Waldemar Ratajczak, it is argued that, despite the explosive growth of large cities, the economic and social role of small and medium-sized towns is still considerable, especially at local and regional scales. This is because they form part of the continuum that stretches from urban agglomerations to the countryside. It is shown that the rank of a particular town of this group of towns still depends on its centrality in the sense of Christaller's Central Place theory, and also that the socio-economic rank of a small or medium-sized town depends to some extent on its location relative to metropolitan areas and on the quality of the rural space.

Next, in Chapter 4, *Market Potential and New Firm Formation*, Jenny Grek, Charlie Karlsson and Johan Klaesson show how the conditions for entrepreneurship vary between regions of various sizes. They test the theoretical arguments as to why, in general, large regions should generate more entrepreneurship. The empirical study analyses the role of regional size in explaining variations in total entrepreneurship in different sectors across functional regions, using data from Sweden for the period 1993 to 2004. Using fixed effects vector decomposition regressions, the authors conclude that the market potential, as measured by local and external accessibility to gross regional product, has a strongly significant impact on both the entry of new firms and on firm exit. Further, the presence of many small firms in the different sectors has also had a strong positive significant impact on new firm formation in all sectors of such regions.

Chapter 5, *New Economic Geography and Rural Development; the Importance of Corporate Strategy for Economic Development of Rural Regions* by José António Porfírio, suggests the need to rely on new economic concepts to better understand and guide effective rural development policies. The text emphasizes the primary sector in order to propose the integration of the new concept of Agriculture District in the framework of the New Economic Geography, so as to produce more successful business strategies by entrepreneurs in the primary sector.

José Luis Navarro Espigares and José Antonio Camacho Ballesta's Chapter 6, *Public-Private Partnership in Small and Medium-sized Towns*, describes how public-private partnerships may offer expectations of expansion plus a beneficial image in relation to the upgrading of facilities associated with public services when promoted by the local authorities of small towns. The data was basis of the Private Finance Initiative in the United Kingdom, and the findings corroborate a clear predominance in recent years of local services provided through PPP schemes in the UK and in most other European countries as well.

The last Chapter 7 of Part II, *Social and Political Determinants of the Area of Influence of Medium-sized Towns,* by Ana Paula Barreira, discusses whether lack of scale should be considered a restriction to regional development. Relevant variables identify cities' area of influence and help us to evaluate whether political choices have the tools to increase such spaces. A case study of Portugal is used to investigate whether integrated networks between medium-sized towns should be considered as adequate solutions, and, if so, what are the possible hindrances for the strategic implementation of such networks.

Part III, Knowledge Transfers in Rural Environments, emphasizes the specific role of learning for the new concept of rurality, starting with Chapter 8 by Helen Lawton Smith and John Glasson, *Technological Transfer in the Perspective of Town Dimension: the Case of Oxford and Oxfordshire in the U.K.* It is discussed how and why the area in and around the small but important City of Oxford has evolved from a rural economy with several agricultural-based industries, an ailing motor plant, and an ancient university, into one of the most innovative and enterprising economies in the U.K. In exploring how Oxfordshire has emerged as an innovative place, the chapter focuses on the entrepreneurs and the organizations which have driven change and on others which have co-evolved with the increasingly entrepreneurial economy. In addition, the changing functional interfaces between the different actors responsible for the making of this innovative place are analysed, as well as those kinds of communication methods and tools that have been used to overcome problems through the actions of individuals and organizations in filling boundary-spanning roles. Also highlighted are some of the local tensions that exist as a consequence of the evolution of the county as an international centre of high-tech activity which has created pressure on the rural environment.

In the following Chapter 9, *Divided Knowledge on Small and Medium-sized Towns*, Tomaz P. Dentinho, Rita D. Coelho and J. Dias Coelho discuss whether restructuring of space attributable to the new information and communication technologies can lead to divided knowledge systems in the small and medium-sized towns where the value chains of basic and non-basic activities are becoming increasingly detached from each other. They examine this hypothesis by looking at the key value chains of small and medium-sized towns: namely, those of agriculture, tourism, and health, and search for the main factors which are conducive to their competitive unity.

The Role of Universities for Economic Development in Urban Poles is evaluated in Chapter 10 by Clive Winters, John Dodd and Keith Harrison. The authors argue that there are clear and significant gaps in the knowledge of how smaller sized cities, with different levels and types of knowledge institutions and different levels of economic activity, can compete within the Knowledge Economy. Yet such cities are recognized within European Union policy as playing a vital role in the implementation of the Lisbon agenda. The analyses focus on the major role of universities that should engage with their local communities, in particular in the medium-sized cities where the local authorities and municipalities mostly contribute to the Triple-Helix structures by supporting economic development and encouraging entrepreneurship.

Chapter 11, by *Anca Dachin, Daniela L. Constantin and Zizi Goschin, The Influence of the Urban-Rural Gap on the R&D and Innovation Potential in Romania,* contains an analysis of the urban-rural disparities in Romania, followed by an examination of the policy measures designed to ensure higher competitiveness in rural areas and, on this basis, a structural convergence between rural and urban areas in the long run. Special emphasis is put on the role of towns located in the predominantly rural areas. Also discussed are the expected results of the current rural development programme, as well as those of the regional operational programme and the competitiveness sectoral programme funded by the EU.

Chapter 12, The Entrepreneurship Dynamic in Rural Tourism: the Case of the Portuguese Municipality of Almeida proposes a revised plan to deal with controversial impacts of rural tourism on development. The research undertaken by Fernando F. Fonseca and Rui A.R. Ramos presents the main conclusions for the peripheral and rural municipality of Almeida, where tourism is regarded as the most promising activity to overcome the current trend of decline. Data were collected from Rural Tourism entrepreneurs, using a previously applied survey about perceptions of, and attitudes to, tourism development in the Municipality. The findings suggest that the contribution of Rural Tourism in socio-economic regeneration and heritage rehabilitation is limited, contradicting some generalized rhetoric and policies. The main weaknesses are related to the low demand, the lack of essential skills, the ageing entrepreneurs, the reduced returns obtained, and the lack of local cooperation. Because of the common nature of the problems involved, some conclusions of this research can be extrapolated to other peripheral and rural territories.

Part IV is dedicated to Urban-Rural Interdependencies, in an attempt to encourage novel specific functionalities for the rural world in the possible interaction it may achieve with the urban economies. Starting with Chapter 13, *How Knowledge on Land Values Influences Rural-Urban Development Processes*, Emília Malcata Rebelo stresses how important information about land and real estate values is for the development processes of successful regional and urban planning. Knowledge of their underlying variables and valuation processes, the relations between rural and urban land, the temporal perspectives of land-use changes, as well as the behaviour of the agents involved, which all permit control of the appreciation of land and real estate values and assure a fair distribution on behalf of society, may all help to avoid land speculation and permit a more equitable and sustainable growth.

Land values in the rural world do not vary as significantly as in the urbanized areas, but, nevertheless, the intrinsic value of land in small towns may change significantly, depending of their quality of life and the beauty of their surroundings. Chapter 14, *From Depreciation to Appreciation of Rural Areas – 'Beauty Idols' in Europe* by Aliye Ahu Akgün, Tüzin Baycan-Levent and Peter Nijkamp, identifies the most important factors associated with the attractiveness of villages. These factors are compared by means of a newly-generated statistical attractiveness index, and a list of the most important characteristics of such settlements is provided in order to promote the attractiveness image of villages, while maintaining a sense of locality and community.

Chapter 15, by Zbigniew Florianczyk, Adam Wasilewski and Claudia Chlebek, focuses on *ICT's Role in Rural Areas' Neighbouring Towns – Stakeholders' Perception* and investigates the relationship between Information and Communication Technologies (ICT) and economic development processes of, specifically, the rural areas surrounding small town centres. The authors argue that the identification of the potential of ICT is critical for the stimulation of rural areas, particularly by experts and leaders in those municipalities surrounding cities. In order to contradict the picture drawn by the European Commission reports that confirm the exclusion of rural populations in the digital society, the authors propose the concept of a complex interaction between the economy and ICT to the rural world. They apply their model to observe the Polish stakeholders' perception of ICT's role in rural development.

Empirical observation of the forms of agriculture developing on the periphery of cities reveals the generalized presence of peculiar types of production or commercialization, which explains why certain sectors, such as the vegetable growing industry are considered peri-urban industries. In Chapter 16, Ségolène Darly and André Torre discuss in Chapter 16 the *Land Use Conflicts and the Sharing of Resources between Urban and Agricultural Activities in the Greater Paris Region: Results based on Information Provided by the Daily Regional Press.* They compile a quantitative inventory of the conflicts related to the use of agri-urban resources located within the Greater Paris Region, in order to evaluate the scales of action implemented by the local actors according to the space-related issues from which conflict arises, and highlight the socio-economic situations that combine the spatial and social conditions that are conducive to the actors' engaging in conflict.

Part V, the Conclusion is devoted entirely to the final Chapter *Lessons from Successful Small Towns* which alerts the readers to future prospects for rural areas, as well as to their potential opportunities and implications for new spatial developments. In addition, the tendency for what are called agglomeration economies, favourable to the explosion of mega-towns, will be discussed. Nevertheless, on the basis of speculative arguments about the human need for proximity to nature and its romantic associations, the authors Teresa de Noronha Vaz, Eveline van Leeuwen and Peter Nijkamp anticipate a positive trend for the future of European rural towns.

References

Vaz, T.N., Morgan, E. and Nijkamp, P. (Eds) 2006. *The New European Rurality: Strategies for Small Business*. Ashgate, Economic Geography Series: London.
Vaz, T.N., Nijkamp, P. and Rastoin, J.L. (Eds) 2008. *Traditional Food Production and Rural Sustainable Development: A European Challenge*. Ashgate, Economic Geography Series: London.

Vaz, T.N. and Nijkamp, P. 2009. Multitasking in the rural world: technological change and sustainability. *International Journal of Agricultural Resources, Governance and Ecology*, 8(2), 111-129.

Chapter 2

Towns Today and Their Multifunctional Activities

Eveline van Leeuwen

2.1. Introduction: Changing Rural Areas

Just like urban areas, rural areas have undergone significant changes over the last 50 years. In the literature (Bryant, 1989), the main forces that have changed rural areas, in particular, are often identified as population, institutions and technology. Population changes relating to changes in values are seen as key driving forces underlying the urbanization process, drawing people away from rural areas and into urban employment opportunities. Institutional changes alter the parameters within which rural businesses, including farms, function. Interest rates are modified, subsidies and price-support systems and levels are determined, and international trade in commodities, a major component of the production of rural areas, regulated and affected (Bryant, 1989). An important example is the reaction of overproduction due to agricultural policies, falling world prices for agricultural commodities, and growing public concern over the environmentally damaging impacts of modern farming practices (Share *et al.,* 1991). Financial and political pressure to reduce agricultural subsidies has grown, which has resulted in a significant decrease in subsidies devoted to agriculture.

Technological change moves in certain directions, influenced by government spending priorities and perceptions of problems and by the profit-motive of technology- supplying industries. All these alter the mix of technologies available, as well as their prices (Bryant, 1989). In particular, technological developments in agricultural and industrial activities have had a great impact on local economic linkages and employment.

In many rural areas, these developments have led to a decline in the importance of not only 'traditional' rural economic activities, such as agriculture, but also forestry, fishing, mining and quarrying. At the same time, employment has risen overall in rural areas in the manufacturing, tourism and service sectors. However, like agriculture, the rural service sector has experienced considerable change in its form and function. The transition to larger production units in agriculture has resulted in progressively smaller numbers of farms and a shrinking farm population (Smithers *et al.*, 2005). Transportation and communications technology have reduced the historical reliance of local households, including entrepreneurs, on their local community for goods and services (Fuller, 1994). In this more 'open' society, many services (*e.g.* banks, schools) traditionally available in rural settlements have been consolidated and centralized, with implications for the employment base of rural towns and villages and for rural service users with limited mobility (Joseph, 2002). On the other hand, changes in the relative costs of housing, travel and transport have encouraged a diverse range of individuals, households and firms, often unrelated to agriculture or agricultural service industries, to relocate to rural settlements (Smithers *et al.,* 2005; van Leeuwen and Nijkamp, 2006).

Many (inter)national policies are increasingly concentrating on the multifunctionality and economic diversity of rural areas. Therefore, in this chapter, the focus will be on the contemporary functions of European towns and their hinterlands. The functions of towns will be assessed from a household perspective, as well as from a more macroeconomic point of view.

First, in Section 2.2 some theoretical perspectives will be given about multifunctional rural areas, describing both their ecological and socio-economic functions. Section 2.3 deals with the importance of towns and their hinterland for households as places to shop and work. Then, in Section 2.4 the economic diversity of small and medium-sized towns is shown, followed by the conclusions.

2.2. Multifunctional Rural Areas

The recent reforms of the Common Agricultural Policy (CAP) introduced the decoupling of subsidies to production, and the possibility to reduce the direct payments to the farmer if sustainability standards are not respected (cross-compliance). This includes the recognition of the multifunctionality of agriculture and a multi-sectoral and integrated approach to the rural economy in order not only to diversify activities and create new sources of income and employment but, also to conserve the rural heritage and landscape.

The most common definition of multifunctionality is based on the idea of the joint production of commodity and non-commodity outputs by farms. However, the term also applies to the overall diversification of the economy in rural areas, *i.e.* the regional level (Rodríguez Rodríguez *et al.*, 2004).

The new farming context, with a variety of goals and actions, is bringing about a more diversified use of rural areas, partly similar to the use of rural areas before the productivism period, but with a less significant role for the agricultural sector (see Wilson, 2001). The increasing leisure time and mobility of residents is leading to a higher number of visits to rural areas. As well as that, environmental qualities attract residents who want to live in the countryside. The renewed awareness of the value of nature, culture and landscapes is encouraging the conservation of these elements. This has resulted in an increasing interest in what are called ecosystem-functions. These functions can be defined as the capacity of natural processes and components to provide goods and services that satisfy human needs, directly or indirectly (de Groot et al., 2002). They are often grouped into four classes: production, habitat provisions, regulation, and information.

Ecosystem services maintain biodiversity through the provision of habitats and the production of ecosystem goods, such as seafood, forage, timber, biomass fuels, natural fibre, and many pharmaceutical and industrial products. These products are also important inputs to our economy. In addition, ecosystem services also include life-support functions such as cleansing, recycling, and renewal, as well as the conservation of many intangible aesthetic and cultural benefits (Daily, 1997).

In general, it is the rural areas that hold those precious services. But, of course, rural areas provide more services apart from ecosystem services. Williams (1969, in Bryant *et al.*, 1982) divides the functions of open spaces (rural areas) into six classes:

- Functions involving activities that are primarily located in the production function (such as agriculture or mineral production);
- Functions involving especially natural and cultural values (such as sites with particular biological or cultural values);
- Functions related to health, welfare and well-being, including 'protection' functions and 'play' functions (such as maintenance of groundwater quality and recreation areas);
- Functions related to public safety and natural or man-made hazards (such as flood control and aircraft flight paths);
- Space for corridors and networks (such as infrastructure and nature networks);
- Space for urban expansion.

Although most of those functions are somehow related to ecosystem services, Williams also recognizes the importance of the need to make space available for infrastructure and urban expansion. Often, it is particularly those functions that threaten the ecological values present. However, in order to protect them, it is necessary that the (local) socio-economic system is in balance and that institutional regulations can be executed. Therefore, towns are indispensable elements in nature conservation and rural development.

Towns used to have a symbiotic relationship with their surrounding area, acting as a source of firm and farm inputs (both goods and services), as a first market destination for farm outputs, as a provider of (supplementary) employment and income to households, and as a source of consumer goods and services for households (Tacoli, 1998). Furthermore, they are often the place where the local authority is located and from which several policies are regulated. From this we can distinguish four important advantages or functions of towns:

- Concentration of firms (agglomeration advantages);
- Concentration of consumers (residents and visitors);
- Concentration of facilities;
- Concentration of institutions.

When looking at the importance of small and medium-sized towns today, there is, on the one hand, a trend for such towns to become less important for local households as a result of, for example, the globalization of markets, the centralization of health and education services, the growth of new types of shopping facilities, the reduced cost of transport services, and the development of telecommunication networks. Most of these factors have reduced the transaction costs that in the past encouraged rural firms and households to conduct most of their transactions in the immediate locality. However, on the other hand, the development of telecommunication networks, technological changes, and reduced transport costs also provide opportunities for a more diverse range of firms and individuals to relocate to some of the rural settlements. Over the years, the symbiosis between towns and their hinterland has certainly changed, but towns can still be considered as important tools in rural development, not only in peripheral areas but also in the vicinity of cities. Towns are locations where rural activities meet and where (often) organizational advantages are found (van Leeuwen, 2010).

2.3. Towns as a Place to Shop and Work

In this section, the focus is on the importance of towns for local households. Our empirical analysis concerns 24 towns with between 5,000 and 20,000 inhabitants, located in England, the Netherlands, Poland and Portugal. In addition, the direct hinterland is also taken into account in order to understand more about the urban-rural interactions and the symbiosis between town and hinterland.

2.3.1. Data collection

For this study, data has been used that was collected as part of a transnational project, the European Union research project 'MARKETOWNS'. This project studied the role of small and medium-sized towns as growth poles in regional economic development. For this purpose, it was necessary to measure the flow of goods, services and labour between firms and households in a sample of 30 small and medium-sized rural towns in five EU countries.

In each of the participating countries, six small and medium-sized towns were selected with reference to a set of relevant, predefined criteria: for instance, the condition that no other town with more than 3,000 inhabitants should be located in their hinterland within a radius of approximately 7 km from the edge of the town. In this contribution we will focus on 24 towns in England, the Netherlands, Poland and Portugal.[1]

Primary data were collected using self-completion survey techniques to measure the spatial economic behaviour of households living in town or in the direct hinterland within a 7 km radius. The questionnaire focused on the spatial

---

1   France was excluded from the analysis due to data problems.

patterns of consumer purchases by distinguishing between different categories of goods and services and expenditure patterns across the town, the hinterland (within the 7 km radius) and the rest of the world. In addition, households were questioned about the location and kind of job(s) they have. Surveys were carried out between September 2002 and May 2003 (Terluin *et al.*, 2003). For this analysis almost 5,000 household questionnaires were used (see Appendix A2.1 for more information about the towns).

2.3.2. Towns as a place to shop

Towns act as a concentration point of facilities, both for households living in town (T-HH) and for the households living in (often) more remote locations in the hinterland (H-HH). The functional relationship between a town and its hinterland can be indicated by a specific flow of products and services from the central place to its hinterland, or by a reverse flow of demand from the hinterland to the central place (Klemmer, 1978).

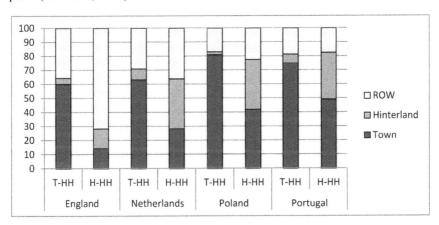

Figure 2.1   **Share of purchases done by town households (T-HH) and in the hinterland households (H-HH) in the three distinguished zones**

Figure 2.1 shows the percentages of purchases made in town shops, hinterland shops, or in shops outside the local economy, in the rest of the world (ROW). To derive these shares, all purchases (including groceries, medicines, health services, insurance, furniture, etc.) of both T-HH and H-HH have been taken into account. It appears that, in general, the towns are the most important location for T-HH to do their shopping: around 60 per cent of the English T-HH purchases are made in town, and even as much as 80 per cent of the Polish T-HH. Except for England, the H-HH also do a lot of shopping in the hinterland, closer to their home. However, they also visit the towns, in particular for durable goods such as clothing and furniture, and for more specific services such as medical care. In England, the local economy is less important, and in particular the H-HH tend to do their shopping further away from the town, often in a bigger city.

2.3.3. Towns as a place to work

Nowadays, with an increasing population, the consumption function of the countryside is becoming more and more important for all kind of citizens. Rural areas close to larger cities are considered as the backyard of thousands of urban residents. At the same time, the increasing accessibility of city and hinterland allow rural residents to work and enjoy cultural activities in the city.

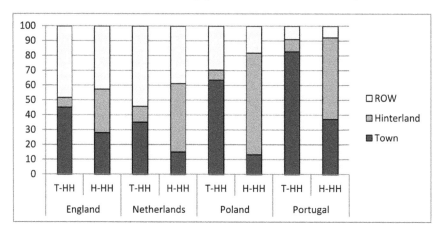

Figure 2.2   Share of households living in town (T-HH) or hinterland (H-HH) that have (a) job(s) in one of the three distinguished zones

Figure 2.2 shows the share of households living in town or hinterland with a job in the town, the hinterland, or in the rest of the world (ROW).

Considering towns as a place to work, it appears that, in all four countries towns, but particularly in Poland and Portugal, towns are an important place of work for the T-HH. In addition, not more than 10 per cent of the T-HH work in the hinterland. On the other hand, only in England and Portugal are towns also important for the employment of H-HH. In general, the hinterland seems to be more important for H-HH as a place to work than as a place to shop. In addition, in Portugal the local economy (town and hinterland) is the most important to the households, in England it is the least.

Overall, we can conclude that towns are still important places for facilities and jobs for local households. It appears that only between 2 and 15 per cent of the T-HH do not shop[2] or have no job in town. Furthermore, between 26 and 69 per

---

2   Less than 30 per cent of their total shopping.

cent of the H-HH do not shop or do not practise their profession in the hinterland. In fact, for most of these H-HH, the town has a central function for shopping or working. Although considerable differences between the countries are found, it can be concluded that the towns with their facilities and jobs are vitally important for the households that reside in town, as well as in the hinterland.

2.4. Economic Diversity in Town and Hinterland

The regional literature offers the hypothesis that more industrially-diverse areas should experience more stable economic growth and less unemployment than less-diverse areas. An important argument is the robustness of the economy (Pasinetti, 1981). Dissart (2003) argues that economic diversity should be fostered, since there is a concern that economic cyclical fluctuations could adversely affect industries, workers, and their communities. The presence of multiple economic sectors in a given region reduces employment fluctuations in that region. Pasinetti (1981) also supports this positive long-term effect of diversity on the economic system. He argues that an economy that does not increase the diversity of sectors over time will ultimately suffer from structural unemployment and stagnate. In addition, the development of new sectors in an economy is required to absorb redundant labour from pre-existing sectors (Malerba, 2006).

$$(1) \quad S = \sum_{i=1}^{n} P_i \log_2 \left(\frac{1}{P_i} \right)$$

To assess the diversity level of small and medium-sized towns and their hinterland we use the Shannon index with a classification into 22 industries:[3]
were P is the share of jobs in a specific industry. The measure can run from 0 to infinity, and higher numbers indicate higher levels of diversity.

Figure 2.3 shows the level of diversity of European towns according to their size and typology: a large share of employment in agriculture, a large share of employment in tourism, or a location close to a city. Furthermore, the small towns have a population between 5,000 and 10,000, and the medium-sized towns between 15,000 and 20,000. The darker bars show the diversity in employment in the towns, the lighter bars the level of diversity in the hinterland areas.

---

3   We adopt Frenken's (1999, 2004) version of the entropy measure, which uses a log with base 2, rather than the natural log, since the sectors we use are mutual by exclusive, and log base 2 captures this distinct difference better.

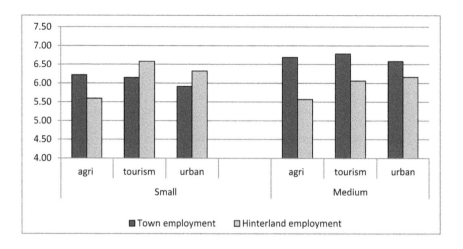

Figure 2.3   Economic diversity of European small and medium-sized towns according to their typology

First of all, it appears that, apart from the more agricultural areas, the hinterland economy is more diverse than the small town economies. However, the town economies in agricultural areas are on average the most diversified amongst the small towns. Apparently, in these areas, even the small towns still have an important function in providing complementary services to their hinterland. On the other hand, the towns located close to a bigger city (the urban towns) are on average less diversified.

The larger towns, referred to as medium-sized towns, have in general a more diversified economy than the smaller towns. In addition, their hinterlands are less diversified than the hinterlands of smaller towns.

Apart from differences between different types of towns, also significant differences appear between the four countries in which the towns are located (see Figure 2.4). Again, it appears that the larger towns have a more diversified economy compared with the small towns. In addition, the level of diversity in the medium-sized towns is quite similar in the different countries. The picture for the hinterland is, however, less clear.

Clearly, the Polish hinterlands are the least diversified, due to the large number of jobs in the agricultural sector. In general, the Dutch hinterlands are most diversified. Here, there are many small settlements located in the rural areas, and the level of facilities is in general high. From this perspective, the English hinterlands are very different, with often a very limited number of shops or other facilities available. The number of jobs is half of the number available in the Dutch situation. However, the jobs in England are spread over many different sectors and not concentrated in, for example, only the agriculture or service sectors.

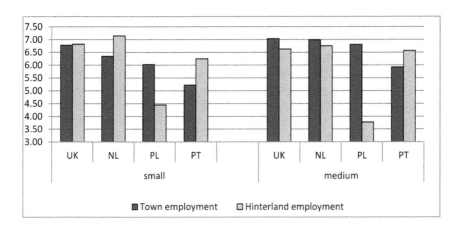

Figure 2.4   Economic diversity of small and medium-sized towns per country

Note: UK= United Kingdom; NL=Netherlands; PL=Poland; PT=Portugal.

When the economic diversity level of the towns and their hinterland is compared with the national diversity levels (which range from 7.2 in the Netherlands to 7.7 in England), it appears that, in particular, the economic diversity of the medium-sized towns is quite comparable. However, in the small towns, the economy is less diverse which could be a reason for concern for the future. Particularly in countries such as Poland and Portugal, where households and firms are still very dependent on the local economy, the economy could be more vulnerable to shocks in a particular sector.

2.5. Conclusions

An important characteristic of many rural areas still is the dominant position of the agricultural sector. Not only is the production process of farms different from that of firms, but also the lifestyle of those persons active in the agricultural sector often differs from the rural lifestyle of those who are engaged in other non-farm activities. With the decreasing economic importance of agriculture, new economic activities are possible and needed in rural areas in order to achieve more consistency between urban and rural areas.

In this chapter, we have focused on the multifunctionality of rural areas and towns. When rural areas are seen as places that contain important functions such as (agricultural) production, biodiversity, regulation, storage and networks, and towns as places with a concentration of facilities and institutions, then it is easy to understand that they complement each other.

The analysis of 24 European towns showed that towns are important places for local households to shop and to work. Especially in Poland and Portugal, households are still very dependent on the local economy. However, it is also in those countries that the economic diversity is relatively low. In particular, the Polish rural areas still have a large share of total employment in agriculture. This means that new developments, such as new farming regulations, new technologies or modernization will have very strong local effects. People who lose their jobs will have few opportunities to find a new one and thus will have less money to spend in the local economy.

However, towns, in particular, are very important places from which to start new economic activities and local development projects, and, at the same time, preserve the indispensable ecosystem services.

References

Bryant, C.R. 1989. Entrepreneurs in the rural environment. *Journal of Rural Studies*, 5(4), 337-348.

Bryant, C.R., Russwurm, L.H. and McLennan, A.G. 1982. *The City's Countryside: Land and Its Management in the Rural-Urban Fringe*. Longman: London.

Daily, G.C. 1997. *Nature's services: societal dependence on natural ecosystems.* Island Press: Washington D.C.

Dissart, J.C. 2003. Regional economic diversity and regional economic stability: research results and agenda. *International Regional Science Review*, 26, 423-446.

Frenken, K. 1999. Entropy statistics as a methodology to analyse the evolution of complex technological systems. Application to aircraft, helicopters and motorcycles Prepared for the European Meeting on Applied Evolutionary Economics Grenoble, France.

Frenken, K. 2004. Entropy and information theory, in *The Elgar Companion to Neo-Schumpeterian Economics*, edited by H. Horst and A. Pyke. Edward Elgar: Cheltenham.

Fuller, T. 1994. Sustainable rural communities in the arena society, in *Towards Sustainable Rural Communities: The Guelph Seminar Series*, edited by J.M. Bryden. University of Guelph: Guelph, 133-139.

Groot, de R.S., Wilson, M.A. and Boumans, R.M.J. 2002. A typology for the classification, description and valuation of ecosystem functions, goods and services. *Ecological Economics*, 41(3), 393-408.

Joseph, A.E. 2002. Rural population and rural services, in *The Sustainability of Rural Systems: Geographical Interpretations*, edited by I.R. Bowler, C.R. Bryant and C. Cocklin. London: Kluwer, 211-224.

Klemmer, P. 1978. Methods for the determination of centrality, in *The Analysis of regional structure: essays in honour of August Lösch*, edited by R. Funck and J.B. Parr. London: Pion Limited.

Leeuwen, E.S. van 2010. Urban-Rural Interactions: Towns as Focus Points in Rural Development. Heidelberg: Physica Verlag.

Leeuwen, E.S. van and Nijkamp, P. 2006. The embeddedness of small enterprises to the rural economy of small and medium sized towns, in *The New European Rurality, Strategies for small firms,* edited by Teresa de Noronha Vaz, Eleanor Morgan and Peter Nijkamp, London: Ashgate.

Malerba, F. 2006. Innovation and the evolution of industries. *Journal of Evolutionary Economics,* 16(1), 3-24.

Marsden, T. 1998. Theoretical approaches to rural restructuring: economic perspectives, in *The Geography of Rural Change*, edited by B. Ilbery, Essex: Longman, 13-30.

Pasinetti, L.L. 1981. *Structural change and economic growth.* Cambridge: Cambridge University Press.

Rodríguez Rodríguez, M., Galdeano Gómez, E. and Céspedes Lorente, J. 2004. *Rural multifunctionality in Europe: the concept and policies*: Paper presented to the 90th EAAE Seminar: Multifunctional Agriculture, Policies and Markets: Understanding the Critical Linkages, Rennes, 28–29 October.

Share, P., Gray, I. and Lawrence, G. 1991. *Rural sociology and the sociology of agriculture: research priorities for rural sociologists in the 1990s*: Proceedings of the Rural Economy and Society Section of the Sociological Association of Aotearoa (N.Z.), 113-157. Discussion Paper n.º 29, Agribusiness and Economics Research Unit.

Smithers, J., Joseph, A.E. and Armstrong, M. 2005. Across the divide (?): Reconciling farm and town views of agriculture–community linkages. *Journal of Rural Studies*, 21(3), 281-295.

Tacoli, C. 1998. Rural-urban interactions: a guide to the literature. *Environment and Urbanization*, 10, 147-166.

Terluin, I.J., Leeuwen, M. van and Pilkes, J. 2003. *Economic linkages between town and hinterland: a comparative analysis of six small and medium-sized towns in the Netherlands.* LEI: The Hague.

Williams, E.A. 196). *Open Space: the Choices before California.* Report to the California State Planning Office, San Francisco: Diablo Press.

Wilson, G.A. 200). From productivism to post-productivism... and back again? Exploring the (un)changed natural and mental landscapes of European agriculture. *Transactions of the Institute of British Geographers*, 26, 77-102.

Appendix A

Table A2.1 Towns used in the analysis

Country	Towns	Size	Type
England	Leominster	Small	Agriculture
	Swanage	Small	Tourism
	Towcester	Small	Urban
	Tiverton	Medium	Agriculture
	Burnham-on-Sea	Medium	Tourism
	Saffron Walden	Medium	Urban
The Netherlands	Dalfsen	Small	Agriculture
	Bolsward	Small	Tourism
	Oudewater	Small	Urban
	Schagen	Medium	Agriculture
	Nunspeet	Medium	Tourism
	Gemert	Medium	Urban
Poland	Glogówek	Small	Agriculture
	Duzniki	Small	Tourism
	Ożarów	Small	Urban
	Jędrzejów	Medium	Agriculture
	Ultsroń	Medium	Tourism
	Lask	Medium	Urban
Portugal	Mirandela	Small	Agriculture
	Tavira	Small	Tourism
	Lixa	Small	Urban
	Vila Real	Medium	Agriculture
	Silves	Medium	Tourism
	Esposende	Medium	Urban

PART II
Rural Networks and Partnerships

Chapter 3

The Role of Small and Medium-Sized Towns in Local and Regional Economies

Waldemar Ratajczak

3.1. Introduction

In the contemporary landscape of each country, small and medium-sized towns (SMESTOs) are a very common phenomenon. This is due to the urbanization processes of the past and those still occurring today that are connected with the social division of labour and the emergence of settlements of a peculiar kind, differing from villages primarily in functional terms – that is, towns.

Without going into the details of chartering a settlement as a town, whether in the past or today, let us note that this status is not conferred on it once and for all, especially in the case of small and medium-sized units; it can be retracted. For instance, in Poland with its 897 towns in 2009, as many as 206 of them, or about 23 per cent, have once received, then lost, and then had their municipal rights reinstated. The largest group of such towns, about 15 per cent, embraces those with a population of under 5,000, while no such vagaries of fate have ever happened to those with over 100,000 inhabitants. This process can be found to occur with varying intensity in every country.

In the 21st century, a further increase in the urban population is anticipated at the global scale, but primarily in giant cities which offer much more promising lifestyle opportunities not only to individuals, but also to entire communities with a specified political, cultural, ethnic, economic, etc. identity of their own (see Nijkamp, 2008). But advances in knowledge, including the development of various kinds of technology, affect the organization of socio-economic life at practically every spatial scale, and hence also in small and medium-sized towns. What is, therefore, their future? An answer to this question has been sought by a great number of authors, for instance Courtney et al. (2000, 2007), *Economic Linkages ...* (2005), ESPON (2006), de Noronha Vaz et al. (2006), Tacoli (2004), Tacoli et al. (2002), and others.

It goes without saying that small and medium-sized towns do not make a uniform category; they differ in many respects. Ignoring the historical aspect, we can state that the main factors determining the rank of a small or medium-sized town today are: its links with the surrounding agricultural areas; its location with respect to a metropolis (thus making it easier or harder to be included in innovative economic processes); the presence of the creative class as a dominant group in the town's social capital; and the extent to which it follows the rules of sustainable development (see Kunzmann, 2007; Lorenzen and Andersen, 2009; Trutkowski and Mandes, 2005).

Small and medium-sized towns that fill the continuum between big cities and villages also have to draw on the resources offered by rural areas, which should be seen in a perspective broader than merely the agricultural sector. They usually account for more than 90 per cent of the area of a country or region. That is why the European Union initiatives for rural development, like LEADER, play a significant part in moulding the future of those towns.

The chief aim of this chapter is to identify factors shaping the role that small and medium-sized towns play today in local and regional economies. An additional goal is to present the conception of sustainable development as a condition for successful development of this category of urban places.

3.2. Small and Medium-Sized Towns in Europe

Social processes of the division of labour are responsible for the fact that the biggest set of units in the settlement system of almost every country is that of rural ones, followed by the set of small and medium-sized towns and then that of large and very large cities. The smallest set, altogether absent from some countries, is that of global cities. This regularity was observed by Zipf (1935, 1949) in the 1930s and 40s. Thus, in 2009 in Poland, the set of small and medium-sized towns (of up to 50,000 inhabitants) with its 813 units accounts for 90.6 per cent of all urban places, but constitutes a mere 1.47 per cent of rural settlements. Since the transformation of rural units into towns is a continuous rather than a discrete process, there are urban settlements without municipal rights (Figure 3.1), in Poland and other countries, that are a potential set of future small towns. Figure 3.2, constructed as a result of geographical-historical studies, illustrates the growth process of urban settlements located in Poland's present territory over the period 1870-1931.

A comparison with Figure 3.3 shows that between 1931 and 2009 many of those urban settlements were chartered as towns, while a substantial number of small towns lost their municipal status. At this point it would be well to observe that the terms 'small town' and 'medium-sized town' have not been given a clear definition, either in science or economic practice.

The most penetrating research on the understanding of SMESTOs in science and the economy is presented in the ESPON 1.4.1 Final Report (2006) prepared under the leadership of the Austrian Institute for Regional Studies and Spatial Planning (ÖIR). It shows that in most countries small and medium-sized towns are defined in terms of both quantitative and qualitative variables. The chief criteria employed include population size, centrality, and territorial impact, supported by an analysis of functions of units that are likely candidates for the SMESTO group.

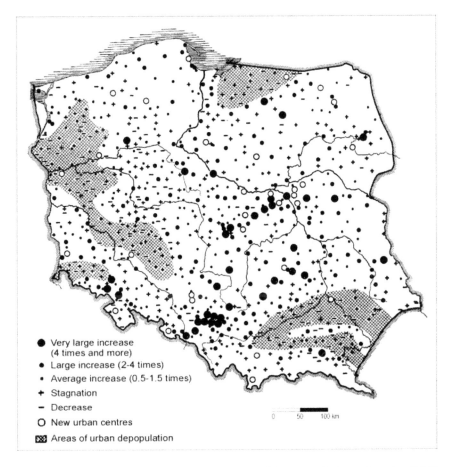

Figure 3.1   Towns and urban settlements with a population of under 5,000 (voivodeship capitals included for clarity. Administrative division as of 1950)

Source: Kiełczewska-Zaleska (1957, p. 41).

The ESPON Report proposes an ingenious ex-ante algorithm to identify SMESTOs. Its application, however, requires considerable preparatory work. In other reports on small and medium-sized towns the categories for delimiting the SMESTO group are simpler and of an ex-post nature. For instance, the MARKETOWNS project, coordinated by Mayfield et al. (2005), identifies such towns on the basis of their population: 5,000-10,000 (small) and 15,000-20,000 (medium-sized). In turn, in the Economic Linkages project (2005), small towns are those with a population of 3,000-10,000. Naturally, those are purely formal definitions. From the social and economic perspectives, small towns are specific communities with specific internal and external functions. The interpersonal

Figure 3.2   Types of urban growth from 1870 to 1931 on present-day Polish territory

Note: A voivodeship is the Polish equivalent of a county or province.

Source: Dziewoński (1964, p. 48).

system of relations makes human links stronger in them, respect for tradition deeper, and cultural assets preserved with special care. Small towns display a social relativism of time: in them it passes 'slower'.

These examples show that, owing to the complexity of socio-economic and historical processes occurring in various countries, it is impossible to establish a single, universal definition of SMESTOs (Bell and Jayne 2006, pp. 1-18). The socio-economic rank of such towns also depends on other factors operating in different countries with different strength, such as total population, level of development of the settlement system, type of the national economy, etc. However, since characteristics like small, medium or large usually refer to the size of the object studied, small and medium-sized towns are understood as those whose

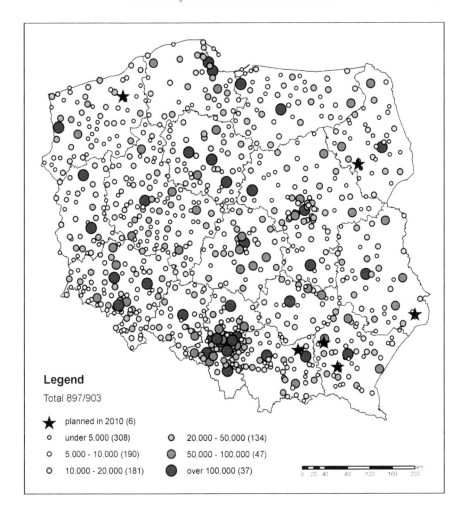

Figure 3.3   Towns of Poland, 2009/2010

Source: Own compilation.

population figures are lower than those of other towns (of the given spatial unit) and range within an interval established by, for example, an expert method. The population number must be treated as the principal factor when deciding about the size of a town (its area is of minor importance), because there simply are no towns without residents. And other factors determining the rank of a town, competitiveness included, derive from the abilities, talent and skills, not only of individuals, but of entire social groups and their capacity for self-organization.

Understandably enough, the arbitrariness of the definition of a SMESTO makes international comparisons somewhat difficult. An example is the map in Figure 3.4 presenting the distribution of towns /municipalities with a population of 5,000-10,000. In some situations it may generate some confusion. For instance, the

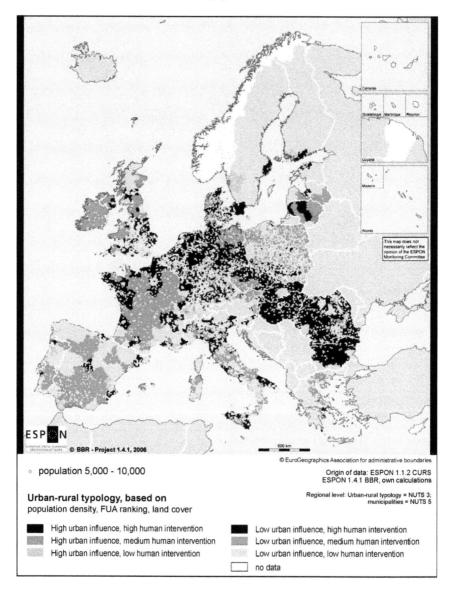

Figure 3.4   European towns with a population of 5,000 to 10,000

Source: ESPON (2006).

distribution of Polish towns within the same population interval, 5,000 – 10,000 and 10,000 – 20,000, are presented in Figures 3.5 and 3.6, respectively.

Naturally, there are fewer of them than suggested by the map in Figure 3.4. Rather, they can be interpreted as presenting the distributions of localities among which are both, actual and potential SMESTOs. This is because in the landscape of Europe there are many places that are not towns, but that, on meeting certain criteria, may become towns. A similar situation for Poland in a historical approach was presented in Figure 3.1.

The current situation in Europe is such that the most numerous spatial units are those described as towns /municipalities (ESPON, 2006, p. 30-32) inhabited by 5,000-10,000 and 10,000-20,000 people. They account for as many as 81.8 per cent of all the towns /municipalities embraced by the research. This corroborates

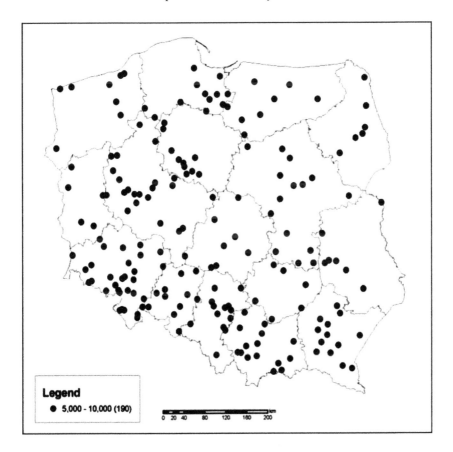

Figure 3.5   Small towns of Poland, 2009/2010

Source: Own compilation.

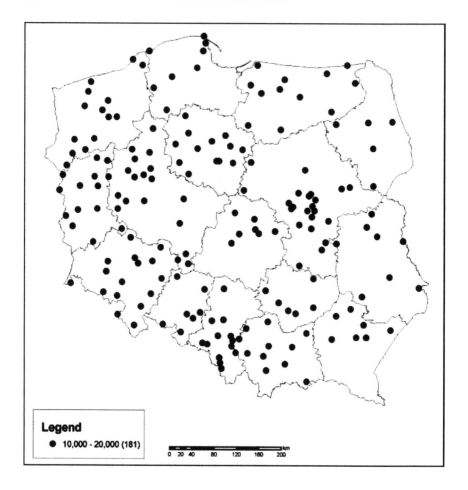

Figure 3.6   Medium-sized towns of Poland, 2009/2010

Source: Own compilation.

the significance of both the existing and potential SMESTOs in the continent's settlement system and, to some extent, in its economy.

Figure 3.7 presents a power model describing the dependence between the proportion of towns /municipalities and population classes. Immediately visible is that this is, in fact, Zipf's model giving a good fit to real data sets.

In turn, Figure 3.8 shows that the proportions of the population living in the European towns/municipalities belonging to the 5,000-10,000, 10,000-20,000 and 20,000-50,000 classes are constant and amount to 19.6 per cent, 19.9 per cent and 19.8 per cent, respectively. Jointly, those classes account for 59.3 per cent of the population of all the units considered. The proportion of people living in the 50,000-100,000 class is markedly lower, at 12.6 per cent, while the figure is the

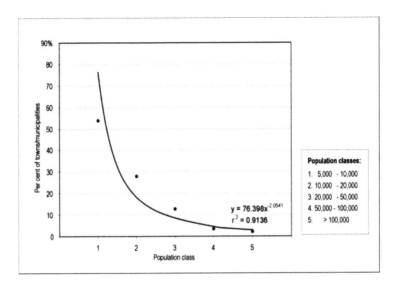

Figure 3.7   Proportion of towns/municipalities in Europe by size-class, 2006

Source: Based on ESPON (2006, p. 30) data.

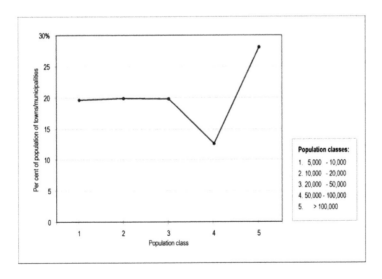

Figure 3.8   Proportion of the population of towns/ municipalities by size-class in Europe, 2006

Source: Based on ESPON (2006, p. 30) data.

highest, at 28.1 per cent, for the class with more than 100,000 inhabitants. In other words, predominant in Europe's settlement system are towns with a population of up to 50,000 and cities with more than 100,000, while much fewer people live in units from the 50,000-100,000 interval. Figure 3.8 also corroborates the exceptional role of SMESTOs in this system.

3.3. Theory of the Development of a Network of Small and Medium-Sized Towns

The existence of small and medium-sized towns in the landscape of each country or region is an undeniable fact (Figure 3.4). They have appeared as a result of urbanization processes that transform urban settlements without municipal rights into small towns. An explanation of why this happens requires the construction of a suitable scientific theory that would accommodate both the economic and the social aspect of this transformation; both, because towns (including small and medium-sized ones) are not merely the sum total of functions, houses, streets and squares, but primarily they are people, their hopes and expectations. This view has been held for centuries.

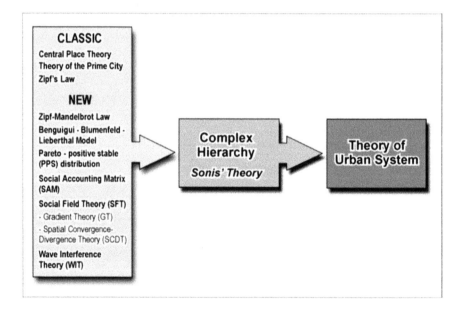

Figure 3.9   Theories of the SMESTO network

Source: ESPON (2006), modified.

Today there is no such general theory. Instead, we have theories focusing on the economic aspect: Christaller's central place theory, the prime city theory, and to some extent Zipf's theory (Figure 3.9).

These theories were worked out in the previous century, hence they do not fully match the growth processes of contemporary towns and world-scale megatrends (see Taylor et al. 2008). Even so, central place theory is still the basic theoretical frame of reference when explaining changes in the structure of the network of towns of various sizes. That is also why the notion of centrality remains the chief element in assessing the attractiveness of small and medium-sized towns (see ESPON, 2006). In this case centrality is understood:

1. in terms of functional analysis, treated as a study of a town's functions performed for the area surrounding it (its hinterland); this is a more general and prevailing approach;
2. in terms of a functional analysis of towns based on the concept of basic/non-basic functions; this is a more restricted functional approach (Wróbel, 1964); or
3. as a spatial-geographic perspective in which the position of a SMESTO located at the central point of the surrounding area plays an important role in minimizing distances to consumers (see ESPON, 2006).

Establishing the degree of centrality and ranges of hinterlands in which the influence of those functions is felt still poses a major research problem. Hence, new methodological solutions keep appearing in the literature concerning the identification of the most significant characteristics of a system of variously sized towns. Among them are new approaches to Zipf's phenomenological law, the identification of the most important functions of towns, and the delimitation of hinterlands. For instance, the Social Accounting Matrix (SAM) is employed to explore intra- and interregional flows in order to establish the structure of a local economy. In turn, the delimitation of the zones of influence of towns (including SMESTOs) can be carried out more precisely using methods of social physics and econophysics, such as spatial convergence-divergence analysis, gradient analysis, and wave interference analysis (Chojnicki, 1999, pp. 101-174).

Figure 3.10 presents the spatial distribution of gradients of the population potential function determined for the Wielkopolska region on the basis of the populations of 100 towns located there. As can be noted, the region divides naturally into several areas of influence delimited by borderlines that form where the gradients meet. Those areas can be regarded as approximate hinterlands of the towns.

More detailed information about areas surrounding the towns is presented in Figure 3.11. Here towns with high population potentials are surrounded by divergent areas, and those with low potentials, by convergent ones. Their spatial distribution can be interpreted in terms of functions performed by the urban centres.

The process of formation of small and medium-sized towns can be explained to some extent by the wave interference theory (WIT) outlined by Arida (2002) in

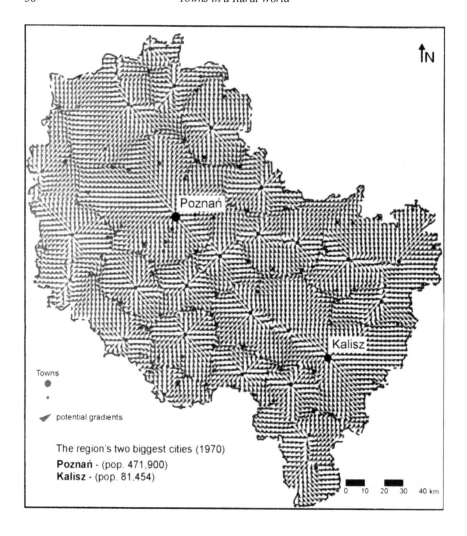

Figure 3.10   Gradients directed towards the highest increase in the potential function

Source: Ratajczak (1999).

a quantum theory context. Figure 3.12 illustrates this mechanism. In this approach, a significant role is played by urban-rural complementary duality. According to Arida (2002, p. 212), 'In the quantum metaphor every element is a duality and part of a higher order duality, which is qualitatively and quantitatively different from its two complementary aspects.' Figure 3.13 presents hinterlands where the propagation of waves from their central places is stopped by sharp boundaries of whatever nature (social, economic, cultural, etc.). By contrast, Figure 3.14

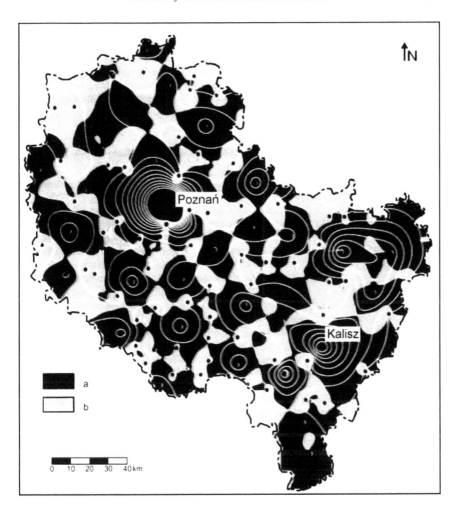

**Figure 3.11   Areas of spatial divergence (a) and convergence (b) in the
potential field of the Wielkopolska region**

Source: Ratajczak (1999).

presents an overlap and interference of the towns' waves. Some borders that
naturally delimit the hinterlands of the different towns can also be identified.

Another important issue that should be taken into account when considering
the spatial distribution of hinterlands of variously sized towns is the fact that the
hexagonal lattice providing the geometrical basis of Christaller's theory is in fact a
deterministic fractal. This characteristic has been demonstrated in an unequivocal
way by Arlinghaus (1985), Arlinghaus and Arlinghaus (1989), and Ratajczak (1998).

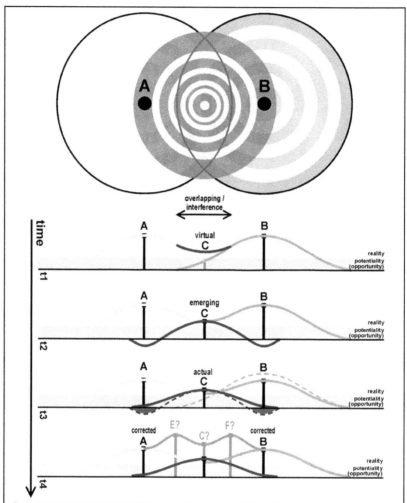

Periphery emerges as centre. The waves of events A and B overlap to produce an interference system wave at t1. The new wave raises the potentiality of event C (which is at the periphery of both A and B), making it 'jump' into reality: C emerges at time t2 as a new potential centre. If acted upon by a human, it can be activated and sustained in reality, and automatically creates its own wave. Notice the negative values of C's wave near the centre of events A and B. We can think of this as 'competition due to the relative novelty of event C'. The C wave now interferes with the original waves of A and B, leading to a new state in t3, where the effects of A and B are slightly diminished to compensate for the emergence of C, and the 'negative' effects of C have flattened out. At this point, the waves interfere together again (feedback loop), resulting in a whole new 'vibration' in t4, potentially triggering events E and F, as the potentiality wave at their position goes beyond the 'existence barrier' between potentiality and reality etc.

Figure 3.12   SMESTO emerging on the periphery

Source: Arida (2002, p. 211).

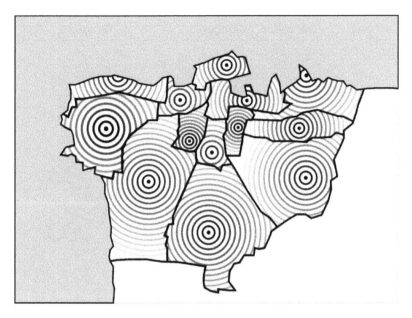

Figure 3.13 The waves passing through different hinterlands are 'attenuated' by borders. There is no wave interference

Source: Own compilation on the basis of Arida (2002, p. 213).

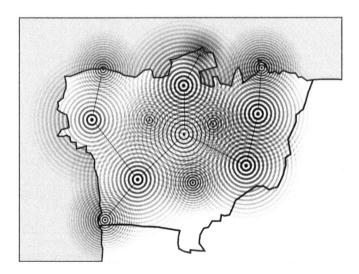

Figure 3.14 The waves of the different central places overlap and interfere, creating naturally delimited hinterlands

Source: Own compilation on the basis of Arida (2002, p. 214).

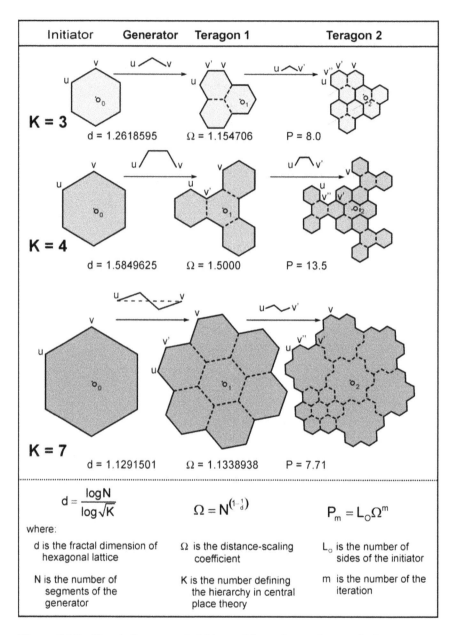

Figure 3.15   Fractally generated hierarchic systems of central places

Source: Arlinghaus (1985) modified, and Ratajczak (1998).

Figure 3.15 demonstrates that the hexagonal lattice and the hierarchical level of central places depend, in the geometrical sense, on the shape of the lattice generator. The lattices generated differ in their fractal dimension (d), scaling factor (Ω) and, understandably enough, circumference length (Pm).

The methodological worth of fractal geometry in modelling the spatial development of towns and their surrounding areas has been proved in a great number of works (see e.g. Batty and Longley, 1994; Peters, 1994; Caglioni and Giovanni, 2004; Batty, 2005).

3.4. SMESTOs and the Economy

The economic importance of SMESTOs has long been an object of much research (see Parr, 1973, Barkley et al., 1996; Courtney and Errington, 2000; Tacoli and Satterthwaite, 2002; van Leeuwen and Nijkamp, 2006; de Noronha Vaz et al., 2004; Rosner, 2004; Tacoli, 2004,;Courtney et al., 2005, 2007; van Leeuwen, 2005). This is because SMESTOs, like any other element of the settlement system and the economy, keep changing under the influence of both, global processes (megatrends) and those of a regional or even only local range.

It is the 'logic of location' that small and medium-sized towns are primarily connected with the rural economy. That is why transactions are of fundamental significance for those units conducted along the SMESTO-hinterland-SMESTO lines. A model of this type of interaction is presented in Figure 3.16 (another interesting one can be found in *Economic Linkages* 2005, p. 90). It conceptualizes the relations that hold between a town and its hinterland based on values, actors, and activities. Their intensity varies over time and space, and can be analysed using the Social Accounting Matrix (SAM) (see, e.g., van Leeuwen, 2005; *Economic Linkages,* 2005; Courtney et al., 2007; van Leeuwen, 2010).

The model in Figure 3.16 illustrates an activity that can be termed an 'economy of place', which, when external links are taken into account, assumes the properties of a 'local economy'. According to Courtney and Errington (2000, p. 283), a local economy can be defined as 'a bounded spatial form within the web of wider economic activity where local income generation within, and leakage through, this "pervious" boundary is variable'. Thus, the location of SMESTOs relative to larger metropolitan regions and to one another plays a major role in developing economic and social relations that are crucial to them (Kunzmann, 2007).

In their work, Courtney and Errington (2000) clearly showed that small towns situated in remote rural areas could be better integrated with their locality than those lying in more accessible parts of the countryside. As a consequence, small towns in remote rural areas can be an appropriate focus for rural development initiatives. In turn, the results based on a SAM led Courtney et al. (2007) to the conclusion that, in terms of town-hinterland flows of goods and services with their spillover effects, SMESTOs did not seem to play the role of sub-poles, at least in the English rural economy. It should be noted, however, that: (1) the analysis

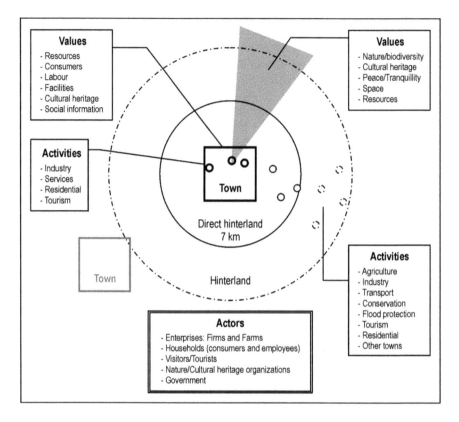

Figure 3.16   Actors, activities and values in the town and hinterland

Source: van Leeuwen (2010).

did not cover any cultural effects that the observed patterns of economic activity might have produced, as the authors stress themselves; and (2) relations between SMESTOs and their hinterlands may be different in other countries.

To clarify the latter problem, Courtney et al. (2005), Mayfield et al. (2005) and ESPON (2006) analysed the role of SMESTOs in local economies in an international context. Their in-depth studies embracing from 5 to 7 countries and from 14 to 30 towns of the SMESTO category provided a basis for a great number of conclusions on the role of those units in the rural economy. The major findings can be summed up as follows.

According to Courtney et al. (2005): (1) Retail trade and personal services sell locally and rely on the local workforce, but tend to seek their supplies in regional and even national markets. (2) Branch plants tend to be less embedded in a locality than independent firms. National branches are usually more oriented towards national markets and regional labour markets, and international branches, towards international markets and supra-regional sources of inputs. (3) Local production linkages vary in strength and nature according to the size and location of a town, and here substantial differences were found to occur between the five countries studied. (4) Some of the local factors shaping the local economic activity may be outside the control of planners and policy makers. (5) Firms most deeply embedded in their locality are 'traditional' rural businesses, usually small, old, operated by local managers, relying on unskilled labour, and reaching rather low levels of productivity.

In turn, the findings of Mayfield et al. (2005), which is a report on the MARKETOWNS project, include the following: (1) The key industries contributing the most to the growth of local economies through local multipliers are almost exclusively those of the service sector, whatever the type of town. This might be taken as implying that the local economy would be given a bigger boost by the development of services rather than manufacturing. (2) The actual employment impact of a sector is highly variable and depends on linkages within the given locality. This suggests that business clustering might be important. (3) Town-based firms sell more locally than those situated in the hinterland, while the local consumption of households in the town is higher than that of those in the hinterland. (4) The flows of inputs and employment from town to hinterland appear to be smaller than those in the reverse direction. This means that, in terms of purchases and labour, town-based firms depend on their hinterlands less than hinterland-based firms depend on towns. (5) Generally, the flows of outputs, inputs, labour and income tend to be greater from hinterland to town than in the reverse direction. Within-town flows will also exceed town-hinterland ones. (6) In most towns that retain local income, it is being retained in the towns themselves rather than in their immediate hinterlands. Still, this need not be taken to imply that SMESTOs cannot be potential foci of future rural development initiatives. This holds especially for towns located in areas with agricultural employment exceeding the national average, because in them initial and subsequent round linkages are likely to generate the greatest trickle-down effects in the local economy (in both the town and its hinterland), with larger towns producing the greatest multiplier effects.

The research launched under the ESPON project was intended to identify the regional and supra-regional roles of SMESTOs. A total of 28 working hypotheses had been formulated, 14 for each of the contexts, viz. regional and national / transnational. On verification, the highest degree of confirmation was obtained for hypotheses H4, H7, H9, and H11 concerning the regional role of SMESTOs, as well as H23 and H26 referring to their national /transnational significance. The hypotheses were formulated as follows (ESPON, 2006, Annex A.1, p. 7-12):

'Hypothesis 4: Rich in built patrimony and the natural environment, SMESTOs offer a high quality of life. SMESTOs combine the advantages of land and city, eliminating its contradictions. Towns and landscape can often still be seen as a unit and SMESTOs are the ecological continuum of the landscape. These towns are marked by their landscape (cultural landscape - vinery towns, health resorts, etc.) and there are rigid personal ties and connections to these cultural landscapes.'

'Hypothesis 7: SMESTOs can be successful when finding production niches (Porter theory) embedded in an innovation scheme which enforces the advantages of low transaction costs and thus facilitates knowledge spill-over. On the other hand, it outweighs the potential disadvantages of a lack of growth-facilitating amenities.'

'Hypothesis 9: SMESTOs show generally a mix of the following basic functions:

- Supply function – this means the provision of a region's population with necessary goods and services.
- Labour market function whereby an aim is to keep small structures and renew local economic entities.
- Housing function which corresponds with the provision of enough habitat and building grounds.
- Cultural functions which include leisure and tourism. They can be reinforced by city marketing and branding.'

'Hypothesis 11: In SMESTOs cultural functions such as leisure, tourism etc. show increasing significance. In order to be competitive, cities need to show their best face. By city branding and city marketing tourism shall be supported and outside investors should be attracted. City types are shifting and SMESTOs are searching for new roles and identities.'

'Hypothesis 23: Smaller and medium sized towns present a rich and diverse cultural heritage for Europe.'

'Hypothesis 26: SMESTOs show an increasing willingness and self-organization to set up international networks and enforce political lobbying in order to strengthen their position vis-à-vis the metropolitan areas.'

Some of the other hypotheses have also gained a relatively high level of confirmation. Therefore, on the basis of this interesting project, a tentative conclusion can be drawn that, generally speaking, SMESTOs in Europe follow a trajectory which may start a virtuous circle, at least in the rural-urban development of their area (see Figure 3.17).

The issue of the role of SMESTOs in rural and regional development was surveyed against a broad international context by Satterthwaite and Tacoli (2003), as well as by Tacoli (2004), although the authors employed a different terminology, referring to medium-sized towns as 'intermediate urban centres'. In both works the authors focused their attention on developing countries in North Africa, Sub-Saharan Africa, South-East Asia, Southern and Western Asia, and Latin America. The authors' special goal was to determine to what extent small and intermediate urban centres alleviated, or could alleviate, poverty in the countries in question. The works provide a large number of conclusions and findings, the most significant being:

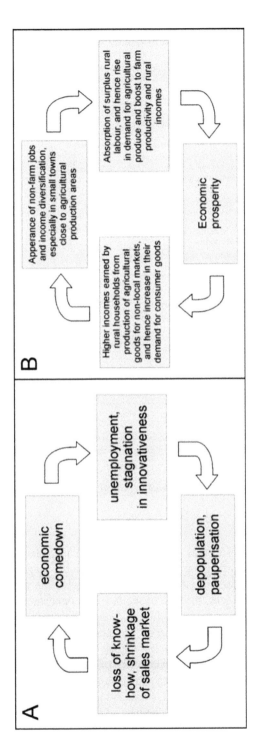

Figure 3.17 SMESTOs and their potential vicious circle (A); Potential virtuous circle of rural-urban development involving SMESTOs (B)

Source: ESPON (2006) (A); Satterthwaite and Tacoli (2003) (B).

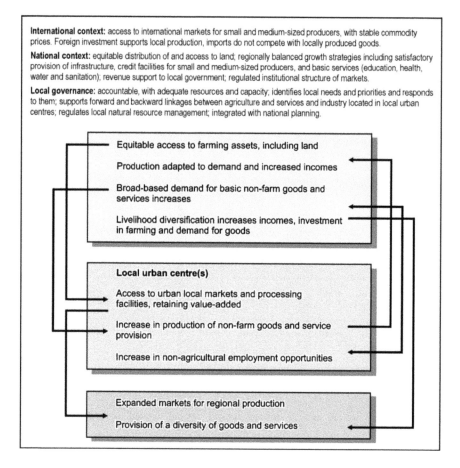

International context: access to international markets for small and medium-sized producers, with stable commodity prices. Foreign investment supports local production, imports do not compete with locally produced goods.

National context: equitable distribution of and access to land; regionally balanced growth strategies including satisfactory provision of infrastructure, credit facilities for small and medium-sized producers, and basic services (education, health, water and sanitation); revenue support to local government; regulated institutional structure of markets.

Local governance: accountable, with adequate resources and capacity; identifies local needs and priorities and responds to them; supports forward and backward linkages between agriculture and services and industry located in local urban centres; regulates local natural resource management; integrated with national planning.

Equitable access to farming assets, including land

Production adapted to demand and increased incomes

Broad-based demand for basic non-farm goods and services increases

Livelihood diversification increases incomes, investment in farming and demand for goods

Local urban centre(s)

Access to urban local markets and processing facilities, retaining value-added

Increase in production of non-farm goods and service provision

Increase in non-agricultural employment opportunities

Expanded markets for regional production

Provision of a diversity of goods and services

Figure 3.18   Positive rural-urban interactions and regional development.

Source: Satterthwaite and Tacoli (2003, p. 3), modified.

Small and intermediate urban centres play an important role as providers of basic services to a large part of the urban population, as well as to the majority of the rural population. Equally importantly, these urban centres give the rural population access to government services, the rule of the law, and opportunities for fulfilling civil and political rights.

Many urban businesses rely on demand from rural producers or consumers. What is more, they often need to resort to rural commodities while agricultural producers rely on urban traders and markets. The majority of rural populations rely on retail shops, as well as on service enterprises and economies.

From the point of view of regional development, small and intermediate urban centres are largely conducive to the economic development of the regions (areas)

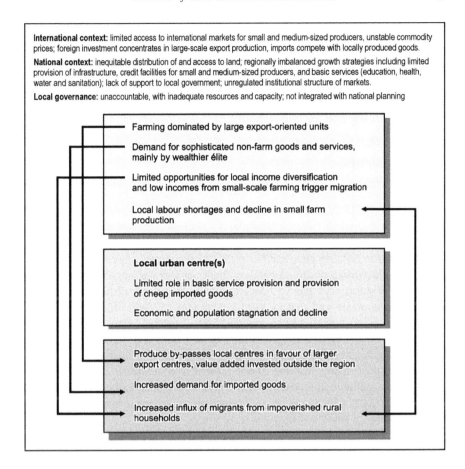

International context: limited access to international markets for small and medium-sized producers, unstable commodity prices; foreign investment concentrates in large-scale export production, imports compete with locally produced goods.

National context: inequitable distribution of and access to land; regionally imbalanced growth strategies including limited provision of infrastructure, credit facilities for small and medium-sized producers, and basic services (education, health, water and sanitation); lack of support to local government; unregulated institutional structure of markets.

Local governance: unaccountable, with inadequate resources and capacity; not integrated with national planning

Farming dominated by large export-oriented units

Demand for sophisticated non-farm goods and services, mainly by wealthier élite

Limited opportunities for local income diversification and low incomes from small-scale farming trigger migration

Local labour shortages and decline in small farm production

Local urban centre(s)

Limited role in basic service provision and provision of cheap imported goods

Economic and population stagnation and decline

Produce by-passes local centres in favour of larger export centres, value added invested outside the region

Increased demand for imported goods

Increased influx of migrants from impoverished rural households

Figure 3.19   Negative rural-urban interactions and regional development.

Source: Satterthwaite and Tacoli (2003, p. 4), modified.

of their operations. The local urban markets can match producers with national and international markets and hence boost rural economies.

The unprecedented diversity of small and intermediate urban centres as to size, economic base, functions and administrative boundaries has an immediate effect on the role of the local authorities and the nature of governance.

Small and intermediate urban centres are capable of playing a key role in spurring regional development and alleviating poverty in urban and rural settlements alike. This area tends to be wider than that typically administered by a single local authority, and as such requires even more capacity on the side of the local civil servants and local politicians.

Local authorities operating in small and intermediate urban centres can and should play a vital role in ensuring that services (health-related, educational and emergency services, post and telephones [over 5 per cent of the global population have never talked over the phone], water supply, sanitation and drainage) are provided to the urban residents and the communities in their area of operations. They can also be of assistance in providing better access to markets for the urban poor.

Local authorities seem incapable of solving fundamental problems related to rural povert, namely, land tenure and access to land, access to credit and the transformation of the agricultural sector, which in many countries has been falling under increasing control of large commercial producers with direct interests with retailers and exports.

Local authorities located in small and intermediate urban centres have the potential to build up the capacity of their local communities and businesses to succeed in, among other things, improving their residents' education level and skills, and therefore to relieve the health-related encumbrance of easily prevented or curable diseases.

What is more, Satterthwaite and Tacoli (2003) also suggest that the role of small and intermediate urban centres depends on both positive and negative rural-urban interactions. Figures 3.18 and 3.19 depict in detail the impact of the international and national contexts and that of local governance on rural-urban interactions and the role of local small and intermediate urban centres. These figures are of a conceptual nature, emphasizing that the role of SMESTOs depends on spatial, social, economic and cultural factors.

It is worth stressing that the above-presented conclusions and statements resulting from studies conducted by various authors are of an inductive nature, but they still contribute a lot to our body of knowledge concerning what is called the spatial economy of small and medium-sized towns.

3.5. SMESTOs and the New Economy

Successful development of small and medium-sized towns, as well as their importance in the settlement system, also depends upon their capability to adopt and apply the rules of the New Economy. This has been confirmed in numerous works (see Budge and Butt, 2007; Siegel and Waxman, 2001; Nelson, 2005; Waitt and Gibson, 2009; Markusen, 2007; Evans, 2007; Foord, 2008; Evans and Foord, 2008; Christopherson, 2004; Brown-Graham and Lambe, 2008).

The New Economy emerged as a result of a transformation of the classical economy and, according to Atkinson and Court (1998), can be interpreted as follows:

'The term New Economy refers to a set of qualitative and quantitative changes that in the last 15 years have transformed the structure, functioning, and rules of the economy. The New Economy is a knowledge- and idea-based economy where the keys to job creation and higher standards of living are innovative ideas and technology embedded in services and manufactured products. It is an economy where risk, uncertainty and constant change are the rule rather than the exception'.

Obviously, issues related to the New Economy include the creative class, human capital, and social capital (see Florida, 2005, 2008; Landry, 2000; Field, et al. 2000).

Various factors are responsible for the limitations and barriers that hinder small and medium-sized towns from adopting the rules of the New Economy. The research conducted on American towns by Siegel and Waxman (2001) suggests that the major challenges include: (1) obsolete infrastructure; (2) dependence on traditional industry; (3) transformation of their human capital base; (3) regions experiencing declining competitiveness; (4) feeble civic infrastructure and capacity; and (5) more limited access to resources.

The adoption of the principles of the New Economy by small and medium-sized towns necessitates primarily a search for creative solutions concerning: (1) creating and enhancing local amenities; (2) building on institutions of tertiary education; (3) engaging in regional collaboration; (4) establishing an effective civic infrastructure; and (5) promoting diversity as a source of strength.

While not undertaking an evaluation of the suggested solutions, special attention should be paid, however, to the need to locate and develop in SMESTOs various types of higher education institutions (HEIs). Regardless of a town's size, the fact that it hosts a university invariably offers it a strong impulse for developing human capital and, in broader terms, social capital as interpreted by Field et al. (2000, see Table 3.1) and by Lopez-Rodriguez et al. (2007). However, the location of a university in a SMESTO, or quite rarely, in an urban place devoid of municipal rights, gains special significance.

Universities provide codified knowledge and provide opportunities for building up tacit knowledge and, as a result, for developing creative space (see Wierzbicki and Nakamori, 2006; Ratajczak and Weltrowska-Jęch, 2008; Chojnicki, 2001). Drucker and Goldstein (2007) identified eight chief functions of universities and subjected them to analysis. Russo et al. (2007) analysed a sustainable relationship between cities and universities, confirming the key role universities play in creating regions of knowledge.

From the point of view of SMESTOs, the work by Rego and Coleiro (2009, p. 11, 15) offers interesting conclusions; the authors proved that a university located in a medium-sized town in Portugal (Évora: 55,000 inhabitants) 'has contributed to fulfil the needs of the job market in Évora and throughout all the Alentejo region through its graduates'. Hence, 'this migration of human capital, therefore of knowledge, towards Évora (and the Alentejo region) can be viewed as complementary to the economic-base relevance of the University of Évora'. Another important result of this work was the confirmation that 'the University of Évora is an important source of knowledge diffusion in terms of the small/medium-sized town where it is located (i.e. Évora)', despite that town's insignificance in terms of the rest of the country.

Table 3.1   Individual and social capital resources

	Human Capital	Social Capital
Object	individual	relations among individuals
Indices	(life expectancy), skills, powers	level of trust, membership of associations, civic engagement
Effects	direct: income, productivity indirect: health, public activity	social cohesion, economic development
Model	linear	circular /relational
Policy (practical recommendations)	education, human resources management, work efficiency	extending citizen rights and powers, easier access to public sphere, enhanced sense of agency

Source: Field et al. (2000: 250), after Trutkowski and Mandes (2005, p. 69).

Scientific research and plain observation alike give grounds for the cautious conclusion that the process of locating universities or, speaking more broadly, HEIs (higher education institutions and their branches) in small and medium-sized towns will gain in intensity. Figure 3.20 presents the spatial distribution of HEIs located in SMESTOs in Poland in 2009. The total number is impressive: a substantial 148. Privately-owned institutions prevail in the group of HEIs, while public institutions tend to provide the majority of HEI branches. It is worth noting that 10 universities in Poland are located in urban places that do not enjoy municipal rights. Therefore, Poland is an obvious example to support the hypothesis of the growing importance of knowledge in developing the social group of well-educated and creative individuals (the creative class) in both big cities and medium-sized and small towns. This may result in the successful social and economic growth of those cities and their hinterlands. It is also in accordance with the ideas presented by Florida (2002, 2005) and confirmed by numerous studies (see, e.g. Beckstead et al., 2008; Waitt, 2006, p. 178; Mommaas, 2009).

Although he does not quite identify the creative class with human capital, in Florida's opinion the creative class is the source of economic growth in a country. While Florida suggests that 'the creative class tends to locate in metropolitan areas with particular amenities', McGranaham and Wojan (2007, p. 214) claim that 'the creative class is diffusing outward from central cities, growing most rapidly in sparsely settled suburbs'.

The role of the creative class in the growth of big cities (and regions) manifests itself right now as the emerging new urban hierarchy in Europe. Research conducted by Lorenzen and Andersen (2009), employing an original database of 444 European cities in 8 countries, proved that: 'The urban hierarchy of the European general population and the urban hierarchy of the European creative

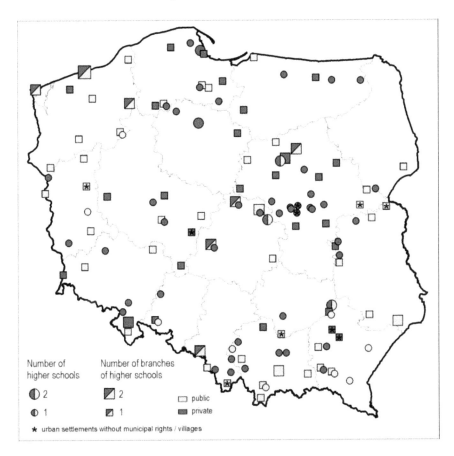

Figure 3.20 State-sponsored and non-state higher schools in towns and municipalities with a population of under 50,000 in Poland, 2009

Source: Own compilation.

class are quite distinctive. The rank-size distribution of the creative class indicates greater proportionate growth (it has a steeper overall slope) than that of the general population, and the slope across the creative class distribution suggests that it has greater diseconomies of small cities' (Lorenzen and Andersen, 2009, p. 21).

Hence, the importance of locating universities and HEIs in general in SMESTOs is high. It can be assumed that SMESTOs, primarily those located within larger metropolitan regions, will first be the destination and later on the source of the creative class, triggering off waves of a new economy (see Figures 3.12 and 3.14). This process will be even more dynamic and sustainable if universities and other HEIs, including those located in SMESTOs, are increasingly incorporated into creative clusters. Flew (2009/2010) offers a full analysis of this issue in his work.

Obviously, this is only a possible scenario, as the role of the creative class in stimulating social and economic development (even with reference to large cities and their regions) has also been criticized in the literature (see, e.g., Glaeser, 2004; Peck, 2005; Markusen, 2006; and, most recently, Hoyman and Faricy, 2009). The results of Hansen's research (2009) do not favour either Florida or his opponents.

Critical reflections concerning the New Economy in general are contained in the book by Daniels et al. (2007).

3.6. The Future of SMESTOs

Because of the roles small and medium-sized towns play in all economies and regions, they certainly need economic, social, cultural etc. development, in compliance with the expectations and determinants of contemporary and future societies. As the future cannot be predicted, it is equally impossible to foresee the precise future of SMESTOs at various spatial scales. However, it is possible to identify the chief drivers which may affect the successful growth of SMESTOs, understood as their strong economic performance, their inhabitants' quality of life and improved welfare, etc. With these drivers in mind, it is possible to create diverse scenarios of the growth of SMESTOs. Brooke (2003; p. 28-29) compiled a list of such factors with reference to cities in general. These factors can, however, also be applied to the group of towns under analysis, as presented below:

Diversity. One of the most significant drivers of urban development today. Narrowly specialized SMESTOs (e.g. agricultural, industrial, service providers, etc.) are going to be more vulnerable and more easily trapped in the vicious circle. Therefore, the diversification of their economic structure (base) should be the main goal of the growth strategy of SMESTOs. Because 'cities that embrace diversity in all its forms, including cultural and ethnic diversity, seem better equipped to generate the creativity that cities need, making themselves attractive to the skilled migrants' (Brooke, 2003, p. 28).

Good governance. Governance stands for a decision-making process where the participant bodies (public, NGOs and private) are interdependent, while implementation of these decisions stems from consensus rather than enforcement. 'Good governance demands strong civic leaders with a vision of where they want to take their city and economic strategy that embraces partnership with local business'.

Quality of life – liveability. Quality of life 'is a broad concept concerned with the overall well-being within society'. Its aim is to enable people, as far as possible, to achieve their goals and choose their ideal lifestyle. In this sense, the quality-of-life concept goes beyond the living-conditions approach which tends to focus on the material resources available to individuals (see Alber et al. 2004; p. 1). With reference to a specific place of residence, hence also SMESTOs, quality of life is strictly related to the notion of liveability which, according to Jones et al. (2003), can be interpreted as: 'All those aspects of a place which make people happy to live and work here, but it embraces a complex and inter-related set of issues including poverty and inequality, housing conditions, safe working environments, environmental pollution, policing, personal security and safety issues, transport facilities, cultural and recreational amenities, and the quality of the public realm'.

Both quality of life and liveability tend to play important roles in contemporary societies, especially in societies existing within the New Economy. Owing to the special bonds and traditions among the inhabitants, SMESTOs are urban centres which can and should raise their level of liveability. All the more so, as the two developing movements for enhancing urban liveability, i.e. Slow Cities and Smart Growth, pertain primarily to SMESTOs (Figure 3.21). These movements result from the 'increasing disenchantment with lifestyles focused on material acquisition within some segments of the population, particularly the young. The values of simplicity, tranquillity and community begin to displace those of consumerism, competition and individualism' (Gallopin et al. 1997; Haughton and Hunter, 2003).

Connectivity – accessibility. Due to their present multifunctionality, SMESTOs should strive to enhance their transport-related accessibility. The

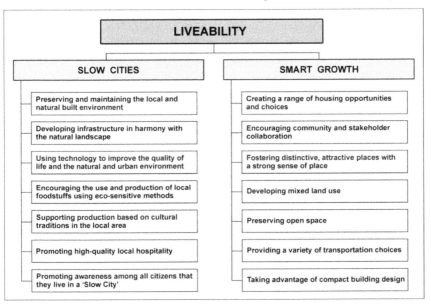

Figure 3.21   View of liveability

Source: Jones et al. (2003).

great contemporary social mobility and the economy's transport-related needs are contributing to growing congestion in cities and on the roads connecting them.

SMESTOs, especially those located in metropolitan areas, can only be reached in rush hours with great delay. Whenever possible, medium-sized towns should also develop a network of local airports. No city can successfully compete with others without good communication with the outside world.

Physical renewal – revitalization. Public amenities, the infrastructure and the condition of the housing stock are invariably significant factors which improve the competitiveness of SMESTOs. Therefore, their physical regeneration and revitalization combined with social regeneration need to be included in strategies for SMESTO growth, especially in the less developed countries.

Culture of innovation. Innovation is the chief driver behind the knowledge-based economy – the New Economy, which, in turn, is the source of welfare in contemporary societies. For this reason SMESTOs should become active elements of Regional Innovation Systems (RIS) by incorporating the local HEIs into these RIS. Establishing networks involving both the public and private sectors may be another activity aimed at creating and sharing innovation in SMESTOs. On top of that, the creation of the Local Innovation Systems (LIS) may be a new venture (Komninos, 2002; Barkley et al., 2006).

Business-friendly culture. Apart from basic friendly legal regulations and low taxes, effective and pro-society business activity in SMESTOs requires a friendly business milieu. This new concept is referred to as 'civic entrepreneurship' (Johnson Jr. 2002, p. 766). Civic entrepreneurship may be described simply as a coalition of business, government, and community leaders who skilfully blend new business models of venture capital and networking with the job of solving public problems (Stafford, 2006, p. 21).

Distinctive brand. Just like big cities, SMESTOs have their history, tradition and idiosyncrasies which differentiate them in the settlement system and the geographical landscape. However, for them no methodology of ranking their brand has yet been developed (see, for example, the Anholts City Brands Index for large cities). The ranking should include their most essential and attractive attributes in order to magnify their own unique identity. This is of key importance from the point of view of the New Economy rules. The construction of a SMESTO Brands Index (SBI) should take place in cooperation with, for example, ECOVAST (the European Council for the Village and Small Town – NGO), APURE (Association for European Rural Universities), as well as other national organizations dealing with SMESTOs. What may facilitate the formulation of an SBI are the results provided by ASSETs (Action to Strengthen European Small Towns – a project proposed by ECOVAST) and those of the PICTURE project whose 'aim was to develop a strategic urban governance framework for the sustainable management of cultural tourism within small and medium-sized European cities'.

The town-hinterland-region relationships. These are key relationships for SMESTOs as their existence largely depends on the types of functions that they perform for their hinterland (their spatial reach) as well as for the region, the country or, broadly speaking, 'the rest of the world' (ROW) (see van Leeuwen 2010, Chapter 2 and Figure 22). A SMESTO strategy should therefore include not

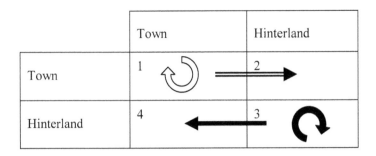

	Town	Hinterland
Town	1	2
Hinterland	4	3

Figure 3.22   Four systems of endogenous accounts (output-oriented)

Source: van Leeuwen (2010).

only activities for a town's successful growth (the economy of place) but also that of its hinterland (the local economy).

At the European scale, a closer SMESTO-hinterland-SMESTO relationship may result from measures and programmes launched in the European Union countries and aimed at Village Renewal (VR) and, more broadly, Rural Development (RD). 'Rural areas are described as territorial entities with a coherent economic and social structure of diversified economic activities, and may include villages, small cities and regional centres' (Dwyer and van Deopele, 2003, p. 3).

Reinforcing the importance of SMESTOs for their hinterlands may take place (is necessary) because: (1) agriculture remains the primary land use; (2) no viable agriculture is possible without a living countryside; and (3) the socio-economic vitality of rural areas needs local employment beyond agriculture, such as: microbusiness, small and medium-sized enterprises, crafts, artisan activities, etc. (Dwyer and van Deopele 2003, p. 4).

Rural development is being stimulated by a movement referred to as Village Renewal: activities aiming to shape living conditions in rural areas, initiated by and targeted at local communities. This movement affects standards of living, the quality of life, and the inhabitants' sources of income, at the same time maintaining the countryside's identity as manifested in the values of country life, and reinforcing and developing rural cultural and material heritage (Wilczyński, 2003, p. 12). The chief objectives of the movement include: (1) strengthening ecological agriculture and forestry and integrating it into regional economic flows while respecting the character of the man-made landscape; (2) maintenance and creation of employment opportunities adequate for the locality; (3) responsible resource management and use of renewable raw materials; (4) symbiosis between valuable old and good quality new buildings; resource-efficient and traffic-reducing development of settlement patterns; (5) strengthening the sense of identity and the self-assurance of village residents; (6) revitalization of traditional socio-cultural qualities and social institutions, and creation of new ones; and (7) encouragement of the participation of all age groups, nationalities and minorities and of both genders in the economic,

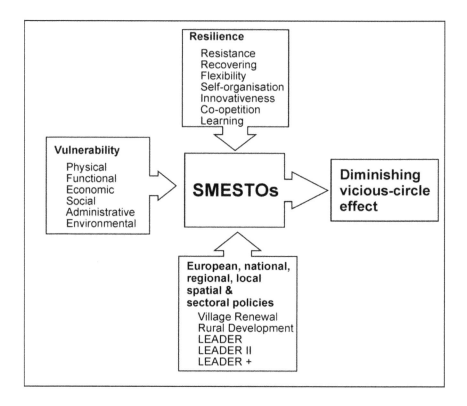

Figure 3.23   SMESTOs: breaking out of a vicious circle in the European context

Source: ESPON (2006), modified.

social and cultural life. One can readily note that the Village Renewal and Rural Development movements not only positively affect the relationship between SMESTOs and their hinterlands, but also the other drivers of SMESTOs, i.e. diversity, good governance, quality of life – liveability, etc.

Reinforcing the SMESTO-hinterland-SMESTO relationship also occurs via the formal EU LEADER programme and its variants, LEADER II and LEADER +. Its goals are similar to those of VR and RD, with the underlying assumption of bottom-up cooperation between the public, social and private sectors in the form of a Local Action Group (LAG) for enhancing rural innovativeness and quality of life, improving the quality of local products, and supporting local natural and cultural resources (Heffner, 2007;,p. 61).

The drivers characterized above may positively affect both, the present and the future situation of SMESTOs and ensure their success in the social and economic exchange. As Figure 3.23 demonstrates, SMESTOs are also subjected to factors that facilitate their growth in the settlement system, but also those that degrade them. Sometimes they form a vicious circle. This is the worst-case scenario: an effect of vulnerability which describes a specific dimension of the socio-economic and environmental disadvantage of SMESTOs. The vulnerability effect may be alleviated, on the one hand, through SMESTOs' ability to self-organize, control their function and structure, and build and increase their learning and adopting capacity, i.e. through resilience. On the other hand, this may be achieved through bottom-up movements and initiatives launches by NGOs like VRRD, as well as formal programmes carried out at the regional and national levels and on a wider scale, e.g. as part of the LEADER programme in Europe. They may also be considered to be a certain form of resilience, but owing to their significance they have been presented separately in the figure.

Non-governmental activities, so characteristic of civil societies, and programmes instigated by local and regional authorities need to be complementary. This is because any social group, authority or even individual must be held responsible for the present and future condition of the place of their residence. This may not only eliminate the vicious circle, but also initiate and put in full swing a virtuous circle (see Figure 3.23). This conclusion obviously also holds true for larger towns and other aspects of life in contemporary societies.

3.7. Conclusions

In contemporary societies, small and medium-sized towns are an important element of the global settlement system. In terms of the biggest proportions of the world's population, large cities are followed by SMESTOs. Big cities, as well as small and medium-sized towns, result from the specific human atavism: big cities result from the human propensity to live in a group. On the other hand, small towns reflect the human yearning to live in harmony with broadly defined nature (at least to some extent). Nature's rhythm makes individuals and groups pursue their goals in the most effective way possible. Small towns gain special importance in this respect. Because 'the small city is an extension of home and homesickness, its powerful seductions are resonant beyond time' (Van Herk, 2005, p. 139). The roles SMESTOs play in the social and economic systems are diverse and depend upon the location and the research context.

The literature on the subject suggests that the role of SMESTOs is interpreted as:

- expectation of: efficient performance within the socio-economic system at the local, regional, national, and even global level; measures taken to achieve a high level of liveability; the creation of a prosperous future for a variety of entities; their function as sub-poles for surrounding rural hinterlands, etc.;

- (multiple) functions, i.e. manufacturing, services, transport, retailing, housing, education, culture, recreation and tourism, the labour market, etc.;

- activity in the social sphere, economic sphere, cultural sphere, etc.

This chapter has explained the fundamental role of SMESTOs in developing the economy of place, the local economy, and the regional economy. No city can operate without close relationships with the surrounding area: its region, its sphere of influence, and its hinterland. Similarly, the area needs to have an opportunity of exchange with the local city (cities). SMESTOs are an important element of the continuum between rural and urban areas. At present a feature of this continuum is tolerant complementarity and duality rather than dualism. The most important relationship between SMESTOs, hinterlands and regions tends to occur in this particular continuum. The concept of self-organization and related theories (including Christaller's theory) explain, albeit not in an entirely satisfactory way, the power, structure and spatial distribution of these relationships.

SMESTOs have also been included in global mega-trends. Globalization-related processes and the emergence of the New Economy pose challenges, but at the same time offer opportunities to SMESTOs. The creative class which is growing as a result of the diffusion of knowledge, talent and entrepreneurship offers such opportunities to SMESTOs.

Cultural diversity necessitates understanding on top of tolerance; the latter is a prerequisite, albeit insufficient, for a social group's harmonious growth. Florida failed to notice that. Due to attachment to tradition and other cultural determinants, both tolerance and understanding may encounter resistance in SMESTOs. They face another challenge: that of softening that resistance.

An impulse for change usually comes from higher education institutions (HEIs). Therefore, locating universities in SMESTOs is always an advantageous and desirable activity as confirmed by this chapter's conclusions.

To ensure that SMESTOs face global challenges, a close cooperation between their local authorities, NGOs, the inhabitants and business people is a must. This is why in this group of towns the rules of governance not only have to be merely applied but also creatively developed. SMESTOs can and should be a laboratory where new public-private partnership (PPP) rules emerge.

SMESTOs will never disappear from the landscape of various geographical units; they will continue to grow under the influence of both external and internal factors and be influenced by trends operating in the global social and economic system. Since SMESTOs are in a symbiotic relationship with rural areas, their growth will be greatly affected by development programmes for rural areas.

On the other hand, the future role of SMESTOs in the settlement system will also depend on the dominant paradigm of growth of the entire global economy. According to Ruskin et al. (2002), two paradigms are plausible under the Great Transition: (1) Eco-Communalism, which 'incorporates the green vision of bio-regionalism, localism, face-to-face democracy, small technology and economic autarky', and (2) the New Sustainability Paradigm, which 'shares some of the goals of the Eco-Communalism scenarios, but would seek to change the character of the urban, industrial situation rather than to replace it, to build a more humane and equitable global civilization rather than retreat into localism'. In either case, SMESTOs will play new important roles in the territorial socio-economic system. What remains an open question is to what extent the two paradigms could affect the emergence of SMESTOs complying with Nijkamp's (2008) conception of XXQ – SIC, i.e. cities (small and medium-sized in this case) with exceptionally high quality of life and existing as self-organizing innovative complexes.

References

Alber, J., Delhey, J., Keck, W. and Nauenburg, R. 2004. *Quality of life in Europe.* European Foundation for the Improvement of Living and Working Conditions. Dublin.

Aleksander, J.W. 1954. The Basic-Nonbasic concept of urban economic functions. *Economic Geography* 30, 246-261.

Arida, A. 2002. *Quantum City.* Oxford: Architectural Press.

Arlinghaus, S.L. 1985. Fractals take a central place. *Geografiska Annaler* 67B, 83-88.

Arlinghaus, S.L. and Arlinghaus, W.C. 1989. The fractal theory of central place geometry: A Diophantine analysis of fractal generators for arbitrary Löschian numbers. *Geographical Analysis* 21(2), 103-121.

Atkinson, R.D. and Court, R.H. 1998. *The New Economy Index: Understanding America's Economic Transformation.* The Progressive Policy Institute Technology, Innovation, and New Economy Project. Washington. *Available at: http://*www.neweconomyindex.org/NewEconomy.pdf.

Barkley, D.L. et al. 2006. *Innovative Activity in Rural Areas: The Importance of Local and Regional Characteristics.* Community Development Investment Review. Available at: http://www.frbsf.org/publications/community/review/122006/barkley.pdf.

Barkley, D.L., Henry, M.S. and Bao, S. 1996. Identifying "Spread" versus Backwash: Effects in Regional Economic Areas: A Density Functions Approach. *Land Economics*, 72(3), 336-357.

Batty, M. 2005. *Cities and Complexity.* Cambridge: The MIT Press.

Batty, M. and Longley, P. 1994. *Fractal Cities: A Geometry of Form and Function.* London: Academic Press Limited.

Beckstead, D., Brown, M. and Gellatly, G. 2008. *Cities Growth: The Left Brain of North American Cities: Scientists and Engineers and Urban Growth.* Research Paper. The Canadian Economy in Transition Series 11-622-MIE, n°.17. Statistics Canada. Ottawa.

Bell, D. and Jayne, M. 2006. Conceptualizing Small Cities, in *Small Cities: Urban Experience Beyond the Metropolis*, edited by D. Bell and M. Jayne. Routledge: Oxon, 1-18.

Besson, E. et al. 2006. *Brakes and Difficulties Faced by Small and Medium Sized Cities in the View of Developing European Cultural Networks.* Available at: http://www.cultureroutes.lu/uploaded_files/infos/posts/108/2a73a6a4fbfb2c0 b81f004c288c7b097.pdf

Boschma, R.A. and Fritsch, M. 2007. *Creative Class and Regional Growth – Empirical Evidence from Eight European Countries.* Jena Economic Research Paper n°. 2007-066.

Boschma, R.A. and Fritsch, M. 2009. *Creative Class and Regional Growth – Empirical Evidence from Seven European Countries.* Forthcoming in *Economic Geography* 85(4), 391-426.

Bretagnolle, A. et al. 2000. Long-Term Dynamics of European Towns and Cities: Towards a Spatial Model of Urban Growth. *Cybergeo*, 131.

Bretagnolle, A., Paulus, F. and Pumain, D. 2002. Time and Space Scales for Measuring Urban Growth. *Cybergeo*, 219.

Brooke, N. 2003. What Makes for a Successful City. *Real Estate Issues*, 28(4), 28-29.

Brown-Graham, A. and Lambe, W. 2008. *Measures and Methods: Four Tenets for Rural Economic Development in the New Economy. Policy Brief*, 9.

Budge, T. and Butt, A. 2007. *What about Australia's Small Cities: Do they have their own Planning and Development Agenda?.* Paper presented to the State of Australian Cities Conference, Adelaide, South Australia. Available at: http:// www.fbe.unsw.edu.au/cityfutures/SOAC/whataboutaustraliassmallcities.pdf

Caglioni, M. and Giovanni, R. 2004. Contribution to fractal analysis of cities: A study of metropolitan area of Milan. *Cybergeo: European Journal of Geography*. Available at: http://www.cybergeo.eu/index3634.html

Chojnicki, Z. 1999. *Modele grawitacji i potencjału (Gravity and potential models)*, in *Podstawy metodologiczne i teoretyczne geografii (Methodological and theoretical fundations of geography)*, edited by Z. Chojnicki. Poznań: Bogucki Wydawnictwo Naukowe.

Chojnicki, Z. 2001. Wiedza dla gospodarki w perspektywie OECD. (Knowledge for the economy in the OECD perspective), in *Gospodarka oparta na wiedzy (The knowledge-based economy)*, editeb by A. Kukliński. Warszawa: KBN 80-91.

Christopherson, S. 2004. *Creative Economy Strategies For Small and Medium Size Cities: Options for New York State.* Available at: http://www. nycreativeeconomy.cornell.edu/downloads/reports/Creative_Economy_ Strategies.pdf

Courtney, P. and Errington, A. 2000. The Role of Small Towns in the Local Economy and Some Implications for Development Policy. *Local Economy*, 15(4), 280-301.

Courtney, P., Lepicier, D., Schmitt, B. 2005. *Rural firms and the local economy- A focus on smali and medium-sized towns.* Available at: http://www-sre.wu- wien.ac.at/ersa/ersaconfs/ersa05/papers/128.pdf

Courtney, P., Mayfield, L., Tranter, R., Jones, P. and Errington, A. 2007. Small towns as 'sub-poles' in English rural development: Investigating rural-urban linkages using sub-regional social accounting matrices. *Geoforum*, 38, 1219-1232.

Daniels, P., Leyshon, A., Bragshaw, M.J. and Beaverstock, J. (eds) 2007. *Geographies of the New Economy: Critical reflections.* Regional and Cities Series. Routledge: London and New York.

Drucker, J. and Goldstein, H. 2007. Assessing the regional economic development impacts of universities: a review of current approach. International Regional *Science Review*, 30(1), 20-46.

Dwyer, J. and van Depoele, L. 2003. *A Living Countryside.* The European Conference on Rural Development, Salzburg, 12-14 November.

Dziewoński, K. 1964. Urbanization in Contemporary Poland. *Geographia Polonica*, 3, 37-56, Warsaw.

Economic Linkages Between Small Towns And Surrounding Rural Areas In Scotland. 2005. Final Report. Scottish Agricultural College et al. Available at: http://www.scotland.gov.uk/Resource/Doc/37428/0009554.pdf

ESPON. 2006. *1.4.1. The Role of Small and Medium-Sized Towns (SMESTO).* Final Report. Austrian Institute for Regional Studies and Spatial Planning (ÖIR). Vienna. Available at: http://www.espon.eu

Evans, G. 2007. Creative Cities, Creative Spaces and Urban Policy. *Urban Studies*, 46(5/6), 1003-1040.

Evans, G. and Foord, J. 2008. Cultural mapping and sustainable communities: planning for the arts revisited. *Cultural Trends*, 17(2), 65-96.

Field, J., Schuller, T. and Baron, S. 2000. Social capital and human capital revisited, in *Social Capital: Critical perspectives*, edited by S. Baron, J. Field and Schuller T. Oxford: Oxford University Press.

Flew, T. 2009. Creative Clusters and Universities. To be published in *Education in the Creative Economy, edited by* Araya, D. and Peters, M.. Peter Lang Publishers, 2010 (forthcoming). Available at: http://www.scribd.com/doc/18323224/Creative-Clusters-and-UniversitiesFlew

Florida, R. 2002. *The Rise of the Creative Class.* New York: Basic Books.

Florida, R. 2005. *Cities and Creative Class.* New York: Routledge.

Florida, R. 2008. *A Creative Manifesto: Why the Place You Choose to Live is the Most Important Decision of Your Life. ChangeThis*, 44(01). Available at: http://www.changethis.com/44.01.CreativeManifesto.

Foord, J. 2008. Strategies for creative industries: an international review. *Creative Industries Journal*, 1(2), 91-113.

Gallopin, G. et al. 1997. *Branch Points: Global Scenarios and Human Choice.* Stockholm: Stockholm Environment Institute.

Gertler, M.S., Wolfe, D.A. and Garkut, D. 2000. No place like home? The embeddedness of innovation in a regional economy. *Review of International Political Economy*, 7(4), 688-718.

Glaeser, E. L. 2004. *Review of Richard Florida's The rise of the creative class.*
Available at: http://www.creativeclass.com/rfcgdb/articles/GlaeserReview.pdf

Hansen, H.K., Asheim, B. and Vang, J. 2009. The European Creative Class and
Regional Development: How Relevant Is Florida's Theory for Europe?, in
Creative Economies, Creative Cities: Asian-European Perspectives, edited by
L. Kong And J. O'Connor. The GeoJournal Library, 98. New York: Springer,
99-120.

Haughton, G. and Hunter, C. 2003. *Sustainable Cities.* Regional Development and
Public Policy Series, London and New York: Routledge.

Heffner, K. 2007. Fundamenty procesu przemian aktywizacyjnych na obszarach
wiejskich. (Fundations of the transformation process connected with the
simulation of rural countryside), in *Odnowa wsi w integrującej się Europie.*
(Rural Renewal in an Integrating Europe), edited by M. Kołodziński et al.
Instytut Rozwoju Wsi i Rolnictwa Polskiej Akademii Nauk. Institute of Rural
land Agricultural Development, Polish Academy of Science. Warszawa.

Henderson, J.V. and Mitra, A., 1996. The new urban landscape: Developers and
edge cities. *Regional Science and Urban Economics,* 26, 613-643.

Herdon, M. and Houseman, I. 2008. *ICT and Innovation in Rural Areas.* Available
at: http://www.mtakpa.hu/kpa/download/l213111.pdf

Hohenberg, PM. 2004. The Historical Geography of European Cities: An
Interpretive Essay, in Handbook of Regional and Urban Economics, edited
by Henderson, J.U., and Thisse, J.F., 4, Cities and Geography, Elsevier.
Amsterdam: North-Holland.

Hoyman, M. and Faricy, C. 2009. It Takes a Village: A Test of the Creative Class,
Social Capital and Human Capital Theories. *Urban Affairs Review,* 44, 311-
333.

Johnson, J.H. Jr. 2002. A Conceptual Model for Enhancing Community
Competitiveness in the New Economy. *Urban Affairs Review,* 37 (6), 763-779.

Jones. P., Hillier. D. and Comfort, D., 2003. *Liveability – Slow Cities and Smart
Growth: Peter Jones, David Hillier, and Daphne Comfort look at the concepts
of 'Slow Cities' and 'Smart Growth' and, drawing on some illustrative
examples of embryonic thinking and practice, ask how applicable they are to
development and regeneration in the UK.* Town and Country Planning.

Kiełczewska-Zaleska, M. 1957. Problemy geograficzno-gospodarcze małych
miast w Polsce w świetle dokonanych opracowań. (Main economic problems
of small towns in Poland in the light of research), in *Studia Geograficzne nad
aktywizacją małych miast.* (Geographical studies of development of small
towns), edited by Kiełczewska-Zaleska, M. et al., Geographical Studies n°. 9,
Warszawa: PWN, 37-60.

Kłodziński, M. 2006. *Aktywizacja społeczno-gospodarcza gmin wiejskich i małych
miast* (*Stimulation of Socio-Economic Activity of Rural Communes and Small
Towns*) Warszawa: Instytut rozwoju wsi i rolnictwa Polskiej Akademii Nauk.

Kołodziński, M. et al. 2007. *Odnowa wsi w integrującej się Europie. (Rural
Renewal in an Integrating Europe).* Instytut Rozwoju Wsi i Rolnictwa Polskiej

Akademii Nauk. Institute of Rural land Agricultural Development, Warszawa: Polish Academy of Science.

Komninos, N. 2002. *Intelligent Cities: Innovation, Knowledge Systems and Digital Spaces.* London and New York: Spon Press.

Kunzmann, K.R. 2007. *Medium-sized Towns Strategic Planning and Creative Governance in the South Baltic Arc.* Available at: http://www.sebco.eu/wmfiles/wm_pdf/kunzmann_discussion_paper.pdf

Landry, C. 2000. *The Creative City: A toolkit for urban innovators.* 7th Edition. London: Comedia.

López-Rodríguez, J., Faíña, J.A. and López-Rodríguez, J. 2007. Human Capital Accumulation and Geography: Empirical Evidence from the European Union. *Regional Studies*, 41(2), 217-234.

Lorenzen, M. and Andersen, K.V. 2009. Centrality and Creativity: Does Richard Florida's Creative Class Offer New Insights into Urban Hierarchy? *Economic Geography*, Published Online: 1 Jun 2009.

Markusen, A. 2006. Urban development and the politics of a creative class: Evidence from a study of artists. *Environment and Planning A*, 38, 1921-1940.

Markusen, A. 2007. *A consumption Base Theory of Development: An Application to the Rural Cultural Economy. Agricultural and Resource Economics Review*, 36(1), 9-23.

Matczak, A., 2007. Małe miasta w badaniach geograficznych. (Small cities in geographical researches), in *Podstawy i perspektywy rozwoju małych miast.* (Foundations and prospects of development of small towns), edited by Rydz, E. Słupsk: Wydawnictwo Naukowe Akademii Pomorskiej w Słupsku, 11-30.

McGranaham, D. and Wojan, R. 2007. Recasting the Creative Class to Examine Growth Processes in Rural and Urban Counties. *Regional Studies*, 41(2), 197-216.

Mommaas, H. 2009. Spaces of Culture and Economy: Mapping the Cultural-Creative Cluster Landscape, in *Creative Economies, Creative Cities: Asian-European Perspectives*, edited by Kong, L.and O'Connor, J., The GeoJournal Library, 98, New York: Springer, 45-59.

Nelson, R. 2005. A Cultural Hinterland? Searching for the Creative Class in the Small Canadian City, in *The Small Cities Book: On the Cultural Future of Small Cities*, edited by Garrette-Petts, W.. Vancouver: New Star Books.

Nijkamp, P. 2008. *XXQ* Factors for Sustainable Urban Development: A Systems Economics View. *Romanian Journal of Regional Science*, 2(1), 1-34.

de Noronha Vaz, T. et al. 2004. *Innovation in Small Firms and Dynamics of Local Development.* Warsaw: Scholar Publishing House.

de Noronha Vaz, T., Morgan, E. and Nijkamp, P. 2006. *The New European Rurality. Strategies for Small Firms.* Ashgate Economic Geography Series.

Parr, J.B. 1973. Growth Poles, Regional Development, and Central Place Theory. *Papers of the Regional Science Association*, 3, 173-212.

Peck, J. 2005. Struggling with creative class. *International Journal of Urban and Regional Research*, 29, 740-770.

Peters, E.E. 1994. *Fractal Market Analysis.* New York: John Wiley & Sons.

Ratajczak, W. 1998. *Metodologiczne Aspekty Fraktalnego Modelowania Rzeczywistości (Methodological Aspects of the Fractal Modelling of Reality).* Poznań: Zakład Graficzny UAM.

Ratajczak, W. 1999. *Modelowanie sieci transportowych (Modeling Transportation Networks).* Poznań: Wydawnictwo Naukowe UAM.

Ratajczak, R. and Weltrowska-Jęch, J. 2008. Knowledge Regions – The European Future, in *Modelling the European Future: Integrating the Old and the New,* edited by S. Vaitekūnas et al. The 4th Scientific volume. Klaipėda: Klaipėdos universiteto leidykla, 61-72.

Rego, C. and Caleiro, A. 2009. *On the spatial diffusion of knowledge by universities located in small and medium sized towns.* MPRA Paper 16241, available at: http://mpra.ub.uni-muenchen.de/16241/1/MPRA_paper_16241.pdf

Rosner, A. 2004. *Modernizing Rural Areas.* Institute of Rural and Agricultural Development. Available at: http://www.english.pan.pl/images/stories/pliki/publikacje/academia/2004/03/46-47_rosner.pdf

Satterthwaite, D. and Tacoli, C. 2003. *The urban part of rural development: the role of small and intermediate urban centres in rural and regional development and poverty reduction.* Available at: http://www.iied.org/pubs/pdfs/9226IIED.pdf

Siegel, B. and Waxman, A. 2001. Third-Tier Cities: Adjusting To The New Economy. *Reviews of Economic Development Literature and Practice.* Economic Development Administration, 6.

Stafford, J. 2006. *What successful cities have to say to Fort Wayne.* Quest Club Paper. Available at: www.ipfw.edu/cri/reports and presentations/Quest.pdf

Tacoli, C. 2004. *The Role of Small and Intermediate Urban Centres and Market Towns and the Value of Regional Approaches to Rural Poverty Reduction Policy.* Available at: www.oecd.org/dataoecd/24/29/36562990.pdf

Tacoli, C. and Satterthwaite, D. 2002. *The Urban Part of Rural Development: the Role of Small and Intermediate Urban Centres in their Regional and Local Economies, Including Rural Development and Poverty Reduction.* Available at: www.ruralforum.info/papers/tacolien.pdf

Taylor, P.J., Moyer, M. and Verbruggen, R. 2008. *External* Urban Relational Process: Introducing Central Flow Theory to Complement Central Place Theory. *GaWC Research Bulletin,* 26.

Trutkowski, C. and Mandes, S. 2005. *Kapitał społeczny w małych miastach (Social capital in small towns).* Warszawa: WN Scholar.

van Herk, A. 2005. The City Small and Smaller, in *The Small Cities Book: On the Cultural Future of Small Cities,* edited by Garrett-Petts, W.F.. Vancouver: New Star Books, 135-144.

van Leeuwen, M. 2005. *Importance of agro-food industry for small and medium-sized towns in EU countries; an inter-regional SAM analysis.* Available at: www.ageconsearch.umn.edu/bitstream/24548/1/pp05va04.pdf

van Leeuwen E.S. and Nijkamp P. 2006. The embeddedness of small enterprises to the rural economy of small and medium sized towns. In: Vaz T., Morgan E. and Nijkamp P. (eds.), *The New European Rurality, Strategies for small firms*, Ashgate, Aldershot.

van Leeuwen, E.S. 2010. Urban-Rural Interactions: Towns as Focus Points in Rural Development. *Contributions to Economics*, Heidelberg: Physica Verlag.

Waitt, G. 2006. Creative Small Cities: Cityscapes, Power and the Arts, in *Small Cities: Urban Experience Beyond the Metropolis*, edited by Bell, D. and Jayne, M.. Oxon: Routledge, 169-183.

Waitt, G. and Gibson, C. 2009. *Creative Small Cities: Rethinking the Creative Economy in Place. Urban Studies*, 46(5-6), 1223-1246.

Wierzbicki, A. and Nakamori, Y. 2006. *Creative Space: Models of Creative Processes for the Knowledge Civilization Age.* Berlin-Heidelberg: Springer-Verlag.

Wilczyński, R. 2003. *Odnowa wsi perspektywą rozwoju obszarów wiejskich w Polsce (Village renewal as prospect for the development of rural areas in Poland).* Fundacja Fundusz Współpracy, Krajowe Centrum Doradztwa Rozwoju Rolnictwa i Obszarów Wiejskich Oddział w Poznaniu. Poznań.

Winter, M. 2003. Embeddedness, the new food economy and defensive localism. *Journal of Rural Studies*, 19, 23-32.

Zipf, G.K. 1935. *Psycho-Biology of Language: An Introduction to Dynamic Philology.* Boston: Houghton Mifflin Company.

Zipf, G.K. 1949. *Human Behavior and the Principle of Least Effort.* Addison-Wesley, Cambridge: MA.

Chapter 4

Market Potential and New Firm Formation

Jenny Grek, Charlie Karlsson and Johan Klaesson

4.1. Introduction

Today there is an extensive research literature on entrepreneurship and firm demography. However, even if many studies have identified substantial and persistent variations in entrepreneurship rates across regions in a variety of countries (Georgellis and Wall, 2000), most attempts that try to explain entrepreneurship variations have been restricted to industry determinants (Arauzo-Carod and Manjón-Antolín, 2007). As a matter of fact, location factors are neglected in most studies trying to explain variations in entrepreneurship.[1] This is astonishing, since there are studies, which show that location factors matter.[2] There are numerous examples of location factors that might explain spatial variations in entrepreneurship in the literature on regional economics and economic geography including institutional framework, size of region, industrial and firm structure, in-migration, demand growth, employment specialization, unemployment rates, educational level, university R&D, the availability of financing, and population density. However, our understanding of the empirical structure of the regional variations in entrepreneurship, as well as the underlying theoretical explanations, is still incomplete. Thus, "the economics literature on regional dimensions of entrepreneurship looks ripe for further investigation and extension" (Parker, 2004).[3] In a similar manner, Audretsch and Feldman (2004) remark that the life cycle of spatial units, such as agglomerations, clusters and regions, with regard to the role of entrepreneurship is a relatively unchartered area.

A better understanding of the drivers of entrepreneurship is important, since many authors assume a relationship between entrepreneurship and growth at both the national and the regional level (Plummer and Acs, 2004; Fritsch and Mueller,

---

1   "Entrepreneurial management, or the study of the creation and growth of new companies, has become a prominent field in the literature on management. This field has developed largely independently of location considerations." Porter (2000, 269)

2   See, e.g., Reynolds, Miller and Maki (1993), Audretsch and Fritsch (1994), Garofoli (1994), Guesnier (1994), Malecki (1993), Saxenian (1999), Fotopoulos and Spence (1999 and 2001), Berglund and Brännäs (2001), Armington and Acs (2002), Arauzo and Tereul (2005), and Karlsson and Backman (2008).

3   "It is surprising to observe that the geography of entrepreneurship has indeed received far less attention [than other aspects of entrepreneurship]." Nijkamp (2003).

2004; van Stel and Storey, 2004; Audretsch et al., 2006).[4] It is imagined that the continual entry and exit of firms and plants is a necessary condition for regional growth. The entry of new firms and plants tend to be connected with productive innovation, *i.e.* the introduction of new or improved products and/or production methods (Baumol, 2002). The entry of new actors in the market place increases competition and forces incumbents to become more effective, *i.e.* to increase their productivity, move to another region or to go out of business. Thus, when new innovative firms enter, some existing businesses are displaced in a process of creative destruction (Schumpeter, 1934; Robinson, O'Leary and Rincon, 2006). However, above all, entry of new firms generates entrepreneur-driven Schumpeter-type creative destruction (Manjón-Antolin, 2004). Instead, new firm formation is a heterogeneous phenomenon where innovative entrepreneurs are mixed with more normal entrepreneurs in the form of passive followers, over-optimistic gamblers and people trying to find an alternative to unemployment (Vivarelli, 2007). Cabral (2004) even claims that most entrepreneurial ventures are 'entry mistakes'. However, there seems to be a considerable consensus that entrepreneurship plays a critical role for the introduction of radical innovations.

However, disregarding the large diversity of entrepreneurial ventures, entrepreneurship has been identified by many authors as an important driver for economic growth, competitiveness and job creation (Thurik and Wennekers, 2004; Friis et al., 2006), even if there are authors, such as Acs and Storey (2004), who claim that the evidence remains inconclusive. However, Karlsson and Nyström (2007) present a survey of empirical studies since 1996 of the relationship between entrepreneurship and productivity, employment and economic growth that shows that two-thirds of the studies find a significant positive relationship.

The focus in this paper is on how the conditions for entrepreneurship vary between regions. Our starting point is the functional region, approximated by the commuting region. Our prime motivation for this is that the functional region for almost all businesses makes up their market but also offers most of the supply conditions, in terms of labour, business services, infrastructure, that are critical for both the start-up of firms and for the efficient operation of firms. Since both the market and the supply conditions vary with the size of functional regions, we have strong reasons to believe that there are not only significant variations in the entry and exit of firms between regions of different size but also differences in terms of both the sectoral composition and the size distribution of entering and exiting firms. A better understanding of how and why the entry and exit of firms vary between different functional regions is important as a knowledge base to develop regional policies that support the entry and exit of firms in regions of various sizes. Since the background conditions vary with the size of functional regions, so must

---

4   Chinitz (1961) has already argued that the existence of many small firms and a culture of entrepreneurship could explain why New York has been much more successful than Pittsburgh.

the regional policies that directly and indirectly are targeted at supporting the entry and exit of firms to stimulate regional economic growth.

The theoretical and empirical literature gives strong support to the idea that the agglomeration of population and jobs in large urban regions offers favourable incubator conditions for creative entrepreneurship and innovation (Hoover and Vernon, 1959; Thompson, 1968; Leone and Struyck, 1976; Pred, 1977; Davelaar, 1991), and has a positive effect on the location of firms and entrepreneurship (Hansen, 1987; Guimarães, et al., 2000; Figueiredo, et al., 2002). The clustering of economic activities in geographical space (Audretsch and Feldman, 2004; Porter, 1998) suggests that there are positive agglomeration economies that influence the location of new firms, and that these economies may compensate for the negative effects, in terms of higher rent and wage costs, in agglomerations, and of potential competition from incumbent firms located in the agglomeration. However, earlier studies use administrative regions rather than functional regions as their spatial units. We claim that a better understanding of the role of size of regions can be achieved if the empirical analysis is based on functional regions. We also claim that incomes are a better measure of size than either population or jobs, since they represent a measure of the potential market demand in different regions. Furthermore, this potential market demand can for each locality within a functional region be divided into three components: the intra-locality, the intra-regional, and the inter-regional demand potential, respectively. This offers an opportunity to highlight the relative importance of these three demand (=size) measures in general for entrepreneurship as well as for entrepreneurship, in different sectors.

The purpose of the current chapter is to analyse the theoretical arguments as to why large regions generally should generate more entrepreneurship, and empirically analyse the role of regional size in explaining variations in total entrepreneurship and entrepreneurship in different sectors across functional regions using data from Sweden.

The chapter is organized as follows. In Section 4.2 we develop our theoretical framework and our hypotheses. Our empirical approach and our data are presented in Section 4.3. The empirical analyses are performed in Sections 4.4 and Section 4.5 provides the conclusions.

4.2. Regional Size as a Stimulus for Formation of New Firms: Theoretical Arguments

The variations in entrepreneurship between large and small functional regions are related to variations in, on the one hand, demand conditions and, on the other, supply conditions. Regional variations in demand conditions, in terms of regional market potential and regional demand for new products, generate spatial variations in entrepreneurial opportunities. On the supply side, there are similar differences between regions of different sizes in the number of economic agents with a capacity to discover, create, and exploit entrepreneurial opportunities due to differences in educational achievements, work experiences, networks, and so on. On the supply side there are also variations between regions of various sizes as regards conditions such as the knowledge base, information supply, industrial structure, company structure, supply of inputs and producer services, supply of financial services and capital, infrastructure supply. At an aggregate level the differences in demand and supply conditions between regions of different size create differences in the agglomeration economies offered by different regions.

The interest in the effects of agglomeration economies goes back at least to Marshall (1920), who identified three types of external economies: a common labour market; information spillovers; and the development of specialized input suppliers. However, it was Ohlin (1933), who by his classification of agglomeration economies illustrated how individual firms and thus potential entrepreneurs are affected by being localized to regions of varying size:[5]

- Internal economies of scale associated with the production function of the firm. Since many products are distance-sensitive or have high geographical transaction costs, the size of the regional market is critical for many firms to be able to breakeven and make a profit.
- Location economies, which are external to the individual firm but are derived from the size of its industry in the region where it is located.
- Urbanization economies, which are external to both the firm and its industry, and which are dependent upon the size of the total regional economy.
- Inter-industry linkages of input-output type where proximity to input suppliers reduces the price of inputs due to scale advantages and reduced transport costs.

These factors explain why entrepreneurs may choose to locate in large urban regions, and accept increased land and labour prices, in situations where simple location analysis would suggest a decentralized location. However, the localization and urbanization economies are in principle static concepts. If we ask about the spillovers entrepreneurs look for we need to turn to the dynamic version of the localization economies, *i.e.* Marshall-Arrow-Romer's (MAR) and Porter's theories of specialization, and the dynamic version of urbanization economies, *i.e.* Jacobs's theory of diversity (Glaeser *et al.*, 1992). MAR's and Porter's theories stress that the industrial specialization of urban regions is the most important source of spillovers, an attractor for entrepreneurs in the same industry. On the other hand, it is claimed that the most important spillovers come from outside the industry with industrial diversity being an attractor for entrepreneurs. Henderson et al. (1995) show that the importance of the two types of spillover varies between industries. Regarding manufacturing industry, they find that diversity does not really matter. However, the diversity of an urban region attracts new industries

---

5   A similar classification of agglomeration economies has been provided by Hoover (1948).

and more particularly high technology industries. Below, we discuss in more detail how agglomeration economies in general and urbanization economies in particular influence entrepreneurial behaviour.

4.2.1. Entrepreneurship and Regional Variations in Demand Conditions

The best opportunities for entrepreneurial initiatives are offered by functional regions, which combine a large home market with high accessibility to markets in other regions, *i.e.* large functional regions. Firstly, generally speaking, the larger the functional region, the higher the per capita income. Entrepreneurs who launch start-ups in large functional regions may take advantage of proximity to a concentration of (potential) customers, *i.e.* of purchasing power, which of course can be other firms.

Under certain conditions, entrepreneurs may capture incumbents' market share if they locate near them (Hotelling, 1929). Admittedly, this gain may be short-lived if more entrepreneurs enter, or if incumbents react to this unwanted competition. When the competition in the product market is imperfect, geographical proximity increases competition in the product market (Fujita et al., 1999), which implies that entrepreneurs may suffer from proximity to firms offering similar products, in particular if the demand is thin. However, when there is a demand for variety among customers, large regions always offer entrepreneurs a greater possibility to successfully launch a new product.

A third motive for entrepreneurs to locate start-up firms in large functional regions may be more longterm. Entrepreneurs may choose to locate in a large functional region because they are more likely to be better exposed to customers. The underlying reason is that searching is costly for customers who, *ceteris paribus*, prefer to minimize search cost by purchasing in areas of concentrated (and varied) supply. This is particularly relevant in product markets with discerning potential customers with specific demands and requirements, who wish to search and inspect before purchasing. Such product markets are to a high extent concentrated in large functional regions. It is these regions, which host the most demanding customers in the form of company headquarters, R&D and product development units of large companies, as well as other advanced establishments, such as research universities, university hospitals, R&D institutes, and specialized R&D firms.

A fourth advantage for entrepreneurs of locating in large functional regions is the positive information externality in such regions, through which individual (potential) entrepreneurs receive signals about the strength of the regional demand by observing the successful trades of incumbent firms. Such observations also provide information about varieties of existing products, which also might trigger the development of new varieties that might be complements or substitutes to existing product varieties.

From a different angle, a fifth advantage for an entrepreneur of a location in a large functional region might be the signalling effect to potential customers in the form of an indication or image of quality.

A sixth advantage for entrepreneurs to locate in large functional regions is risk reduction (Mills and Hamilton, 1984). To the extent that fluctuations in demand are imperfectly correlated across customers, demand can be stabilized since some customers are buying while others are not.

A seventh advantage is that, finally, when an entrepreneur chooses a location in a large functional region, he can expect a local economic milieu of qualified and demanding customers, which is important for entrepreneurs engaged in innovation processes and product development.

4.2.2. Entrepreneurship and Regional Variations in Supply Conditions

On the supply side, the regional economic milieu (including its culture, knowledge-base, and attitudes to businesses) often appears to act as a critical success factor for new forms of entrepreneurship (Camagni, 1991). Large functional regions offer advantages to entrepreneurs in terms of knowledge flows that are particularly important when the product and/or process knowledge is complex and perhaps tacit in nature (Karlsson and Manduchi, 2001). Tacit knowledge, which is vital to found new firms, is best communicated informally through frequent face-to-face interactions, hence the importance of the proximity offered by large functional regions. Major research universities and research laboratories are normally located in large functional regions. This implies that these regions offer a larger and more varied knowledge base for potential entrepreneurs to draw upon (Audretsch et al., 2006).

A special type of information externality accrues to potential entrepreneurs from observing a large number of successful incumbents in large functional regions, *i.e.* there is large potential for product and production knowledge to spillover in large regions.[6] This implies that the start-up rate for each industrial sector should increase with the existing density of firms in each sector. Large and dense regions offer physical proximity, which facilitates the integration of multidisciplinary knowledge that is tacit and therefore person-embodied rather than information-embodied as well as allowing the rapid decision making needed to cope with uncertainty (see Patel and Pavitt, 1991). Due to urbanization economies, these regions also offer diversity, that is, economies of scope, in information, skills, knowledge, competence, producer services, and other inputs, which are crucial for innovative entrepreneurial processes. Furthermore, they offer advantages in terms of access to a large pool of well-educated and specialized labour (Marshall, 1920), particularly specialized workers in accounting, law, advertising and different

---

6   We thus have a spatial version of what is called "knowledge spillover theory of entrepreneurship" (Audretsch and Lehman, 2005).

technological fields.[7] This is partly because most leading higher education institutions are located in large functional regions. This reduces the costs of starting-up and expanding new businesses (Krugman, 1993). It probably also leads to a higher proportion of high-quality start-ups, but may also be an important success factor for new firms following the start of operations.

Large, densely populated functional regions are also conducive to a greater provision of non-traded inputs, *i.e.* their service infrastructure is more developed. These regions provide these inputs both in greater variety, with a higher degree of specialization at lower costs (Krugman, 1991a, b). This implies that entrepreneurs who start firms in large regions can take full advantage of all potential substitution possibilities inherent in available production functions, *i.e.* taking full advantage of the outsourcing of functions and activities. One special aspect of the greater provision of non-traded inputs is the larger and more varied supply of financial services in large regions. Risk capital investors prefer to locate in large urban regions since they try to lower their risks by investing in several new projects and by keeping a hands-on relationship with the entrepreneurs and their new companies, which demands geographical proximity and frequent face-to-face interactions (Thornton and Flynn, 2003). A larger and more varied supply of financial services in large regions tends to stimulate the start-up of new firms in such regions (Backman, 2008). The reason is that face-to-face contacts are normally required to obtain funding for starting new firms, since there are normally no physical assets that can serve as collateral.

There are also physical infrastructure benefits for entrepreneurs to locate in large functional regions in terms of, for example, access to major highways, international airports and broadband capacity. A final reason for large functional regions providing advantages for entrepreneurs arises from the reductions in spatial transaction costs that are made possible by locating in a large and dense region (Quigley, 1998).[8] In particular, search costs for customers, suppliers, services, and knowledge are lower in large and dense functional regions.

The information-flow economies (Acs et al., 1992) on both the supply and the demand side are greater in large functional regions than small ones. Information and knowledge is a *sine qua non* for entrepreneurial success. Learning-by-doing supported by inter-firm network collaboration enhances, for example, the competitive potential of new firm initiatives (Malecki and Poeling, 1999). Since large urban regions are the leading communication and transport network nodes, they are the primary locations of the emission and reception of information and knowledge. Because these regions contain concentrations of complex communication equipment and transport terminals, much information

---

7   Florida (2002) has suggested that creative capital rather than human capital is the source of entrepreneurship and economic growth in regions.

8   It may be observed that, while in some respects spatial transaction costs have fallen over time, there are other aspects in which spatial transaction costs appear to have actually increased over time (McCann and Shepard, 2003).

and knowledge diffuse more easily from urban region to urban region than to the hinterland around each urban region (Florax and Folmer, 1992; Guillain and Huriot, 2001). Thus, new firms are likely to be started where such economies are greatest. Large functional regions, in particular, offer favourable conditions for innovative entrepreneurship as a result of a larger and more varied access to knowledge and to skilled and educated labour, economics of density and entrepreneurial opportunities generated by the large functional regions which are the nucleus of innumerable networks with a scale ranging from local to global (Nijkamp, 2003). Regional economic milieus which offer a rich supply of various types of networks (*i.e.* mainly large functional regions) tend to encourage entrepreneurship, since participation or involvement in regional or broader economic networks makes it possible to externalize some of the risks involved (Shapero, 1984).[9] This implies that conditions that can generate potentially synergetic situations and support for learning are mostly available in large functional regions.

Besides general demand and supply conditions, one may assume that the larger and richer a functional region, the larger the number of potential entrepreneurs, since individuals in such regions in general are better educated, have more varied work experience, and so on. We may even assume that large (and dense) functional regions offer increasing returns in the acquisition of entrepreneurial skills and entrepreneurial competence as a result of the more numerous, more varied and more effective interactions between individuals in such regions (Glaeser, 1999; Desmet, 2000). Since larger functional regions offer greater opportunities and higher capacity for entrepreneurship, they are bound to experience a build-up of entrepreneurial knowledge, which will stimulate further entrepreneurial action.

Furthermore, entrepreneurs are change agents who will not only make decisions to start firms but they will also actively try to shape the regional economic milieu and regional institutions by trying to influence political decision makers in the region or try to take their own initiatives (Stimson et al., 2006). They will spend resources and develop relationships that further their own interests, as well as those of potential entrepreneurs, through the creation of a positive regional entrepreneurial environment (Feldman, 2001). Good conditions for entrepreneurial actions and good conditions in general in large functional regions will stimulate potential entrepreneurs, often well-educated people, in smaller regions to move to larger regions.[10] When more potential entrepreneurs gather in larger function at

---

9   This does not exclude the possibility that some smaller functional regions may offer favourable seed-bed conditions for entrepreneurship within, for example, specialized industrial clusters.

10   The concept 'potential entrepreneurs' is used here to stress that when well-educated people move into larger regions from smaller ones the major attractor is probably the dynamic labour market in larger functional regions. However, as soon as the in-migrants are established in the larger region, they become potential entrepreneurs who sometimes are better at discovering business opportunities than people who have lived in the larger region for a long time. It seems, on the other hand, to be well-established in the literature that

regions, the conditions for entrepreneurial actions will improve due to the increased availability of entrepreneurial knowledge. This will further induce entrepreneurial initiatives and encourage in-migration of potential entrepreneurs from other (smaller) regions. In this sense, entrepreneurial spatial behaviour generates a dynamic cumulative concentration process of entrepreneurial knowledge, skills and competence.

It is clear that new enterprises in a functional region contribute significantly to its economy and employment but, in particular, to its renewal. It is important in this connection to understand that all entrepreneurial start-ups can be seen as experiments. All potential and active entrepreneurs benefit from learning the outcome of such experiments, and the knowledge spillovers from such experiments are proportional to the number of experiments. Since larger functional regions normally host many more such experiments than smaller ones, they also benefit proportionally more from such entrepreneurial learning. Thus, they accumulate a larger stock of entrepreneurial knowledge over time, which implies that externalities from entrepreneurial knowledge are dynamic in nature. In a multi-regional context, each functional region may build up a stock of regional entrepreneurial knowledge based upon past and current entrepreneurial activity (Glaeser, *et al.*, 1992), involving sets of cumulative experiments. Such regional accumulation of entrepreneurial knowledge affects the probability that entrepreneurial actions will take place and be successful, and, since large functional regions accumulate more entrepreneurial knowledge, they will also generate more entrepreneurial activities.

Even if there are many reasons why larger regions should be expected to offer better supply-side opportunities for entrepreneurship, it is not clear in the available literature whether more diversified or more specialized regional economic milieus offer the best conditions for entrepreneurship and firm growth (Glaeser, *et al.*, 1992; Henderson, Kuncoro and Turner, 1995). In this connection, it has been suggested that firms and thus entrepreneurs prefer different regional economic milieus depending upon the stage of the life cycle of their products (Duranton and Puga, 2001). However, the distinction between diversified and specialized regions is no easy issue, since large diversified regions also exhibit many different specializations.

4.2.3. Entrepreneurship and Agglomeration: The Empirical Picture

The general relationship between agglomeration economies and location has been analysed extensively from both a theoretical and an empirical point of view. However, the more specific relationship between agglomeration economies and entrepreneurship has been less extensively analysed.

---

entrepreneurs rarely move when they establish new (Stam, 2007) and, in particular, new high-tech firms (Cooper and Folta, 2000). However, they may have migrated to the region well before they become entrepreneurs.

In van Oort and Stam (2006) the relationship between agglomeration economies and entrepreneurship is analysed. The authors find evidence that agglomeration effects have a stronger effect on new firm formation than on growth of incumbent in the ICT industry. According to Van Ort and Stam (2006), there are two reasons that can explain this relationship. The first reason is that incumbent firms usually have a wider spatial orientation, and the second is that the incumbent firms usually tend to keep their knowledge inside the company as much as possible compared with new firms. According to Acs (2005), the geography of innovation and the new economic geography suggest that the extent to which a country is entrepreneurial and its economic system is agglomerated can be a factor that explains technological change. He concludes that entrepreneurial activity and agglomeration have a positive effect on technological change in the EU. McCann (1995) analyses the characterization of various types of agglomeration economies, *i.e.* internal returns to scale, localization economies and urbanization economies. Intermediate locations are indeed the norm regarding agglomeration economies. Agglomeration factors are available in a larger metropolitan area, such as sheer size of medium-sized agglomerations and access to high-level knowledge in local universities. Both, agglomeration economies, and footlooseness, are likely to increase in the future, based on growing globalization. This would mean that medium-sized agglomerations at some distance from the large cities are anticipating additional opportunities for economic growth.

4.2.4. Hypotheses

Based upon the above discussion we now formulate our first hypothesis:

H1: We expect that the higher the regional income level, the larger the gross rate of firm formation.

However, it must be stressed that start-ups and newly established firms face substantial risks for numerous reasons. As a consequence, the death rate among start-ups is relatively high but tends to decrease rather rapidly over time.[11] A high death rate among newly formed firms is natural since they are involved in the introduction of new products and/or new production processes in the market place. Accordingly, they provide a major challenge to established firms and encourage or force them to improve product quality and services, or to reduce prices or to leave the market. This means that entrepreneurs play a fundamental role in the renewal of regional economies by strengthening competition and initiating competitive processes that end in the creative destruction of existing modes of production. Thus, we shall expect regions with extensive entrepreneurial activities to also be characterized by extensive firm exits, *i.e.* we expect entry and exit rates across regions of various sizes to be correlated (see Keeble and Walker, 1994;

---

11   Naturally, the survival or success rates of new entrepreneurs show large variations between sectors and regions (Acs, 2000).

Reynolds et al., 1994). Earlier studies show that high population density leads to relatively low survival rates of new businesses, but to higher average employment in those start-ups that do manage to survive (Fritsch et al., 2006; Weyh, 2006). This implies that higher intensity of competition in larger agglomerations results in more rigorous market selection in these regions with the surviving businesses performing relatively well there.

This discussion allows us to formulate our second hypothesis:

H2: We expect that the larger the regional income, the larger the rate of firm deaths.

The idea here is that entries, among other things, can be expected to generate a displacement effect that causes exits to increase. However, exits might free niches in the market place and economic resources that might increase the ability and willingness of potential entrepreneurs to enter the market (Acs and Audretsch, 1990; Nyström, 2006; Arauzo *et al.*, 2007). If we consider hypotheses H1 and H2 together, we run into uncertainty concerning the effects of regional size on the net entry of firms. However, the basis of our basic arguments about the importance of regional size for new firm formation we launch the following hypothesis concerning the net entry of firms:

H3: We expect that the larger the regional income, the larger the net entry of firms.

In the introduction to this paper, we made the remark that it is possible to work with a more sophisticated representation of the regional income and its influence on entrepreneurship. Our starting point is that the geographical space of any nation can be divided into a number of functional regions, where each functional region contains a number of localities. For practical reasons these functional regions can be approximated by the labour market, *i.e.,* commuting, regions. Entrepreneurs start their firms in a locality and, depending upon their type of product, they market their product within the locality, within the region and/or within the whole national economy.[12] Thus, the different markets are not of equal importance for all products. In this chapter, excluding the primary sector and the public sector, we make a distinction between four types of products or industries: primary products, manufacturing products, ordinary services, and advanced business services, where ordinary services have a high content of household services. For these four product groups, we now formulate the hypotheses H4-H6:

H4: We expect entrepreneurship in advanced business services to have the highest dependency on the size of the intra-regional market potential.

---

12   The international market is of course also an alternative, but an alternative that we disregard here.

The motivation for this hypothesis is the general tendency among advanced business services to locate in large functional (urban) regions, where their major customers are located and where they can interact face-to-face with their customers.

H5: We expect entrepreneurship in manufacturing to have the highest dependency on the size of the inter-regional market potential.
Producers of manufacturing products have, on average, a lower need for face-to-face contacts with their customers than producers of advanced business services. Manufacturing production is also more space demanding. This induces entrepreneurs in manufacturing to start their enterprises in regions with plenty of space but with a good location in the logistical networks to be able to deliver efficiently to the customers in the most important markets.

H6: We expect entrepreneurship in ordinary services to have the highest dependency on the size of the intra-locality market potential.
Most enterprises in the household service sector operate with a very small market area. Thus, entrepreneurs starting firms that deliver household services will prefer to locate in localities with a high market potential.

4.3. Empirical Approach and Data

This chapter uses FEVD regressions, *i.e.* fixed effects vector decomposition regressions, to investigate the market potential and new firm formation in industrial sectors at the local level.[13]

The regional concept in focus in this study is the functional region, which for practical purposes is approximated by the commuting region. A functional region normally consists of a central municipality surrounded by a number of hinterland municipalities.

To model size, we measure for each municipality its total accessibility to Gross Regional Product (GRP), which we interpret as accessibility to market potential and thus to potential demand. For each municipality we break down the total accessibility to GRP into two components:

*   Local accessibility to GRP; and
*   External accessibility to GRP.

This makes it possible for us to make statements about which accessibility that matters most for gross entries, exits, and net entries of firms in different sectors in the economy. In this study we make a distinction between four sectors: (i) the primary sector, (ii) the manufacturing sector, (iii) the ordinary service sector; and (iv) the advanced service sector. Gross entry of firms in a municipality is defined

---

13   See Plümper and Troeger (2007) for further details.

as (number of entering firms + 1)/(population of working age in 1000s). Exit of firms in a municipality is defined as (number of exiting firms + 1)/(existing firms). Net entry of firms in a municipality is defined as (number of entering firms minus number of exiting firms)/(existing firms +1).[14]

To control for the influence on gross entries, exits and net entries from other factors, we also include a number of control variables in our analysis. These control variables are (i) the employment rate; (ii) the share of the labour force with more than three years of university schooling; (iii) the share of small firms with 1 to 4 employees in all sectors; (iv) local accessibility to GRP; and (v) external accessibility to GRP.

The data used in this chapter comes from Statistics Sweden and spans the years 1993-2004.[15] Tables 4.1 and 4.2 below give a short presentation of the data.

Table 4.1   Variable descriptions

Variable	Description /Explanation
Population in working age	Population in the ages between 20 and 64 years of age
Entry	(Number of entering firms + 1) / (Population in working age in 1000s)
Exit	(Number of exiting firms + 1) / (Existing firms + 1)
Net entry	(Number of entering firms - number of exiting firms) / (Existing firms + 1)
Local accessibility to GRP	Accessibility to Gross Regional Product in municipality *m* coming from economic activity in municipality *m*
External accessibility to GRP	Accessibility to Gross Regional Product in municipality *m* coming from economic activity in all other Swedish municipalies
Education	Population with more than three years of university schooling / Population in working age
Employment rate	Population holding a job / Population in working age
Share of small firms	Number of firms with 1 to 4 employees / all firms

Table 4.2   Descriptive statistics

Variable	Mean	Median	Std. Dev.	Min	Max
Entry in the primary sector	0.346	0.256	0.310	0.012	3.256
Entry in the manufacturing sector	0.980	0.885	0.489	0.092	4.889
Entry in the ordinary service sector	1.857	1.741	0.780	0.202	8.160
Entry in the advanced service sector	1.533	1.395	0.808	0.170	8.537
Exit in the primary sector	0.228	0.179	0.199	0.014	3.000
Exit in the manufacturing sector	0.108	0.098	0.051	0.012	0.571
Exit in the ordinary service sector	0.137	0.132	0.045	0.017	0.533
Exit in the advanced service sector	0.193	0.175	0.086	0.016	1.000
Net entry in the primary sector	-0.006	0.000	0.365	-0.857	0.889
Net entry in the manufacturing sector	-0.059	-0.060	0.255	-0.900	0.875
Net entry in the ordinary service sector	-0.051	-0.046	0.189	-0.857	0.857
Net entry in the advanced service sector	0.037	0.037	0.237	-0.889	0.900
Local accessibility to GRP	0.006	0.003	0.017	0.001	0.289
External accessibility to GRP	0.026	0.011	0.044	0.001	0.319
Education	0.098	0.087	0.043	0.040	0.366
Employment rate	0.749	0.750	0.044	0.514	0.882
Share of small firms	0.606	0.602	0.056	0.417	0.809

Note: N = 3420

14   We add 1 to all observations to avoid any zeros in entries and exits in any municipality. This 'transformation' will only have a very slight influence on our econometric results.

15   See tables of correlation matrix in the Appendix A 4.1 for further details/ characteristics of the variables.

4.4. Empirical Results

Here we present our empirical results. We start by analysing the determinants of firm entry in our four different sectors during the time period 1993 to 2004 (see Figure 4.3). Then we analyse the determinants of firm exit in our four different sectors (see Figure 4.4), and thereafter we investigate the determinants of the net entry of firms in the different sectors (see Figure 4.5).

4.4.1. Firm entry

The dependent variable is defined as the entry of firms in each one of our four sectors, for the time period 1993-2004.

Table 4.3   Results from the FEVD regressions for firm entry (in the period 1993-2004)

Dependent variable	FEVD (fixed effects vector decomposition)			
	Entry (1)	Entry (2)	Entry (3)	Entry (4)
	(Primary sector)	(Manufacturing sector)	(Ordinary service sector)	(Advanced service sector)
Local accessibility to GRP	-2.547	-0.979	9.274	12.991
	(11.08)***	(2.35)**	(16.18)***	(24.38)***
External accessibility to GRP	-1.590	0.577	3.292	5.556
	(15.50)***	(3.08)***	(12.89)***	(23.33)***
Education	-0.666	-3.266	-6.380	1.643
	(5.92)***	(16.03)***	(22.26)***	(5.86)***
Employment rate	-1.073	-3.192	-3.778	-2.385
	(12.17)***	(19.19)***	(17.30)***	(11.94)***
Share of small firms	0.997	1.687	2.227	2.484
	(15.31)***	(14.22)***	(13.82)***	(16.79)***
Constant	0.669	2.660	3.817	1.421
	(8.54)***	(18.11)***	(19.56)***	(7.97)***
Observations	3420	3420	3420	3420
R-squared	0.61	0.48	0.62	0.70
* significant at 10%; ** significant at 5%; *** significant at 1%				

Local accessibility to GRP has a strongly significant impact on the entry of new firms. For the primary sector and the manufacturing sector, this impact is negative, and for the ordinary service sector and the advanced service sector, it is positive. External accessibility to GRP also has a strongly significant impact on the entry of new firms. However, the negative impact is only valid for the primary sector and positive for the three other sectors. Further, the strongly significant impact on new firm formation can be interpreted as follows. In municipalities with high external accessibility to GRP, potential entrepreneurs tend to form new firms. A high employment rate implies that there is a strong negative impact of firm entry in all sectors. This is in line with what one could expect, since there is less need for individuals to start their own business when compared with situations where the employment rate is low. If a municipality or a region has a high level of education among its citizens, there is a strong negative impact on the entry of new firms in all sectors except in the advanced service sector where the impact is positive. Further, the presence of many small firms in different sectors also has a strongly positive significant impact on new firm formation in all sectors.

4.4.2. Firm exit

The dependent variable is defined as the exit of firms in each of our four sectors, for time period 1993-2004. The results are presented in Table 4.4.

Table 4.4 **Results from the FEVD regressions for firm exit (in the period 1993-2004)**

| Dependent variable | FEVD (fixed effects vector decomposition) | | | |
| | Exit (1) | Exit (2) | Exit (3) | Exit (4) |
	(Primary sector)	(Manufacturing sector)	(Ordinary service sector)	(Advanced service sector)
Local accessibility to GRP	-0.877	-0.134	0.071	-0.355
	(4.80)***	(2.84)***	(1.63)	(4.19)***
External accessibility to GRP	0.945	0.197	0.293	0.116
	(11.50)***	(9.22)***	(14.60)***	(3.04)***
Education	-0.492	-0.112	-0.267	-0.253
	(5.50)***	(4.84)***	(12.21)***	(6.13)***
Employment rate	-0.997	-0.718	-0.463	-0.673
	(14.10)***	(33.92)***	(25.33)***	(20.00)***
Share of small firms	0.060	0.237	0.142	0.191
	(1.16)	(17.58)***	(11.44)***	(7.95)***
Constant	0.968	0.508	0.416	0.604
	(15.41)***	(27.85)***	(26.04)***	(20.49)***
Observations	3420	3420	3420	3420
R-squared	0.40	0.38	0.32	0.31

* significant at 10%; ** significant at 5%; *** significant at 1%

Local accessibility to GRP has a strongly negative significant impact on firm exit in all sectors except in the ordinary service sector. External accessibility to GRP also has a strongly significant impact on the entry of new firms for all sectors. In this case, the impact is positive, which means that, given that a municipality has a high degree of external accessibility to GRP, firm exit is assumed to increase. As in the case of firm entry, a high employment rate and a high level of education implies that there is a strong negative impact of firm exit in all sectors. Further, the presence of many small firms in the different sectors also has a strongly positive significant impact on firm exit in all sectors, *i.e.* the higher the share of small firms, the higher the exit of firms, for all sectors.

4.4.3. Net entry of firms

The dependent variable is defined as the net entry of firms in our four sectors, *i.e.* firm entry – firm exit in each sector, for the time period 1993-2004 (see Table 4.5).

Both local and external accessibility to GRP have a strongly positive significant impact on net entry of new firms in all sectors. There is no such significant impact for the primary sector in the case of external accessibility to GRP. A high employment rate implies that there is a strongly positive impact of net firm entry in the primary sector, the manufacturing sector, and in the ordinary service sector. A high level of education implies a strongly negative significant impact on net entry of new firms in all sectors. As in the case of new firm formation and firm exit, the presence of many small firms in the different sectors also has a strongly positive significant impact on new firm formation in all sectors except for the primary sector.

Table 4.5   Results from the FEVD regressions for net entry of firms (in the period 1993-2004)

	FEVD (fixed effects vector decomposition)			
Dependent variable	Net entry (1)	Net entry (2)	Net entry (3)	Net entry (4)
	(Primary sector)	(Manufacturing sector)	(Ordinary service sector)	(Advanced service sector)
Local accessibility to GRP	0.851	1.927	1.278	0.694
	(2.02)**	(6.03)***	(5.78)***	(2.52)**
External accessibility to GRP	0.199	0.618	0.649	0.528
	(1.05)	(4.54)***	(6.64)***	(4.23)***
Education	-0.568	-1.683	-0.748	-0.656
	(2.74)***	(8.97)***	(6.25)***	(4.64)***
Employment rate	0.273	1.237	0.438	-0.095
	(1.68)*	(8.77)***	(5.10)***	(0.91)
Share of small firms	0.129	0.283	0.159	0.137
	(1.07)	(3.38)***	(2.61)***	(1.76)*
Constant	-0.244	-1.021	-0.426	0.071
	(1.69)*	(8.78)***	(5.70)***	(0.76)
Observations	3420	3420	3420	3420
R-squared	0.05	0.06	0.08	0.05

* significant at 10%; ** significant at 5%; *** significant at 1%

4.5. Conclusions

The purpose of this chapter was to show how entrepreneurship conditions vary between regions of various sizes, and to analyse the theoretical arguments as to why large regions generally should generate more entrepreneurship. The purpose also covered empirically analysing the role of regional size in explaining variations in total entrepreneurship and entrepreneurship in different sectors across functional regions, using data from Sweden for the period 1993 to 2004.

Using FEVD regressions, we estimate how the conditions for entrepreneurship vary between regions of various sizes. The empirical results from the estimated FEVD regressions show that both local and external aaccessibility to GRP have a strongly significant impact on both entry of new firms and firm exit. For the primary sector and the manufacturing sector this impact is negative, and for the ordinary service sector and the advanced service sector it is positive. Hence, both local and external accessibility to GRP are of great importance for the two different service sectors. However, accessibility to GRP is not that important for new firm formation in the primary sector and the manufacturing sector. Further, a high employment rate implies that there is a strongly negative impact of firm entry in all sectors. This is in line with what we would expect, since there is less need for individuals to start their own businesses compared with times when the employment rate is low. The presence of many small firms in the different sectors also has a strongly positive significant impact on new firm formation in all sectors. Hence, the more small firms there are, the higher the potential for new firm formation.

References

Acs, Z.J. (ed.) 2000. *Regional Innovation, Knowledge and Global Change.* London: Frances Pinter.

Acs, Z.J. and Audretsch, D.B. 1990. *Innovation and Small Firms.* Cambridge: The MIT Press, MA.

Acs, Z.J., Audretsch, D.B. and Feldman, M.P. 1992. Real Effects of Academic Research: Comment. *American Economic Review, 82,* 363-367.

Acs, Z.J. and Storey, D.J. 2004. Introduction: Entrepreneurship and Economic Development. *Regional Studies, 38,* 871-877.

Arauzo-Carod, J.M. and Manjón-Antolín, M.C. 2007. Entrepreneurship, Industrial Location and Economic Growth: An Appraisal, in *Entrepreneurship, Industrial Location and Economic Growth*, edited by J.M. Arauzo-Carod and Manjón-Antolín, M.C., Cheltenham: Edward Elgar, 3-17.

Arauzo, J.M. and Teruel, M. 2005. An Urban Approach to Firm Entry: The Effect of Urban Size. *Growth and Change, 36,* 508-528.

Arauzo, J.M. *et al.* 2007. Regional and Sector-Specific Determinants of Industry Dynamics and the Displacement-Replacement Effects, *Empirica, 34,* 89-115.

Armington, C. and Acs, Z.J. 2002. The Determinants of Regional Variation in New Firm Formation, *Regional Studies, 36,* 33-45.

Audretsch, D.B. and Feldman, M.P. 2004. Knowlege Spillovers and the Geography of Innovation, in *Handbook of Urban and Regional Economics*, edited by V.J. Henderson and J.-F. Thisse, Amsterdam: Elsevier, 2713-2739.

Audretsch, D.B. and Fritsch, M. 1994. The Geography of Firm Births in Germany, *Regional Studies, 28,* 359-365.

Audretsch, D.B., Keilbach, M.C. and Lehmann, E.E. 2006 *Entrepreneurship and Economic Growth.* Oxford: Oxford University Press.

Audretsch, D.B. and Lehman, E.E. 2005. Does the Knowledge Spillover Theory Hold for Regions. *Research Policy,* 1191-1202.

Backman, M. 2008. Financial Accessibility and New Firm Formation, Department of Economics, Jönköping International Business School (mimeo).

Baumol, W. 2002. *The Free-Market Innovation Machine: Analysing the Growth Miracle of Capitalism.* Princeton: Princeton University Press.

Berglund, E. and Brännäs, K. 2001. Plants' Entry and Exit in Swedish Municipalities. *The Annals of Regional Science, 35,* 431-448.

Cabral, L. 2004. Simultaneous Entry and Welfare. *European Economic Review, 48,* 161-172.

Camagni, R. 1991. *Innovation Networks: Spatial Perspectives.* London: Belhaven Press.

Chinitz, B. 1961. Contrasts in Agglomeration: New York and Pittsburgh, *American Economic Review, 71,* 279-289.

Cooper, A. and Folta, T. 2009. Entrepreneurship and High-Technology Clutsers, in *The Blackwell Handbook of Entrepreneurship*, edited by D.L. Sexton and H. Landström, Malden MA: Blackwell, 348-367.

Davelaar, E.J. 1991. *Incubation and Innovation. A Spatial Perspective.* Aldershot: Ashgate.

Desmet, K. 2000. A Perfect Foresight Model of Regional Development and Skill Specialization. *Regional Science and Urban Economics, 30*, 221-242.

Duranton, G. and Puga, D. 2001. Nursery Cities: Urban Diversity, Process Innovation and the Life Cycle of Products. *American Economic Review, 91*, 1454-1477.

Feldman, M.A. 2001. The Entrepreneurial Event Revisited: Firm Formation in a Regional Context. *Industrial and Corporate Change, 10*, 861-891.

Figueiredo, O., Guimarães, P. and Woodward, D. 2002. Home-field Advantage: Location Decisions of Portuguese Entrepreneurs. *Journal of Urban Economics, 52*, 341-361.

Florax, R. and Folmer, H. 1992. Knowledge Impacts of Universities on Industries: an Aggregate Simultaneous Investment Model. *Journal of Regional Science, 32*, 437-466.

Florida, R. 2002. *The Rise of the Creative Class.* New York: Basic Books.

Fotopoulos, G. and Spence, N. 1999. Spatial Variations in New Manufacturing Plant Openings: Some Empirical Evidence from Greece. *Regional Studies, 33*, 219-229.

Fotopoulos, G. and Spence, N. 2001. Regional Variations of Firm Births, Deaths and Growth Patterns in the UK, 1980-1991. *Growth and Change, 32*, 151-173.

Friis, C., Karlsson, C. and Paulsson, T. 2006. Relating Entrepreneurship to Growth, in *The Emerging Digital Economy. Entrepreneurship, Clusters, and Policy*, edited by B. Johansson, C. Karlsson and R.R. Stough. Berlin: Springer, 83-111.

Fritsch, M., Brixy, U. and Falck, O. 2006. The Effect of Industry, Region and Time on New Business Survival – A Multi-dimensional Analysis. *Review of Industrial Organization, 28*, 285-306.

Fritsch, M. and Mueller, P. 2004. Effects of New Business Formation on Regional Development over Time. *Regional Studies, 38*, 961-976.

Fujita, M., Krugman, P. and Venables, A. 1999. *The Spatial Economy. Cities, Regions and International Trade.* Cambridge MA: The MIT Press.

Fujita, M. and Thisse, J.F. 2002. *Economics of Agglomeration: Cities, Industrial Location, and Regional Growth.* Cambridge: Cambridge University Press.

Garofoli, G. 1994. New Firm Formation and Regional Development: The Italian Case. *Regional Studies, 28*, 381-393.

Georgellis, Y. and Wall, H. J. 2000. What Makes a Region Entrepreneurial? Evidence from Britain. *Annals of Regional Science, 34*, 385-403.

Glaeser, E. 1999. Learning in Cities. *Journal of Urban Economics, 46*, 254-277.

Glaeser, E. *et al.* 1992. Growth in Cities. *Journal of Political Economy, 100*, 1126-1152.

Guesnier, B. 1994. Regional Variations in New Firm Formation in France. *Regional Studies, 28*, 347-358.

Guillain, R. and Huriot, J.-M. 2001. The Local Dimension of Information Spillovers: A Critical Review of Empirical Evidence in the Case of Innovation. *Canadian Journal of Regional Science, 24*, 313-338.

Guimarães, P., Figueiredo, O. and Woodward, D. 2000. Agglomeration and the Location of Foreign Direct Investment in Portugal. *Journal of Urban Economics, 47*, 115-135.

Hansen, E.R. 1987. Industrial Location Choice in São Paulo, Brazil: A Nested Logit Model. *Regional Science and Urban Economics, 17*, 89-108.

Henderson, J.V., Kuncoro, A. and Turner, M. 1995. Industrial Development in Cities, *Journal of Political Economy, 103*, 1067-1085.

Holl, A. 2004. Transport Infrastructure, Agglomeration Economies and Firm Birth: Empirical Evidence from Portugal. *Journal of Regional Science, 44*, 683-712.

Hoover, E.M. 1948. *The Location of Economic Activity*. New York: McGraw Hill.

Hoover, E.M. and Vernon, R. 1959 *Anatomy of a Metropolis*. Cambridge: Harvard University Press, MA.

Hotelling, H. 1929. Stability in Competition. *Economic Journal, 39*, 41-57.

Karlsson, C. and Backman, M. 2008. Human Capital and New Firm Formation. *Technological Forecasting and Social Change* (forthcoming).

Karlsson, C. and Manduchi, A. 2001. Knowledge Spillovers in a Spatial Context – A Critical Review and Assessment, in *Knowledge, Complexity and Innovation Systems*, edited by M.M. Fischer and J. Fröhlich, Berlin: Springer-Verlag, 101-123.

Karlsson, C. and Nyström, K. 2007. *Nyföretagande, näringslivsdynamik och tillväxt i den nya världsekonomin*. Underlagsrapport nr 5 till Globaliseringsrådet, Regeringskansliet, Västerås.

Keeble, D. and Walker, S. 1994. New Firms, Small Firms and Dead Firms: Spatial Patterns and Determinants in the United Kingdom. *Regional Studies, 28*, 411-427.

Krugman, P. 1991a. Increasing Returns and Economic Geography. *Journal of Political Economy, 99*, 483-499.

Krugman, P. 1991b. History and Industry Location: The Case of the Manufacturing Belt. *American Economic Review, 81*, 80-83.

Krugman, P. 1993. First Nature, Second Nature and Metropolitan Location. *Journal of Regional Science, 33*, 129-144.

Leone, R.A. and Struyck, R. 1976. The Incubator Hypothesis: Evidence from five SMSAs. *Urban Studies, 13*, 325-333.

Malecki, E.J. 1993. Entrepreneurs, Networks, and Economic Development: A Review of Recent Research, in *Advances in Entrepreneurship, Firm Emergence and Growth*, Vol. 3, Greenwich: JAI Press, CT, 57-118.

Malecki, E.J. and Poehling, R.M. 1999. Extroverts and Introverts: Small Manufacturers and their Information Sources. *Entrepreneurship and Regional Development, 11*, 247-268.

Manjón-Antolin, M.C. 2004. Firm Size and Short-Term Dynamics in Aggregate Entry and Exit. *CentER Discussion Paper*, Tilburg: Tilburg University.

Marshall, A. 1920. *Principles of Economics*. 8th Edition. London: Macmillan.

McCann, P. 1995. Rethinking the Economics of Location and Agglomeration. *Urban Studies, 32*, 563-578.

McCann, P. and Sheppard, S. 2003. The Rise, Fall and Rise Again of Industrial Location Theory. *Regional Studies, 37*, 649-663.

Mills, E.S. and Hamilton, B.W. 1984. *Urban Economics*. 3rd Edition. Glenview: Scott, Foresman and Co, IL.

Nijkamp, P. 2003. Entrepreneurship in a Modern Network Economy. *Regional Studies, 37*, 395-405.

Nyström, K. 2006. *Entry and Exit in Swedish Industrial Sectors*. JIBS Dissertation Series. n°. 32, Jönköping International Business School, Jönköping.

Ohlin, B. 1933. *Inter-regional and International Trade*. Cambridge: Harvard University Press, MA.

Parker, S.C. 2004. *The Economics of Self-Employment and Entrepreneurship*. Cambridge: Cambridge University Press.

Patel, P. and Pavit, K. 1991. Large Firms in the Production of the World's Technology: An Important Case of 'Non-Globalisation'. *Journal of International Business Studies, 22*, 1-21.

Plümper, T. and Troeger, V. E. 2007. Efficient Estimation of Time-Invariant and Rarely Changing Variables in Finite Sample Panel Analyses with Unit Fixed Effects. *Political Analysis, 15*, 124-139.

Porter, M. 1998. Clusters and the New Economics of Competition. *Harvard Business Review*, November-December, 77-90.

Porter, M.E. 2000. Location, Clusters and Company Strategy, in *The Oxford Handbook of Economic Geography*, edited by G.L. Clark, M.P. Feldman and M.S. Gertler, Oxford: Oxford University Press, 253-274.

Plummer, L.A. and Acs, Z.J. 2004. Penetrating the 'Knowledge Filter' in Regional Economics. *Discussion Papers in Entrepreneurship, Growth and Public Policy*, Jena: Max Planck Institute for Research into Economic Systems.

Pred, A. 1977. *City-Systems in Advanced Economies*. London: Hutchinson.

Quigley, J.M. 1998. Urban Diversity and Economic Growth. *Journal of Economic Perspectives, 12*, 127-138.

Reynolds, P., Miller, B. and Maki, W. 1993. Regional Characteristics Affecting Business Volatility in the United States, 1980-1984, in *Small Business Dynamics*, edited by C. Karlsson, B. Johannisson and D.J. Storey, New York: Routledge, 78-115.

Reynolds, P., Storey, D.J. and Westhead, P. 1994. Cross-National Comparisons of the Variation in New Firm Formation Rates. *Regional Studies, 28*, 443-456.

Robinson, C., O'Leary, B. and Rincon, A. 2006. *Business Start-ups, Closures and Economic Churn: A Review of the Literature*. BERR: Enterprise Directorate, UK.

Rosenthal, S.S. and Strange, W.C. 2003. Geography, Industrial Organization and Agglomeration. *The Review of Economics and Statistics, 85*, 377-393.

Saxenian, A. 1999. *Silicon Valley's New Immigrant Entrepreneurs.* San Fransisco: Public Policy Institute of California.

Schumpeter, J.A. 1934. *The Theory of Economic Development.* Cambridge: Harvard University Press, MA.

Shapero, A. 1984. The Entrepreneurial Event, in *The Environment for Entrepreneurship*, edited by C.A. Kent, Lexington: Lexington Books, MA, 21-40.

Stam, E. 2007. Why Butterflies Don't Leave: Locational Behaviour of Entrepreneurial Firms. *Economic Geography, 83*, 27-50.

Stimson, R.J., Stough, R.R. and Roberts, B.H. 2006. *Regional Economic Development. Analysis and Planning Strategy.* 2nd Edition. Berlin: Springer.

Thurik, R. and Wennekers, S. 2004. Entrepreneurship, Small Business and Economic Growth. *Journal of Small Business and Enterprise Development, 11*, 140-149.

Thompson, W.R. 1968. Internal and External Factors in the Development of Urban Economeis, in *Issues in Urban Economics*, edited by H.S. Perloff and L. Wingo, Baltimore: John Hopkins Press, MD, 43-62.

Van Ort, F.G. and Stam, E. 2006. Agglomeration Economies and Entrepreneurship in the ICT Industry. *ERIM report series*, 016-ORG, Erasmus University.

Van Stel, A. and Storey, D.J. 2004. The Link between Firm Births and Employment: Is There an Upas Tree Effect?. *Regional Studies, 38*, 893-909.

Viladecans, E. 2004. Agglomeration Economies and Industrial Location: City-Level Evidence. *Journal of Economic Geography, 4*, 565-582.

Vivarelli, M. 2007. *Entry and Post-Entry Performance of Newborn Firms.* London and New York: Routledge.

Weyh, A. 2006. What Characterizes Successful Start-up Cohorts?, in *Entrepreneurship in the Region*, edited by M. Fritsch and J. Schmuck, Berlin: Springer, 61-74.

Appendix

Table A4.1   Correlation matrix for the primary sector

	Entry (1)	Exit (1)	Net entry (1)	Local accessibility to GRP	External accessibility to GRP	Share of small firms	Employment rate	Education
Entry (1)	1.0000							
Exit (1)	0.0798	1.0000						
Net entry (1)	0.3344	-0.3124	1.0000					
Local accessibility to GRP	-0.2259	-0.0614	0.0119	1.0000				
External accessibility to GRP	-0.3087	0.0843	0.0043	0.1571	1.0000			
Share of small firms	0.1571	0.0396	0.0119	-0.1655	0.1445	1.0000		
Employment rate	-0.1571	-0.0887	0.0054	-0.1175	0.2449	0.0462	1.0000	
Education	-0.3581	-0.0436	-0.0088	0.3806	0.5519	0.0926	0.2695	1.0000

Note: N = 3420

Table A4.2   Correlation matrix for the manufacturing sector

	Entry (2)	Exit (2)	Net entry (2)	Local accessibility to GRP	External accessibility to GRP	Share of small firms	Employment rate	Education
Entry (2)	1.000							
Exit (2)	0.3088	1.000						
Net entry (2)	0.4577	-0.4388	1.000					
Local accessibility to GRP	-0.1341	-0.0255	0.0053	1.000				
External accessibility to GRP	-0.1550	-0.0057	0.0319	0.1571	1.000			
Share of small firms	0.1677	0.2565	0.0396	-0.1655	0.1445	1.000		
Employment rate	-0.1841	-0.3346	0.0223	-0.1175	0.2449	0.0462	1.000	
Education	-0.2994	-0.0959	0.0163	0.3806	0.5519	0.0926	0.2695	1.000

Note: N=3420

Table A4.3   Correlation matrix for the ordinary service sector

	Entry (3)	Exit (3)	Net entry (3)	Local accessibility to GRP	External accessibility to GRP	Share of small firms	Employment rate	Education
Entry (3)	1.000							
Exit (3)	0.2709	1.000						
Net entry (3)	0.4365	-0.4410	1.000					
Local accessibility to GRP	0.1019	-0.0004	0.0573	1.000				
External accessibility to GRP	-0.0062	0.0625	0.1068	0.1571	1.000			
Share of small firms	0.1108	0.1707	0.0385	-0.1655	0.1445	1.000		
Employment rate	-0.2040	-0.2006	0.0329	-0.1175	0.2449	0.0462	1.000	
Education	-0.0097	-0.0594	0.0983	0.3806	0.5519	0.0926	0.2695	1.000

Note: N=3420

Table A4.4   Correlation matrix for the advanced service sector

	Entry (4)	Exit (4)	Net entry (4)	Local accessibility to GRP	External accessibility to GRP	Share of small firms	Employment rate	Education
Entry (4)	1.000							
Exit (4)	0.0415	1.000						
Net entry (4)	0.3619	-0.4745	1.000					
Local accessibility to GRP	0.3484	-0.0909	0.0180	1.000				
External accessibility to GRP	0.3857	-0.0889	0.0401	0.1571	1.000			
Share of small firms	0.1723	0.1179	0.0263	-0.1655	0.1445	1.000		
Employment rate	-0.0069	-0.1916	0.0050	-0.1175	0.2449	0.0462	1.000	
Education	0.5701	-0.1809	0.0202	0.3806	0.5519	0.0926	0.2695	1.000

Note: N=3420

Critique of New Economic Geography to Understand Rural Development: The Influence of Corporate Strategy

José António Porfírio

5.1. Introduction

The economic development of societies has been, in general, from the agricultural to the services sector, making economies less real and more dependent on the intangible sectors. Agriculture was an important component of economic geography through the 1950s. But with the rise of model-building and quantitative methods, especially after the 1960s, the focus shifted to studies of industry. Most of the first studies about farming were in the sub-field of agricultural geography. *'The result was that studies of agriculture within geography were cast either as old fashioned and backward looking or derivative of industrial geography (...) In any case, the secondary status of agriculture within economic geography was cemented into place'* (Page, 2000 [2003]).

From the late 1970s, regional development theories became most oriented to the high technology industries. Economic theory was particularly concerned to explain the uneven income distribution between regions and the apparently better propensity of some regions to develop high-tech economic bases (Storper, 1997), related to both industry and the services sector. At the same time, associated with these tendencies, the economic theories that studied this evolution became more urban and less rural. In this sense, it is possible to say that, nowadays, there seems to be a kind of dogmatic position in economics that the evolution of societies should be made from the agricultural to the services sector.

As a consequence, we see that the majority of the main economic theories that are available in the literature, and that can be heard in presentations made at international conferences, are dealing with the manufacturing or the services sector, while only a few theoretical papers in economics are dedicated to agriculture or primary sector activities.

The 1990s saw the emergence of the New Economic Geography (NEG). NEG is mainly a 'theoretical body of knowledge' (Krugman, 1991b) – in the 'new' wave of economic theories – that asserts that the world is divided between a certain number of 'centres' and a huge number of 'peripheral regions' that surrounds these 'centres'.

According to the principles of NEG, it may be argued that the agricultural activities represent a burden for the regions, once the NEG's authors were able to show, through the development and use of complex mathematical models, that the development dynamics of regions, heavily dependent on agriculture or agriculture-related activities –, even if we are talking about industries with the same characteristics as agriculture – will push them to the peripheral condition of less developed regions in contrast with any developed centre.

The present financial and economic crisis that is affecting most of the world economies has increased the relevance of transaction costs as determinants of economic development and, at the same time, has thrown into question economic development patterns. We believe that this change will make the primary sector a vital sector in future economic development of each country and in particular it will be crucial in terms of the development of certain regions where these activities are more predominant.

In accordance with this train of thought, in this chapter we try to explain a different possible view of development. We propose that, under certain conditions and armed with an adequate theoretical framework, it may be possible to see an alternative path of development for regions dependent on agriculture.

This chapter is divided into four sections. Section 5.2. presents a brief overview of the evolution of economic theories explaining growth and development. In this section, we aim to show how the development of economics has led to the emergence of the NEG body of knowledge.

Section 5.3. is dedicated, in particular, to the NEG's 'body of knowledge'. We start by briefly presenting NEG theory and its principles. Knowledge about the principles of NEG is very important in order to understand our view that the conclusions of NEG about the agricultural sector are of limited relevance if we take into consideration, first what should be the real importance of agriculture for societies in the near future; and, second, the impacts of introducing strategy (considered from the point of view of the individuals, the enterprises, the regions, or the country as a whole) into our analysis of rural development. This job is done in Section 5.4, where we analyse what we call the pitfalls of NEG concerning agriculture and their consequences regarding the conclusions of rural development theories. In Section 5.5, we explain the limitations of the present theories, and present a possible new framework for economic analysis of agricultural and rural regions that might leverage these new insights. To this end we propose the new concept of Agricultural District.

5.2. Evolution of Economics concerning Growth and Development

Growth and decline has been a characteristic of human societies, ever since mankind learned to use fire and invented stone tools (Findlay, 1996). As Cameron (2003) stated, between the discovery of agriculture, more than 10.000 years ago, and the beginning of Industrial Revolution, in the mid-18th century, world population grew from 5 to 10 million to 700 to 800 million. However, living standards for the great majority of the world's population were stable, at the subsistence minimum.

By contrast, in the two and a half centuries that followed the mid 17th century, standards of living almost doubled from generation to generation and there were substantial historical improvements in health, education and even wealth all over the world (Castells, 1998 [2000]). At the same time, the difference between income growth rates between these two periods was impressive and was followed by an incredible evolution concerning reductions in the rates of mortality, birth and population growth. As a result, the world's population reached more than 6 billion by the year 2000.

One of the most astonishing facts that marked these extraordinary evolutions in the world economy and society is related to the big increase in inequality among groups of world countries with regard to both their growth dynamics and their income levels (Brander, 1992), and this remains one of the central questions of our times (see Brander, 1992, Rodrik, 2003; Pritchett, 1997; Fujita et al., 1999 [2001]).

Since David Hume's (1741) passionate debates about economic growth in the 18th century, the search for the reasons that explain these differences has fascinated economists. This search has expanded since economics started to have a significant number of serious and competent practitioners.

The main issue here was that, in a perfectly competitive world, where trade is based on the principles of comparative advantage, one should expect convergence among countries according to the Heckscher-Ohlin-Samuelson Theorem. However, empirical analysis showed the contrary.

More recently, in the era of what are called 'new economic theories', it is considered that trade, as well as specialization and growth, should be seen as a result of the action of economic agents, in general, and companies, in particular, trying to explore the advantages of economies of scale. The New Growth (and Trade) Theories consider that economic growth happens as the outcome of a system's economic agents' actions and not as a result of specific forces coming from outside the system itself. This kind of endogenous growth explanation is the main difference between the 'new' theories and the neoclassical ones (Romer, 1994).

In general, it is possible to observe that the evolution of economics concerning growth and specialization has brought into the analysis the clear influence of the action of economic agents, institutions and public policies and, at the same time, the power of markets to act, in order to adjust to natural differences that arise from market imperfections. The preoccupation with market structure is also one of the main features of this 'new' wave of economic models.

By considering the possibility of increasing returns coming, fundamentally, from within a company, new trade theory breaks with the classical and neoclassical ideas of perfect competitive markets, and has become adapted to a new reality that was at the origin of the process of globalization. Specialization patterns and differences among countries is the result of the different actions and capacities of enterprises in each region.

Structural changes within a country or a region, regarding the sectors' influence on its economy, are usually the result of economic agents' turning to more value added activities, with higher productivity levels, than just the characteristics of each sector by itself. So, from our perspective, agriculture by itself should not be considered synonymous with underdevelopment.

In this chapter we defend the case that different growth patterns between regions (as well as countries), which could explain income differentials, are more related to the capacity to conceive and implement Corporate Strategies (seen as the catalyst of globalization movements) than with intrinsic sector differences, regarding their importance in GDP.

That is to say, we consider that the success of regions (as well as countries), in terms of both economic growth and income increase, is mainly the result of corporate movements, and is to a certain extent independent of the sectors of economic activity in which a country or a region is more specialized. In other words, comparative advantage may be seen as the condition for trade and specialization. However, comparative advantages should be seen with regard to different specialization patterns between countries that are mostly the result of corporate decisions and not just the existence of different factor endowments and sector composition. So, if there is a structural change regarding the value given to certain products (such as those coming from agriculture), it is possible to effect a change in specialization of regions (and countries).

Countries' specialization movements from agriculture to industry, and then to the services sector (in that order) are usually seen as synonymous with development. However, from a theoretical point of view at least, there is nothing against the idea that the contrary movement may also be true. Ultimately, as some authors argue, income differentials are always the result of the potential (at each moment in time, and space) of the sectors in which one invests (in terms of both technological progress and productivity increases) as well as of the choices that are made in terms of intra-sector composition, more than the result of existing differences in inter-sector composition, in general terms (Castells, 1996 [2000]).

If one considers the importance of technology for income growth, we should also pay attention to the concept of social capital that could be considered to be at the origin of growth processes, and where technology will produce its effects. Moreover, we should be aware that these effects will always be dependent on the economy's particular stage of development, which will increase or limit the potential synergies that could contribute to the process of development itself. In addition, one must consider that the technological level associated with each sector of economic activity may be a rather broad concept, since we may see, inside the same sector of activity, a very large spectrum of technological intensity, depending on the different industries within the sector as a whole.

This leads us to conclude that a region's (or a country's) potential for rapid growth is strong, not when it is backward and its population is without qualifications, but rather when it is technologically backward but socially advanced (Abramovitz, 1986), independently of the particular sector that it is at the basis of the regional development.

In summary, local economic development of territories is a large-spectrum phenomenon that depends mainly on production and commercial activities, which is the result of three main variables: *'(1) regional strategies for development; (2) entrepreneurial strategies; and (3) technological networks organising inter-firm co-ordination through and outside markets'* (Noéme and Nicolas, 2004, p. 124).

Our ideas are supported by a deeper analysis of what agriculture is and what it can be. First of all, agriculture should be seen as a part of a large agro-food system. This means that, in spite of our broad view concerning development deriving from agriculture, we should be aware that agriculture, maybe more than the manufacturing or the services sector, is an economic activity that must be considered in the light of social agency theory (Sheppard and Barnes, 2003). That is to say, any analysis of this particular sector of activity – very deep in terms of culture and tradition – must consider not just the individual but also the collective actions and interests of people, i.e. the 'social agents'. Any analyses, regarding agriculture potential and effects will be incomplete if they do not consider the role played by human actors across the whole range of activities, linking food production to food consumption.

The economic agents' capacity to act should be then considered a must. They are the main factor in determining specialization patterns. Besides the region's social capital levels, this also depends on the enterprises' intrinsic capabilities, as well as on their capabilities to interact within networks of firms, or even to reap gains from both local institutions policies and government or regional development policies.

In summary, if one believes that the primary sector's economic agents (especially enterprises), and the regions where this sector of activity prevails, do not show similar capabilities, by comparison with what one sees in other sectors (for instance, because it is a sector more reliant on small and medium sized companies or its entrepreneurs do not have the same qualifications) or regions, it is arguable whether we will arrive at conclusions like those proposed by the NEG's theorists.

Notwithstanding this, even if the conclusions are the same, the implications may be completely different, especially if one considers the chance to use these conclusions for policy conception and implementation directed toward a region's capability-building instead of policies directed to structural sector changes that may face even greater challenges to succeed.

5.3. New Economic Geography in Brief

The New Economic Geography (NEG), a theory first formulated by the 2008 Nobel laureate Paul Krugman (Krugman and Venables, 1990; Krugman, 1991b), argues that the organization of the economic landscape occurs between some core and several peripheral regions that emerge as a result of the interaction between different centrifugal and centripetal forces. These forces cause, or reinforce, externalities at the level of each firm. By taking into consideration the effects of transport (and transaction) costs, they will affect all economic activities, reinforcing or limiting the capacity of regions to develop.

Operating within a framework of imperfect monopolistic competition, core (or centre) regions represent the places where the most interesting industries are located, where we may see the main economic activities and the majority of the population and where there are the biggest markets (both for consumers and for intermediate goods) and the best possibilities to leverage economies of scale for each industry, a situation that tends to reinforce concentration processes.

This theory argues that there are economies of scale that are purely internal to firms but, at the same time, the action of some 'centripetal forces' (mainly coming from transportation costs, knowledge spillovers, or factor mobility) is able to oppose certain 'centrifugal forces' (such as wage increases, increasing land rents, and so on) that equilibrium forces are generated. These forces, complemented by the effects caused by the existence of forward and backward linkages among economic agents located in the same region, tend to promote manufacturing concentration. So, by this, it is possible to explain the development of certain regions that tend to become centres, in opposition to other regions where this 'virtuous cycle' does not occur – or it occurs only on a small scale – and that tend to decline and become peripheral regions.

In a seminal paper by Krugman and Venables (1990), one can see that the main distinctive characteristics of NEG are the following:

- Framework of Imperfect Monopolistic Competition (a la Dixit-Stiglitz);
- The result of this being the division of the space between core and peripheral regions;
- Consideration of the spatial mobility of manufacturing firms but immobility for factors of production (especially labour);[1]
- Consideration of transportation costs that represent barriers to trade and give NEG models the necessary spatial dimension and operability;
- Economies of scale considered at the level of each firm (differing from Marshallian externalities);
- Use of General Equilibrium Models to model spatial economies;
- Consideration of 'circular causation', which incorporates the temporal and spatial dimensions of the general equilibrium models.

The NEG theory shows, for example, how a country can endogenously become organized in an industrialized 'core' and an agricultural 'periphery' as a result of the action of firms when trying to achieve scale economies while minimizing transportation costs. According to the dynamics, it is considered that manufacturing firms will choose to locate near the regions with big markets (both in terms of consumer and intermediate goods) (Krugman, 1991b).

---

1   These restrictions were first considered and, then, in more recent models, were dropped.

Attracted by better conditions for growth and prosperity, the centre gains the more important industries and a big share of the population – generating what are called 'home market effects'[2] – and the generation of economies of scale tend to reinforce this process of accumulation by producing higher incomes and so better standards of living for its population.

In contrast, the periphery – where economic activities are not able to generate such important levels of economies of scale, and show a certain lack of capacity to generate externalities – represents the poorest regions, with fewer capabilities to develop and to break with this 'fatal destiny'. According to this body of knowledge in economics, this is the case for regions more dependent on agriculture, or on any other marginal industries.[3]

There is no doubt that, this vision represents a big advance in economic theory since it breaks with the traditional vision of perfect competition, and its models consider imperfect monopolistic competition from a Dixit-Stiglitz (1977) perspective.

To these characteristics, NEG – following the principles of what we may call the 'New wave' of economic theories[4] – adds two more very important 'tricks': i) Samuelson's (1952) iceberg transportation costs;[5] and ii) evolutionary computational models, where in more recent models, factors of production have the ability to move between different locations, generating different and multiple equilibrium points in time and space. All this means that NEG has become a very important body of knowledge to explain the pathway of regional development.

NEG started its development and application about 20 years ago, in the landscape of the European Union, curiously a region where regional development policies in general, and rural development policies, in particular, assume a very important and relevant role, especially with the aim to reverse those polarizations arising from distinctive economic capacities to grow.

We consider that the role given to the European policies for Cohesion and Rural Development, more than just the usual redistribution of wealth, derives from the European belief that the joint action of individuals, families as well as governments (at a local, national or at an European level) should be able to modify development pathways. This can be achieved if their actions are supported by enough European funds and developed within a favourable context, in order to

---

2   We may understand the home market effect as 'the tendency of countries to export goods for which they have a relatively large domestic market' (Krugman, 1991a [2000], p. 5).

3   A marginal industry, in this sense, is an industry that shows the same characteristics as agriculture, which means: constant returns of scale and operations occurring in perfectly competitive markets.

4   This 'new wave' of economics started with the New Industrial Organization, developed later through New Growth Theory and 'finished' with New Trade Theory. All of them represented a breakdown of the old paradigm of economic theories, in trying to adjust the theories to the new realities of economic development.

5   Transportation costs are assumed to be of the 'iceberg type' if only a fraction g of any good shipped arrives, with 1-g lost in transit (Krugman, 1991a [2000], p. 27).

leverage the actions of these economic agents. Unfortunately, if we accept the basic conclusions of NEG models, then rural regions will not be able to develop if they continue to be rural.

5.4. The Pitfalls of NEG Models for Agriculture and their Implications for Rural Development

In human affairs, like in any other thing in life, it is very important to distinguish between what happens due to chance and what is a result of certain causes. If an event is derived from chance, people will not inquire about its reasons, and will not progress from a certain level of ignorance. But, if there is reason to suspect that there are causes at the origin of some event, then we may believe that, as Hume assumed, *'if I were to assign any general rule to help us in applying this distinction, it would be the following: what depends upon a few persons is, in a great measure, to be ascribed to chance, or secret and unknown causes; what arises from a great number, may often be accounted for by determinate and known causes'* (Hume, 1741: I.XIV.1).

In the sense of the NEG's body of knowledge, the 'centres' that we may see around the globe are mainly specialized in urban service or highly industrialized regions, whether peripheral regions consist mainly of regions dependent on rural and agriculture, or regions where economic activities are based on decadent industries or industries with weaker capacities to generate economies of scale.

We argue that, notwithstanding the fact that this vision may represent an empirical analysis of – or a justification for – the present reality, this also represents a very static and abstract way to look at economics, since it appears to be embedded in a great determinism and does not consider economies as the result of the actions of economic agents. That is to support that chance, more than causes, is at the origin of development.

Our ideas are based on the assumptions of what we call some pitfalls in the foundations of NEG models, and on the belief that future will bring us different pathways for development based on the strategic actions taken by economic agents, independently if they are individuals, families, companies or governments, or all of them together.

The initial NEG model developed by Krugman (1991a [2000]; b) was based on two different industries: agriculture and manufacturing. Agriculture is seen – besides consisting of agriculture itself – as a broad representation of industries where markets are perfectly competitive and work in constant returns to scale regime. On the contrary, manufacturing, which works in an imperfectly (à la Dixit-Stiglitz) monopolistic competition framework, presents a capacity to work with increasing returns to scale.

In this sense, manufacturing should be seen as a group of many firms in a specific location, producing differentiated products. In manufacturing, increasing returns ensure that each plant produces a unique good in a single location. So, *'all that firms need to do is choose an optimal location, taking into account the spatial distribution of demand and the transportation costs they must pay'* (Krugman, 1995 [2002], p. 61). At the same time, these assumptions are not incompatible with the monopolistic competition behaviour that is assumed by NEG models.

Moreover these models assumed that: 'The agricultural good was produced by immobile farmers, but manufactures were produced by workers who could move to the region that offered the higher real wage. And manufactures (but not agriculture) were subject to iceberg transportation costs' (Krugman, 1998, p. 166).

As a result, we may say that, according to NEG theory, the capacity to generate externalities seems to be remote regarding the agricultural sector, especially if we take into consideration that NEG models consider that agriculture works in a perfectly competitive market with constant returns to scale, and sells homogeneous products to the market (Fujita et al., 1999 [2001]).

It is the dynamics implicit in each sector of activity (manufacturing versus agriculture) that creates 'successful locations' that tend to cast a kind of 'agglomeration shadow' over nearby locations (Krugman, 1995 [2002]). Thus, we will see space organized between several rival centres – at a more or less characteristic distance –surrounded by nearby locations with peripheral characteristics, that is, mainly dependent on agriculture.

From our point of view, this represents a very restrictive and backward-looking vision of the primary sector and, at the same time, a vision that conceives the macro-economy as an independent variable of the microeconomic performance and business management capabilities, not to talk of the capacity of individuals to influence the way economies develop.

By this we mean that this mechanism renders almost worthless any actions taken by economic agents to change what seems to be an 'economic determinism' that creates certain path dependencies, in particular those that allow companies in the primary sector to put in place effective business strategies capable of going against these trends of economic development.

We argue that NEG models present some pitfalls regarding at least two aspects related to agriculture: the first concerns the non-consideration of transport costs; and the second concerns the capacity of the agricultural sector to produce differentiated products and, hence the ability of the agents engaged in agriculture to put in place effective business strategies.

Regarding transport costs in agriculture, the role of these costs 'in acting as a break on urban development is well documented (the 'tyranny of distance', as Bairoch (1988) calls it).' Fujita et al. (1999 [2001], p. 110).

Moreover, these authors did not just capture the effects of agricultural transport costs for regional development. They were also able to demonstrate how the reduction in agricultural transport costs can cause agglomeration to occur; just as it can cause a reduction in manufacturing transport costs. They were even able to conclude that: *'adding costs of transporting agricultural goods not only reminds us that these costs themselves may play an important role in shaping the economy's spatial structure, it also leads us to conclude that the effects of the gradual abolition of distance – of declining transport costs – need not be monotonic (...)'* Fujita et al. (1999 [2001], p. 111).

The second aspect relates to the differentiation capacity in agriculture. And this is important, not just regarding the development implications arising from the capacity to put in place real competitive strategies for the agents within agriculture but also because, as is recognized, the transportation cost effect in agriculture could be even stronger, if one considers the capacity of the agricultural sector to produce differentiated goods, once: *'assuming homogeneity of agriculture turns out to have the peculiar implication that even infinitesimal transport costs have a major qualitative impact on the economy's dynamics'* (Fujita et al. (1999 [2001], p. 105).

Surprisingly, however, and after all these considerations, these authors ended up by neglecting the idea and the importance of differentiated products in agriculture, based on their assumptions that Agriculture works in a framework of constant returns to scale and within perfectly competitive markets which is an idea that, as stated before, we reject.

Just by doing this, they were able to justify that forward and backward linkages in the manufacturing sector are capable of overcoming the joint effects of transport costs and non-homogeneous products in agriculture in terms of agglomeration movements. At the same time, this prevents agriculture-related activities from achieving economies of scale and from having significant externalities that, otherwise, unlike the situation in the manufacturing sector.

In our view, it is also possible to see economies of scale and the appearance of externalities in the primary sector, if we make the more realistic assumption that economic agents dedicated to the primary sector may be able to put in place competitive differentiation strategies. These are related, for instance, to the development of certain types of food processing industries, the exploitation of products' 'natural' differentiation arising from different soil and climate characteristics, etc.

By breaking with the assumption of perfectly competitive markets in agriculture, and assuming the capacity of their economic agents to put in place true competitive strategies, we believe that this situation, if it reaches certain levels, may even overcome the forces that derive from similar movements of factors in manufacturing, and take former peripheral regions away from a condition of periphery, by turning them into new centres.

Moreover, from an aggregate perspective, as in Harris's (1954) and Pred's (1966) theories – which Krugman's (1991b) NEG seminal paper tries to formalize (Krugman, 1998) – we believe that, if the right conditions are to be created, the actions of self-interested individual economic agents interact to produce an aggregate behaviour that is more than the simple sum of its parts.

That is to say, the development of a region is mainly dependent on the capabilities that this region shows at a microeconomic level, independently of the sector that accounts more for the region's income and growth. And this *'microeconomic foundation'* of development relies on two interrelated domains: the sophistication of company operations and strategy, and the quality of the microeconomic business environment. In our analysis we adopt Porter's new vision of strategy, where strategy is based on an advanced form of competition that relies on the capacity to produce and market differentiated products and services, and is capable of creating unique competitive positions in opposition to a primitive form of strategy, which mostly relies on factor (input) costs (Porter, 2000 [2003]).

This idea becomes even more crucial if we consider that, in light of the vision of the industrialization of agriculture (Page, 2003, p. 246), firms in the primary sector usually make efforts to transform basic foodstuffs into a wide array of processed and packaged food products that are more easily differentiated.

We also share, in our vision, Myrdal's idea that every successful businessman 'has the principle of the cumulative process as a built-in theory in his approach to practical problems; otherwise he will not be successful' (Myrdal, 1957 [1972], p.21).

These ideas, however, seem to have been neglected in NEG theory, by recognizing that, in spite of this being a central point in Henderson-type urban systems theory, NEG's 'thrust is to pursue the implications of atomistic action, and that will not be a very appealing solution' (Fujita et al., 1999 [2001], p. 105).

Assuming this principle, bringing strategy to the spatial economic analysis, and at the same time considering a theoretical framework of analysis for the rural development phenomenon like the proposed 'Agricultural District' (Porfírio et al., 2009) we believe that we are increasing the explanatory power of the theories for regional and particularly for rural development.

In spite of the significant advance to economics brought by the NEG, we consider that it may be imprudent to watch regional and rural development only from the NEG perspective since this is a phenomenon that depends on a variety of factors (Martin, 1999; Noéme and Nicolas, 2004) and can/must be seen from a wide range of perspectives and schools of thought (Storper, 1997).

As we have already mentioned, among the main drivers of regional (including rural) development, besides the question of localization and the economic aspects related to it, we may find social, institutional, cultural and political characteristics embedded in local and regional economies. As we know, these types of characteristics are usually stronger and more evident in rural communities and, in particular, in each inhabitant of rural and agricultural communities. In these territories, tradition usually assumes a greater importance compared with the situation that we may observe in urban regions.

For Vaz and Cesário (2008), the regional innovation is the result of: the interaction between regional and local development conditions; the technological learning and the entrepreneurial strategy of firms within a region; and the institutional proximity.

Moreover, when talking about regional (or rural) development, it is arguable that we should enlarge our vision in order to include institutions in a broader sense, and to reinforce the role of social (and civil) capital, as well as the importance of regional/rural policies for development.

The importance of institutional factors for development is also very well documented in the literature.[6] There is also no doubt about the importance of geography for development, since it plays a major role in determining income, based on the existence of natural-resource endowments, and, at the same time, it can shape (in part) the existing institutions. However, *'geography is not the destiny'* (Rodrik, 2003, p. 12) and institutions, considered in terms of the quality of formal and informal socio-political arrangements (ranging from the legal system to the broader political institutions), may well *'play a major role in promoting or hindering economic performance'* (Rodrik, 2003, p. 5)[7] and *'might well be the most critical determinant of economic performance'* (Rodrik, 2003, p. 230).

The question in rural regions is that, in these territories we usually observe certain characteristics regarding their social capital[8] levels, considered in terms of social relations and social networks, and including cultural factors (Fukuyama, 2002), that may reduce the chance to reap the gains of all these aspects.

Another point of divergence between our vision of rural development and that of NEG occurs at the concept level. Differences start with such an important issue as the simple consideration of what is understood by the concept of economy. We assume, in our vision, a Marshallian definition of economy as *'the study of mankind in the ordinary business of life'* (Marshall, 1890 [1920], book I) and this, from our perspective, relates directly to the importance of corporate actions for regional development, and their implications concerning market structure.

From our point of view, it is unquestionable that Krugman and other NEG theorists were able to break with the neoclassical rigidity to deal with markets. Moreover, we do not question that, as already mentioned, in NEG models they *'tried to consider the real implications of atomistic strategic actions'* (Fujita et al, 1999 [2001], p. 105).

However, as Penrose states about business studies in general, in our opinion, they failed when they 'start to taking over the analysis of the firms almost entirely, leaving the traditional microeconomics to concentrate on perhaps its most useful function as the theoretical foundation of the theory of macroeconomic behaviour of the economy, for which the 'firm' as an organization is thought to be irrelevant' (Penrose, 1959 [1995], p. x). In this sense, strategy and related strategic actions, being the basis for the monopolistic competition markets – ultimately, the great

---

6   See, for instance, Rodrik (2003) or Storper (1997).

7   A good explanation about institutions and their role in development can be found in Storper (1997) and in Rodrik (2003).

8   The concept of social capital first began to be used in the 1960s, mainly by the sociologist Pierre Bourdieu (1980). However, it was above all in *Foundations of Social Theory* by the American James Coleman (1990), that it came into wider use and was linked to problems of development.

operational achievement of NEG regarding market structure – becomes more or less irrelevant, and determinism in terms of economic development takes root[9].

It is important to note that some micro questions, such as the relative price of commodities or the behaviour of individuals, firms or households cannot be discussed 'in the air', without any reference to the structure of the economy in which they exist, and to the processes of cyclical and secular change. The same applies to macro-theories when they represent generalizations about micro-behaviour. For instance, as Robinson (1977, p. 1320) argues: *'The relation of (...) wages to the level of prices results from reactions of individuals and social groups to the situations in which they find themselves (...).'*

In line with these thoughts, we believe that increasing returns, as well as economies of scale per se are not so central to history as Krugman and Venables (1993) argue. If we 'add' corporate, or government strategy, to the action of economic agents in a certain region that is facing problems in its economic activity (like an increase in unemployment, insolvency of certain industries and the consequent slowdown in GDP growth, or even a decrease in GDP), it is possible to expect that these agents (independently if we are talking about individuals, families, companies, local or national governments) will start to conceive, develop and put in place strategies to fight the difficulties that the adverse environment is adding to their life.

In other words, strategy will bring a little more rationality to the economic agent's actions. This rationality is based on the information obtained in order to conceive and execute the right strategies for the changing environments where companies operate.

It is well known that the choices that each individual economic agent makes depend "on the information at his disposal. In a perfectly static society, relevant knowledge might be handed down to everyone by tradition, but their behaviour also would be governed by tradition and no one could be conscious of ever making choices at all. In the world we are living, choices have to be made in the light of more or less inadequate information" (Robinson, 1977, p. 1322).[10]

Only by accessing information are managers able to act to anticipate the evolution of the markets and their consumers' problems. Therefore strategy will make economic agents sufficiently informed to break with what Krugman (1991a [2000]) calls the *'unreasonable idea of rational expectations driving economic agent's actions'*.

---

9   As Penrose stated: 'we are not saying that they are wrong, only that, being theoretical economists, they saw reality differently from other people and asked different questions about it' (Penrose, 1959 [1995], p. x).

10   Or, as Loasby (1977, p. 21) states: 'there is no certain knowledge about the future, not even certain knowledge of probability distributions. There are expectations (or guesses) formulated with greater or less care; and unfortunately those formulated with the greatest care are by no means always the most accurate' (In Robinson, 1977, p. 1322).

By assuming this we are open to the assumption of the *'self-fulfilling prophecies'* (Krugman, 1991a [2000]) that may arise from the conjunction of rational expectations and information, through strategic actions. Altogether these will allow the anticipation or, at least, the reaction of economic agents in response to adverse expected market conditions and hence, their ability to resist to any development path dependencies will be increased. However, this is something that we should only observe if we were able to analyse the real implications of considering atomistic strategic actions.

This line of thought is valid in general but, in particular, it is valid for rural regions, especially in the present context of the world economic crisis where food supply is becoming a must in the future strategy of countries, and where the increase in the prices of energy is also having a big impact on the increase of transaction costs.[11] To this idea we must also add the worries about the environment and the importance that rural regions have regarding this crucial subject.

Moreover, differentiation arising from the simple fact of being present in a certain region, or the capacity to produce certain type of products that can only be produced in a single region, may unleash competitive forces that might well work as ways to break with the historic determinism or the path of development that constantly relegate rural regions for the 'second division of development'.

A different issue regarding NEG principles is related to factors of production movements that are at the basis of economic adjustments between regions. *'NEG models typically assume an ad hoc process of adjustment in which factors of production move gradually toward locations that offer higher current real returns'* (Krugman, 1998, p. 165). We could consider that the world is changing the forces that are at the origin of these production factors' movements and this may well change NEG models' results. This is mainly related to the following subjects:

First, it is important to notice that NEG models assume the capacity of the factors of production to move between different locations, but this is not the case for the main factors of production in agriculture: soil, as well as climate factors.[12] This could represent a big issue in NEG models, especially if we link them to the gravitational models theory of trade;

- Secondly, it depends on what we consider to be 'real returns'. The upgrading in living standards among urban citizens brings new ideals about quality of life for societies. Therefore, what we mean by 'real returns' is that, nowadays, development is not measured just in terms of GDP (especially in

---

11   Rural regions might have the potential to be more or less self-sufficient in energetic terms.

12   Certain unique climate conditions may allow the production of unique food products or, at least, food products with unique characteristics that markets will able to value differently, should the capacity of companies allow their adequate marketing and commercialization. This will also reinforce the importance of forward and backward linkages related with agricultural activities.

the developed world), but it must consider other aspects of human life such as living conditions, happiness of citizens, wellbeing, capacity to spend time with family, stress, health and medical conditions, etc. However, today in economic developed regions – usually urban regions - exactly the other side of the coin is in evidence: stress, criminality, unhappiness, lack of time, etc, things that are more difficult to find in the agricultural/rural regions.

- The main consequence of this is that we must add to the traditional economic measure of real returns (usually very dependent on the GDP measure), the conditions of a good life (real or adjusted cost of living; quality of life, happiness, etc…) that were previously the basis of the population exodus from rural regions to cities. This will have a significant impact on what are called 'home market effects', a very important issue in NEG models, in particular reflecting the relationship between forward and backward linkages with transport costs that these models incorporate.
- The third thing to consider is the world's adoption of the sustainable development principles and their environmental implications, with consequences for the increased importance of rural regions and territories. The need to rationalize the use of land by reconciling the needs of housing, food and, environment and energy production, and the restrictions regarding the use of the land, as well as their importance regarding the fight against greenhouse gas emissions (and the solution of carbon dioxide capture), will inevitably have an increased impact on the value of rural territories making them more desirable as places to live.

It is uncontroversial that we should support the general increase in the wealth of people – in spite of all the inequalities that remain – in developed nations, making them more aware of those aspects related to their quality of life. In the future, with the continuous increase in citizen's wealth, it is probable that we will witness a big increase of centrifugal forces in developed regions, mainly coming from the aforementioned new intangible factors. So, it is natural that we will observe a search for housing in regions outside big cities, thus increasing the competition for land.

This movement will tend to create or to reinforce the network of towns, but it will also put pressure on the environment and energy prices. All these aspects are domains in which rural development is very rich. These, in turn, are factors that will raise food prices, increasing pressure on the land and, at the same time, that will increase enormously the real value of rural regions for the economic development of countries.

Besides these issues, the present financial and economic crisis, that is changing the future trends of world development, has called our attention not just to the problems that could arise from the growing dependency of countries and regions (at a supra or at a sub-national level) on food and energy imports but also to the growing concern about the need for a more equal redistribution of wealth around the globe, which is essential for the continuation of globalization.

In this connection, we believe that the present financial and economic crisis that is affecting most of the world economies has increased the relevance of transaction costs (here including transportation costs that have naturally increased with the increase in oil prices[13]) as determinants of economic development, and, at the same time, is questioning traditional economic development patterns by putting pressure on the primary sector, whose industries are becoming more relevant and whose products are also becoming more and more valued for the future of societies.

In line with these thoughts, we are able to understand the problem with the whole theory that derives from the fact that 'the sort of dynamic process that NEG considers was initially proposed apologetically, since it neglects the role of expectations. But it is possible to regard models of geography as games in which actors choose locations rather than strategies – or rather, in which locations are strategies' (Krugman, 1998, p. 165).

When strategy is applied in this way to a specific location, it is our belief that, sooner or later, we will lose the basis and the real sense of strategy, since this makes strategy something rather abstract instead of being embedded in some rationality. It is good to remember that strategy usually has a specific purpose: to help agents (and, ultimately, regions), put an end to the determinism that arises from the development of other competitors – whether they are other firms located in other regions or also other regions – and hence point the way to success.

If we consider that the capacity to conceive, to put in place and to develop strategies may be a characteristic of each economic agent in each region, and if this happens generally – at least for the majority of economic agents in one region – the strategy impact for the whole region will be more than the sum of the results of each individual strategy. At the same time, if the beginning of individual (reactive or pro-active) strategies starts producing visible results for several agents at the same time, we may expect that this will produce a virtuous cycle of development (a la Myrdal) for the whole region.

This could be considered a paradigmatic situation, since Krugman's concerns about building multiple equilibrium models (where the goal is a better resource allocation, price equilibrium and an increase in welfare) but where, in due course, companies' actions, as individual economic agents, are more or less irrelevant, represents a situation where one may assume that an enterprise's strategies are more or less uniform. In the end, this is contrary to the principles of corporate strategy theory itself. As a corollary, we may say that, if firms do not put in place strategies – or their strategies are irrelevant for the analysis – it will be very difficult to talk about imperfectly competitive markets.

---

13   Even the recent slowdown in oil prices does not affect this. However, everybody is aware that in the near future we will again experience an increase in energy prices, once resources are scarce and consumption is still growing as new developed economies continue to grow.

Concerning the tertiary sector, at present we observe a general decrease in prices for services, as a result of strong economies of scale and the decrease in communication costs. Also, there is a present feeling that economies must become more real and less dependent on intangibles. This will, in the near future, relegate the tertiary sector to second place regarding its importance for regional development, and we believe that this change will then make the primary sector a crucial sector for the future economic development of each country.

In summary, we may say that economies of scale that previously paved the way for geographic concentration of some economic activities, and that present a very important role in NEG theory, may, in the near future, be the driving forces of the dispersion of economic activities. The main reasons for this are as follows:

- The assumption that there are economic activities that depend heavily on the particular conditions and characteristics of certain places and that this will produce unique capacities for strategic differentiation;
- The development of the social capital of rural and agricultural regions, which will allow their economic agents to play a more active part in the development of regions and countries.
- An awareness of the need to reconcile food and energy production with environmental protection, and to maintain certain standards of living, in order to comply with the necessary sustainable development principles, which is very difficult to achieve if we pursue the present patterns of development.

5.5. The Need for a New Theoretical Framework Regarding Rural Development

Throughout the last century, we have observed a structural change in the capitalist system, especially related to the way companies are managed and operated. Management has become more flexible, companies have started to be more decentralized and, to obtain success in a faster and sustainable way, firms have started to operate in networks, increasing the interdependency among main economic agents (Castells, 1996 [2000]).

Moreover, at the same time that capital has become stronger vis-à-vis labour, we have seen a decrease in the importance and the scope of state interventions, accompanied by a decrease in the weight of the welfare state. This trend started to change, however, by the beginning of the 21st century, where we have witnessed a gradual increase in the level of state intervention in order to regulate markets and support critical institutions that previously have supported the capitalist system itself, as a consequence of the crisis which the world is now experiencing.

A permanent tendency seen during the last century was also a 'stepped-up global economic competition, in a context of increasing geographic and cultural differentiation of settings for capital accumulation and management' (Castells,

1996 [2000], p. 2). This sharply divided the world into an industrial and services developed Northern hemisphere and a less developed, agriculturally dependent Southern hemisphere.

In this scenario, agriculture, understood in its singularity, became the poor relation of economic theory. However, it is our understanding that the study of agriculture can not be undertaken without considering the link that it must establish with manufacturing (Page, 2000 [2003]). And this reinforces the idea of agricultural activities embedded in the concept of territorialization and in light of the territorialized economic development, which is something quite different from mere localizations of economic activities (Storper, 1997)[14] considered in NEG.

We must be conscious that, apart from the fact that soil or sunlight do not have direct industrial substitutes, and that we consider that we should link agriculture to industry in our analysis, agricultural activities can not be considered to operate by the same principles as industrial activities (Page, 2000 [2003]), since one of the most important production factors of agriculture is land which, by definition, is immobile and may present some productivity constraints, independently from the inputs used for production. This means that in agricultural activities in general, and in contrast to other economic activities like manufacturing, "capital cannot be applied to the labor process at a single site when production is expanded or intensified. Instead, increased production requires a spatial extension. (...) But because land is a fixed and limited resource, and because land markets are deeply colored by localized social conditions, farmers cannot easily or quickly adjust their investment in land" (Marsden et al., 1986, in Page, 2000 [2003], p. 245).

Moreover, according to Page (2000 [2003]): "albeit it is true that locational constraints can be overcome via the transformation of nature and the location of new agricultural systems through irrigation, plant and animal breeding, improved production facilities, new transport modes and so on, indeed, spatial divisions of labour surrounding agriculture are never static (...)" (Page, 2000 [2003], p. 248).

From our point of view, the concept of territorialization is crucial when we are talking about agriculture and rural regions since it captures the territory, as well as the social and cultural systems linked with an agricultural region.

According to this concept, an activity is fully territorialized: "when its economic viability is rooted in assets (including practices and relations) that are not available in many other places and cannot easily or rapidly be created or imitated in places that lack them. Locational substitutability is not possible, and feasible locations are small in number, making locational 'markets' highly imperfect" (Storper, 1997, p. 170).

Agricultural territories represent very particular production systems that usually may not be replicated at all in other places since they rely on certain crops that are difficult to grow in other places since they are very dependent on climate and soil characteristics. These particular production systems usually are the cement for a region's culture and traditions, shaping institutions' quality and

---

14   After all, this is the main idea underlying the dynamics of NEG models.

characteristics and network relationships among the main economic agents of that region. These characteristics could be the basis for differentiation, and for the development of differentiation strategies, issues that will reject the assumption of NEG models regarding agriculture operating under perfect competition and constant returns to scale.

Moreover, as already expressed, the economic development of regions is a very complex process. Besides geography it involves important features, such as factor endowments (that in part can also be seen as dependent on geography), institutions, as well as policies, as drivers for productivity, market dynamics, and the resilience of regions, as determinants of regional income.

All these aspects must be seen as determinants for the generation of virtuous cycles of development or vicious cycles of underdevelopment, based on the cumulative processes first proposed by Myrdal (1957 [1972]) and explored later in the framework of NEG models. In spite of the vague consideration of 'historical accidents', it seems that these NEG models are not, however, able to predict the factors that, by causing some kind of 'accidental changes' (Myrdal, 1957 [1972]), can at the same time break out of the vicious cycles of underdevelopment that they foresee (and confirm) regarding the rural regions.

Corporate strategies related to the capacity of firms to generate and explore network effects, as well as the role of certain regional development policies, may well be seen as sources of accidental changes for the otherwise 'condemned' rural regions.

First, we argue for the importance of strategy for the development of rural regions. Strategy is considered as one of the most effective ways for firms, regardless of size or sector, to cope with the changes in the business environment (Hart and Banbury, 1994).

However, we must be aware that strategies are first the result of management capabilities. Generic organizational capabilities have a positive impact on strategy deployment and on the achievement of the overall performance of organisations. Generic capabilities, in fact, are the main drivers that enable firms to manage for the future by focusing on customer's needs and requirements, while at the same time managing crises and problems arising in their operating environment (O'Reagan and Ghobadian, 2004).

Within each firm we assume that "managers qua managers are primarily interested in the profitable expansion of the activities of their firm. Profits were treated as a necessary condition of expansion – or growth – and growth, therefore, was a chief reason for the interest of managers in profits" (Penrose, 1959 [1995], p. xii).

Moreover, we consider that these actions from managers are taken to achieve the execution of a strategy, which brings them the needed rationality and, of course, an awareness of what is happening outside the firm, and what are the causes for those changes to happen. Only by assuming this will we be able to argue that growth could be an evolutionary process, and that it is based on the cumulative growth of collective knowledge, in the context of a purposive firm, as defended by Penrose (1959 [1995]).

In order for all this to happen, we must be able to develop human resources and their linkages in each rural/agricultural region.

Secondly, the impact of individual firm's strategies for development and growth of the region where they are located is dependent on the capacity of the region to promote regional synergies. This in turn is dependent on the capacity of firms to establish strong local networks, as well as on the capacity for local authorities to put in place policies that support individual efforts of firms and bring resources available at the supra-regional level to the region, in order to leverage regional efforts for development. Finally, this also depends on the quality of the institutions influencing the region.

Networks imply multiple connections and alternative paths in order to reinforce their 'interconnection power'. This also implies rules and collective or individual actors to assure system functioning on the basis of information and knowledge sources, financial, logistic and human resources and specific conditions (technical, economic, social, political and environmental). The system is functionally built up by the network and is organized in order to maintain a certain regularity, in spite of several changes which occur in the conditions referred to above (Carrilho et al., 2007).

From the perspective of the industrialization of agriculture, we may think of a liaison between manufacturing and agriculture, through the expansion of industrial activities that surround a farm. These processes of 'appropriationism' and 'subsitutionism' (Goodman et al., 1987, in Page, 2000 [2003]), which are generally embedded in what is called the agro-industrialization process, have moved forward slowly, but over time natural constraints have been successfully (albeit incrementally) eroded, as technological and organizational innovations have been introduced by suppliers of farm inputs and processors and marketers of farm output (ibidem).

So, we must admit that it is very important to develop linkages between firms, universities and other research institutions, to transmit knowledge and develop innovation, as well as build up the capacity of regional institutions to supply skilled personnel and venture capital to feed the growth of local firms (Ardy et al., 2002).

Also it is important to be aware that, by bringing strategy to our theoretical framework, we must depart from the traditional economic idea of equilibrium, which supports that *'an economy is in equilibrium when it generates messages which do not cause agents to change the theories which they hold or the policies which they pursue'* (Hahn, 1973; 1984, p. 59, in Penrose, 1959 [1995], p. xiv).

Strategy is, in principle, a constant change in the art of doing business. In spite of looking for consistency in the actions of firms, the dynamics implicit in strategic management processes means that it is impossible to have any stable scenario for action: 'in management terms to stop is to die'. So we must expect constant changes in the position of companies and, consequently, in the growth of regions deriving from the results of individual strategies played in the field by firms.[15]

---

15   In this sense, equilibrium is just a question of time. More important than taking a picture of the moment of equilibrium should be the knowledge of the evolutionary trend of

We need to better understand the patterns and dynamics that characterize the agricultural sector of activity, as well as the relations that are established among their main actors, and between them and the environment where they operate. Only by doing this will we be able to put in place policies that are in accordance with the role that is reserved to the primary sector in the developed economies of the world.

But, for policies to be effective, they must be conceived in an adequate framework that is able to cope with this new vision of development. We propose that a new economic concept like the Agriculture District (Porfirio et al., 2009) could be able to achieve this end since it will help us to better understand the dynamics that we can observe among enterprises that work in the primary sector and will also help us to guide effective rural development policies.

We believe that, if we adapt the concept of Industrial District to the reality of the rural regions and, in particular, to those most dependent on Agriculture, we would have at our disposal a particular framework that would help economists and politicians to become more aware of the kind of relationships that are established between economic agents in these regions. This will allow us to make better use of regional development and innovation policies to leverage the strategy results of the individual development efforts of those economic agents.

If we think about short-term growth, geography may provide a good explanation for development pathways. However, as recognized by Acemoglu et al. (2000), after controlling for institutions, *"geography does not matter"*.

In fact, long-term growth is something that goes beyond the explanation of ordinary business. If we think of long-term growth and development, we must be aware that one of the key variables that must be considered is the quality of institutions (Rodrik, 2003). In this sense, institutions must be seen as the capacity to manage conflicts, maintain law and order, provide defendable property rights, and align economic incentives with social costs and benefits. All these aspects are crucial regarding the long-term growth of territories.

Furthermore, the capacity to understand the reality of territories, to conceive and implement adequate regional policies that promote long term growth is crucial for the development of less favoured territories and this can represent a kind of 'accidental change' (Myrdal, 1957 [1972]) that can change certain path dependencies regarding development. However, we must be aware that institutions, like geography, are variables that change very slowly, or even hardly, over the course of time (Rodrik, 2003).

If we can incorporate this concept within the framework of NEG theory, we will be able to verify the following. If the primary sector's agents are able to put in place effective development strategies – strategies oriented to the market, and

growth and expectations regarding the improvement of standards of living in a particular region. For this, equilibrium must be seen more as something like the Schumpeterian idea of 'creative destruction': as a process that incessantly revolutionizes the economic structure from within, incessantly destroying the old one, incessantly creating a new one'. However, this revolution occurs in 'discrete rushes', and not suddenly.

capable of creating more value added for the companies, for the individuals, and for the region, as a whole – and, if these strategies are fuelled by proper social capital within the regions and accompanied by institutions, we are promoting the generation of externalities in these industries. We will then have the ingredients to promote the regional development of previously potentially condemned peripheral territories.

By doing this on a certain scale and within a certain time frame, we are, ultimately, resisting a certain pre-determined economic tendency for a vicious cycle of underdevelopment, and we might be able to promote the resurgence of new centres, mainly based on the primary sector.

If one applies these principles to the less developed countries, which are usually very dependent on the agricultural sector, we believe that we will be able to obtain the conditions to promote virtuous cycles of development and contribute to the progress of human kind by transforming regions once condemned to be peripheral, in new centres.

5.6. Conclusions

NEG's vision of regional development paints a black and white future world, where rural, and particularly regions dependent on agriculture, are more or less condemned to stay on the dark side of development by being part of a periphery which is much less interesting for people to live in.

Notwithstanding the considerations made in the course of this chapter, we are aware that the questions raised are controversial, difficult to prove in practice, and quite complex to answer easily. However, when trying to clarify these issues, apart from very detailed empirical work on rural regions, any answer to these questions, must be based on the following considerations:

- The composition and characteristics (in terms of capabilities) of the primary sector agents;
- The capacity of the primary sector agents (mainly enterprises) to put in place effective competitive business strategies;
- The characteristics (regarding competition, transport costs, etc.) that are present in commodity markets;
- The capacity for differentiation in the primary sector, arising from different climate and soil conditions;
- The dynamics and characteristics of both regional, and national institutions that are associated with regional development,

Regional (whereby we include rural) development is a complex phenomenon, difficult to represent by any model. It is also known that, "once you have a model, it is essentially impossible to avoid seeing the world in terms of that model – which means focusing on the forces and effects your model can represent and ignoring or giving short shrift to those it cannot. (...) A successful model enhances our vision, but it also creates blind spots, at least at first" (Krugman, 1995 [2002], p. 71).

In this chapter we argued that Krugman's NEG model representing a great advance in economics can, in fact, shed new light on the development of rural regions. However, in our view, rural regions must be seen more on the basis of the territorialization concept advanced by Storper (1997).

Moreover, in principle, we must reject any dogmatic position, especially if we are talking about economics as a science. In this chapter we have expressed the belief that, by developing endogenous resource capabilities able to put in place real development strategies – starting with firms – then regions, in particular rural/agricultural regions will be able to break away from this apparent fatal destiny regarding their development pattern.

There seems to be no doubt that the new paradigm of development coming out of what is called the 'reinvention of capitalism', as a reaction to the present financial and economic crisis, will bring a new and qualitatively rather different stage of development for post-capitalist society. Farming can be seen as a critical interface between nature and society (Page, 2000 [2003]) and the human use of the environment and nature preoccupies governments, business, and the ordinary citizen as never before.

Moreover, latest statistics are optimistic about the capacity of the agricultural sector to continue to grow. From 1980 to 2004 Gross Domestic Product (GDP) in Agriculture expanded globally by an average of 2.0 per cent a year, which exceeds the population growth of 1.6 per cent a year (World Bank, 2008). And curiously, it is in the developing countries that the most interesting progress has been made in this field. These countries had a growth of 2.6 per cent a year in agriculture, compared with a modest 0.9 per cent a year in the developed world, which means that developing countries contributed an impressive 79 per cent of overall agricultural growth during the period in question. This means that their share in agricultural GDP rose from 56 per cent in 1980 to 65 per cent in 2004.

If we think, for instance, of the capacity that derives from the use of biotechnology or the exploitation of differentiation in food production and agri-business, we should be aware that the majority of the traditional constraints imposed on agricultural production before are now, one way or another, no longer valid or, at least, do not have the same level of importance. All the changes already seen and forecast will put into question the vast majority of existing economic theories related to spatial economics and will create pressure for the restructuring of economic theory (Martin, 1999).

One of the main issues of this chapter was to show that agriculture no longer needs to be seen to work in a framework of perfectly competitive markets and, by demonstrating this, we believe we have contributed to giving a certain hope to rural regions – a hope that was more or less taken away according to the principles of NEG theory that 'condemns' rural regions to a condition of underdevelopment.

We have shown that the new paradigm of the techno-economic society, based on information (Castells, 1996 [2000]) will accelerate the increase of the tertiary sector's weight in most economies, and this will have stronger effects regarding the change of production structure and consumption, as well as resulting in a new division of labour within each country.

One of the implications of this tendency is that the tertiary sector, accompanied by an increased size of urban areas, will bring more downward pressure on the standards of living of their populations, and this will cause a new exodus of people: this time from big cities to smaller towns, usually located in rural regions. We believe that these movements will increase the pressure for land use and will result in a new type of forward and backward linkages, not just because of the 'intangibility' of relationships between economic agents, but also because of the characteristics of immobility of such an important factor of production as land.

We are sure that this, in turn, will result in a new decentralization of activities and create opportunities for the development of rural regions where food and energy supply is easier and their contribution to the environment and sustainability of countries is, without doubt, very important.

As a corollary, rural regions in general, instead of being just a space to launch the initial stage of a development process (that will inevitably end with the end of agricultural activities in that region), may represent, according to our vision of the future, the arrival of a new paradigm of territorial development. Our belief is based on the following assumptions:

- The primary sector's firms are able to conceive and put in place business strategies like any firm in the other sectors of economic activity;
- The firms within the commodity sector (where we may include some agricultural goods, as a particular subset of the primary sector), are able to play differentiation strategies within international markets;
- Climate and soil peculiarities cause a kind of 'natural differentiation' within agricultural products that form the basis for firms in the primary sector to put in place differentiation strategies;
- Usually, agriculturally dependent and rural regions have weaker levels of social capital, which handicaps their development. It is these aspects that are more important for the development of these regions than just the characteristics of the businesses that these regions develop;
- The primary sector's firms are mainly small and medium sized which also handicaps regional development, especially if we consider the weaker capability of these types of firms to conceive and implement business strategies.

In summary, there is no doubt that NEG represents a huge advance in economics concerning the development of regions and the study of the origins of this development. Moreover, NEG raises very important questions about unequal regional development.

However, we must be careful about incorporating the conclusions of this theory in policy making since we may be focusing on the wrong issues if we adhere too closely to the NEG's conclusions about the development of rural regions.

References

Abramovitz, M. 1986. Catching Up, Forging Ahead, and Falling Behind. *The Journal of Economic History*, 46(2), *The Tasks of Economic History*, 385-406.

Acemoglu, D., Johnson, S. and Robinson, J.A. 2000. The Colonial Origins of Comparative Development: An Empirical Investigation, *NBER Working Paper* n°. WP/00/7771.

Ardy, B., Begg, I., Schelkle, W. and Torres, F. 2002. *EMU and Cohesion: Theory and Policy*. 1st Edition. Principia.

Arthur, B.W. 1989. Competing Technologies, Increasing Returns, and Lock-in by Historical Events. *Economic Journal*, 99 (394), 116-31.

Arthur, B.W. 1994. *Increasing Returns and Path Dependence in the Economy*. Ann Arbor, MI: University of Michigan Press.

Bourdieu, P. 1980. Le capital social. *Actes de la Recherche en Sciences Sociales*, 3, 2-3.

Brander, J.A. 1992. Comparative Economic Growth: evidence and interpretation, *Canadian Journal of Economics*, 25(4), 792-818.

Cameron, G. 2003. Economic Growth. *Mimeo*. Department of Economics, Oxford University.

Carrilho, T., Jacquinet, M. and Porfirio, J. 2007. O conceito de Distrito Agrícola e a sua Adequação aos Problemas de Desenvolvimento Regional em Portugal: O caso do Alto Douro Vinhateiro, in *2°. Congresso Nacional da Ordem dos Economistas*, Lisboa.

Castells, M. 1996 [2000]. *The Information Age: Economy, Society and Culture, Volume I - The Rise of the Network Society*. 2nd Edition. Massachusetts: Blackwell Publishers.

Castells, M. 1998 [2000]. *The Information Age: Economy, Society and Culture, Volume III - End of Millenium*, 2nd Edition. Massachusetts: Blackwell Publishers.

Clark, G.L., Feldman, M.P. and Gertler, M.S. (eds) 2000 [2003]. *The Oxford Handbook of Economic Geography*. United States: Oxford University Press.

Coleman, J.S. 1990. *Foundations of Social Theory*. USA: Harvard University Press.

Diniz, F. and Gerry, C. 2005. A Problemática do Desenvolvimento Rural, in *Compêndio de Economia Regional*, edited by J. Costa. 2ª Edição. Colecções APDR, 529-561.

Dixit, A. and Stiglitz, J.E. 1977. Monopolistic Competition and Optimum Product Diversity. *The American Economic Review*, 67(3), 297-308.

Findlay, R. 1996. Modeling Global Interdependence: Centres, Peripheries, and Frontiers. *The American Economic Review*, 86(2), *Papers and Proceedings of the Hundredth and Eighth Annual Meeting of the American Economic Association*, San Francisco: CA, 47-51.

Fujita, M., Krugman, P. and Venables, A.J. 1999 [2001]. *The Spatial Economy – Cities, Regions and International Trade*. Cambridge, Massachussetts: MIT Press.

Fukuyama, F. 2002. Social Capital and Development: The Coming Agenda. *SAIS Review*, 22(1), (Winter-Spring).

Gallup, J.L., Sachs, J.D. and Mellinger, A. 1998. Geography and Economic Development. *CID Working Paper, WP n°. 1*, Forthcoming in *Annual World Bank Conference on Development Economics*, edited by B. Pleskovic and J.E. Stiglitz, The World Bank: Washington, DC.

Harris, C. 1954). The Market as a Factor in the Localization of Industry in the United States. *Annals of the Association of the American Geographers*, 64, 315-348.

Hart, S. and Banbury, C. 1994. How Strategy Making Processes can make a difference. *Strategic Management Journal*, 15(4), 251-69.

Helpman, E. and Krugman, P. 1985. *Market Structure and Foreign Trade - Increasing Returns, Imperfect Competition and the International Economy*. Cambridge, MA, London: The MIT Press.

Hume, D. 1741 [1995]. Of The Rise And Progress Of The Arts And Sciences, in *The Writings of David Hume*, edited by J. Fieser, (Internet Release, 1995).

Krugman, P.R. 1991a [2000]. *Geography and Trade*. Eight Printing.

Krugman, P.R. 1991b. Increasing Returns and Economic Geography. *The Journal of Political Economy*, 99(3), 483-499.

Krugman, P.R. 1995 [2002]. *Development, Geography and Economic Theory*. Cambridge: MIT Press.

Krugman, P.R. 1998. Space: The Final Frontier. *Journal of Economic Perspectives*, 12(2), 161-174.

Krugman, P.R. 1999. The Role of Geography in Development. *International Regional Science Review*, 22(2), 142–161.

Krugman, P.R. 2000. Where in the World is the 'New Economic Geography', in *The Oxford Handbook of Economic Geography*, edited by G. Clark, M. P. Feldman and M.S. Gertler, New York: Oxford University Press, 49-60.

Krugman, P.R. and Venables, A.J. 1990. Integration and the Competitiveness of Peripheral Industry. *CEPR, Discussion Paper Series*, 363.

Krugman, P.R. and Venables, A.J. 1993. Integration, Specialization and Adjustment. *NBER Working Paper Series*, 4559.

Loasby, B.J. 1977. Imperfections and Adjustment. *University of Stirling Discussion Paper*, 50.

Maddison, A. 2001. *The World Economy – A Millenial Perspective*. OECD - Development Centre Studies.

Maddison, A. 2005. *Growth and Interactions in the World Economy: The Roots of Modernity*. Washington D.C.: AEI Press.

Malthus, T. 1798. *An essay on the principle of population, as it affects the future improvement of society, with remarks on the speculations of Mr. Godwin, M. Condorcet, and other writers*. London: printed for J. Johnson, in St. Paul's Church-yard, available at: http://www.library.adelaide.edu.au/etext/m/m26p/ m26p.zip.

Martin, P. 1999. Are European Regional Policies Delivering, *EIB Papers*, 4(2).

Marshall, A. 1890 [1920]. *Principles of Economics*. 8th Edition, MacMillan and Co. Ltd., available at: http://www.econlib.org/, on 16 October 2003.

Myrdal, G. 1957 [1972]. *Economic Theory and Underdeveloped Regions*. University Paperbacks, Methuen & Co. Ltd., London.

Noéme, C. and Nicolas, F.M. 2004. The Processes of Technological Learning and co-operation in small firms, in *Innovation in Small Firms and Dynamics of Local Development*, edited by M.T. Vaz, J. Viaene and M. Wigier. Warsaw: Scholar Publishing House.

O'reagan, N. and Ghobadian, A. 2004. The importance of Capabilities for Strategic Direction and Performance. *Management Decision*, 42(2), 292-312.

Page, B. 2000 [2003]. Agriculture, in *A Companion to Economic Geography*, edited by E. Sheppard and T.J. Barnes, Blackwell Publishing.

Penrose, E. 1959 [1995]. *The Theory of the Growth of the Firm*. New York: Oxford University Press.

Porfírio, J.A. 2005. *Portugal e a Integração Europeia à luz da Nova Geografia Económica – As implicações no Domínio da Estratégia Empresarial*. PhD Thesis, Universidade Aberta.

Porfírio, J., Carrilho, T. and Jacquinet, M. 2007. Regional Innovation Policies: The Case of the Upper Douro. *International EAEPE Conference Papers*, Porto.

Porfírio, J., Carrilho, T. and Jacquinet, M. 2009. The Concept of Agricultural District and the question of Rural Development. *Spatial and Organization Dynamics – CIEO Discussion Papers Nº 1*, 43-61, CIEO: Universidade do Algarve.

Porter, M. 2000 [2003]. Locations, Clusters, and Company Strategy, in *The Oxford Handbook of Economic Geography*, edited by G.L. Clark, M.P. Feldman and M.S. Gertler, United States: Oxford University Press.

Pred, A.R. 1966. *The Spatial Dynamics of U.S. Urban Industrial Growth, 1800-1914*. Cambridge: MIT Press.

Pritchett, L. 1997. Divergence, Big Time. *Journal of Economic Perspectives*, 11(3), 3-17.

Robinson, J. 1977. What are the Questions? *Journal of Economic Literature*, 15(4), 1318-1339.

Rodrik, D. (ed.) 2003. *In Search of Prosperity - Analytic Narratives and Economic Growth*. Princeton and Oxford: Princeton University Press.

Romer, P. 1994. The Origins of Endogenous Growth. *The Journal of Economic Perspectives*, 8(1), 3-22.

Samuelson, P.A. 1952. The Transfer Problem and Transport Costs: The Terms of Trade when Impediments are Absent. *The Economic Journal*, 62(246), 278-304.

Samuelson, P.A. 1954. The Transfer Problem and Transport Costs, II: Analysis of Effects of Trade Impediments. *The Economic Journal*, 64(254), 264-289.

Sheppard, E. and Barnes, T.J. 2003. *A Companion to Economic Geography*. UK: Blackwell Publishing.

Storper, M. 1997. *The Regional World - Territorial Development in a Global Economy*. New York, London: The Guilford Press.

Triglia, C. 2001. Social Capital and Local Development. *European Journal of Social Theory*, 4(4).

Vaz, M.T. and Cesário, M. 2008. Driving Forces for Innovation: Are they measurable? *International Journal of Foresight and Innovation Policy*, 4(1/2).

World Bank 2007. *World Development Report 2008 – Agriculture for Development*. The International Bank for Reconstruction and Development/The World Bank, Washington D.C.

Chapter 6

Public-Private Partnership in Small and Medium-Sized Cities

José Luis Navarro Espigares and José Antonio Camacho Ballesta

6.1. Introduction

Goods and services can be delivered by governments in a number of different ways. Governments that previously both produced and provided services now tend to rely increasingly on the market either for inputs to government production and provision or for direct provision of goods and services. This change has occurred for ideological reasons and to obtain better value for money, i.e. how to improve the use of resources. Public-private partnership (PPP) is part of this trend. Through PPP the government enters into a long-term contract with a private partner to deliver a good or service. The private partner is responsible for building, operating and maintaining assets that are necessary for delivering the good or service.

Although private firms have been involved in public service delivery for a long time, the introduction of public-private partnership in the early 1990s established a mode of public service delivery that redefined the roles of the public and private sectors. Throughout the 1990s and early 2000s, increasingly more countries started using this mode of delivery. The early participants in this trend were Australia and the United Kingdom, but since 2004 the list has also included France, Germany, Ireland, Italy, Japan, Korea, Portugal, Spain, Turkey, Argentina, Brazil, South Africa, and several other countries. Governments introduced PPP for various reasons: to improve the value for money in public service delivery projects, or because PPP had the potential of bringing private finance to public service delivery. Because many governments experienced the pressure of fiscal deficits and increasing public debt burdens, by the mid-1990s, private finance partnering was perceived to be attractive, especially for large infrastructure projects. During the last decade in particular, governments increasingly recognised that PPP is an instrument to improve value for money, although not necessarily constituting an additional source of finance. Nevertheless, there is still a lack of clarity about the definition of public-private partnerships, as well as about the relationships regarding affordability, budgetary limits and access to private finance.

The development of PPP also raised a series of political and economic questions. Firstly, at issue would be the reasons for active participation of the private sector in the provision of services that have traditionally been provided by the public sector. The answers to this question involve economic and political choices that depend in a given country on the relative efficiency of public services, on the potential availability of capital, and on the social consensus about acceptable ways of delivering certain services. The public and social acceptability of such partnerships is often a key factor. The economic questions concern issues such as contract management and risk sharing which pertain to maximizing value for money. A number of tests are involved, relating to affordability, risk sharing and competition, as well as the provision of a benchmark with a public sector comparator. In these decision processes and tests, budget decisions are a key factor. In the opinion of some public authorities PPP may be seen as a way to shift part of the public debt off their books, particularly when they are faced with fixed ratios of acceptable public sector indebtedness.

At a more general level, engaging in a PPP process will require governments to define clear legal and policy frameworks, and to make certain that the *appropriate capacity exists within the government to initiate and manage PPPs*. Ensuring an enabling environment for PPP also has implications from the perspective of public governance, so that the public sector, needs to establish itself as a credible partner with appropriate regulatory and oversight mechanisms. This condition is particularly important, as public-private partnerships are often managed by decentralized authorities or local governments that must deal with major private sector participants.

In 2005 the European Commission published the Green Paper on PPP (EC, 2004). This Green Paper discusses the phenomenon of PPP from the perspective of Community legislation on public contracts and concessions; however Community law does not lay down any special rules covering PPP. First in Section 6.2, we present a summary of the main highlights found in the specialized literature on PPP. This review is structured around three topics relevant to our work: definition and concept; development and trends; and those particular aspects of PPP in local services. In section 6.3 we present a descriptive analysis of the Private Finance Initiative in the United Kingdom. This analysis was carried out utilising the list of signed projects offered by HM Treasury and focuses on the role played by investment in this new model for contracting facilities and infrastructures at a local level. While most studies on PPP adopt a perspective based on sectors and financial issues, our work pays special attention to project promoters (local authorities, health authorities, and ministers) and geographical distribution of PPP projects. Finally, in Section 6.4 we present our conclusions. On the one hand, we offer a warning about the risk that PPP could entail for the public provision of local services, with special emphasis on the risks and critical visions published by various authors. On the other hand, we suggest that PPP could play a new role as a mode of regulation to prevent public services provision from being moved into the private sector.

6.2. Background

6.2.1. PPP definition

Public service provision does not imply that government also has to be the producer of the services. Most government services are provided with assets that are procured from the private sector or through contracts where private companies furnish the assets, usually according to government specifications. These assets may include buildings, computers, dams, roads, hospital equipment or military equipment. Governments may also contract private companies to supply certain services such as maintenance or advisory services. However, none of these arrangements may necessarily qualify as public-private partnership. They could all still be categorized as traditional public procurement.

There is currently no clear definition of what constitutes public-private partnership; the literature offers several possibilities (Table 6.1):

Table 6.1   Definitions of public-private partnerships (OECD, 2008)

The OECD (OECD, 2008) defines a public-private partnership as an agreement between the government and one or more private partners (which may include the operators and the financers) according to which the private partners deliver the service in such a manner that the service delivery objectives of the government are aligned with the profit objectives of the private partners and where the effectiveness of the alignment depends on a sufficient transfer of risk to the private partners.
A Public-Private Partnership (PPP) is a contractual agreement between a public agency (federal, state or local) and a private sector entity. Through this agreement, the skills and assets of each sector (public and private) are shared in delivering a service or facility for the use of the general public. In addition to the sharing of resources, each party shares in the risks and rewards potential in the delivery of the service and/or facility (The National Council for Public-Private Partnerships http://www.ncppp.org/howpart/index.shtml#define).
PPPs describe a form of cooperation between the public authorities and economic operators. The primary aims of this cooperation are to fund, construct, renovate or operate an infrastructure or the provision of a service. PPPs are present in sectors such as transport, public health, education, national security, waste management, and water and energy distribution (EC, 2004). http://europa.eu/legislation_summaries/internal_market/businesses/public_procurement/l22012_en.htm

According to the International Monetary Fund (IMF, 2006), public-private partnerships (PPPs) refer to arrangements where the private sector supplies infrastructure assets and services that traditionally have been provided by the government.

A cooperative venture between the public and private sectors, built on the expertise of each partner that best meets clearly defined public needs through the appropriate allocation of resources, risks and rewards (The Canadian Council for Public-Private Partnerships http://www.pppcouncil.ca/resources/about-ppp/definitions.html).

Public-Private Partnership is a generic term for the relationships formed between the private sector and public bodies often with the aim of introducing private sector resources and/or expertise in order to help provide and deliver public sector assets and services (EIB, 2004).

Given that public-private partnerships occupy a middle ground between traditional public procurement and privatization, it is necessary to distinguish them clearly from those two. It is also necessary to distinguish PPP from concessions (though they are closely related). To define PPPs and to distinguish them from all other forms of public and private sector interaction, it is necessary to first understand the main reasons for their implementation.

The main reason is to improve service delivery – that is, to create better value for money in comparison with a government delivering the service. Thus, even if delivery through traditional procurement is effective, the service may neither be of high quality nor delivered efficiently (i.e. at least cost). Thus governments may decide to initiate PPP contracts and draw on the capacity of the private sector to efficiently deliver quantity and quality. However, although private sector participation in PPP frequently contributes to higher levels of efficiency, its participation does not guarantee improvement in service delivery and efficiency. Such improvements depend crucially on a sufficient transfer of risk from the public sector to the private partner. In the absence of a sufficient transfer of risk, service delivery could still be viewed as public procurement even if a private company is involved. Therefore, the distinguishing feature that determines whether a project is defined as traditional public procurement or as a public-private partnership should be whether or not a sufficient amount of risk has been transferred.

If a PPP contract implies that the private partner will maximize its profit by delivering a service efficiently and effectively, then the contract constitutes a partnership, in view of the fact that both parties – the government and the private partner – will achieve their objectives. This broader definition of the term partnership helps to distinguish PPP from privatization. Privatization does not involve strict alignment of objectives since the government does not usually participate in the output specification of the privatized service.

PPPs are situated between traditional public procurement and full private provision. Usually the government sets the quality and quantity requirements, and allows the private partner to design and build the asset and service aspects (Corner, 2006). In contrast to traditional procurement, the government does not buy the capital asset directly from the private partner. Rather, it purchases the stream of services that the private partner generates with the asset. To the government, value for money represents an optimal combination of quality, features and price, calculated over the whole of the project's life. The United Kingdom government (HM Treasury, 2006) defines it as: ...the optimum combination of whole-life cost and quality (or fitness for purpose) to meet the user's requirement.

There is one remaining question. What distinguishes PPPs from concessions? The OECD (2006b) points out two distinguishing characteristics concerning risk and payment:

- The level of risk transferred, especially that of demand risk, might in general be higher in the case of a concession. The distinction between supply and demand risks is important since the presence of externalities and the public good nature of some goods create demand risk due to the free rider problem. The extent of demand risk might be such that a private operator is unwilling to deliver unless the government (and not the direct recipient) remunerates it for its services.
- Concessions usually depend on user charges for the majority of their income, and many do not receive any payment from the government. In fact, instead of the government paying the private operator for services delivered, in the case of a concession the private operator pays the government for the right to operate the asset.

Having made this distinction, it should also be mentioned that much of the literature does not draw a clear line between PPP and concessions regarding affordability and value for money.

Public-private partnership in local services can take a variety of forms with differing degrees of public and private sector responsibility and risk.

- Design, Build and Operate (DBO) contracts. Under this form of PPP, the contractor undertakes designing, building, operating and maintaining the asset for a period specified in the contract, normally 20-25 years. The design and build element of the contract is financed by the Exchequer, while the operations and maintenance element of the contract is the responsibility of the contracting authorities i.e. the local authorities. At the end of the contractual period, the asset reverts to state ownership. Contracts under this form of PPP are mainly in the Water Services sector.
- Design, Build, Operate and Finance (DBOF) contracts. Under this form of contract the contractor undertakes designing, building, financing and operating and maintaining the facility for the duration of the contract.

The contactor recoups the capital and operational cost through a series of unitary payments made by the contracting authorities over the duration of the contract. At the end of the contract period the asset reverts to state ownership.

- Design, Build and Finance (DBF) contracts. Under this form of contract the contractor agrees to design, build and finance the scheme. This form of contract is widely used in the housing sector, where the contractor recovers his costs through the sale of the private element of the scheme.

In practice, several key types of PPP are frequently encountered in local services. Although the majority of PPP contracts are in the water/wastewater sector, other sectors involved include waste management, housing, local services, urban development and alternative energy.

Private Financing Initiatives (PFI), which normally involve a concession contract, have evolved in practice as a distinct means of funding major capital investments in local services through financing provided by private partners. In the United Kingdom's PFI, which is probably the best-known example, private consortia enter into long-term contracts with the government to finance, build, and, less frequently, manage new projects. PFIs have been the subject of an ongoing cost-benefit debate. Their applicability and use need to be evaluated carefully both as a matter of policy and on a case-by-case basis.

In Ireland, the majority of PPP contracts are in the water /waste-water sector, with the design, build and operate (DBO) as the predominant form of contract. There is however an increasing number of long-term operation and maintenance (O+M) contracts being advanced. Almost all of the DBO PPP water/wastewater contracts for the cities and larger towns are currently operational or under construction, and the focus is now on the remaining towns and smaller villages. To ensure competition in the tendering process, particularly through the participation of international companies, local authorities are bundling a number of smaller schemes into a single DBO contract to achieve an economic mass (http://www.environ.ie/).

The specific format of PPP in any given situation will depend on the regulatory framework. Beyond enabling PPP, the regulatory framework plays a critical role in assuring and promoting the quality of services resulting directly or indirectly from any such arrangements. Quality regulation at all levels, but particularly at the national and local levels, is a prerequisite to ensure a successful public-private partnership. The multilevel governance aspects also require an adequate interface between local authorities and national governments. This issue can be significant in some federal countries where, in specific cases, different layers of regulations may be superimposed.

In general, partnering with the private sector implies potential benefits, but there are also important risks to be managed. Although, in contrast with conventional public procurement, PPP seems to offer greater returns, some PPP disadvantages should also be carefully considered, such as higher costs, reduced competition, and loss of flexibility.

6.2.2 Recent evolution of PPP

During the past two decades, some countries have seen a huge increase in the use of PPP as a mode of public service. In the experience of most countries, the trend has been to begin with PPP in the transportation sector and then move gradually into other sectors. Other services that governments deliver through PPP in the early stages of their use are water and waste management and healthcare (PricewaterhouseCoopers, 2005). The majority of the projects undertaken by OECD countries have been within the transportation infrastructure, e.g. airports, railroads, roads, bridges and tunnels. Other projects include public utilities and services such as waste and water management, educational and hospital facilities, care for the elderly, and prisons. In addition, governments of both OECD member and non-member countries have often used PPPs to build new assets or upgrade deteriorating ones. Despite the rather extensive rollout of PPP in some countries, it should not be seen as a mechanism that will largely replace public procurement in the future. For a number of years in the United Kingdom, PFI deals have made up a mere 10-15 per cent of the total annual public investment expenditure, that is, a small proportion in the country with a relatively extensive use of PPP.

Between 1985 and 2004, worldwide public-private financing occurred in 2096 projects and totalled nearly $ 887 billion (AECOM, 2005). Of this total, $ 325 billion went to 656 transportation projects. Several developed countries, as well as some emerging market economies, increasingly engage in public-private partnership to deliver services that were previously delivered through traditional procurement (Grimsey and Lewis, 2005).

Developed countries with extensive PPP experience include Australia and the United Kingdom. Recent large players include Korea, Portugal and Spain, while countries such as France, Germany, Hungary, Italy, Japan and the Nordic countries also have experience with public-private partnership. Table 6.2 lists the top-ten countries engaged in PPP/PFI project finance deals in 2004.

Table 6.2   Top-ten countries with the largest PPP/PFI project finance deals, 2004

Rank	Country	Value (USD Millions)
1	United Kingdom	13,212
2	Korea	9,745
3	Australia	4,648
4	Spain	2,597
5	United States	2,202
6	Hungary	1,521

Rank	Country	Value (USD Millions)
7	Japan	1,473
8	Italy	1,269
9	Portugal	1,095
10	Canada	746

Source: Own elaboration from OECD, 2006.

The European Investment Bank (EIB, 2004) reported that, by 2004, the United Kingdom had 650 projects of which 400 were in operation. Total capital expenditure was GBP 48 billion or approximately 12 per cent of total annual capital expenditure (KPMG, 2007). Over the past 15 years, more than one thousand PPP contracts have been signed in the EU, representing a capital value of almost 200 billion €. While in recent years PPPs have become increasingly popular in a growing number of European countries, they are of macroeconomic and systemic significance only in the UK, Portugal, and Spain. In all other European countries, the importance of investment through PPPs remains small in comparison with traditional public procurement of investment projects (EIB, 2007).

The list of signed PFI projects of HM Treasury as of July 2008 shows 628 projects with a total capital value of £ 58.56 billion, or £ 40.96 billion if the three London Underground projects with the value of £ 17.6 billion are excluded. These three contracts constitute the largest PPP arrangements in the United Kingdom. Of the remaining contracts, the two largest PFI projects concern defence (the largest with a total capital value of £ 1.26 billion, and the second largest with a value of £ 1.08 billion), while the third largest is a healthcare contract (with a total capital value of £ 1 billion) (HM Treasury, 2008).

PPP in Spain focus on transportation, with private sector participation set to be a key element in the 2005-20 transportation plan of the government. That plan entails an investment of € 248 billion over the 15-year period, of which the private sector is supposed to contribute approximately 20 per cent (Sevilla, 2008). In Spain activity regarding PPP is concentrated with national and regional authorities. Allard and Trabant (2007) pointed out that during the period 1975-2000 the distribution of PPP projects between national and regional governments was 69 per cent and 31 per cent respectively. In recent years (2000-2005) these ratios have changed significantly in favour of regional authorities with 86 per cent of projects overall. The Allard and Trabant list does not include any PPP projects promoted by local authorities.

In 2001 the French government concluded a 62-year concession contract with ALIS (Autoroute de Liaison Seine-Sarthe) to design, build, finance and operate a 125 km motorway in the northwest of France at a total cost of € 900 million (OECD, 2006a). The motorway opened in October 2005. In addition, the French government announced 35 PPP projects that include part of the TGV Rhine-Rhone high-speed train line (train grande vitesse), the renovation of the zoo at

Vincennes, and the rebuilding of the Maison d'arrêt de la Santé (Santé prison) in Paris (OECD, 2006a, p. 58). The French government also plans to use PPP to construct 18 prisons and for 30 schemes in healthcare (Poulter, 2005).

In Germany, the federal government, as well as several of the Länder, became interested in using public-private partnerships, in particular to deliver infrastructure services (OECD, 2006a). In addition, several municipalities in Germany also use PPPs to deliver local government services; ten new projects with the value of EUR 500 million entered the market in 2005, with the total market estimated to be worth € 1 billion (OECD, 2006a).

Portugal has also extensively expanded partnership projects across various sectors. With a ratio of between 1.2 per cent and 1.3 per cent of GDP, Portugal has the highest PPP-to-GDP ratio in Europe (nearly double the United Kingdom ratio of between 0.6% and 0.7%) (PricewaterhouseCoopers, 2005). In addition to several large transportation projects, Portugal also initiated PPP projects in water and waste management.

In addition to transportation projects, Ireland has seen several water and waste projects (PricewaterhouseCoopers, 2005). The Irish government also announced PPP deals in relation to prisons, courts, and the health and education sectors.

In Italy, PPP projects focus especially on transportation, but there are also projects regarding health, water and central accommodation (PricewaterhouseCoopers, 2005, p. 38).

The countries using PPP are not limited to developed countries, but also include several emerging market economies such as Brazil, Chile, China, and South Africa (IMF, 2006).

6.2.3. Local services and PPP

Privatization of public services became more widespread in the 1980s with the emergence of a neoliberal consensus that sought to reduce the role of the State. In general, comprehensive privatization was rejected because of the existence of market failures. Instead, various quasi-market solutions were developed, typically the separation of purchaser and provider roles within the public sector. The logical next step was to move the delivery of these services out of the public sector. This was seen as a means to increase value for money, innovation, and responsiveness to users.

Although several reasons may explain why local privatization leads to cost savings, there is no agreement in the empirical literature about the relationship between privatization and costs. In fact, recent surveys about local privatization and costs do not reveal a systematic superiority in private production (Hodge, 2000; Sclar, 2000; Bel and Warner, 2007). A possible explanation for the unclear relationship between privatization and costs relates to the dynamics of the markets for local services, which are typically characterized by a lack of effective competition (Bel and Costas, 2006; Dijkgraaf and Gradus, 2007). This lack can be especially severe in small municipalities, as they usually have fewer numbers of private contractors available (Warner and Hefetz, 2003). In their study of the solid waste sector in Spain, Bel and Costas (2006) find descriptive evidence that suggests a highly concentrated sector, with the major contracts in the hands of the leading firms at one extreme, and a high degree of small firms and contracts at the other.

Empirical studies about the impact on costs of the private delivery of local services do not find a robust positive relationship between costs savings and privatization. One possible explanation for this ambiguous relationship is that privatization implies some transaction costs due to the use of external firms to deliver the service. However, evidence concerning the expected cost savings from privatization of local services that are not affected by a high degree of transaction costs, such as solid waste collection, is not conclusive either. An additional explanation is the lack of competition in the markets for local services, as several studies have shown.

Bel and Fageda (2008) found that competition may be weak in solid waste collection when there is an intensive use of private service delivery. Empirical data utilized in this study were obtained from a survey on local services production. The questionnaire asked about different organizational aspects of the delivery. It was directed at municipalities with over 1,000 inhabitants in the Spanish region of Catalonia. These municipalities include 97.2 per cent of the total population of Catalonia. The questionnaire was designed by researchers at the University of Barcelona and it was implemented by Catalonia's Competition Commission in late 2006 and early 2007. The implementation of the survey has provided complete and sufficient information regarding the year 2006 for 255 municipalities. The sample included 56 per cent of the municipalities in Catalonia that have a population of over 1,000 inhabitants. The population included in the sample represents 82.4 per cent of the total population of municipalities of more than 1,000 inhabitants, and 80.1 per cent of the total population of Catalonia.

The waste collection market analysed is characterized by a high degree of concentration and the number of firms that have participated in contract tenders is relatively low. More importantly, the authors found empirical evidence in favour of the dual market hypothesis. Large firms that operate at a national level dominate the market for contracts in highly populated municipalities and, it would appear, in municipalities that belong to the same urban area. Although the number of firms that participate in contract tenders may be higher in these municipalities, major firms very often seem to win the contract award process. Smaller firms that operate at a regional or local level dominate the market for contracts in less-populated municipalities and in rural area municipalities isolated from big cities. In these cases, the number of firms that participate in contract tenders may be particularly low, so that the scope of competition for the market is very modest.

In the United Kingdom, the Private Finance Initiative (PFI) is the main model of PPP. Since 1996, the Public Private Partnerships Programme (4ps), established by the Local Government Association (LGA), has provided support to local authorities. This Programme is the local government's partnership and project delivery specialist. As part of the LGA, 4ps works in partnership with all local authorities to secure funding and accelerate the development, procurement and implementation of PFI schemes, public private partnerships, complex projects and programmes. The 4ps multidisciplinary team provides hands-on support, gateway reviews, skills development and best-practice know-how. 4ps provides support to projects across nine key sectors: Corporate Property & Regeneration, Housing & Sustainable Communities, Culture & Sports, Fire & Police Services, Corporate & Transactional Shared Services (CATSS), Social Care, Transport & Regeneration, Schools, and Waste Management.

Any PFI scheme must demonstrate value for money (VFM) for expenditure by the public sector. In order to achieve the optimum combination of whole life costs and benefits, the guidance *Public Private Partnerships in the National Health Service: The Private Finance Initiative* (1999) details the phases of the PFI process, alongside the procurement process set out in HM Treasury's *Step by Step Guide to the Procurement Process*. This guidance provides practical advice for government bodies involved in, or contemplating, PFI schemes, highlights the main issues and procedures in PFI procurement, and indicates what is required at various points in the process. The guidance applies to both small and large schemes involving the provision of facilities and services. It may also be useful to the private sector as well, and can be accessed via the Internet at www.doh.gov.uk/pfi.htm.

In France PPP is currently in its early stages in comparison with the development of these markets in the UK. Domestic law has not, until very recently, provided sufficient flexibility to encourage their growth. PFI healthcare and prison projects currently lead the field in France. The healthcare sector is the first to take advantage of a recent wave of liberalizing legislation and has now implemented its first PPPs and continues to generate new deals as part of the French Government's investment programme, *Hôpital 2007*. When analysing the state of the PPP market in France, what becomes immediately clear is that while the overall objectives are common to all sectors, the legal basis and commercial maturity differ significantly from one sector to another.

The French Ministry for the Economy is also supported in its PPP objectives by a task force (*Mission d'appui à la réalisation des contrats de partenariat publics privés – MAPPP*). The primary purpose of the MAPPP is to provide assistance in the preparation and negotiation of "partnership contracts" and also to provide its expert opinion on the overall economics of a transaction or to assist the relevant public authorities (both at central and local government levels) in their initial feasibility study. This taskforce has already issued an initial practical guide (*Les Contrats de Partenariat- principes et méthodes*), but does not currently intend to follow the UK Treasury's precedent of issuing standardized documentation.

Those responsible for PPP projects can be found at both the national and local level depending on the specific sector involved. In the case of prisons, for instance, the authorities in charge fall within the jurisdiction of the central government (Ministry of Justice) as do those responsible for military procurement projects (Ministry of Defence), whereas projects serving more local needs, such as healthcare projects, are managed locally (through the *Enterprises Publiques de la Santé, EPSs*).

Decentralization clearly represents an opportunity to closely tailor service provision to local needs and thereby improve efficiency of public services. In this light the government is currently in the process of decentralizing important sectors such as airports and roads.

Since 2005 the Ministry of Economy, Finance and Industry has encouraged local authorities (*collectivités locales*) to systematically consider the *contrat de partenariat* option in any major procurement project. The inclination, at the local government level, to turn to these contracts is likely to be pivotal in relation to their overall success.

The French Support Unit regularly publishes a list of PPP signed projects. The list of signed projects from 2004 to August 2008 numbered 178 projects. 25 per cent of the projects have been promoted by the State, while the remaining 75 per cent are from the local administration. Since 2006 the evolution of PPP projects in France has been clearly determined by local authorities' activities. Table 6.3 classifies the projects into eight categories:

Table 6.3   List of published PPP projects since 2004

Type	No. Projects	%
Buildings	53	30%
Transportation	18	10%
Culture and sport	25	14%
Telecommunication	12	7%
Information Systems	3	2%
Urban Equipment	37	21%
Energy	27	15%
Education	3	2%
TOTAL	178	

Source: http://www.ppp.bercy.gouv.fr/

Apart from the previously mentioned list, Andriani et al. (2006) identified 26 additional projects (representing the vast majority of the *Hôpital 2007* programme) which are procurement processes currently underway. Among the key deals that are expected to be tendered in the near future in the healthcare sector we may note the implementation of the Electronic Medical Record (*Dossier médical personnel*).

In introducing PPPs, Spain was facilitated by its multi-level governance structure, particularly suited for the implementation of these types of contractual arrangements. Besides the effectiveness of central administrations in providing public services and assets, regional authorities, the *Comunidades Autónomas*, also have the power to implement projects, including PPPs, in their areas of competence. As a result, PPP initiatives could be tailored to the specific needs of local communities and also lead to the creation of cross-regional projects, monitored by the government itself. Among other sectors, PPPs are also booming in the health sector: the programme Madrid Nuevas Infraestructuras Sanitarias 2007 has projected nine new hospitals in Madrid (Renda and Schrefler, 2006). In 2005 there were 15 signed PPP healthcare projects (16.5 per cent of the total), which concentrated 8.4 per cent of total capital value invested by means of this contracting mode (Allard and Trabant, 2007).

In Germany where PPP is already well established, the German Institute of Urban Affairs (Difu) has carried out a study on behalf of the PPP Task Force at the Federal Ministry of Transport, Building and Housing (BMVBW). This study is a comprehensive and up-to-date review of PPP projects at federal, *Land* and municipal levels. It includes information on the distribution of PPPs, project types, investments, obstacles and prospects of success. The survey's main focus was on projects which had been planned or implemented since 2000 (http://www.difu.de/english/occasional/06ppp.pdf).

The survey's most important findings revealed that PPP infrastructure projects are now widespread in Germany, particularly at the municipal level. PPP projects have been around for many years, but such cooperation has only really taken off since around 2004. Despite the growing popularity of PPP projects, their share of total public fixed investment remains low (PPP investment averaged 2 per cent of municipalities 2000-2005 fixed investment). By 2005, 143 projects had been contractually agreed on, and a further 57 are currently in various stages of preparation. Estimates suggest that at least 300 ongoing projects are now being planned or implemented, of which about 80 per cent are at the municipal level.

Expectations of PPP regarding higher efficiency and faster implementation go a long way towards explaining the increase in the number of PPP projects. Thus, the survey did not find much evidence to suggest that PPPs are primarily seen as instruments to bridge widening gaps in public finances. Municipalities that have anticipated greater efficiency as the main advantage from PPP projects are not generally disappointed by the result. Using a method of calculation which considers the interest and compound interest effects of future payment flows, average efficiency gains reached 10 per cent.

6.3. PFI and Local Services in the United Kingdom

The Private Finance Initiative (PFI) is a form of public-private partnership (PPP) in which local authorities can gain access to new or improved capital assets (most commonly, but not always, buildings). Unlike in the practice of traditional procurement, the public sector does not buy the assets, but rather pays for their use, together with associated services (for example, security, cleaning, etc). Capital investment in the assets is made by the private sector, which recovers its costs over a long contract period (often 25 years or more).

In the UK, HM Treasury publishes an updated list of PFI projects. The last published list (last consulted in July 2008) contains a total of 628 projects signed until April 2008. For each project it provides information on the Department, Commissioning Body, Project Name, Location, Constituency, Region, Data of Financial Close, Operational Project (Yes/No), Capital Value Scores on the Departmental Balance Sheet (On/Off), Total Capital Value, Period of Operational Contract, and Annual Payments from 1992 to 2060.

Apart from the availability of data, we have chosen the UK case because this country, a pioneer in PPP implementation, offers the most extensive example of participation by local authorities. So its experiences can be seen as a case study by other countries. Some institutional instruments such as the 4ps or the Operational Taskforce (HM Treasury) were conceived to provide the dissemination of knowledge from central to local governments plus free expert advice and support to public sector partners within operational PFI projects.

While most studies on PPP adopt a perspective based on sectors and financial issues, our work pays particular attention to project promoters and the geographical distribution of PPP projects. In order to analyse in a systematic manner the information provided in the list, we have distinguished three groups of signed projects: projects related to the provision of health services, projects promoted by local authorities, and other projects. In the third category are grouped, among others, projects promoted by the Police Departments, the Ministry of Transport (Highways Agency), the Ministry of Defence, and the Ministry of Justice. This category brings together 32 per cent of the total projects included in the list. The remaining 68 per cent are split between health projects (25 per cent) and local projects (43 per cent). We distinguished between local and health services because in the latter case local and central governments make joint decisions. So these services have a special status that makes it impossible to classify them *sensu stricto* as either local or central.

20 Departments have promoted 628 projects in total, although the participation of many of them is merely symbolic. Eleven departments administered more than 95 per cent of the projects [Department for Children, Schools and Families (119), Scottish Government (103), Health (98), Department for Communities and Local Government (54), Ministry of Defence (53), Department for Transport (51), Northern Ireland Executive (35), Home Office (25), Welsh Assembly Government (24), Ministry of Justice (22), Department for Environment, Food and Rural Affairs (18)].

The majority of the health projects are concentrated in the Health Department and the Scottish Government. In the group promoted by local authorities, activities developed by three Departments must be highlighted (Department for Children, Schools and Families, Department for Communities and Local Government, and the Scottish Government). Finally in the group of Others, the Ministry of Defence is the Department with the greatest number of projects, 53 of the 199 included in this group.

In absolute terms, the Department with the largest number of projects is the Department for Children, Schools and Families (119 projects), followed by Health

(97 projects). Schools and hospital building are the star projects within the variety of contracts: more than one-third of the projects included in the list pertain to one of these two categories.

The relative importance of the three identified groups of projects changes considerably when we analyse their capital value (Figure 6.1). Projects included in the list of those signed (628) have a total capital value of £ 58,560 million.

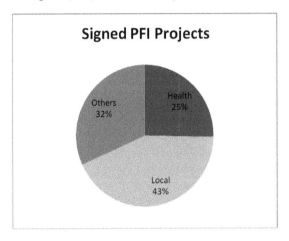

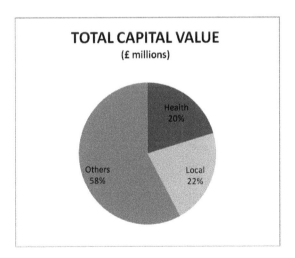

Figure 6.1   Signed PFI Projects and Total Capital Value

The relative share in the group of Others projects are enhanced significantly when we consider the capital value of projects. The health group is the only one that remains relatively stable, the gain of the Others group comes at the expense of the group of projects promoted by local initiative, which reduces its share from 43 to 22 per cent.

The Departments most active, such as, those in the local area (Department for Children, Schools and Families, 39 per cent) and in the health group (Health, 88 per cent), remain the same when we use the capital value of projects such as variable grouping. However, in the group of Others, the group's leadership passes to the Department of Transport (63 per cent), relegating the Department of Defence to second position.

Globally computed, the Department of Transport (38 per cent), Health (18 per cent), and Defence (10 per cent) account for 67 per cent of the total number of signed projects.

Table 6.4 shows the breakdown by number of projects, amounts and total amounts of projects signed in each group.

Table 6.4   Health, Local and Others PFI in the UK 2008

Type	Total Capital Value (£ millions)	Number of projects	£ millions / project
Health	11,957.23	159	75.20
Local	12,720.43	270	47.11
Others	33,882.45	199	170.26
Total	58,560.10	628	93.25

In addition to the average values, it is interesting to observe the relative size of projects promoted by the most active Departments within each group. In the case of the health group, the Department of Health offers an average capital value of £108.16 million. In the local group, the average capital value of the Department for Children, Schools and Families amounts to £41.53 million. Finally, in the group Others, the average values are affected by the high value of the Department of Transport (£763.16 million). However, the Department of Defence, which has a greater number of projects, presents an average value of £114.65 million. These values and those in Table 6.4 show the lowest amount of capital value for the projects promoted by local authorities.

At any rate, there is no relationship whatsoever between the number of projects initiated by each Department and their average monetary value. This lack of relationship shows that the average value of projects depends more on the type of project than on the activity of each Department (Figure 6.2).

In the group of projects promoted by local authorities, nearly half of them are furthered by localities with fewer than 300,000 inhabitants, typically known as

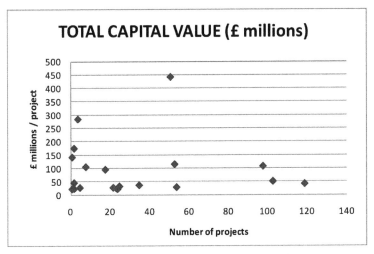

Figure 6.2 Number of PFI projects and £ millions/project

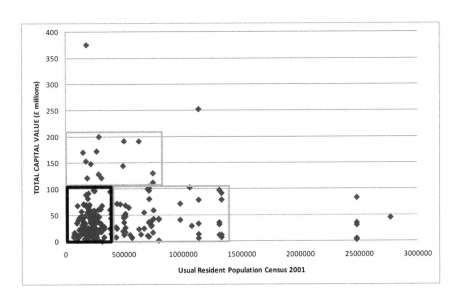

Figure 6.3 Relationship between the size of cities and capital value of PFI projects

small and medium-sized cities. In terms of capital value, these initiatives represent just over 37 per cent of all local projects.

The comparison of the resident population in the localities with the value of capital projects initiated in each of them shows the complete absence of correlation between both series. The graph below (Figure 6.3) displays the relationship between the size of cities and the capital value of projects undertaken by their local authorities. In principle, we are able to distinguish three areas with a different density of projects. In the area closest to the axes, we observe the highest density of projects. Cities of less than 400,000 inhabitants and projects with a capital value less than 100 million pounds are located in this area (Figure 6.3).

With respect to the number of active projects, approximately 80 per cent of the projects are in an operational phase. The situation is very similar when we use capital value of operational projects as a grouping variable. The only notable exception is found in health projects where the capital value of functioning projects represents 45 per cent of the total. That state of affairs can be described as exceptional and is due to there being a small number of projects with a high capital value that will become operative in 2010.

This leads us to wonder about the implementation trajectory of PFI projects. Taking as reference the "Year of Financial Closed", we note that this type of initiative was begun in the early 1990s. Until 1995 PFI experiences were merely occasional, although since 1996 there has been a sharp rise that has stabilized since 1998 with a figure of between 50 and 60 new projects annually. Although the number of projects has remained very stable from 2000, figures of annually bidden capital show a rather more unstable an evolution. In the group of health projects the growing and sustained trend should be highlighted, observing maximum numbers commissioned annually. This observation is equally valid in local projects although the beginning of the PFI experience started later than 1995. Despite the criticism that this practice has received from some sectors, evidence shows a strong upward trend in its use as a new form of financing and delivery of public services involving a large component of physical assets.

One of the reasons often argued to justify the use of PPP is the hiring investment linked to the public sector that is not reflected in public budgets, and thus does not enlarge the public debt. The Departments of Transport, Justice and Defence are the ones that recorded their PFI projects in their departmental budgets. This phenomenon can be analysed from one of the fields of the database of PFI signed projects in which the question arises of whether Value Capital is ON or OFF the Scored Departmental Balance Sheet. Overall, 86 per cent of the projects fall outside of departmental budgets, although in terms of capital value the proportion is reduced to 59 per cent. This percentage is distributed unevenly among the three groups of projects that we have been differentiating. 98 per cent of capital employed in local and health projects is not registered on departmental budgets, whereas projects classified in the group of Others present a high percentage of official records that amounts to 70 per cent of capital employed.

Table 6.5 presents the geographical distribution of the contracted amounts and the number of PFI projects at a regional level. Depending on capital value contracted, the regional sets which show a certain similarity are shown in different colors. It should be noted that the leading position is the London area, which concentrates almost half of the total capital value contracted. The primacy of the London region is not observed in either local or health projects. Projects grouped in these two categories are distributed much more uniformly across regions.

Table 6.5   Regional distribution of PFI projects

REGION	Signed Projects	CAPITAL VALUE (£ millions)
London	84	24,762.93
National/More than one region	34	5,926.83
Scotland	110	5,498.36
West Midlands	39	3,478.57
North West	46	2,921.62
Yorkshire & The Humber	42	2,659.78
South West	44	2,429.98
South East	48	2,397.20
East of England	27	2,165.64
East Midlands	35	1,958.01
North East	41	1,787.01
Northern Ireland	35	1,288.71
(n.a.)	14	667.78
Wales	29	617.67
Total	628	58,560.10

Regarding the regional distribution of projects, we are interested in determining whether this distribution is stable regardless of the authority promoting the projects. To do this, we utilized the Pearson's Chi-square (χ^2) test. From the data of Table 6.6, we calculated possible similarities among regional distributions of projects and capital value involved in relation to the origin of the projects' promotion (health, local, other).

Table 6.6   Regional distribution by promoting authorities

REGION	Total Signed Projects	TOTAL CAPITAL VALUE (£m)	Health Signed Projects	HEALTH CAPITAL VALUE (£m)	Local Signed Projects	LOCAL CAPITAL VALUE (£m)	Other Signed Projects	OTHER CAPITAL VALUE (£m)
East Midlands	35	1,958.01	8	802.50	19	961.03	8	194.48
East of England	27	2,165.64	9	847.60	10	351.19	8	966.86
London	84	24,762.93	20	2,649.50	46	1,531.75	18	20,581.68
North East	41	1,787.01	12	823.72	22	664.39	7	298.90
North West	46	2,921.62	7	1,358.40	28	1,196.72	11	366.50
Northern Ireland	35	1,288.71	8	167.06	0	0.00	27	1,121.65
Scotland	110	5,498.36	43	1,183.15	43	3,274.51	24	1,040.70
South East	48	2,397.20	13	895.20	19	1,006.75	16	495.25
South West	44	2,429.98	6	270.20	18	863.38	20	1,296.40
Wales	29	617.67	11	115.03	10	261.45	8	241.20
West Midlands	39	3,478.57	12	1,944.67	19	891.30	8	642.60
Yorkshire & The Humber	42	2,659.78	10	900.20	27	1,222.38	5	537.20
National/More than one region	34	5,926.83	0	0.00	0	0.00	34	5,926.83
(n.a.)	14	667.78	0	0.00	9	495.58	5	172.20
Total	628	58,560.10	159	11,957.23	270	12,720.43	199	33,882.45

Chi-Square tests demonstrate that geographical differences exist depending on whether PPP projects were promoted by local, health or state authorities. Nevertheless, the regional distribution of PPP projects is more homogeneous than the distribution of the quantities invested.

Table 6.7 presents the previous distributions adjusted by population. In this case, both variables have been divided by population. Consequently, the number of projects is expressed in projects per million inhabitants, and capital value is expressed in £'s per inhabitant.

Table 6.7   Per capita regional distribution by promoting authorities

REGION	Total Signed Projects/ mlnh	TOTAL CAPITAL VALUE (£/inh)	Health Signed Projects/ minh	HEALTH CAPITAL VALUE (£/inh)	Local Signed Projects/ minh	LOCAL CAPITAL VALUE (£/inh)	Other Signed Projects/ minh	OTHER CAPITAL VALUE (£/inh)
East Midlands	8.39	469.30	1.92	192.35	4.55	230.34	1.92	46.61
East of England	5.01	401.93	1.67	157.31	1.86	65.18	1.48	179.44
London	11.71	3,452.68	2.79	369.42	6.41	213.57	2.51	2,869.69
North East	16.30	710.42	4.77	327.47	8.75	264.13	2.78	118.83
North West	6.84	434.13	1.04	201.85	4.16	177.82	1.63	54.46
Northern Ireland	20.77	764.69	4.75	99.13	0.00	0.00	16.02	665.56
Scotland	21.73	1,086.20	8.49	233.73	8.49	646.88	4.74	205.59
South East	6.00	299.63	1.62	111.89	2.37	125.83	2.00	61.90
South West	8.93	493.05	1.22	54.82	3.65	175.18	4.06	263.05
Wales	9.99	212.76	3.79	39.62	3.44	90.06	2.76	83.08
West Midlands	7.40	660.41	2.28	369.20	3.61	169.21	1.52	122.00
Yorkshire & The Humber	8.46	535.72	2.01	181.32	5.44	246.21	1.01	108.20
National/More than one region (n.a.)								
Total	11.50	1,072.20	2.91	218.93	4.94	232.90	3.64	620.36

Table 6.8 shows the p-value obtained in Chi-Square tests. By means of this statistical test we have contrasted the null hypothesis for both variables, number of projects and capital value. The null hypothesis assumes that there are no differences between the regional distributions of variables. When the p-value is lower than the significance level (0.0500) we reject the null hypothesis and accept the existence of differences.

The right side of Table 6.8 presents p-values after the number of projects and their capital value were associated with the population of each region. We can observe that the number of PPP projects has a very homogeneous regional distribution and statistically significant differences only appear when we compare the number of projects promoted by local and central governments. The main divergences are located in two regions, London and Northern Ireland.

One of the specific characteristics of PPP that differentiates it from traditional public procurement is the long-term nature of relationships between the public sector and private partners. With regard to the length of signed contracts, the high frequency of contracts with an operational period of 25 and 30 years should be noted. Figure 6.4 shows the frequency of these two periods in UK signed deals.

A total of 376 projects amounting to £36,443 million have been signed for 25 or 30 years. As is shown in the chart, the distribution of total projects between the two periods is very homogeneous. When we break down the database into various groups of projects, this homogeneity is segmented, and it is possible to distinguish between health projects in which 30 years dominate and local projects where 25 year deals prevail.

The main criticism raised against the PPP mode is the potential financial overload that this practice may impose on public finances in the future. Figure 6.5 presents the evolution of Charge Unitary Payment (£ million) in the coming years. Taking into account all PFI projects as a whole we can observe a peak in the expected payments for the period 2017-18. This maximum is different for each of the various groups of projects (health 2030-31, local 2023-24, others 2010-11).

The impact of PPP in public finance can be clearly observed in the case of healthcare services. The existing PFI schemes are a source of financial difficulty for NHS trusts. Prior to contracts being signed, NHS trusts prepare business cases which purport to show that their PFI plans are 'affordable' within projected budgets. Since PFI costs are higher than historical capital costs, all business cases contain plans to sell assets and cut service capacity to offset the shortfall. But these cuts have been insufficient to bridge the funding shortfall. The cost of PFI contracts for most trusts is greater than the capital they are provided with through the NHS resource allocation mechanism. This underfunding has led to the emergence of crucial financial deficits, and, under government pressure to balance the books, plans for further cuts to services (Hellowell and Pollock, 2007).

The current system of resource allocation for England's NHS is called 'Payment by Results' (PbR). Under PbR, trusts receive the bulk of their income through a standard tariff for each patient who receives treatment. This standard tariff for treatments includes an element for capital costs, designed to equal the

Table 6.8   Chi-Square Test (P-value)

Absolute values

Chi-Square Test P value	Total Signed Projects	Health Signed Projects	Local Signed Projects	Other Signed Projects
Total Signed Projects		0.4461	0.0159	0.0020
Health Signed Projects	0.4461		0.0008	0.0024
Local Signed Projects	0.0159	0.0008		0.0000
Other Signed Projects	0.0020	0.0024	0.0000	

Chi-Square Test P value	Total Capital Value (£m)	Health Capital Value (£m)	Local Capital Value (£m)	Other Capital Value (£m)
Total Capital Value (£m)		0.0000	0.0000	0.0000
Health Capital Value (£m)	0.0000		0.0000	0.0000
Local Capital Value (£m)	0.0000	0.0000		0.0000
Other Capital Value (£m)	0.0000	0.0000	0.0000	

Per capita values

Chi-Square Test P value	Total Signed Projects	Health Signed Projects	Local Signed Projects	Other Signed Projects
Total Signed Projects		0.9973	0.4546	0.4263
Health Signed Projects	0.9973		0.4515	0.5600
Local Signed Projects	0.4546	0.4515		0.0041
Other Signed Projects	0.4263	0.5600	0.0041	

Chi-Square Test P value	Total Capital Value (£m)	Health Capital Value (£m)	Local Capital Value (£m)	Other Capital Value (£m)
Total Capital Value (£m)		0.0000	0.0000	0.0000
Health Capital Value (£m)	0.0000		0.0000	0.0000
Local Capital Value (£m)	0.0000	0.0000		0.0000
Other Capital Value (£m)	0.0000	0.0000	0.0000	

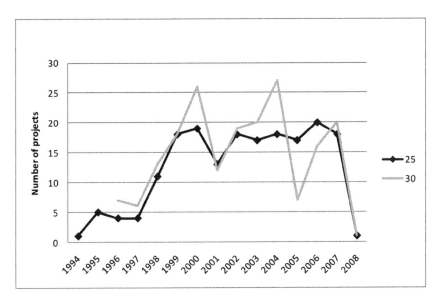

Figure 6.4   Operational period of PFI contracts

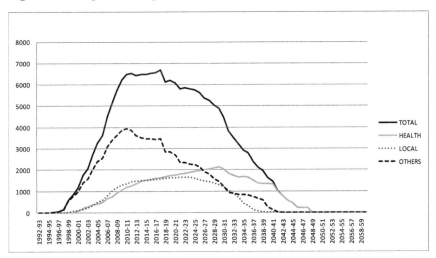

Figure 6.5   Temporal distribution of PFI payments

average capital cost across all English trusts, based on 5.8 per cent of trust income. However, the capital costs of trusts with PFI schemes average 8.3 per cent, with the result that they are underfunded. The problem is even more serious for trusts with large or multiple schemes. Trusts with operational PFI schemes with capital values of over £50 million have average capital costs of 10.2 per cent – a shortfall in income of 4.4 per cent. This underfunding has created serious financial difficulties for many trusts, which can only be reconciled by further service reductions.

Drawing on the experience of countries such as Australia, Spain, and the United Kingdom McKee et al. (2007) points out that new facilities have, in general, been more expensive than if procured by using traditional methods. Although it is true that compared with the conventional system, new facilities are more likely to be built on time and within budget, this often seems to entail compromises on quality.

From a budgetary standpoint, financial problems posed by the financing of new assets in healthcare or local services via PPP are exactly the same as those related to the introduction of new health technologies. Specifically in healthcare services, cost-effectiveness analyses linked to the emergence of new health technologies often demonstrate an improved cost-effectiveness ratio, so the introduction of the technologies into regular clinical practice is usually recommended. However, although new treatments and technologies are more cost-effective, they have an incremental budgetary impact, so decisions regarding their introduction into the portfolio of services should also be supported by studies of budgetary impact and financial sustainability.

Ultimately, the controversy that arises over the financing of new assets associated with the delivery of health services is none other than the traditional dispute between quality and quantity in providing public health services. The PPP strategy favours a volume of investments in the health sector that, from a budgetary point of view, would not be able to be sustained in the traditional model of public procurement. However, the financial burden that these investments are imposing on the budgets of current expenditure in the coming years will force a decrease in the quantity or variety of benefits, except in the unlikely case that an increase in the volume of health financing might happen.

From the standpoint of managers and regional authorities it is logical to expect an increasing trend in improving and modernizing health facilities and services. However, from the perspective of financial authorities it would be desirable to have greater concern about the affordability and financial sustainability of projects underway.

One of the main demands that we must impose on the PPP model as a new formula for financing investments in health funding is its profitability. To analyse this requirement we compare the capital value of each project with the total annual payments. In projects for which the data on total annual payments were available, we found that the sum of annual payments collected on average exceeded the amount of investment involved by a factor of 5.54. This multiplier is surpassed slightly (a factor of 5.62) in the case of health projects, those closest to the average value. The projects that offer a more favourable financial relationship were initiated by local authorities (a factor of 4.45). The projects listed in the category of Others presented a factor well above average (a factor of 6.19).

Figure 6.6 shows the relationship between financial leverage and the number of PFI projects promoted by each department. The distribution points in the graph indicate a certain learning effect, so that the two departments (the Department

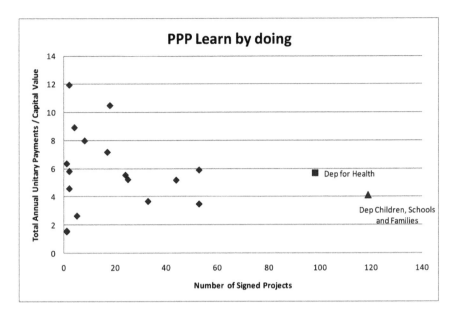

Figure 6.6   Departmental financial leverage

of Health and the Department of Children, Schools and Families) with a greater number of projects offer the smallest financial multipliers.

The average internal rate of return (IRR) for the total of signed projects is 16 per cent. Projects promoted by the Department of Health offer an internal rate of return of 15 per cent and projects from the Department of Children, Schools and Families are at 13 per cent, both below the overall average, although well above the price of money in monetary markets. Projects initiated by local authorities present the lowest IRR (13 per cent).

Healthcare and education are two main social objectives closely related to economic growth. Sometimes the development of these two objectives is compromised by resource shortfall. In the British case we have shown how PPP became a driver in both healthcare and educational projects. Thus indirectly PPP is helping to promote the European Strategy of Growth and Competitiveness that was set out by the European Council in Lisbon in March 2000 with the aim to make the EU 'the most dynamic and competitive knowledge-based economy in the world capable of sustainable economic growth with more and better jobs and greater social cohesion, and respect for the environment by 2010'.

6.4 Conclusions

In accordance with the results of our empirical work on the British PFI, the conclusion drawn from the German case could be perfectly valid for most European countries where the PPP practice offers high expectations and a beneficial image in the upgrading of facilities related to public services. Up to now, most of the tests carried out on PPP have been concerned with ensuring proper management of contracts, especially through the dissemination of good practice models and guides which provide the necessary requirements at each stage of the contractual process. That is, the main concern about PPP projects has been value for money (efficiency). However, this new model of public service delivery can result in major problems for public finances, which could ultimately limit the actual level of provision. Finally, this list of precautions should not omit the negative effect that PPP has on the labour market, i.e. the generating of segments that, from an economic and social perspective, is considered inadvisable.

So far, the majority of regulations concerning the new PPP procedures have focused on the need to ensure efficiency improvement: namely 'value for money'. Typically, as many studies testify, the PPP procedure offers notable improvements in efficiency and effectiveness when we use the traditional procurement as a reference (public sector comparator). However, the increased efficiency of individual projects does not mean that at the aggregate level the financial burden of such projects is bearable by the public purse.

Therefore, in order to prevent the PPP strategy from becoming a source of public deficit that would be unacceptable by budgetary limits, it is imperative that practice guidelines and national regulations on PPP procedure incorporate the overall budget restriction as a prerequisite over the efficiency of individual projects, to be regarded as a necessary but not sufficient condition.

As we have shown, operational, labour, and financial problems related to PPP are relevant but preventable issues.

Finally, we would like to point out a very pertinent aspect regarding regulation. The relationship between PPP and regulation can be observed from two different perspectives.

On the one hand, national regulation can cause PPP strategy to be successful or not. Firstly, the legal environment and methodological procedures in relation to PPP should be adapted to fit each country. The establishment of PPP Central Unit or Task Force, whose mission is to apply the best practice knowledge in governance and preparation of PPP projects, has demonstrated good results in many countries. These centres are responsible for guaranteeing the successful implementation of PPP projects, ensuring best practice in developing, procuring and appraising projects, and for ensuring transparency and setting up ethical standards. Furthermore, PPP central units must cooperate with the Ministry of Finance, which is usually responsible for monitoring and regulating long-term future liabilities of public budgets resulting from the realization of PPP projects.

On the other hand, PPP can also be viewed as a new form of regulation of private activities. Some services traditionally provided by the public sector may be converted to private services owing to the scarcity of resources, the low quality level, or low efficiency in the public sector. The tendency towards privatization could be considered a political project under the auspices of globalization.

Globalization is the flipside of deregulation, (a system without rules or institutions), and deregulation means that public institutions withdraw from the provision of public goods, in order to make way for private providers and the working of the market mechanism, which is usually considered much more efficient than the public provision of public goods. During recent years, the combination of technical possibilities, market strategies combined with financial power, and political trends has reinforced strategies to privatize public goods all over the world.

With regard to public services we can compare provision by public suppliers with private ones and thus evaluate whether the provision of certain public goods by public institutions is better and more efficient in satisfying public needs than their provision by private providers. There are many examples of an improvement in the provision of public goods by private firms, especially in the telecommunications sector, in countries where people have money to spend. But there are also many examples where privatization of the provision of public goods has had negative effects, from the British railway system to the drinking water supply in Latin-American and African cities. In all cases, deregulation and privatization has reduced the capacity of state institutions to intervene in economic processes.

Although sometimes PPP is seen primarily as a way to privatize public services, PPP implementation could actually deter excessive pressure from building up within public systems to move towards privatization. We should not forget that PPP is a type of public procurement, in the sense that the combination of market efficiency and public interest in satisfying the needs of the population is made possible through this model. This combination allows for private production along with guarantees of public rules and institutions.

References

Allard, G. and Trabant, A. 2007. Public-Private partnership in Spain: Lessons and Opportunities. *IE Business School Working Paper WP10-07*.

Andriani, B., Lignières, P. and Ratledge, S. 2006. PPP in France – 2006. Linklaters' Projects, Paris. www.linklaters.com.

AECOM Consult, Inc. 2005. Synthesis of Public-Private Partnership Projects for Roads, Bridges and Tunnels from Around the World, 1985-2004. United States Department of Transportation, Washington DC.

Bel, G. and Costas, A. 2006. Do public sector reforms get rusty? Local privatization in Spain. *Journal of Policy Reform*, 9 (1), 1-24.

Bel, G. and Fageda, X. 2008. Privatization and competition in the delivery of local services: An empirical examination of the dual market hypothesis. Document de treball XREAP2008-4, Universitat de Barcelona.

Bel, G. and Warner, M. 2007. Privatization of solid waste and water services: What happened to costs savings?. *Working Paper Universitat de Barcelona & Cornell University*.

Corner, D. 2006. The United Kingdom Private Finance Initiative: The Challenge of Allocating Risk. *OECD Journal on Budgeting*, 5(3), 37-55.

Dijkgraaf, E. and Gradus, R. 2007. Collusion in the Dutch Waste Collection Market. *Local Government Studies*, 33 (4), 573-588.

EC (European Commission) 2003. Guidelines for Successful Public-Private Partnerships. *Directorate General Regional Policy*, European Commission, Brussels, http://ec.europa.eu/regional_policy/sources/docgener/guides/pppguide.htm.

EC (European Commission) 2004. Green Paper on Public-Private Partnerships and Community Law on Public Contracts and Concessions, COM (2004)327 Final, European Commission, Brussels.

EIB (European Investment Bank) 2004. The EIB's Role in Public-Private Partnerships (PPPs), *European Investment Bank*, Luxembourg. Available at: www.eib.org/Attachments/thematic/eib_ppp_en.pdf.

Grimsey, D. and Lewis, M.K. 2005 Are Public Private Partnerships Value for Money? Evaluating Alternative Approaches and Comparing Academic and Practitioner Views. *Accounting Forum*, 29(4), 345-378.

Hellowell, M. and Pollock, A.M. 2007. Private finance, public deficits. A report on the cost of PFI and its impact on health services in England. Centre for International Public Health Policy, University of Edinburgh.

HM Treasury 2006. PFI: Strengthening Long-term Partnerships. *The Stationery Office*, London.

HM Treasury 2008. PFI Signed Projects List, July. Available at: www.hmtreasury.gov.uk/documents/public_private_partnerships/ppp_index.cfm .

Hodge, G. 2000. Privatization. An International Review of Performance. Boulder, CO: Westview Press.

IMF 2006. Public Private Partnerships, Government Guarantees, and Fiscal Risk. *Fiscal Affairs Department, International Monetary Fund*, Washington DC.

KPMG (Klynveld, Peat, Marwick and Goerdeler) 2007. Effectiveness of Operational Contracts in PFI 2007. KPMG LLP, London. Available at: www.kpmg.co.uk.

McKee, M., Edwards, N. and Atunc, R. 2006. Public–private partnerships for hospitals. *Bulletin of the World Health Organization*, 84 (11).

NHS Executive 1999. Public Private Partnerships in the National Health Service: The Private Finance Initiative. *Good Practice*, Overview, Treasury Taskforce.

OECD 2006a. *Interim Report on the Role of Private Participation in Major Infrastructure Provision.* Intermediary report submitted to the Working Party on Territorial Policy in Urban Areas at its 8th session in Bilbao, Spain, 5-6 June, GOV/TDPC/URB(2006)5, Public Governance and Territorial Development Directorate, OECD, Paris.

OECD 2006b. *Concessions.* Global Forum on Competition, Directorate for Financial and Enterprise Affairs, OECD, Paris.

OECD 2008. *Public-private partnerships: in pursuit of risk sharing and value for money*. GOV/PGC/SBO(2008)1/REV1, Public Governance and Territorial Development Directorate Public Governance Committee, OECD, Paris.

Poulter, T. 2005. Middle Age for the PPP Market?. *Infra-News*, 13-15.

PricewaterhouseCoopers 2005. Delivering the PPP Promise: A Review of PPP Issues and Activity. London: PricewaterhouseCoopers.

Renda, A. and Schrefler, L. 2006. Public – Private Partnerships National Experiences in the European Union. *DG Internal Policies of the Union - Directorate A – Economic and Scientific Policy*, European Parliament.

Sclar, E. 2000. You don't always get what you pay for. The economics of privatization. Ithaca, NY: Cornell University Press.

Sevilla, J. 2008. Public-private Partnerships: Affordability, Value for Money and the PPP Process. *Personal communication at the OECD Symposium*. Winterthur, Switzerland, 21-22 February.

Warner, M.E. and Hefetz, A. 2003. Rural-Urban Differences in Privatization: Limits to the Competitive State. *Environment and Planning C: Government and Policy*, 21(5), 703-718.

Chapter 7

Social and Political Determinants of the Area of Influence of Medium-sized Cities in Portugal

Ana Paula Barreira

7.1. Introduction

Nowadays the urban influence as a device for the establishment of networks that can improve economic development is at the centre of attention. The main studies on these issues are concerned with large cities as an anchor for knowledge spreading, creating the big city as the required scale for innovation, thus influencing the development of adjacent urban and suburban areas.

However, little attention has been paid to medium-sized city dynamics. Medium-sized cities lack dimension and their interactions are the central key for agglomeration economies generation. This implies that medium-sized cities have to be positioned as partners rather than as competitors. Only with cooperative behaviour can medium-sized cities achieve the required agglomeration effect that generates positive economic spillovers. Although the scope of this chapter did not allow checking to see whether cities cooperate or compete, it evaluates whether cities spread influence over their adjacent territories, as an indicator of agglomeration economies generation. Moreover, the chapter tests if cities are affected by neighbouring effects, i.e. by the influence over the population that a neighbouring city achieves. In the chapter, the greater the city influence is, the larger the population who benefit from public and private amenities relative to the city's residents.

This issue is even more relevant for Portugal, where cities are, in the main, of relatively small size when compared with European medium-sized average cities. Moreover, the Portugal's neighbouring country Spain has much bigger cities, with which typical Portuguese cities, in isolation, cannot compete because of their lack of dimension.

In a context where the lack of scale (dimension) of most of the Portuguese cities is considered as a restriction to regional development, the definition of integrated networks between medium-sized cities appears to be a natural solution, but is not always easy to implement. As a matter of fact, in Portugal, on average, the cities have only 28,000 inhabitants, the median being around 14,000 inhabitants, which indicates a large gap between the two largest cities: Lisbon and Oporto, with, respectively, 510 thousand and 228 thousand inhabitants, and the rest of the country.

To understand how territorially diffused individuals have access to specific amenities highlights how populations interact even when individuals do not belong to, or are near, a big city. These dynamics can be a sign of knowledge spread, in the sense that small and medium-sized cities can have a coordinating activity that can achieve the same benefits emerging from large cities, i.e. agglomeration economies.

As such, the main goal of this chapter is to understand if cities, as providers of a mix of public and private amenities, are positively or negatively influenced by similar provisions in neighbouring cities. This kind of influence can result either from a balance found between neighbouring cities that leads to a cooperative behaviour or, from the dominance of self-interest that leads to competitive behaviour. The purpose of this chapter is not to identify whether the driving forces behind cities interaction are cooperation or competition but whether such interaction functions as a stimulus or as a restriction for the influence achieved by neighbouring cities.

Understanding the way cities relate has relied on a differentiated theoretical and empirical framework. There are various reasons to explain why the population sorts out in accordance with the presence of certain amenities, such as those focusing on private interests for a certain place of residence, on public choice as the main driving force, and on agents' network establishment.

Typical work on this subject relies on the explanatory effect of both socio-economic and geographic variables. Apart from the literature on local government behaviour in what concerns public good provision, political variables have not been taken as an explanation for inter-local relations. Moreover, nor is the role of political variables explicitly considered as determining the number of population served by those amenities. Trying to fill this gap, this chapter attempts to understand whether political variables do play a role in the degree of influence spread by medium-sized cities. As such, a model is estimated where the city's influence is explained by socio-geographic characteristics, as well as by political factors.

In this sense this chapter has two major goals: first, to understand whether the area of influence of medium-sized cities is affected by neighbouring cities when these cities offer a set of similar private and public amenities to their population; second, to identify the role played by political variables in the promotion of cities' influence, thus with public actors, as promoters of the benefits of agglomeration economies.

The first finding is that, when neighbouring cities' behaviour in providing public and private amenities is considered by the population (and not the political behaviour, which cannot be aligned with population), the population's demand for amenities in a certain city is negatively affected. Thus, cities' influence constrains the neighbouring cities' influence. This result can be twofold. Society reacts to amenities provided in other cities located in proximity, avoiding the duplication of amenities, and exploiting the agglomeration economies advantage, thus being economically rational and conductive to the necessary volume of amenities.

Alternatively, cities can be negatively affected by neighbouring cities because society looks at the closer amenities and chooses to have such amenities as well, thus leading to inter-city competitive behaviour, thus compromising the achievement of agglomeration economy effects.

Another result of the chapter is that political variables are important for studies regarding cities' connectivity. The consecutive number of years that a political party is in office is relevant for the degree of influence that a city attains. It appears that, for a greater number of individuals to benefit from a city's amenities, it requires a higher number of years for one political party to be in office on the municipal council.

It is also found that geography has a crucial role on city's influence since cities are not equally distributed over the territory. Cities near the coastal each tend to have a smaller influence, since that is where most of them are concentrated. This proximity can be seen as an advantage to explore network channels and, by joining them, increase the scale of such territorial space. An agglomerate of cities appears to be a natural solution, and in this chapter there is a proposal for the formation of 3 clusters of medium-sized cities, each with approximately 500,000 inhabitants: one around the city of Lisbon; the one around the city of Oporto; and the one comprising the remaining not agglomerated medium-sized cities.

Finally, a positive parameter is estimated for the number of inhabitants in a city, which has a significant effect on the city's influence, thus providing evidence of the advantage of the integration of cities in a broader network that allows them to explore agglomeration economies, and hence, achieve gains in competitiveness. As a matter of fact, without a critical mass of population in a globalized world, the survival of medium-sized cities could be compromised. Development which relies on medium-sized cities' connectivity allows us to explore the main advantages of big cities – the agglomeration effect – without their main disadvantages, such as congestion and crime.

The chapter is organized as follows. Next, Section 7.2 presents a literature review of the main areas in the study of inter-city relations, as well a description of the institutional arrangement of Portuguese cities. Section 7.3 describes the adopted empirical methodology and the estimated results. In Section 7.4 is explained the major empirical findings and their political implications. Section 7.5 concludes.

7.2. Survey Procedures

7.2.1. Related literature

Usually people decide to live in cities because cities have a concentration of a number of important amenities, as well as other economic characteristics, such as the availability of jobs, which are valued by citizens. This behaviour is in line with the pioneer work of Tiebout (1956) in which people vote with their feet by looking at the package of tax/public goods provided by local governments. In a broader sense, people do sort by looking at both the economic opportunities and the well-being offered in cities as a device to select which municipality to belong to, and in which city to reside.

Tiebout's seminal paper considered population sorting only in response to public good provision. However, as pointed out by Bewley (1981), the assumptions inherent in the revealing preferences, present in the Tiebout's work, imply that public goods are almost private goods. The main argument is that, if people prefer to live in a certain place that means that public goods and corresponding fiscal effort are what is most required, given the alternatives of location.

However, when a household moves to a certain jurisdiction or town, such decision usually does not exclusively rely on public goods provided but also on a branch of other private services that signifies a better way of living.

In this sense, several works, such as Krugman (1991), Glaeser et al. (2001) and Rosenthal and Strange (2001), have developed theoretical and empirical foundations to explain the main reasons why people choose to settle in a certain jurisdiction or city. These papers use socio-economic and geographic variables as the main determinants of the attraction of a certain jurisdiction, and do not consider variables that could capture the role of political action. Glaeser et al. (2001) particularly state that high amenity cities tend to grow faster. The authors also find that urban rents, as well as urban wages, are explanatory factors of city expansion.

Putting emphasis on the public goods provided by jurisdictions, others looked at local governments' choices, and how interdependent the adopted local governments' policies are, thus evaluating if jurisdiction relationships are based on competition or on cooperation. The main findings of this branch of the literature are that local governments tend to compete for the attraction of the mobile tax payers, and thus evolve in a process of strategic interaction. In this approach the population's gain in a certain jurisdiction implies a loss on taxes collected by the neighbouring jurisdictions. These findings are presented, for example, by Besley and Case (1995) and Brueckner (1998, 2003).

Analogously, Case et al. (1993) developed a model that sustains mimicking on public expenditures, thus presenting evidence that local governments tend to replicate public expenditures made by neighbouring local governments in an attempt to attract a bigger proportion of population. Baicker (2005) and Ermini and Santolini (2007) find empirical support for such local governments reaction to their expenditure policies of neighbours, for different countries in, respectively, the United States and Italy.

However, Feiock (2004) has pointed out that cooperation between jurisdictions is likely when the transaction costs of bargaining are low. In this approach, local governments can find it more advantageous to find cooperative arrangements than to play a Nash game. Under voluntary agreements, any spillover effect between jurisdictions could be solved by a compensation mechanism. This kind of collective action was merely focused on the local governments' explicit attitude, and did not consider any societal attitude, in general, as an implicit device to find cooperation.

Another branch of the literature looks at economic agents' behaviour, relying on social and natural sciences, and states that repeated interactions between neighbours imposes a spatial Prisoner's dilemma that can lead either to cooperation or to competition. Trust built during the successive interactions is the main driving force for cooperation to be enhanced, bearing in mind the defect action taken in the past by economic interveners. Barr and Tassier (2008) propose a model where, depending on the geographical model specification of local neighbours, a different degree of cooperation can be found. The authors show that a circular or a lattice network tends to promote cooperation. Such cooperation incentive decreases when networks are discretely distributed. Their main argument is that agents receive larger payoffs when they share their neighbourhood with other cooperative agents.

Based on these different approaches the relationship established between cities, thus conditioning their influence, can be expected to be either more cooperative when focus is put on social aspects, or more competitive if public administration selfishness is the most relevant issue in explaining the number of beneficiaries of the city's amenities.

7.2.2. Brief characterization of a Portuguese city's political autonomy

Portugal is a country where the major political decisions are made by a centralized government, which is usually identified by international institutions such as the IMF as a unitary country, meaning that the political levels below central government are not entirely free to set policies. On the Portuguese mainland[a] there are only two political levels: the central government and the local governments, the latter being carried out by an elected mayor (the President of the Municipal Chamber) and his/her executive. A local government in Portugal is usually identified as a Municipality.[b] Portugal contains 308 municipalities, 278 of them on the mainland.

The municipal authorities have more control of expenditures than of receipts. Municipalities can select where to spend but are not allowed to select the taxes to be collected. The municipality has only limited freedom to choose the tax rate of certain taxes, which can vary only within a certain range, previously imposed by central government.

Not all Portuguese local governments are located in cities. Some of them are located in villages because there are no cities within the municipality borders. Only 117 municipalities on the mainland have their councils in cities. Moreover, municipalities with cities have, on average, only one city. There are only 17 municipalities that include more than one city in their borders.

In fact there are 139 cities on the Portuguese mainland, two of which are characterized as exercising aggregative forces, thus leading to the definition of the metropolitan areas: Lisbon and Oporto, with 510,000 and 228,000 inhabitants, respectively; 42 cities that are considered to be of medium-size with 20,000 to 100,000 inhabitants, and 95 cities of effective small size, i.e. below 20,000 inhabitants. The distribution of these cities explains the average and median size of Portuguese cities, respectively, 28,000 and 14,000 inhabitants.

Portugal does not have, as it happens in some countries, any entity with power based exclusively in city or urban areas, that role being played just by the municipality. Moreover, Portuguese cities are mainly located near the coast, which means that the sea borders the two major mainland cities and 55 per cent of the municipalities which have medium-sized cities. If we consider relative proximity to the sea, not necessarily sharing a border with it, this percentage increases to 69 per cent.

7.3. Empirical Analysis

7.3.1. Econometric approach

Given the possibility of the presence of a neighbouring effect between cities, we now check for spatial effects by using a spatial autoregressive model. The regression takes the form $y = \rho Wy + X\beta + \varepsilon$, where y contains a nx1 vector of cross-sectional dependent variable; W represents a nxn spatial weights matrix attached to neighbours according to a certain distance criterion; X is a nxk matrix of regressors; and ε is the error term with $\varepsilon \sim N\left(0, \sigma^2 I_n\right)$.

Since in the presence of spatial dependence, least-squares will produce biased and inconsistent estimates of β 's, here a maximum likelihood estimator developed by Anselin (1988) is used. The characteristics and adequacy of spatial models are explained in works such as Anselin et al. (1995, 1996), Graaff et al. (2001) and Florax and Nijkamp (2005).

In the estimation of the spatial autoregressive model the GEODA software is employed. Several distance-based spatial weights were tested considering different k-nearest neighbours, but, given the asymmetric spatial distribution of cities in the Portuguese territory, this approach does not fit the data adequately since it imposes that all observations have exactly the same number of neighbours. As such, the weighting matrix is adjusted according to a critical distance. The best results are found with a threshold distance of a radius of 1.5 degrees around each city. This implies that cities located up to approximately 167 km apart are considered neighbouring cities[1]. This means that medium-sized cities which are located more closely to each other are included in the neighbouring border of a higher number of cities than when such cities are relatively diffusely distributed.

The presence of spatial dependence is found by an analysis of the Lagrange multiplier associated with the OLS regression, showing the lag multiplier to have a higher value than the error multiplier. That being the case, a better result of the Maximum Likelihood Estimation is expected under a spatial lag model than under

---

[1] The calculus of distance between cities, considered for the definition of the weighting matrix, establishes that one mile is equal to 1.852 km and, the transformation of degrees into kilometres is given by the following expression: 1.5 degrees * 60 minutes * 1.852 km = 166.68 km.

an error lag model. Table 7.2 in subsection 7.3.3 summarizes the main diagnostic results.

7.3.2. Data

The data set comprises 42 observations for medium-sized cities defined as having between 20,000 and 100,000 inhabitants (see list of considered cities and inhabitants in Appendix A.7.1).

The dependent variable is the city influence (CITY INFLUE) determined by the ratio between the number of inhabitants that benefit from a set of specialized city amenities relative to the population residing in the city[2]. The larger the number of beneficiaries of the amenities the bigger the city's influence is. Amenities can be either public or private. Public amenities comprise facilities such as hospital/clinics, centres for treatment of certain diseases (such as AIDS and drug addiction), employment centres and professional training centres. Private amenities include private schools, private clinics, supermarkets and vehicle inspection centres. The number of inhabitants with access to these facilities was retrieved from the 2004 Statistics Portugal (INE) publication: Urban System – Functional Marginality and Influence Areas.

As shown in Figure 7.1, cities around the two major Portuguese cities Oporto and Lisbon have the smallest area of influence. Moreover, cities located on the coast tend to be less influential than those in the interior. In fact, Viseu and Beja (the right-hand map), given the absence of relatively closer medium-sized cities, correspond to cities that have spread their influence to an extensive number of individuals compared with these cities' inhabitants. This implies that when medium-sized cities have several neighbours, they tend to replicate the availability of the same specialized amenities, thus giving rise to two contradictory interpretations: thus observation derives from the fact that these cities are functioning both as competitors and partners. The influence of a medium-sized city located geographically closer to other cities of the same size tends to constrain the influence of the neighbouring cities. Hence, the agglomeration of several cities with a small population influence can be an outcome of either cooperative or a competitive inter-cities' behaviour.

The estimated regression includes six explanatory variables: namely, two socio-economic, three political and one geographical.

The two socio-economic variables are a measure of the municipal concentration of inhabitants in cities (POP CITY WE) and an indicator of city attractiveness evaluated by the average property price in urban areas (PROPERTY VA). The former variable tries to capture how the inner-city concentration constrains its

---

2   City population is distinct from urban population. The latter includes population living in areas around cities. Here, only the population resident in city is considered. The cities' population is retrieved from the following web page: http://pt.wikipedia.org/wiki/Lista_de_cidades_em_Portugal.

sphere of influence for inhabitants outside the city. The expectation is that if a city contains a significant fraction of the municipal inhabitants that would imply a lower city influence, since the major potential beneficiaries of the city amenities were already living near such facilities. The latter variable tries to capture how populations choose to sort. If property has a high value in inner-cities that creates an incentive for the population to reside in peri-urban areas, thus favouring residential zones with lower property prices around cities. In this sense, the expectation is that the higher the property value, the higher the influence of a city, since population will be less tempted to live in the city 'core'. Both municipal inhabitants and property values were retrieved from the 2004 Statistics Portugal (INE) publication: *Annual Statistics*.

Three political variables were considered as regressors: POL ORIENTA, ALIGN CGOV and MAJORITY. The first measures in how many of the 16 years prior to 2004 has the local mayor belonged to the same party as the mayor in office in 2004. The second variable measures in how many of the last 16 years prior to 2004 was the leading party on municipal council the same as that in the central government. The third variable measures the number of years municipal and assembly councils have had a majority of seats belonging to the same party in the 16 years prior to 2004. The municipal information regarding political variables is available at the Portuguese

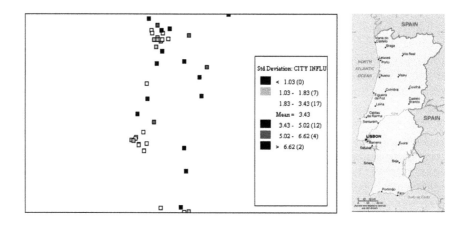

Figure 7.1   City influence of Portuguese medium-sized cities

Source: INE, Wikipedia and calculations by the author. Portugal Map is a file from the Wikimedia Commons, available at http://pt.wikipedia.org/wiki/Portugal. Commons is a freely licensed media file repository. *Permission is granted to copy, distribute and/or modify this document under the terms of the GNU Free Documentation License, Version 1.2 or any later version published by the Free Software Foundation; with no Invariant Sections, no Front-Cover Texts, and no Back-Cover Texts. A copy of the license is included in the section entitled "GNU Free Documentation License".*

National Municipalities Association (ANMP) web page: http://www.anmp.pt/index. php?option=com_content&view=article&id=67&Itemid=58.

In the political variables definition, a temporal lag is used, since there is a consensus that public and private amenities made available in a certain city are the result of policies made over the course of several years and not an outcome exclusively of the present party in office.

The prior expectation for the three political variables is that they are positively correlated with city influence.

The last variable LITTORAL KM is the geographical variable and measures the distance in kilometres between the coast and the city, in order to evaluate if cities located near the coast shows differences regarding population attracted by amenities from those located in the interior.

The expected result is that the nearer the city is to the coast the lower will be the influence generated, since the majority of the cities are located along the coast. Similarly if a city is far away from the coast, a greater influence is anticipated because interior cities are geographically remote. Thus, a positive correlation between a city's influence and a city's distance from the coast is anticipated.

Table 7.1 summarizes the main statistical values for the variables considered.

Table 7.1   Variable statistic values

Variable	Average	Std. Deviation	Maximum	Minimum
CITY INFLU	3.43	1.58	7.5	1.03
PROPERTY VA	86 387	23 134	156 277	44 629
POL ORIENTA	11	5	16	4
ALIGN CGOV	7	4	14	0
MAJORITY	8	5	16	0
LITTORAL KM	42.5	63.38	247	0.3

7.3.3. Estimation Results

As stated above three regressions were run: an OLS estimation and two maximum likelihood estimations using the spatial lag model and the spatial error model. Table 7.2 summarizes the main findings.

The rho coefficient in the spatial lag model is very significant, indicating that the neighbours' influence does affect the influence that each city achieves. In fact, the results show that the influence of each neighbouring city constrains a certain city's influence by almost the same magnitude (the rho coefficient is closer to 1).

This result indicates that the existence of amenities in neighbouring cities imposes a constraint on the number of inhabitants who have access to those amenities. This implies that cities do interact. However, such interaction can be caused by two different types of social behaviour. People can use amenities closer to their residence as a consequence of cooperative behaviour, thus exploring the advantages of agglomeration economies. In this sense, cities behave by exchanging information flows, avoiding the duplication of amenities, and adjusting amenities supply to their demand. In contrast, people can request to have public and private amenities nearby, exhibiting a competitive behaviour, leading consequently to efficiency losses derived from duplication of facilities, not allowing beneficial agglomeration effects to be fully explored. Even when competitive behaviour is in place, information between cities will flow since populations share relevant data relative to available amenities for the purpose of comparison.

The results show that, despite the main driving forces that sustain inter-city relations, cities also establish links between them, thus having the essential mechanisms to share and spread information. Cities do not function in isolation and the way neighbouring cities evolve has an impact in the development of each city.

Table 7.2   Model specification with diagnostics for spatial effects

Variables	OLS	Spatial Lag Model - MLE	Spatial Error Model - MLE
Rho - Spatial Lag City Influ		-0.98	
		(-2.80)***	
Constant	-0.17	3.09	-0.08
	(-0.11)	(1.82)**	(-0.06)
POP CITY WE	1.03	1.58	1.03
	(0.83)	(1.57)*	(0.94)
PROPERTY VA	0	0	0
	(1.45)*	(1.25)	(1.55)*
POL ORIENTA	0.13	0.11	0.13
	(2.67)***	(2.77)***	(2.94)***
ALIGN CGOV	0.06	0.08	0.06
	(1.04)	(1.63)*	(1.13)
MAJORITY	-0.07	-0.04	-0.06
	(-1.34)*	(-1.04)	(-1.46)*
LITTORAL KM	0.01	0.02	0.01
	(3.41)***	(5.09)***	(3.87)***
Lambda			-0.14
			(-0.37)

Variables	OLS	Spatial Lag Model - MLE	Spatial Error Model - MLE
Regression Diagnostics			
Multicollinearity	19.35		
Test on Normality of Errors			
Test Jarque- Bera	1.88		
	(0.39)		
Diagnostic for Heteroskedasticity			
Test Breusch-Pagan Test	3.84	6.88	3.86
	(0.70)	(0.33)	(0.70)
Specification Robust Test			
Test White	33.33		
	(0.19)		
Diagnostics for Spatial Dependence			
Lagrange Multiplier (lag)	4.73		
	(0.03)		
Lagrange Multiplier (error)	2.67		
	(0.10)		
Likelihood Ratio Test		7.53	6.58
		(0.01)	(0.01)
Number of Observations	42	42	42
R^2 - adjusted	0.27	0.51	0.4
Log Likelihood	-68.75	-64.98	-65.46

Notes: T-statistics for OLS estimation and Z-values for MLE are in parentheses. ***, **, * denote significance at the 1%, the 5% and the 10% level, respectively. In the regression diagnostics the p-values are in parentheses.

Of the socio-economic regressors, the population city weight (POP CITY WE) is the only one which is statistically significant but is only relevant in the spatial lag model. Contrary to the prior expectations, the concentration of inhabitants in cities improves the influence of cities, meaning that scale does matter for the spreading of benefits from amenities to a large number of individuals. In this sense the higher population concentration in a city, the more the city's influence is, although with a somewhat disappointing significance (see Figure 7.2).

Again, contrary to the expectation, the second socio-economic variable: property value (PROPERTY VA) also does not have an impact on the city's influence in the spatial lag model specification, being significant only at the 10 per cent level in OLS and spatial error specifications. Looking at Figure 7.2, property value does not appear to have a significant impact on cities' influence.

These findings can result from either a lack of sample dimension or the existence of spatial phenomena. In fact, when the analysis is extended to consider the territorial behaviour between these two variables, and looking in particular for the points on the maps where several cities coexist near to each other, the results change, showing, as can be seen in Figure 7.3, a positive correlation for the coastal centre of Portugal but a negative correlation both in the coastal North and in South.

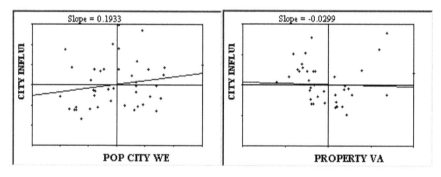

Figure 7.2   Correlations between city influence and socio-economic variables

The political variables have lower coefficients than population city weight but the political orientation of the mayor of the municipality to which the city belongs (POL ORIENTA) is highly significative. This significance is present despite the model specification considered. This leads to the conclusion that, when a certain party remains in office for a longer period, it is tempted to act in order to expand city's influence. This can be interpreted as a way for the leading party to reinforce its power over neighbouring cities, which is only feasible when a certain political orientation of the municipal executive remains in power for a long period.

From the results, it can be stated that competitive behaviour from the municipalities to which cities belong is more expected as long as the leading political party remains in power for long periods. This implies that, the alternation

North

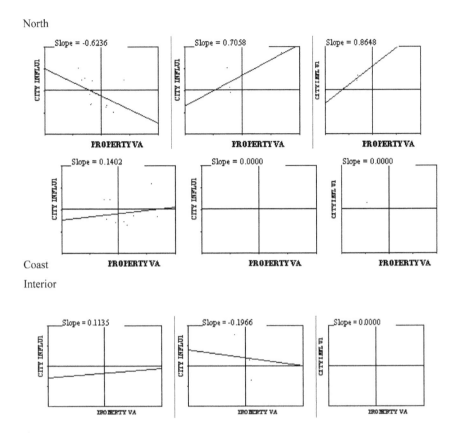

Figure 7.3   Correlation by geographical areas of the city's influence and property value

of the leading political party in a municipality improves cities cooperation, thus leading to a better environment for the generation of agglomeration economies. Municipal leading parties for longer periods tend to privilege more competition between cities, thus leading to a duplication of amenities, with the corresponding negative effects on economic efficiency.

The number of years that the same leading party is in office in local and central government (ALIGN CGOV) is only significant in the spatial lag model, and appears to slightly improve the city's influence, creating a more favourable environment for city competition.

The variable that measures the number of years in which the same party leads simultaneously both the municipal chamber and the municipal assembly (MAJORITY) appears not to have a role in explaining the city's influence when a spatial lag model is considered. In the OLS and the spatial error model specifications this variable is slightly significant.

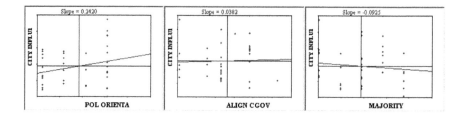

Figure 7.4   Correlation between city influence and political variables

The minor importance exhibited by the variable MAJORITY leads to the conclusion that municipal executive action is not truly constrained by the fact that the leadership of the municipal assembly is of a different party. This result is unexpected since it would be expected that municipal assembly could have a role on the influence that a certain city achieves.

The findings regarding political variables are corroborated by the correlations between the dependent variable and each one of the political variables. Figure 7.4 shows that the only significative positive correlation is found between the maintenance of municipal incumbency and country influence.

The geography variable (LITTORAL KM) is statistically significant in the three specifications. However, the major impact is found on the spatial lag model. Distance from the coast does explain the different city's influence found on the Portuguese mainland. Effectively, the closer to the coast a city is, the lower the city's influence. This is because cities are more concentrated near the coastal zone, thus inducing the cities of interior, because of the absence of nearby cities, to spread their influence into larger areas.

7.3.4. Robustness Analysis

As stated above the OLS estimation will produce biased and inconsistent estimators in the presence of spatial dependency. As such, there now follows an analysis of the regression diagnostics.

The presence of spatial dependence is identified by a simple test of lag specification, significant at the 5 per cent level, but not significant using a simple error test specification.

The model does not suffer from multicollinearity problems, since the test result is below 20. The model also presents normality of errors, a required condition for inference in small samples. The Jarque-Bera critical value of a Chi-square test with two degrees of freedom at the 5 per cent of significance is 5.991. The Chi-square test with six degree of freedom for heteroskedasticity test is 12.592, and therefore regression does not reject the null hypothesis of homocedasticity. Regression also does not reject the null hypothesis of the correct specification test since the White test critical value, corresponding to a Chi-square test with 27 degrees of freedom at the 5 per cent of significance, is 40.113.

As required for finite samples, the Wald test is higher than the Likelihood Ratio Test which is also higher than Lagrange multiplier (lag) test. The Wald test is the square of the z-value and is equal to $(-2.8)^2=7.84$. As such, the corresponding ordering is $7.84>7.53>4.73$.

After considering the lag spatial model, the spatial dependence disappears as can be seen by the Moran's I test statistic on LAG-RESIDU of -0.0496 that is essentially zero. This indicates that including in the model the spatially-lagged dependent variable term has eliminated all spatial autocorrelation. Figure 7.5 shows the absence of spatial effects on the residuals.

7.4. Main Results and Political Implications

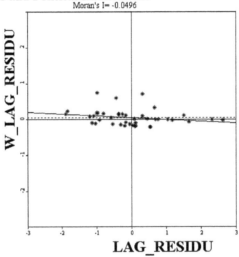

Figure 7.5   Moran's *I* test on spatial lag regression residuals

The way cities interact is important information since it allows us to understand how society behaves in the presence of certain amenities. Usually studies consider the role that public actors have on public goods provided in cities and the main discussion is how local governments interact in the presence of such provision: cooperatively or competitively.

Both public and private agents' intervention plays a role in cities' dynamics. How population has access not only to public facilities but also to private services is an important issue showing how populations act, share relevant information and explore the benefits of agglomeration economies.

The estimation results show that people are rational and try to explore the existing nearby amenities, such choice resulting from either cooperative or competitive behaviour. This is important since it shows that economic partners will find ways to exchange relevant information. Consequently, there are information flows that ensure that knowledge is spread to neighbouring cities. This inter-city behaviour is a good sign because it provides evidence of the existence of a social mechanism for transmitting information, which opens an opportunity for cooperative behaviour, networking individuals of different cities, based on a wider set of issues. The existence of such a mechanism is required in order to ensure that relatively small cities share knowledge and reinforce the agglomeration economy effects that they lack. This implication is of major importance in order to sustain the development of those cities, which compete globally with other cities to enhance the competitive advantage of being large.

Political intervention also plays a role in the achievement of the inter-cities' relationship goal. The regular changing of the political party in the leadership of the municipality to which the city belongs to seems to facilitate interactive solutions. Alternatively, when a leading party is in power for several periods, the executive leaders are tempted to intervene in a way that aims to increase the city's influence, thus compromising the influence of the neighbouring cities. The imposition of term limits, although not preventing party re-election, nevertheless helps to constrain the intervention of a certain executive that could remain in power for too long.

Following the approach by Glaeser and al. (2001), it was tested whether property value as well as wage value explains the number of individuals who have access to cities' amenities. It is found that, for some model specifications, property value is statistically significant, but, with an insignificant coefficient. Although not reported in this chapter, wage value is not statistically significant in any of the models specified.

The explanation for the former result could be that higher property values push households to live in the peri-urban areas, thus increasing the spread of the city's influence to neighbouring areas. This occurs mainly around Lisbon and in the South, leading to the territorial phenomenon that property values force the agglomeration economies effect in the North but does not encourage the population agglomeration of medium-sized cities in the Centre and South of Portugal. These two conflicting results can explain the small statistical significance of by the property value variable. Figure 7.6 shows property value results and how property values affect the city's influence.

Wages are higher in cities near Lisbon and Oporto. Taking into consideration wage effects on a city's influence when neighbour effects are included, only the influence of medium-sized cities around Lisbon appears to benefit from their having higher average wages. Those benefits disappear for cities around Oporto. Figure 7.7 portrays this situation.

In contrast, the city's geographical location has an impact on its influence, presenting a lower value, the closer the city is to the coast. Since the majority of cities are concentrated on the coast, cooperative behaviour could provide

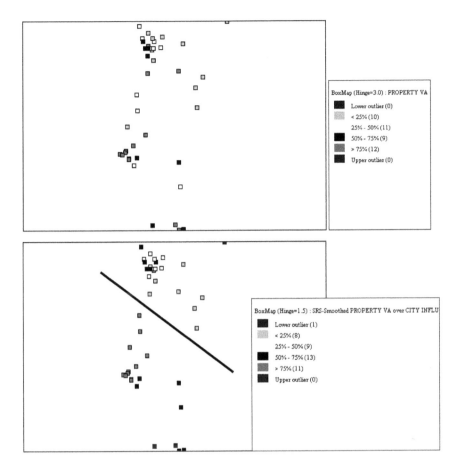

Figure 7.6   Portuguese mainland property values, and the relation between property values and the city's influence

the opportunity for the formation of agglomerations of cities. Such a territorial arrangement could improve cities' relationships and bring extra dimension to cities that in isolation are only of medium size. The result would be an increase in the exploitation of agglomeration economy effects and an increase in the agglomeration competitiveness.

This being the case, given the neighbouring characteristics of closer cities, an agglomeration based on proximity could be a rational solution to overcome the size constraint.

There now follows a proposal for a territorial arrangement of cities into several clusters relying on geographical proximity and on analogous socio-political characteristics.

There is here the assumption that the political agents' actions, regarding medium-sized cities, are driven by the attempt to gain the benefits of agglomeration

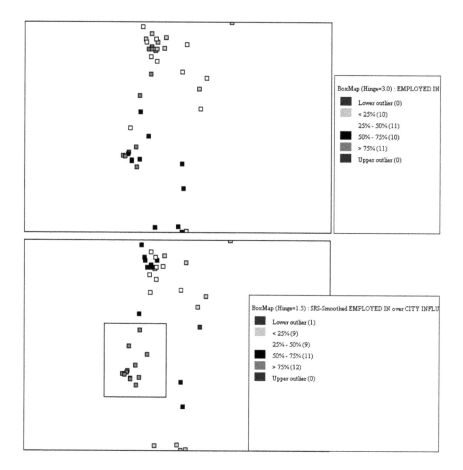

Figure 7.7   Portuguese mainland wage value and wage value in relation to the city's influence

economies, which would be more easily attained if policies were to be focused on only three clusters. This being so, the proposal made here is to focus on public intervention in order to get more inter-city interactions, with policy action concentrated around three attraction poles, one corresponding to the 17 medium-sized cities around Oporto, one to the 9 medium-sized cities around Lisbon; and one to the remaining 16 territorially diffused medium-sized cities (see Figure 7.8).

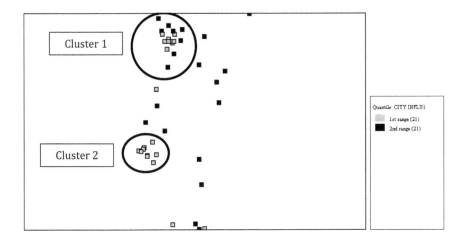

Figure 7.8   Medium-sized cities territorially organized into clusters based on proximity and size

Notes: *Cluster 1* includes: Viana do Castelo, Barcelos, Guimarães, Santo Tirso, Vila Nova de Famalicão, Espinho, Gondomar, Rio Tinto, Maia, Matosinhos, São Mamede de Infesta, Póvoa de Varzim, Valongo, Vila do Conde, Paredes, São João da Madeira e Aveiro. *Cluster 2* includes: Loures, Odivelas, Sintra, Queluz, Vila Franca de Xira, Barreiro, Montijo, Seixal e Setúbal. *Cluster 3* includes the territorially-diffused medium-sized cities, namely, Vila Real, Bragança, Figueira da Foz, Leiria, Viseu, Guarda, Castelo Branco, Covilhã, Caldas da Rainha, Évora, Beja, Santarém, Faro, Loulé, Olhão e Portimão.

This territorial arrangement leads to a concentration of 567,000 inhabitants in Cluster 1, 495,000 inhabitants in Cluster 2, and 484,000 inhabitants in Cluster 3. This proposal for political intervention regarding policy for cities could involve some slight reconfigurations, where the four medium-sized cities on the coast between clusters 1 and 2: Figueira da Foz, Leiria, Caldas da Rainha and Santarém, could be reallocated to either one of those two clusters.

This approach has political implications: namely, it implies a policy for the metropolitan area of Lisbon, another for the metropolitan area of Oporto, and an integrated policy for the other territorially-diffused medium-sized cities. Thus, as this chapter suggest, such a policy regarding medium-sized cities when cities are territorially "diluted" does not sustain regional policies, i.e., a policy for the Algarve region, another for the Central region, and so on. The Portuguese medium-sized cities' territorial characteristics call for a concentration of efforts, requiring a centralized perspective and a centralized policy action.

7.5. Conclusions

An understanding of the way cities are affected by the availability of public and private amenities located in neighbouring cities was the prime goal of this chapter. The findings indicate that cities interact, each one being limited by the inhabitants captured outside cities by the presence of neighbouring cities which have similar amenities. This being the case, when cities extend their influence, they can achieve higher agglomeration economies but also limit neighbour cities from taking such advantage, especially if the cities are closely located.

Given that cities offer a set of public and private amenities, it was tested to see whether political intervention by local governments also plays a role in the influence attained by each city. The literature that relies on political variables as explanatory variables for the attraction of inhabitants usually focuses on public expenditure decisions regarding facilities, and how local governments interact in order to provide them. The purpose of this chapter was to fill this gap and determine whether, when cities comprise public and private actors that offer public as well as private amenities, political variables are still important for the number of beneficiaries of such amenities attracted from outside the city.

The results indicate that the permanency in office of the same party in the local government to which the city belongs has a positive effect on the city's influence. This can be interpreted as follows: to improve a city's influence a higher number of years in office is required. However, if the city's influence is gained by subtracting influence from a neighbouring city, then incumbency for long periods can mean more competitive behaviour between neighbouring local governments, thus inducing efficiency losses. In this framework, cooperation between public actors of different cities seems more likely under alternation of political parties in power. As such, the time span a political party has in office does not improve the likelihood of medium-sized cities cooperating.

Political alternation on local governments (municipalities) appears to be a disciplining mechanism of political self-interest, making the economic gains from cooperation more relevant than individual career concerns, and which could be an incentive to aim to increase cities influence through competitive behaviour. These findings contradict Park and Feiock's (2003) predictions of more cooperative arrangements between local governments, the longer the same executive body is in power. Their argument is that by repeated interactions, local actors build up a reputation that would facilitate agreements.

It was also tested whether social economic variables can explain a city's influence. The number of inhabitants in a city has a positive impact on the city's sphere of influence. Departing from Glaser et al.'s (2001) argument, it was found that only property values determine the influence achieved by a city, although with only a weak significance, which can be due to asymmetries in mainland property values. The wage value only appears to increase the city's influence of medium-sized cities around Lisbon.

Finally, geography plays a major role in determining the influence of a city. This being the case, the benefits of agglomeration economies are most easily explored in medium-sized cities around the two biggest Portuguese cities: Lisbon and Oporto, which form Metropolitan Areas. This raises the possibility of having a policy which is oriented towards the characteristics of such cities. Consequently, a medium-sized territorial organization is proposed around three clusters: the two metropolitan areas and a third cluster comprising the remaining territorially-diffused medium-sized cities which require a specific policy intervention in order to gain the benefits of agglomeration economies. This intervention is best accomplished under a central government policy, and is not therefore attainable either at regional or local level.

References

Anselin, L. 1988. *Spatial Econometrics: Methods and Models*, The Netherlands: Kluwer Academic Publishers.

Anselin, L. and Florax, R. 1995. Small sample properties of tests for spatial dependence in regression models: Some further results, in *New Directions of Spatial Econometrics*, edited by L. Anselin and R. Florax, Berlin: Springer-Verlag, 21-74.

Anselin, L., Bera, A.K., Florax, R. and Yoon, M.J. 1996. Simple diagnostic tests for spatial dependence. *Regional Science and Urban Economics*, 26(1), 77-104.

Baicker, K. 2005. The spillover effects of state spending. *Journal of Public Economics*, 89, 529-544.

Barr, J. and Tassier, T. 2008. Endogenous neighbourhood selection and the attainment of cooperation in a spatial Prisoner's Dilemma Game. *Department of Economics, Fordham University, Discussion Paper 21.*

Besley, T. and Case, A.C. 1995. Incumbent behaviour: Vote-seeking, tax setting and yardstick competition. *American Economic Review*, 85, 25-45.

Bewley, T.F. 1981. A critique of Tiebout's theory of local public expenditures. *Econometrica*, 49(3), 713-740.

Brueckner, J.K. 1998. Testing for strategic interaction among local governments: The case of growth controls. *Journal of Urban Economics*, 44, 438-467.

Brueckner, J.K. 2003. Strategic interaction among governments: An overview of empirical studies. *International Regional Science Review*, 26, 175-188.

Case, A.C., Rosen, H.S. and Hines, J.R., Jr. 1993. Budget spillovers and fiscal policy interdependence. *Journal of Public Economics*, 52, 285-307.

Ermini, B. and Santolini, R. 2007. Horizontal interaction on local councils' expenditures. Evidence from Italy. *Dipartimento di Economia, Università Politecnica delle Marche, Quaderni de Ricerca n°. 278.*

Feiock, R.C. 2004. *Metropolitan Governance: Conflict, Competition and Cooperation*. Washington D.C.: Georgetown University Press.

Florax, R. and Nijkamp, P. 2005. Misspecification in linear spatial regression models, in *Encyclopedia of Social Measurement*, edited by K. Kempf-Leonard. San Diego: Academic Press, 695-707.

Glaeser, E.L, Kolko, J. and Saiz, A. 2001. Consumer city. *Journal of Economic Geography*, 1, 27-50.

Graaff, T., Florax, R., Nijkamp, P. and Reggiani, A. 2001. A general misspecification test for spatial regression models: dependence, heterogeneity, and nonlinearity. *Journal of Regional Science*, 41(2), 255-276.

Krugman, P. 1991. Increasing returns and economic geography. *Journal of Political Economy*, 99, 483-499.

Park, H.J. and Feiock, R.C. 2003. Social capital and formation of regional partnership. Paper presented at the *Annual Meeting of the American Political Science Association*, 27–30 August, Philadelphia MA.

Rosenthal, S.S. and Strange, W.C. 2001. The determinants of agglomeration. *Journal of Urban Economics*, 50, 191-229.

Tiebout, C.M. 1956. A pure theory of local expenditures. *Journal of Political Economy*, 64(5), 416-424.

Appendix

A.7.1   Medium-sized cities in Portugal

Medium-Sized City	No. of Inhabitants
Viana do Castelo	36,148
Barcelos	20,625
Guimarães	52,182
Santo Tirso	24,649
Vila Nova de Famalicão	27,900
Espinho	21,589
Gondomar	25,700
Rio Tinto	47,695
Maia	35,625
Matosinhos	45,703
São Mamede de Infesta	23,542
Póvoa de Varzim	38,643
Valongo	38,270
Vila do Conde	25,731
Paredes	26,547

Medium-Sized City	No. of Inhabitants
São João da Madeira	21,102
Vila Real	24,481
Bragança	20,309
Aveiro	55,291
Figueira da Foz	27,742
Leiria	42,785
Viseu	47,250
Guarda	26,061
Castelo Branco	25,316
Covilhã	34,772
Caldas da Rainha	29,000
Loures	26,300
Odivelas	50,846
Sintra (Agualva-Cacém)	81,845
Queluz	78,040
Vila Franca de Xira	50,787
Barreiro	40,859
Montijo	25,719
Seixal	50,991
Setúbal	89,303
Évora	41,159
Beja	21,658
Santarém	28,760
Faro	41,307
Loulé	21,000
Olhão	24,876
Portimão	32,433

Note: Cities are sorted geographically from North to South of the Portuguese territory.

Endnotes

[a] Portugal is also composed of the archipelagos of the Azores and Madeira. These are not, however, considered in this work, and have an intermediate institutional level between central government and local government: a regional government whose competences find no counterparts on mainland, where there is no such intermediate level.

[b] In Portugal there is another lower government level: the parish level, economically dependent on municipality transfers. There are around 4050 parishes on the Portuguese mainland.

PART III
Knowledge Transfers in Rural Environments

Chapter 8

Technological Transfer in the Perspective of Town Dimension: the Case of Oxford and Oxfordshire, UK

Helen Lawton Smith and John Glasson

8.1. Introduction

The small but important city of Oxford, of some 143,000 people, and its surrounding rural county of Oxfordshire have become one of the most innovative and enterprising economies in the UK. This chapter explores how Oxford and its county has emerged as an "innovative place" over the last 30 years from a city famous for its ancient university and car plant which makes the Mini and surrounded by a rural economy with several agricultural-based industries, such as blanket making and food processing. It identifies the unique features that characterize Oxford and Oxfordshire focusing on the entrepreneurs and the organizations and institutions which in some cases have driven change and in others have co-evolved with the increasingly entrepreneurial economy. It examines the changing interfaces between the different actors responsible for the making of this innovative place, using a conceptual framework developed by Mahroum et al. (2008). This identifies three types of capacities that lead to improved absorptive capacity of firms and as a consequence the potential for technological transfer between firms and firms and research organisations in any particular place. These are access capacity: the capacity to access international networks of knowledge and innovation; anchor capacity: the capacity to anchor external knowledge from people, institutions and firms; and diffusion capacity: the capacity to diffuse new innovation and knowledge in the wider economy. These lead to developmental capacities of knowledge creation and knowledge exploitation.

Using this framework, the chapter examines how some of the asymmetric knowledge problems, whereby "knowledges" in different domains remain unexploited, have been resolved, and where they still exist in the city and the county. It reviews what kinds of communication methods and tools have been used to overcome these problems through the actions of individuals and organizations who have filled boundary-spanning roles (academic leaders, government agencies and so on). It also highlights some of the local tensions that exist as a consequence of the evolution of the county as an international centre of high-tech activity which has created pressure on the rural environment. Finally it presents a case study of Milton Park, a business park, which is itself an innovative place within the county, and provides an example of how micro-level management can influence innovative capacity of a set of firms, its tenants.

8.2. Key Elements in Technology Transfer in Urban and Rural Economies

8.2.1. Innovative capacity

Since the 'Genesis of Silicon Valley' (Saxenian, 1983) various studies have analysed the transformative effects of entrepreneurship on economic development in a small number of places worldwide. These are what Hilpert describes as 'islands of innovation'. The distinctive feature of such places is their capacity (their firms, the science base, and other organisations) both to generate new knowledge and draw in and utilise information from other places and countries. These have been conceptualised as absorption and diffusion capacities (Mahroum et al., 2008) drawing on the concept of absorptive capacity of the firm (Cohen and Levinthal, 1990) applied to local contexts. In Cohen and Levinthal's conceptualization, the ability of a firm to recognize the value of new external information, assimilate it and apply it to commercial ends is critical to its innovative capacities. This is largely a function of the firm's level of prior related knowledge, the development of its absorptive capacity through investment in research and development.

The Mahroum framework shown in Table 8.1 similarly recognizes that a place's innovative capacity often depends on complementarities between internal and external sources of knowledge. If a place is to innovate it needs to combine both a capacity to absorb external knowledge and a capacity to develop this knowledge into new innovations. Absorptive capacity allows (organizations within) a place to identify value and assimilate new knowledge, while the development capacity of a place allows it to develop and exploit knowledge.

Table 8.1 A framework of innovative capacity

Absorptive capacities	Examples
Access capacity: is the ability to connect and link to international networks of knowledge and innovation. This capacity requires agents, resources and culture.	Through universities, firms with global networks, and people with international connections.
Anchor capacity: is the ability to identify and domesticate external knowledge from people, institutions, and firms.	Attracting and retaining overseas people, firms and ideas. Could include the presence of training, networking, transport connectivity and sustainable infrastructure.
Knowledge diffusion capacity: is the collective ability of a place to adapt and assimilate new innovations, practices and technologies and spread them in the economy.	The spread of ideas, information and knowledge between people, firms and institutions in the local economy, involves skills, networks and boundary spanning activities.
Developmental capacities	Examples
Knowledge creation capacity available in a city or region to be a source of new ideas, discoveries and innovations	Through university research, business R&D, and the training of new talent.
Knowledge exploitation: the capacity to use knowledge commercially and extract value from it	Through the creation of innovation enterprises or product innovations.

Source: Mahroum et al. (2008).

In this framework the agents of each capacity and their outcomes are not confined to discrete sets of individuals (e.g. entrepreneurs) or organizations such as firms, universities and science parks. They are also strongly influenced by the national, regional and local regulatory contexts and local institutional capacity (Burfitt and MacNeil, 2008).

We now consider which actors have the capacities, and are the channels, for establishing both inward and outward links. We consider as key elements entrepreneurs, the science base, highly-skilled labour markets, networks and infrastructure.

Key element: entrepreneurs

New enterprises have been described as 'the embodiment of innovation' (Feldman, 2008, 318). The relationship between the 'entrepreneurial event' (Shapero, 1984), the cumulative effects of a growth in entrepreneurship which leads to an entrepreneurial culture in which technological transfer and other networking outcomes occur is complex. On the one hand a well-developed social structure promotes the formation of new firms (Florida and Kenney, 1988); on the other the growth in the number of new enterprises similarly produces the conditions under which networking, including through an expansion in informal and formal networks well as the supply of venture capital and independent suppliers (see

Saxenian, 1994; Benner, 2003) - also flourishes. It has also been argued that some places just have a greater supply of entrepreneurs than others (Chinitz, 1961), that higher rates of entrepreneurship are due to labour intensity and that high amenity places attract entrepreneurs and firms (Glaeser et al., 2009). Therefore there is a reinforcing effect of the growth in the number of entrepreneurs and the potential for absorptive and developmental capacities.

Key element: science base
The impact of universities on their regional economies has been identified as being a result of a number of factors, including size of region, presence of agglomeration economies, industrial structure and entrepreneurial 'culture' of a region. Goldstein reports that regional size is important because: (i) larger economies with more high-tech firms have a higher potential for the absorption of university knowledge; and (ii) because larger regions will have a more developed knowledge infrastructure. 'Entrepreneurial culture' has at least two possible mediating outcomes: first, some firms in some sectors are more likely to seek out and absorb knowledge from universities, and, second, that in such an environment, there is a higher degree of collaboration, cooperation and connectedness among firms, between firms and universities and other knowledge creating institutions. Where there are numerous university spin-offs these potential impacts are increased.

Benneworth et al., (2005) highlighted a number of mechanisms by which university spin-offs come into contact with other regional actors, thereby increasing knowledge exploitation. These include paying good wages and promoting entrepreneurship (Etzkowitz, 2001); stimulating business support services and infrastructure benefitting other start-ups (Lockett et al., 2003); building on global technological and market knowledges in building new networks to access finance, sales and marketing (Lindholm Dahlstrand, 1999), and retaining close linkages back to their parent institution through equity holdings, incubators, technological transfer, recruitment and collaboration. All of these mechanisms improve both anchor and knowledge diffusion capacities and both forms of developmental capacities. They therefore increase the university's impact on local absorptive capacity and on overcoming asymmetric knowledge problems.

Key element: scientific labour markets
The stocks and flows of the highly-skilled personnel within local labour markets are argued to be of collective benefit, as the movement of the highly-skilled within a region is a key mechanism for technology transfer and fostering inter-firm links. Both the nature and quality of jobs available to an individual, as well as the opportunities those jobs provide, are the key elements in the development of high-technology local economies. This also depends on the skills of the individuals in those jobs, hence the capacity of high-technology firms to absorb new information and to retain the individuals who access new information internally and externally. It follows that the larger the concentration of the highly skilled, the more efficient search activity (for employers as well as employees) tends to be due to the

concentration of opportunity in geographical space (Waters and Lawton Smith, 2008), hence the collective potential for innovation.

Key element: networks

Networks are argued in the literature to be the medium by which knowledge flows are facilitated, and their development is a characteristic of innovation-based local economic development. High-tech economies such as Silicon Valley (Saxenian, 1994; Benner, 2003) and Oxfordshire and Cambridgeshire (Lawton Smith, 2010) are characterized by high-levels of both informal networks and numbers of formal, business and professional networks (the latter contributing to the former). Networks have been defined as consisting of nodes (i) firms (and their activities and employees), universities and research centres; (ii) connections – communication channels; and (3) the intensity of transfers of goods, services or ideas (Lambooy, 2004). This definition encompasses informal and formal networking, with implications for the strength and outcome of varying kinds of capacities and outcomes. Localized networks embed organizations and their people in local economic and technological activity.

It follows that, under these conditions, networks have a role to play in several of the innovative capacities, having at least three beneficial effects which affect the ability of firms to select and absorb information. First, networked businesses are likely to be more successful than non-networked business. Membership is linked to small business survival and, through networking with competitors, firms have a greater knowledge of their own strengths and weaknesses and a greater knowledge of the industry (Besser et al., 2006). As networks enable their members to become more competitive through improved marketing and innovation, sharing best practice and access to current research, collective action and infrastructures, the knowledge diffusion capacity of the region/locality is increased by the growth in the stock of successful firms and the scale of interlinkages. Second, networked firms are more innovative (knowledge creation capacity). A review of networking and innovation in the UK by Pittaway et al. (2004) confirmed that networks and networking amongst firms play a pivotal role in innovation, and that these activities have become more relevant as technologies become more complex. The use of networks can be crucially important during venture formation and for small growing firms. Third, not only do individual firms benefit directly but networks also act as 'open gates' bringing in new ideas and practices to the local economy as a whole (Eraydin and Armiatli-Koroglu 2005) (anchor capacity).

Key elements: infrastructure

Property developments, such as science, technology and business parks, have long been recognized as being an important element of national and local innovation policy. This follows from the perceived connection between innovation and high-tech industry and the presence of a science park attached to a university – for example Stanford University (1951) and Cambridge University (Trinity College, 1970 and St John's College, St John's Innovation Centre, 1987) in what here we would call access, anchor and knowledge diffusion capacities. Innovation activities in this sector, identified in various studies of science parks, relate to the value of the supportive park environment, the access to facilities, and the prestige associated with the park infrastructure. Other studies have suggested that there needs to be caution about the causality of those connections. For example Keise (1995), Fergusson (1995) and Doutriaux (1998) all found differences between objectives and reality. Keise's main finding of a study of tenants in the science park of Warwick University in the UK was that the tenants accept paying a premium for the prestigious location, but the association with areas of academic excellence, combined with the 'ambience' of the premises and the active marketing of the science park makes tenants expect a return on their investment. Flexible leases allowing tenants to move into larger (or smaller, if necessary) units as the firm declines were the second most important factor. In all of these studies, visibility and good servicing rather than contacts with the university were the major benefits of a science park location.

To sum up, the various key elements (science base, labour market, networks and infrastructure) can to varying degrees enhance innovative capacity, and lead to knowledge creation and knowledge exploitation. However, we must also be aware of barriers to innovative capacity, including for example infrastructure and planning constraints (e.g. unaffordable housing and congested transport infrastructure), plus lack of synergy between key public and private sector stakeholders, and weak networks.

8.3. The Oxfordshire Economy: Comparisons of Success

We now turn to the particular case of Oxford and Oxfordshire. In Section 8.4, we review the capacities which make Oxford and Oxfordshire such successful high-tech economies, and provide a detailed case study of the Milton Park business park in Section 8.5. But first, in Section 8.3, we provide some comparative evidence of that success, at various scales. We begin by briefly noting some EU-scale and UK-scale comparisons before discussing the urban and rural dimensions of the Oxfordshire high-tech phenomenon.

8.3.1. Some EU comparisons

The innovative capacity of the larger region in which Oxford and Oxfordshire are located is indicated by the statistic that high-tech employment in the Bucks, Berks and Oxon (BBO) (EU-NUTS 2) sub-region accounts for a higher proportion of total employment than in the South East region, UK and EU averages. This is true of employment in both high-tech manufacturing and high-tech services, although the relative strength of the sub-region in high-tech knowledge intensive services is particularly noteworthy. These activities accounted for just over 9 per cent of total employment in the BBO area in 2004, compared with the then EU-15 average of only 3.5 per cent. No other EU-15 region had a higher proportion of its employment in high tech services (Table 8.2).

Table 8.2   EU Regions with the highest proportion of employment in high-tech knowledge intensive services, 2004 (Top 20 EU-15 regions)

NUTS 2 Region	% of Employment in High-Tech Knowledge Intensive Services
1 – Berks, Bucks & Oxon (UK)	9.05
2 – Stockholm (SWE)	7.96
3 – Prague (CZE)	7.57
4 – Oslo (NOR)	7.26
5 – Bedfordshire & Hertfordshire (UK)	6.85
6 – Ile de France (Paris) (FRA)	6.63
7 – Inner London (UK)	6.17
8 – Bratislava (SK)	6.08
9 – Etela-Suomi (FIN)	5.94
10 – Outer London (UK)	5.86
11 – Utrecht (NETH)	5.85
12 – Madrid (SPA)	5.83
13 – Lazio (ITA)	5.75
14 – Flevoland (NETH)	5.56
15 – Darmstadt (GER)	5.41
15 – Hampshire & Isle of Wight (UK)	5.41
17 – Kozep-Magyarorszag (HUN)	5.35
18 – Vlaams-Brabant (BEL)	5.29
19 – Brussels (BEL)	5.20
20 – Bucharest (ROM)	5.05
EU-15 average	3.5

Source: Eurostat, employment in high-tech and knowledge intensive sectors, NUTS 2 regions.
Definitions: High-tech knowledge intensive services = NACE categories 64, 72 & 73.

8.3.2 Some UK comparisons

Counties of the UK can be compared on many economic dimensions, such as GVA, GVA per capita, unemployment rates and many others. On most of these indicators, Oxfordshire performs very well. However, the focus here is on innovation, and the extent to which Oxfordshire's firms are engaged in various types of innovation, including the introduction of new products and processes, hence knowledge creation and exploitation capacities. The evidence is derived from an on analysis by the Oxfordshire Economic Observatory of responses to the Department of Trade and Industry UK Innovation Survey undertaken in 2005. The Oxfordshire results are based on responses from a sample of 155 firms located in the county, and this small size should be borne in mind when interpreting the survey results (see Table 8.3). Nevertheless, the able provides many indicators of innovative firms, including improved products and processes, and acquisition of R&D, advanced equipment, patents and know-how.

Table 8.3   Selected indicators from 2005 UK Innovation Survey

Indicator	Oxfordshire	South East	England
% of Enterprises Introducing:-			
New or significantly improved products, 2002-04	34	33	30
Novel products, 2002-04	19	20	17
% of Product Innovators' Turnover Due to:-			
Novel products, 2004	8	10	9
Other new or significantly improved products, 2004	27	29	28
Unchanged products, 2004	66	61	63
% of Enterprises Introducing:-			
New or significantly improved processes, 2002-04	28	21	20
Novel processes, 2002-04	9	6	6
% of Enterprises Engaged in (During 2002-04):-			
In-house R&D	38	33	31
Acquisition of external R&D	14	14	12
Acquisition of advanced machinery, equipment or software to produce new products or processes	48	46	45
Acquisition of patents, know-how & other types of external knowledge	17	15	14
Training for their staff specifically for the development of innovations	44	41	40
Expenditure on design for the development of new products or processes	23	20	18
Market introduction of innovations	27	27	25

Source: DTI, 2005 UK Innovation Survey responses, analysed by location of respondent firms. All figures are unweighted.

Oxfordshire urban and rural

Oxfordshire is the most rural county in the South East of England. The official Rural and Urban Classification for England and Wales was developed in 2004 to provide a single and consistent definition of urban and rural areas. It defines urban areas as settlements with a population of above 10,000. When this distinction is applied to employment by sector, it is unsurprising that rural Oxfordshire has higher proportions than urban Oxfordshire of employment in the following sectors: agriculture, construction, hotels and catering, real estate and business services but also in public administration and defence. What is perhaps more surprising is the strong performance in the creative industries and knowledge intensive service industries, which are widely seen as important drivers of growth and productivity (DEFRA, 2005; Local Futures Group, 2004). In 2004 there were 6,000 employees in the creative industries in rural Oxfordshire, and over 20,000 in knowledge intensive services (Table 8.4). The latter uses an OECD definition which includes both high-tech services and the knowledge-based services. However, some sectors are used in both the creative industries and the high-tech intensive services, and Table 8.4 includes adjustment for this to exclude double counting.

Table 8.4 Jobs in specific sectors in rural and urban Oxfordshire, 2004

Sector	Rural Oxfordshire		Urban Oxfordshire	
	Number	%	Number	%
Creative Industries	6,000	6.5	14,300	6.4
Knowledge Intensive Services	20,200	21.9	28,700	12.8
Creative Industries + Knowledge Intensive Services (excluding double-counting)	21,200	22.9	33,900	15.2

Source: Office for National Statistics, 2004 Annual Business Inquiry (NOMIS). Figures for rural and urban Oxfordshire are calculated from data for lower layer super output areas (LSOA's), and are rounded to the nearest hundred. Percentages show the number working in the sector, as a proportion of all employees.

8.4. The Oxfordshire Economy: The Science Base and Technology Transfer

Drawing on the concepts in section 8.2, what are the capacities which make Oxford and Oxfordshire such successful high-tech economies? To explain, we first need to consider what kinds of communication methods and tools are present for developing and using those capacities, and where the gaps and barriers are to the exploitation of "knowledges" in different domains in the city and the county. While all three absorptive capacities can be found in Oxfordshire positioning it within a broad international nexus of processes, the evidence suggests that it happens through a limited number of means: there is more direct evidence of developmental capacities. Key mechanisms for the functioning of those capacities are the enterprises, the science base, the labour market, networks and supporting organizations (Glasson et al., 2006). However, technology transfer needs not only the technology to transfer, but also the supportive organizations to facilitate that transfer. As we will show, Oxfordshire has a high number of business networks, business incubation facilities, and its science and business parks. Milton Park is an exemplar of the last.

8.4.1. Enterprises and knowledge diffusion capacities

The county has a range of entrepreneurial businesses, some large, such as Oxford Instruments (industrial and research instrumentation) and Research Machines (computers and software used in education), and many quite small. It is also an increasingly internationalized economy, with a growing number of foreign investors, such as Siemens, Novartis and BMW.

Estimates of total high-tech activities in 2004 indicated that there were some 3500 high tech businesses and 45,000 employees (Lawton Smith et al., 2007). These accounted for about 12 per cent of businesses and 14 per cent of employment in Oxfordshire. As indicated above, the majority of the businesses are in high-tech services, especially in small software consultancies and in architecture, engineering and related technical consultancies. The county is still a very important centre for manufacturing: the largest businesses are in high-tech manufacturing, including pharmaceuticals, medical instrumentation, computers and motor vehicle engineering, the first three sectors being particularly research -and development- intensive and therefore comprise a significant element in the city and county's knowledge-diffusion capacity. Notable high-tech, high-skill motor vehicle engineering is the Mini plant at Cowley in the City of Oxford and a number of component manufacturers which contribute to the skill base in the area.

8.4.2. Science base and absorptive capacities

Oxford and Oxfordshire are part of the 'golden triangle' of Oxford, Cambridge and London, that has the highest density of university, publicly -and privately-funded research in the UK. All three are some of UK's top locations for biomedical research and the bio-pharma sector. Oxford city has two universities, University of Oxford (23,985 students) and Oxford Brookes University (18,035 students). Either associated or co-located with Oxford University are a number of charity supported research institutes, predominately in bio-medical science. They include the Oxford Stem Cell Institute (Oxford University), Institute of Biomedical Engineering (Oxford University, established 2008), and the Oxford Biomedical Research Centre, a partnership between the University of Oxford and Oxford Radcliffe Hospitals, funded by the National Institute of Health Research. Other research laboratories include the Oxford Centre for Cancer Medicine, the Jenner Institute (vaccines, established 2005) and the Wellcome Centre for Human Genetics).

To the south of the county is a cluster of government-funded research laboratories. Much of this development is due to post-World War II developments in the UK's nuclear energy programme (UK Atomic Energy Authority), and the later expansion of Research Council research into science and engineering. Oxfordshire's laboratories are primarily located on the Harwell site at Chilton:

RAL (Rutherford Appleton Laboratory) owned by the Science and Technology Facilities Council; UKAEA Laboratory; the National Radiological Protection Board (NRPB); the Medical Research Council (MRC) Radiation and Genome Stability Unit; and the MRC Mammalian Genetics Unit. Nearby are the NERC (National Environment Research Council) Centre for Ecology and Hydrology, and the UKAEA (United Kingdom Atomic Energy Authority) and JET (Joint European Torus), both at Culham. About 20 miles from these laboratories is Oxfordshire's third university, Cranfield University, which has a main campus about 40 miles away to the north-east of Oxford. Cranfield University acquired the defence research academy which trains students for the military in the 1990s, and is now known as DCMT (Defence Science, Technology and Management) at Shrivenham, which has around a thousand students, mostly post-graduates.

As well as research possibilities, all of these research institutions are further sources of personnel who might potentially be recruited into the local labour market, and whose networks send and receive technological knowledge inside and outside the county (Goldstein, 2009). Over time, these institutions have become more entrepreneurial. For example Oxford University's 'innovation infrastructure' now has four main elements: wealth creation, awareness raising, education and training, and support including a business angels network and a consulting company (Lawton Smith et al., 2007).

Evidence of the importance of the science base in making Oxford and Oxfordshire innovative is, however, mixed, even in the case of the biotech sector which is one of the sectors most closely associated with university research. A study by the Oxfordshire Bioscience Network (OBN) (2002) (see Lawton Smith, 2005) found that the prime locational advantages for dedicated biotechnology firms (DBFs) in Oxfordshire were to be close to a top university (Oxford) and other research institutes possessing 'talent'. These were followed by quality of life, availability of staff and proximity to like-minded companies. Access to hospital units was satisfactory. The study showed that the research strengths in medicine and medical research are reflected in the county's specializations in the related areas of biotechnology/pharmaceuticals and medical diagnostic products (34 per cent and 17 per cent of firms, respectively).

While the impact of the science base seems to be that of attracting and establishing firms in the biomedical sector (only a fifth were spin-offs from Oxford University), the knowledge base as a source of information was seen as much less important. Rather than local information sources being the most important, conferences scored the highest, reflecting the research practice which spans both industry and academia. Other important sources were the Internet, published sources and trade fairs. Universities were ranked 9th in importance along with local sector networks, national trade associations, technology transfer departments and independent research organizations. Moreover, firms generally did not view proximity to Oxford University and the local research base as an important factor in the development of interactions, other than those of an informal nature. This may be an indication of an 'entrepreneurial culture' but not directly of access, anchor capacities, nor even knowledge diffusion capacities - except informally and indirectly.

There was, however, more evidence of a knowledge creation capacity, as the universities contribute to the number of highly-skilled persons, and thus the quality of the local scientific labour market. In both the 2002 and the follow-up 2005 OBN surveys the availability of staff was the most important locational advantage. But availability was also a problem. A shortage of scientists and other appropriately qualified staff was ranked as the 5th most important sector challenge. Nearly a half (44 per cent) had problems with recruitment. In part, this is related to the very high costs of living. Oxfordshire is one of the most expensive places to buy a home in the UK outside London. In the 2005 OBN survey three-quarters of respondents felt this was an issue and impinged on five of the other challenges: cost of living, availability of scientists, the need to pay higher salaries and cost of office and laboratory space.

Knowledge exploitation can be observed directly. A later study (Lawton Smith and Glasson, 2006) identified 114 companies that had their origins in Oxford University primarily (80 per cent) or in the government laboratories. The latter impact has been long established as some of the firms dated back to the 1940s.

8.4.3. The labour market

Further to the role of the quality of the labour market in making innovative places, Oxford and Oxfordshire have high proportions of well-qualified residents compared with the rest of England and Wales and these proportions have grown over time (Waters and Lawton Smith, 2008). In 2008, nearly 40 per cent of Oxfordshire residents were qualified to degree level (National Vocational Qualification (NVQ) level 4+) to rank as the 3rd most qualified county in England. Within the local authorities which comprise the counties, Oxford City, with 42 per cent is ranked 39th of England and Wales' 408 local authorities. In the rural areas to the south of the county, the Vale of White Horse District, in which the majority of the government laboratories are located, is ranked 23rd. With respect to the professional workforce, in 2008, the county ranked 3rd of all county council areas for the proportion of residents employed in professional occupations (SOC2). The figures do reveal a relative shortage of associate professional and technical workers, and hence of overall absorptive capacity, especially in the more rural areas. It is the technical workers who play a crucial role in innovation (Freel, 2003).

8.4.4. Networks and networking

The growth of networks has been identified as one of the distinctive features of the evolution of high-tech economies. Indeed it has been argued that the dynamic success of Silicon Valley's economy since the 1950s is fundamentally linked with the dense social networks within the framework of professional networks (Benner,

2003) that exist between firms. The studies in Silicon Valley and in Oxfordshire suggest that formal networks are associated with innovation-led economies.

The Oxfordshire study followed an observation by one of the members of the Oxfordshire Economic Observatory (OEO) Advisory Council in March 2006 that there were too many networks in Oxfordshire. To investigate this suggestion, a study of business networks in Oxfordshire was conducted in 2006 by OEO, using an online survey conducted on the OEO website. Each identified network was asked to send out an email to their members asking them for information on the value of networks, the kinds of networks they participated in, which they used most, what networks delivered and what initiatives could be traced back to the network(s). It also asked about the limitations/gaps of the networks and opportunities to improve practical operational efficiency.

The study showed that by 2008 Oxfordshire had 65 formal networks, ranging from large and highly specialized networks to smaller networks: for example, breakfast clubs. Many are local branches of national organizations. In Oxfordshire, as in Cambridgeshire, a similar high-tech economy, networks specifically for high-tech firms date back to the mid-1980s. The Oxford Trust, established by the founders of Oxfordshire's leading high-tech firm, Oxford Instruments, in 1985 became established as a key host network for the high-tech economy. This was three years later than the Cambridge Europe Technology Club formed in 1982 but earlier than the St John's Innovation Centre established in 1987 which has developed similar functions for the Cambridgeshire high-tech economy to The Oxford Trust. More recently, Oxford University has become active in hosting networking opportunities. Since 1999, Oxford University's Saïd Business School Science Enterprise Centre, later Entrepreneurship Said, has acted as a host for networking events such as Venturefest (an annual two-day fair for bringing entrepreneurs and funders together) and for high-profile seminars at which companies within and outside Oxfordshire meet with academics, venture capitalists and other professional service providers.

Business networks are funded from a variety of sources including private subscriptions, county councils, regional development agencies and central government (particularly in biotech). Public policy support follows from government intervention to offer businesses access to expert advice from specialist organizations, as well as other businesses, in order to improve their performance.

The kinds of benefit of membership of the various networks are shown in Figure 8.1. Collaboration was by far the biggest advantage, followed by sales contacts reflecting the function of networks as fora for doing business. To a much lesser extent, they were important, as the learning region literature suggests, as the means by which information is shared in 'learning communities' (Benner, 2003), and as a means of raising finance and finding new suppliers.

A further recent development is worth noting. This is the increase in virtual networks. An example is the virtual support network for Oxfordshire. The Oxfordshire component of the South East Innovation Growth Team (IGT) is a partnership led by Oxford Innovation working together with Isis Innovation, Oxford Brookes

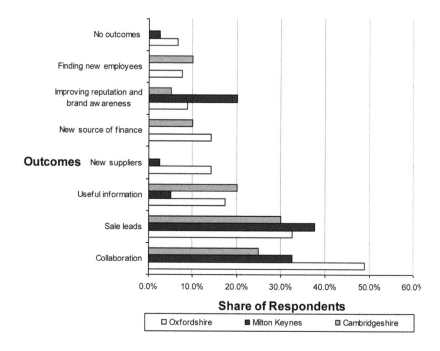

Figure 8.1   Network roles - a comparison of Oxfordshire, Cambridgeshire and Milton Keynes

Source: OEO survey.

University, Science Oxford, LeaderShape, Business Link, the Oxfordshire Economic Partnership, Oxfordshire County Council, Harwell Science and Innovation Campus, NESTA (National Endowment for Science, Technology and the Arts) and the Technology Strategy Board. Partner organizations will provide specialist expertise as part of a virtual and sustainable business community throughout Oxfordshire, including bespoke training and advice on a number of topics, such as starting a high growth enterprise and understanding business finance [1].

8.4.5. Infrastructure

The distribution of major high-technology locations in Oxfordshire (Figure 8.2) is influenced by several factors, including the strong environmental constraints on development in this attractive semi-rural county (see Figure 8.3). It was only in the early 1990s that there was some relaxation of planning controls to allow science park developments near to the universities in Oxford. It was also changes in planning regulations which were significant in the contemporary and rapid development of Milton Park, which is possibly the most important component of the physical infrastructure which contributes to absorptive capacity (Lawton Smith and Glasson, 2010).

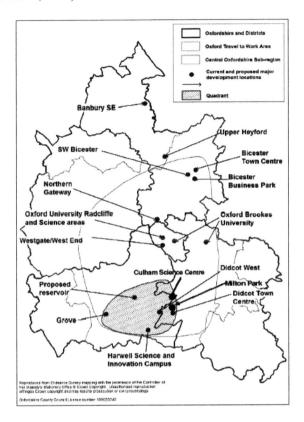

Figure 8.2   The distribution of major high-tech locations in Oxfordshire

8.5. The Example of Milton Park

Milton Park was formerly a 1930s railway supply depot for military supplies; it was then used as an industrial estate – with good railway connections. In 1984 it was acquired by MEPC (Milton Estates Property Company). It grew rapidly after the revision of the Planning Use Class Orders in 1987 (B1-Business Use), which allowed the mix of research and commercial /industrial activities within a single planning consent. It is now one of Europe's largest mixed-use business communities, with more science and biotech companies than anywhere else in Oxfordshire [2]. It is home to some 165 companies which, combined, employ around 6,500 people. To accommodate new firms, and innovation in larger firms, it has an incubation centre and a science centre. Its ethos and activities have been

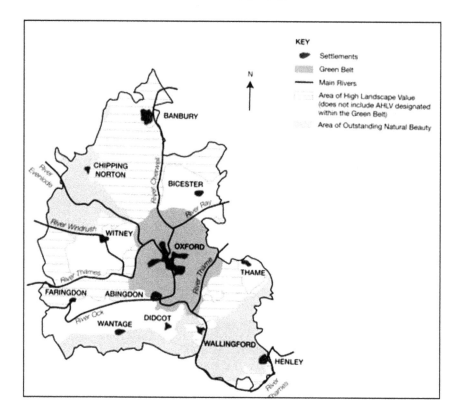

Figure 8.3   Key constraints and influences on high-tech locations in Oxfordshire

critical in incubating some of Oxfordshire's leading high-tech companies and improving the county's innovation knowledge capacity. It is both an 'innovation leader' and an 'innovation absorber'.

Although Milton Park is in the high profile location of Oxfordshire, uniquely its contribution to innovation (technological and social) predates and, in the early stages, was separate from the formal engagement of Oxford's universities and government laboratories in the development of the Oxfordshire high-tech cluster. However, as the cluster has grown, Milton Park has recognized the opportunities for its tenants presented by the changed environment, as an 'innovation absorber' enabling firms to learn from innovations developed elsewhere to create new economic value locally. Moreover, as an 'innovation leader' it has been a driving force in drawing together public and private sectors to stimulate entrepreneurship and innovation in the area to the south of Oxford in an area designated as 'The South Oxfordshire Quadrant'. It has all three types of capacities that lead to improved absorptive capacity in Oxfordshire. Examples of indicators of active diffusion are the high quality skills, networks and 'boundary spanning' activities.

Access capacity is indicated by commitment by the managing company (MEPC) to a long-term single ownership of the development, enabling it to control how the park is developed and to make long-term far sighted decisions. MEPC is not just a land owner and site manager but actively s in clients' business and help plan for growth, or even downsizing. It has a strong commitment to environmental sustainability, (e.g. shuttle bus system, car-share scheme, work with local wildlife trust); and social and economic sustainability (e.g. provision of good service facilities on site; and company contributions to local community well-being via training for staff, involvement with local schools, work experience for students etc).

Anchoring is the capacity to anchor external knowledge from people, institutions and firms which attract high quality people, investment and firms. A distinctive characteristic of Milton Park is a capacity to anchor tenants to the site, thereby retaining external knowledge from people who work their and hence also retaining their networks. As at Warwick University (Keise, 1995), this is achieved by flexibility within provision of accommodation, the support given to tenants, for example in training, the considerable geographical location advantages, networking, social facilities on site, and a more general ethical and social sustainability ethos that is entirely in keeping with – and indeed taking the lead on – firms' increasing recognition of their need to respond to society's changing environmental and social values. The Park has also developed through strong partnerships with the Oxford universities, in research and consultancy advice. In recognition of its profile as a location where innovation happens, the Park has attracted a number of foreign firms, bringing people and investment to it, Oxfordshire, and the UK more generally. Surveys by MEPC tenants show a high level of satisfaction with the Park services and management.

In its diffusion capacity, MEPC is a key player in major high-tech business networks and partnerships - including a leading role in promoting the South Oxfordshire Quadrant initiative to help to deliver one of SEEDA's high-tech Diamonds for Investment and Growth in the SE Region. Its activities include promoting Competitions, e.g. the Greenshoots award for small innovation businesses, and it promotes Networks, e.g. Oxfordshire Bioscience Network, encourages spin-outs: for example, from Oxford University, UKAEA Harwell and Culham and the Rutherford Appleton Laboratory. It occasionally takes Equity stakes in small companies.

8.6. Conclusions

Oxford and Oxfordshire have been used to explore the conditions under which technological transfer takes place in a town or small city surrounded by a rural economy. Using a framework of absorptive and developmental capacities (Mahroum et al., 2008), it is argued that Oxford and its county are an 'innovative place' characterized by strong growth in innovation-led entrepreneurship and an entrepreneurial infrastructure.

The key features that relate to a place's innovative capacity depend on complementarities between internal and external sources of knowledge. Here internal sources of knowledge have been identified as entrepreneurs, the science base, highly-skilled labour markets, and networks and infrastructure. We have shown that collectively these have contributed to developmental capacity, knowledge creation capacity and knowledge exploitation capacities which have allowed it to develop and absorb knowledge, and use that knowledge commercially. Oxford and Oxfordshire have assets that have made them more likely than other places to produce and attract entrepreneurs (Glaeser et al., 2009), including a pre-existing concentration of the highly-skilled, and that in part are due to the presence of a very strong science base. We have also suggested that capacity for technological transfer has grown with the increasing number of entrepreneurs, particularly in the creative industries and knowledge-intensive business services, the increasing size of the highly-skilled labour market which has expanded with the growth in high-tech entrepreneurship, the increasingly entrepreneurial science base, the rapid growth of formal networking opportunities and the supporting infrastructure.

It is, however, easier to find evidence of development capacities: for example, increasing numbers of high-tech firms and university spin-offs, than of the processes by which the absorptive capacities, access, anchor and knowledge diffusion are said to occur, except possibly in the case of the labour market and in infrastructure. For example, the survey of the biotech sector shows that, as in other studies, access to the university (knowledge diffusion capacity) (and similarly local sector networks) was not ranked as highly as the availability of labour. We also suggested that the lack of intermediate skills, which may be a consequence of the high cost of living, may inhibit technological transfer, and hence developmental capacities.

We do, however, find specific evidence of the making of a smaller innovative place, and one which connects Oxfordshire and Oxfordshire to geographically more extensive networks of innovation. A recent study of Milton Park (Lawton Smith and Glasson, 2010), has shown how the actions of the MEPC management have been responsible for increasing absorptive capacities on that business park. The flexibility of its terms of property leasing, active involvement in tenant's business development (access capacity), relationships with the Oxford universities (anchor capacities) and in its role as a major player in high-tech business networks (diffusion capacity) demonstrate ways in which technological and other forms of knowledge transfer can be supported. Thus while innovation-led growth can be a result of self-organization (Feldman, 2008), some parts of the process can be managed.

Websites

http://www.ngagesolutions.co.uk/news/virtual-support-network-opens-for-business accessed 31 January 2010)

http://www.mepc.com/miltonpark/Home.aspx (accessed 2 February 2010)

References

Benneworth, P., Charles, D. and Groen, A. 2005. Bringing Cambridge to Consett? The role of less successful places in the 'knowledge economy. Paper presented at the session on *'Universities and the Knowledge Economy' RGS-IBG conference*, London 2005.

Benner C., 2003. Learning Communities in a learning region: the soft infrastructure of cross-firm learning networks in Silicon Valley. *Environment and Planning A 1809-1830.*

Besser T.L., Miller, N. and Perkins R.K., 2006. For the greater good: business networks and business social responsibility to communities. *Entrepreneurship & Regional Development*, 18(4), 321-340.

Burfitt, A. and Macneill, S. 2008. The challenges of pursuing cluster policy in the congested state. *International Journal of Urban and Regional Research*, 32(2), 492-505.

Chinitz, B. 1961. Contrasts in agglomeration: New York and Pittsburgh. *American Economic Review*, 51(2), 279-289.

Cohen, W.M. & Levinthal, D.A. 1990. Absorptive Capacity: A new perspective on learning and innovation. *Administrative Science Quarterly*, 35, 128-152.

Countryside Agency, DEFRA, ODPM, ONS and Welsh Assembly Government 2005. Rural and Urban Area Classification 2004: An Introductory Guide.

DEFRA 2005. *DEFRA Classification of Local Authority Districts and Unitary Authorities in England: An Introductory Guide.*

Doutriaux, J. 1998. Canadian Science Parks, Universities and Regional Development, in *Local and Regional Innovation Systems of Innovation*, edited by J. de la Mothe and G. Paquet, Chapter 15, Kluwer Academic Publishers, 303-326.

Eraydin A. and Armiatli-Koroglu B. 2005. Innovation, networking and the new industrial clusters: the characteristics of networks and local innovation capabilities in the Turkish industrial clusters. *Entrepreneurship & Regional Development*, 17(4), 237-266.

Etzkowitz, H. 2001. University as a bridge between technology and society. *IEEE Technology and Science Magazine*, 20(2), 209-227.

Feldman, M. and Francis, J.L. 2006. Entrepreneurs as agents in the formation of industrial clusters, in *Clusters and Regional Development*, edited by B. Asheim, P. Cooke and R. Martin, Chapter 6, Abingdon: Routledge.

Feldman, M. 2008. The entrepreneurial event revisited: firm formation in a regional context, in *Handbook of Research on Innovation and Clusters*, edited by C. Karlsson, Chapter 18, Cheltenham: Edward Elgar, 318-342.

Ferguson, D. 1995. Panacea or Let-down? Science Parks in the Literature. Paper published by the *Small Business Research Group, Department of Economics*, Swedish University of Agricultural Sciences and TeknikBroStiftelsen i Stockholm.

Florida, R. and Kenney, M. 1988. Venture capital-financed innovation and technological change in the USA. *Research Policy*, 17, 119-37.

Freel, M. S. 2003. Sectoral patterns of small firm innovation, networking and proximity. *Research Policy*, 32(5), 751-770.

Glaeser, E.L., Kerr, W.R. and Ponzetto, G., A. M. 2009. Clusters of Entrepreneurship. *NBER Working Paper 15377*, available at: http://www.nber.org/papers/w15377 (accessed February, 1, 2010).

Glasson, J., Chadwick, A. and Lawton Smith, H. 2006. The growth of Oxfordshire's high-tech economy. *European Planning Studies*, 14(4), 503-524.

Kiese, M. 1995. University of Warwick Science Park, Survey of Tenants in the Barclays Venture Centre. *A Report for University of Warwick Science Park Ltd*, Warwick.

Lambooy, J.G. 2004. The transmission of knowledge, Emerging Networks and the Role of Universities: An Evolutionary Approach. *European Planning Studies*, 12(5), 643-675.

Lawton Smith, H. 2005. The Biotechnology Industry in Oxfordshire: enterprise and innovation. *European Planning Studies*, 12(7), 985-1002.

Lawton Smith, H., Glasson, J. and Chadwick, A. 2007. *Enterprising Oxford: The Oxfordshire Model*. Oxford: Oxfordshire Economic Observatory.

Lawton Smith, H. and Glasson, J. 2006. *Public Research High-tech Spin-offs: Measuring Performance and growth in Oxfordshire*. Oxford: Oxfordshire Economic Observatory.

Lawton Smith, H. and Glasson, J. 2010. Formal networks and regional contexts: the case of the Oxford to Cambridge Arc. *Regions*, March 2010.

Lindholm Dahlstrand A. 1999. Technology-based SMES in the Goteborg Region: their origin and interaction with universities and large firms. *Regional Studies*, 33(4), 379-389.

Local Futures Group 2004. *The Knowledge Economy in Rural England A report for DEFRA*.

Lockett, A., Wright, M. and Franklin, S. 2003. Technology Transfer and Universities' spin-out Strategies. *Small Business Economics*, 20(2), 185-201.

Mahroum, S., Huggins, R., Clayton, N., Pain, K. and Taylor, P. 2008. *Innovation by Adoption*. London: NESTA.

Pittaway, L., Robertson, M., Munir, K., Denyer, D. and Neely, A. 2004. Networking and Innovation: A Systematic Review of the Evidence. *International Journal of Management Reviews*, 5/6(3&4), 137-168.

Saxenian, A. 1983. The genesis of Silicon Valley. *Built Environment*, 9, 7-17.

Saxenian, A. 1994. *Regional Advantage: Culture and Competition in Silicon Valley and Route 128*. Cambridge, MA: Harvard University Press.

Shapero, A. 1984. The entrepreneurial event, in *The Environment for Entrepreneurship*, edited by C. A. Kent, Lexington, MA: Lexington Books, 21-40.

Waters, R. and Lawton Smith, H. 2008. Social Networks in High Technology Local Economies: The Cases of Oxfordshire and Cambridgeshire. *European Urban and Regional Studies*, 15(1), 21-37.

Chapter 9

Divided Knowledge on Small and Medium-sized Towns

Tomaz P. Dentinho, Rita D. Coelho and J. Dias Coelho

9.1. Introduction

Compared with other European countries, Portuguese small and medium-sized towns still have a major role in the economy (van Leeuwen, 2010). The purpose of this chapter is to understand the role of information and knowledge for the regional competitiveness and welfare of small and medium-sized towns in Portugal, by looking at information flows and knowledge frames of reference along the value chains rooted in those territories.

Section 9.2 develops the conceptual framework of the study. Section 9.3 analyses three case studies. Section 9.4 combines the analysis of the case studies with the existing literature on the development of small and medium-sized towns. Finally, Section 5 presents the main conclusions of the paper.

9.2. Conceptual Framework

9.2.1. Data, information, knowledge and wisdom

Information is commonly considered as a comprehensive idea involving concepts such as data, signals, decisions and knowledge. Information occurs only when data about facts is transformed into a signal and then integrated into knowledge (Information That) or when knowledge informs how to do things (Information How). Knowledge, in its turn, consists of representations of reality, and if 'information that' is data with meaning, knowledge is meaning with sufficient believability to sustain decisions – 'information how'. Wisdom goes beyond that and can be seen as the capacity to jump from data to successful decisions, learned by trial and error in the course of human interaction with an ever-changing environment. In the step from data to decisions, flows (information), stocks (knowledge) and 'open channels' (wisdom) interact in a rather unknown process. The only thing that seems useful to present for the purpose of this chapter is that the shift from data to 'information that' can be seen as a process of codification through which data, e.g. the price of some commodity with virtually infinite different values, is decoded into categories such as cheap, reasonable or expensive, to become meaningful within what is usually called a 'frame of reference'.

These frames of reference – or preconditions, using the words of Vickers (1955) – are constantly built up by the interaction of experiences, aims, facts, problems, methods and, eventually, solutions (Barabba and Zaltman, 1991). For that, it is important to apply what is commonly called a 'trust test', or procedures that generate believability from the meaning of all those elements: experiences, aims, facts, problems, methods and solutions. If the signals received are not believable, even with acute information, then the uncertainty about the environment is not only maintained but can inclusively increase. In the end, these evolving frames of reference not only sustain and shape the shift from data to meaning but they also support the reasonably understandable process leading to decisions. Using the language of information theory (Theil, 1967), those frames of reference can be considered as *a* priori probabilities of signals that, jointly with data, influence the posterior distribution of signals. It is interesting to perceive that, mainly when the entity under consideration is composed of different actors, these frames of reference tend to become a culture specific to the entity or organization under consideration, shaping and being shaped by its internal structure.

Direct causality does not take place only in the interaction between acts and facts that occurs in the environment, but when decisions are a choice among perceived images of the future (Boulding, 1966). From this perspective, time has different speeds, playing an important role in all parts of the cycle composed by facts-data-signals-decisions-acts and, again, facts. Actually time cannot be taken just as a reference or as a cost; more than that, time must be considered as an active element that constantly reveals new opportunities for the actors involved in the system.

9.2.2. The role of information in the economy

This last sentence can be better understood if we look at information from an economic perspective. It is from an economic approach that time is usually taken as a reference that schedules different events, or as a cost that reveals itself in some discount rate. However, it is also from an economic point of view that time is seen as the dimension along which supply and demand adjust to each other, constantly answering to the various signals given by prices and other relevant data. The stimulator of that adjustment is undoubtedly information (Spence, 1974), without which the invisible hand does not work (Stiglitz, 1991).

However, as was pointed out by Rosenstein-Rodan (1934) a long time ago, market adjustments can take many directions with different velocities. It can be from demand to price or vice versa; from supply to price, or vice versa; and from supply to demand, or vice versa. This being so, and because information has a role both in the velocity and the direction of all these adjustments, then we can expect a large range of market effects from the interaction of different entities with their own information-decision structures. In the end, it is conceivable to have: a) a definite equilibrium; b) a delay in the equilibrium; c) a different equilibrium; or d) disequilibrium. Seen from the perspective of market interaction, the role of information in the economy is much more complex and difficult to analyse than if it were viewed as a mere reduction of uncertainty for a particular actor, as Kenneth Arrow (1979) describes it. Nevertheless, looking at singular entities, individuals or organizations, some interesting aspects emerge: i) first, it is possible to conceive the improvement of the information-decision structures of a particular actor, namely by choosing the signals to receive, which is costly, and devising decision strategies that take into account information varying over time; ii) second, it can be expected that, in order to avoid the uncertainty of irregular market interaction, actors will tend to cluster in organizations which can be seen not only as cost-saving behaviour in the acquisition of information for each individual actor (Arrow, 1979) but also as an improvement in group effectiveness (Strassmann, 1990); iii) finally, it is information that guides the combination of production factors to generate higher value goods and services. In this sense, information can be seen as a gravitational force that attracts complementarities of production factors.

9.2.3. The common sense on information and regional development

Quite often the effects of information on space are seen from an outside perspective, as if someone had a bird's eye view of the spatial reconfiguration of some economic phenomenon on the ground below. Nevertheless, this global outlook has been rather inconclusive in terms of the impacts of information flows and knowledge stocks in the development of a particular region. Winners and losers could appear almost anywhere; the heart of the matter seems to be in the reshaping of regional controls and complementarities as a result of changes in information and knowledge systems. Hence, it seems wise to analyse the development effects of information and knowledge including the potential high value services based on them (Nicol, 1985; Akoy, 1991).

Nevertheless, common sense on the development effects of information and knowledge suggests that such factors constitute one of the key elements of any development process. If other basic conditions are fulfilled, then the development constraint concerning information and knowledge is merely financial (Bruce et al., 1988), and this is because limited demand in underdeveloped regions is not enough to stimulate a self-sustained supply of information and knowledge (COM, 1989).

Information and knowledge, it is said, are already available and so the obvious policy is to finance the provision of these factors using the widespread information and communication technologies. If the existence of those elements fails to generate a development process, then other basic conditions are to blame, not the provision of information and knowledge.

This argument, rooted in the unproved assumption that there is some causality able to explain the empirical correlation between the provision of information and knowledge and regional development, entails the implicit belief that regional development is either equal to access to goods and services, from the demand perspective or, from the supply point of view, merely related to the access to capital assets. Therefore, in this perspective, regional policy always means the shrinking of distances constrained by the availability of financial resources within the possible range of technological options.

What happens is that these perspectives often mismatch the development of information and knowledge with the effects of information and knowledge on regional development. This is clear through the analysis of some literature (Vanguard, 1987; Nijkamp *et al.*, 1990; Rietveld *et al.*, 1991), supposedly focused on the economic effects of information and communication technologies, but really more concerned with the constraints on and barriers to the diffusion of information and knowledge. They implicitly assume that the reason why the benefit from the provision of information and knowledge is not clarified is simply the lack of use of these factors. From this perspective, the right policy would be to stimulate the use of technologies that allow access to information and knowledge, or just provide ICT and attract effective users. The confusion between the provision of information with the effects of information and knowledge on development can be so great that indicators of the first could be mixed up with signs of the second. For instance, in a study about the effects of ICT on the Caribbean economy (Demac and Morrison, 1989), the level of development is assessed by the diffusion of those technologies. Another study (Taylor and Williams, 1990) certifies the benefits of ICT implementation on development, just by the reduction of communication barriers between the Scottish Islands and the Highlands. Another less discussed assumption is to distinguish between the various actors with respect to their location. This is the perspective of another study (COM, 1989), which separates the actors according to their urban centrality, and concludes that, at least conceptually, peripheral actors could become relatively less developed through the general provision of information and knowledge.

Therefore, instead of adopting unproved assumptions, or avoiding global assessments, it seems wise to focus on the problems that impede the building up of the missing links between information and knowledge provision and regional development.

9.2.4. A different argument on information, knowledge and regional development

The missing links between the provision of information and knowledge and regional development can be conceptualized at two different levels. One (see a) below) deals with the step that connects the information systems of particular organizations with their competitiveness. A second (see b) below) focuses the relation between organizational competitiveness and regional development.

a) Value Chain Information Systems and Value Chain Competitiveness

The first missing link relates to the step that connects Information Systems, also pervaded by ICTs, with the competitiveness of organizations to which they are specific. In order to frame different sets of literature, we focus on three levels of organizational structures: organizations in general, value chains and value chains, rooted in small and medium-sized towns and territories.

Concerning organizations in general, some authors refer to a suggestive correlation between the modification of information systems pervaded with ICT and the performance of the adopters (Harchill and Wynaczyk, 1990). Nevertheless, correlation does not mean causality and, depending on the type of integration achieved between the information system and the organizations, there can be either successful cases or illustrative failures, as is argued by Peter Keen (1988). In fact, some studies show that US corporations with the most complex decision-making systems made no better decisions than firms making similar decisions with less information (Melody, 1986).

In the end, the change of information systems redefines the role of logistics in competitive strategies not only by positioning time and space as strategic management issues (Keen, 1988) but mainly because information systems constitute a powerful interaction tool that interferes with the results of the competitive game between different organizations.

One of the main assumptions of the present chapter is that such a game can be also played by the main actors of the value chains rooted in peripheral small and medium-sized towns and territories and, this being so, information systems turn out to be a key factor for regional competitiveness (Gillespie *et al.*, 1989).

(b) Value Chain Competitiveness and Regional Development

If the development of small and medium-sized towns and territories is a function of export performance, then the competitiveness of the export value chains is at stake. So it is possible to establish the missing link connecting the change of the information systems of value chains and the development of the regions where these chains are rooted.

More recently, authors have revealed that the effect of new information systems is different when it is rooted in high-tech clusters or in traditional ones. With high-tech clusters, there is a need for geographical proximity (Lawson, 1999) and strong competition between global centres (Basant, 2003). With traditional clusters, skilled labour is also very important, but quite often horizontal linkages break down and the dependence on the outside broker increases (Schmitz, 1999).

The new argument we intend to present and defend in this chapter is that information and knowledge could be crucial elements to support regional development, if the timing of their implementation and the shape of their design is appropriate. Otherwise, the effects could be reduced or even negative.

Assuming this hypothesis, and focusing the development of small and medium-sized towns and territories of regions, it is advisable to understand how the moulding of the information systems of value chains interferes with the competitiveness of the regions where those value chains are rooted. If this is proved to be the case, then it seems possible to highlight the role of information and knowledge in the dynamic development or backwardness (Jussawalla et al., 1989) – of small and medium-sized towns and their territories.

In fact, some studies have proved that modified information systems, apart from reinforcing, with other factors, the pattern of uneven development (Goddard et al., 1990; Goddard and Gillespie, 1988; Hepworth, 1986), can have significant negative effects on peripheral areas, as their businesses will face greater competition for local markets from firms located in urban areas (COM, 1989; Lamberton, 1989; Sabbar, 1985; Thorngreen, 1970). Notice that, despite some positive effects of information and knowledge systems in rural areas, the overall balance, far from being clearly positive or negative, is difficult to measure.

On the same stream of literature, but with a stronger argument, Goddard and Gillespie (1988) claim that negative implications associated with information and knowledge are not just a matter of greater competition from the centre, generated by the shrinking of distances between centre and periphery. They assert that, because of the effect of capital-embedded complementarities, the implementation of new information systems can lead the process of regional development along certain dependency paths which have ambiguous or even detrimental implications for the regions' longer-term development prospects.

According to this new argument, information and knowledge must be optimized and not maximized. Nevertheless, because of the different 'missing' links involved, the optimal level of information input for development always seems to be vague and undecided (Jussawalla and Lamberton, 1980). Therefore, it is necessary to focus on the moulding of information transferred along the links and nodes of value chains rooted in peripheral small regions, and not just change the overall communication access, independently of the specific links which are being affected.

9.3. Case Studies

In order to cover a large spectrum of the Portuguese economy and also to consider sectors strongly rooted in regions, the traditional sectors of agriculture, industry and services were considered as relevant units within which the study sectors could be selected. From these, we identified eight subsectors suitable to be analysed for the purpose of this study: dairy, moulds, footwear, the auto-industry, tourism, education, health, and public services/bureaucracy. Following our selection, we then proceeded to analyze dairy, tourism and health not only to include innovative sectors associated with small and medium-sized towns and territories (Frey and Zimmer, 2001), such as agriculture, tourism and public services (BIS Strategic Decisions, 1992), but also to respect the criteria put forward by Porter (1994) in the identification of the main value chains for the Portuguese regions, taking into account their importance in terms of total production, *i.e.* their role as internal and external links and their degree of uniqueness.

9.3.1. Dairy

Of all the agricultural sectors, the Portuguese dairy sector is an appropriate choice for this study because it has the potential to grow, it has important connections within Portugal, and it has experienced a strong restructuring process closely associated with the uptake and use of advanced communications.

The structure of the dairy value-added chains in the mid-1990s showed information systems very much divided according to the actors involved: farmers, processors, distributors, and customers.

The farmers' decisions about the product mix (beef or milk) and the production factor mix (feed or pasture) were closely associated with the information provided by the processor (milk quality, milk quantity, and milk prices). This information was usually carried by paper and directly exchanged in the milk collection station or in the collective or private dairy parlours.

At the processors' level there were three main information decision structures which had direct consequences up and down the value chain: i) the purchasing policy took into account the margins allowed by the production process and the milk prices set in other areas to decide on the milk price based on the farmers' reaction; ii) in the 1990s, the planning of production used processed internal (inventories, production costs, milk quantity, seasonal variations, and milk quality) and external data (demand by product, prices) to convey decisions concerning the time and the amount of production for each alternative product (cheese, powdered milk, ultra-pasteurized milk, or other); iii) the marketing system received information about the level of inventories, the demand for products and respective market prices, and built decisions related to sales conditions, advertising, choice of alternative customers and the timing of sales. Related to marketing, information technologies in the 1990s were evolving from the utilization of faxes and transference of diskettes (by hand or by mail) to the use of terminal emulation systems that would enable the vertical integration between processors and distributors; iv) the communication between the distributors and the customers – usually large malls located in Lisbon and Porto – was based on paper (sent by mail), telephone and fax. Yet at the time there were good conditions to introduce EDI systems to reduce the transaction costs between these two types of economic actors.

In the late 1990s there was a big restructuring process in the Portuguese dairy value chains with the vertical integration of processors and distributors and also a horizontal integration roughly according to the geographical distribution of the value chains (Azores, Northwest, and Lisbon). This movement was pushed by the greater control exercised by European entities, supported by the capabilities of new information technologies and forced by the increasing market power of giant malls and big banking structures.

The spatial structures of those new chains became completely different from the previous ones, with more coordination activities transferred to central places and less market power at the peripheral level. The restructuring process stimulated the specialization of the production systems and a stronger use of information systems strongly based on information technologies. Furthermore, a better integration between peripheral production and central demand resulted in a reduction of the processing of intermediary products such as powdered milk, and a rise in the production of final goods such as cheese. Better logistics also enlarged the space of competition not only down the value-added chain in the markets of Lisbon and Porto, where the French ultra-pasteurized milk increasingly rivals that of the Portuguese, but also up the value-added chain where there was still space for new entrants with modernized technologies, as exemplified by the creation of new factories in the Azores and the entry of multinationals in the Portuguese market.

The functions, decisions and information flows of these new production systems were similar to those presented before. Nevertheless, there are remarkable differences in the information systems, in the location of control from peripheral to central areas, and in the emergence of new markets and new competitors. Although there is a tendency for the specialization of each one of the spatially rooted dairy value chains according to the source of the raw material (differentiated cheese and milk for France, common cheese, butter and powdered milk for the Azores, and normal milk for the Northwest), there is also some space for competition between the different value chains. This being the case, there is a stimulus to reduce costs, to improve management and to increase the barriers against new entrants along the value chain: namely through the design, adoption, and use of information systems based on new information technologies.

Summing up, the dairy sector has experienced a strong restructuring process leading to the horizontal integration of dairy producers and to the vertical integration of producers and distributors. This phenomena was closely associated with the changes in the information systems of the value chains and the spatial structure of the surviving value chains are becoming significantly different from the previous ones, with more coordination activities transferred to central places and less market power at the periphery, where dairy farming, milk collection and primary processing takes place.

From this it is clear that the modifications of the information systems, allowed by information technologies can, on the one hand, support the better integration of small and medium-sized townsand territories whose economic base is associated with the dairy sector. Notwithstanding this, on the other hand, the diffusion of advanced communication and its effects on the moulding of information systems is also associated with the reduction of the market power of those small and medium-sized townsand territories.

9.3.2. Tourism

The integration of Portugal in the European Community in 1986 reinforced Portugal as a tourist destination and increased the number of European tourists in the country. However, the average tourist stay has been steadily decreasing, from 11 days in the 1980s to 7.4 days in the 1990s, and 3.5 days more recently. Hotel capacity is spread relatively evenly across the country; nevertheless, tourists are more attracted to the Algarve, to Lisbon, and to Madeira; the rest of the country (Northwest, Mountains, Central Coast, Azores and the Southern Plains) is less attractive for tourists despite the great desire of the regions to attract tourism. There is a strong seasonal variation and 40 per cent of the tourists arrive in only three months of the year (July, August and September); UK tourists are more spread over the year than Spanish or German tourists, mainly because they are interested in different attractions like golf and longer retirement holidays.

Notwithstanding this, the spatial structure of the tourist value-added chains rooted in Portugal is evolving. First, despite their small-scale tourism, at least two or more areas are becoming relevant as touristic attractions: the Azores and the Douro valley. Second, the expected networking between Portuguese travel agencies and hotels is enabling the creation of a big national networked operator able to substitute or complement international ones. Third, the national tourism will tend to increase: namely, based on a better distribution throughout the year and using improved road accessibility within Portugal. Finally, a stronger competition between airlines is changing the structure of the transport system: from regular, expensive and overbooked flights to more flexible, cheaper and demand-adjusted flights.

There are two alternative information systems for the tourist value-chain, each one associated with a particular distribution of control and results. One of these alternatives derives from the merging process between agencies and tour operators and their association with airlines and oversea operators, all of this supported on telematic systems. With this expected structure, tour operators are becoming more flexible and, based on an easy booking system run on advanced communication systems, are organizing holiday programmes or tourist routes for any demand size; presently, based on automatic booking and automatic payments, the service can be provided either to one person or to one thousand. Even the allotment system – for hotels or even flights – is becoming less rigid because firms can easily sell and buy rooms through a telematic network connecting operators, agencies, hotel chains and airlines. The other alternative is associated with the adoption and use of information technologies by most of the hotels and also by the final customers using the Internet or some other global network system. In this scenario it is possible for the customer to virtually bypass the system created by the tour operators and book the hotel and the flight directly.

These two solutions can coexist in competition with each other. The imposition of the first leads to the greater dependency of hotels and local operators on the big international operators. The supremacy of the second virtually eliminates the need for tour operators and tour agencies.

9.3.3. Health

The public health system in Portugal has 18 Regional Health Areas on the mainland with 346 health centres (128 with internal patients) and their extensions. Each Regional Health Area has at least one regional hospital and Lisbon, Coimbra and Porto have University Hospitals (2 in Lisbon, 1 in Coimbra and 2 in Porto) and quite a few hospitals for particular clinical specialties. In the Azores, there are 3 regional hospitals and 16 health centres with their extensions. In Madeira, there is 1 regional hospital and 11 health centres and their respective local branches. The islands are ruled by autonomous governments which manage the health system in each one of the archipelagos but with strong clinical relations with the Lisbon central hospitals to secure the treatment of more complicated clinical cases.

These health information systems can be divided into two main sets of structures: those that deal with the interfaces between the various entities along the chain; and the others which focus the internal information systems of the main actors, health centres and hospitals.

Concerning the interfaces between the various entities of the health value chain, the main characteristics are: i) the connection between the base of the health centres and their extensions in small villages, and also between different health centres, if the patient moves from one to another. The information exchanged in these interfaces relates mainly to data about the patients but often there is a duplication of the records whenever the patient goes to a different health centre or even to a different extension of the same centre. The support of that information is paper or the patient himself; ii) the link between the health centres and the support regional hospital constitutes the second interface. The main information flows concern booking for specialist observation or analysis, warning of urgencies and data on patients, related to both diagnosis (health centre => hospital) and assistance (hospital => health centre). The lack of coordination between the two levels creates some problems in this interface: first, data on patients is often misleading and booking for specialist observation does not avoid big queues and related inconveniences for the patients. Once again, the information carrier in this interface is paper, sometimes sent by fax, and the patient; iii) the interface between the different services inside each hospital and between regional and central hospitals is also quite important and even more complex, not only because, at that level, the personal knowledge of the patient is lost but also because there is a significantly different language in each of the various specialties. Patients usually do not complain much about the system, but insiders do know that a lot must be done, and a lot can be done with the use of better information systems; iv) another important interface is with the patient him/herself and the relevant data he/she carries with his story and with his own files. Until now most of the information concerning each patient is within his own body and/or in data stored by himself. Private doctors and specialists also store specific information about their own patients, but this information is not shared with others. All in all, there is no information system to access data about the patients in Portugal; v) finally, there is the interface that connects each entity of the health value chain with the National Health Service. Until now, the health centres have been paid not according to what they do but to what they do theoretically and the same happens with the hospitals. Owing to this, the management of whole system becomes quite difficult and the relation between health costs and health benefits deteriorates. Once more, the use of an advanced communication system has the capability of ameliorating that situation.

For hospitals, the information system that deals directly with the patients can be divided into four blocks: i) identification, where the patient is identified and connected with a sponsor (National Health Service; the Health Care for Public Servants; other Private system; or some insurance company); ii) consulting, where the scheduling and follow-up of specialists' advices is defined; iii) internal treatment, which includes all the information about the clinical, logistic and administrative procedures related to the patients admitted to the hospital; and iv) urgency, which collects all the identification data of those patients who had not been in the hospital before. For health centres, the information system secures only the two first modules above: i) identification; and ii) consulting.

It should be noted that public health information systems are not the same all over Portugal. There are important differences the various Regional Health Areas, although all of them do send the required information to the central services in Lisbon. In some Regional Health Areas, the processing of information is completely manual, while in others there is a broad use of information systems based on new information technologies; in some places files registered by the Health Centres are centralized in the respective Area whereas in others it is completely decentralized in the Health Centres; finally, in some situations the coordination of the information systems is made by the clinical boards, and in others that coordination is controlled by the administration.

Generally the information systems of each Regional Health Area are built up on a bottom up approach, chiefly designed to support sectors like statistics and planning in the Regional Health Area and in the central administrative services in Lisbon. The reliability of that system is not high because the low motivation of the information providers; besides what is the use of providing information that enhances the control of the Health authority without any feedback.

The adoption and use of information technologies is also quite different from one site to another. Some have created their own programmers and produce their own software, eventually with the support of private companies. Others demand computer services from the programmers of the Health Ministry.

As explained above, there are two particular problems: one is the inadequacy of the health value system to compete and cooperate with the private sector in the urban areas; the other is the lack of coordination between the health centres and the regional hospitals.

There are two main sets of political projects designed to face the problems highlighted above: one is the creation of a medical record for each person and the privatization of the management of some hospitals located in metropolitan areas; the other is the implementation of Regional Health Units with the support of advanced communication systems, in order to obtain better coordination between regional hospitals and the health centres located in the respective zone.

The spatial structure of those new chains will tend to be completely different from the previous ones, with more coordination between the different levels of the health value chain and leading to greater competition between central hospitals, private and public. The functions, decisions and information flows of these restructured health value chains vary a little from those existing before. There are, nevertheless, remarkable differences in the location of control and in the competitive environment in the health sector: a patient can change between one central hospital to another in the same metropolitan area, and the hospital with less patients will be penalized; in the rural areas, a patient can also move from one family doctor to another, and the former will receive less payment. There is also a new environment around the private health system. On the one hand, the new financial system is reducing the differences between private and public hospital in the metropolitan areas. On the other hand, the use of new information technologies is expanding the area of influence of the private specialists; presently, they are also competing with the public health system in peripheral areas.

9.4. Value Chains and Small and Medium-sized Towns and Territories

From the restructuring process of the dairy sector it is clear that changes in the information systems can support the better integration of small and medium-sized towns and territories in core regions. Notwithstanding this, those changes are also associated with the reduction of the market power of peripheral producers. The final outcome is the enlargement of the area of influence of larger cities and the creation of a system of divided information and knowledge in small and medium-sized towns and territories.

Regarding the tourist value chains, it is quite clear that the integration of the information systems is increasing the competition between different sites, transferring to the operator the capacity to reduce the margins of the local stakeholders and enlarging their own margins. Simultaneously, the competition between operators is stimulating the concentration of operators by favoring those who are rooted in central cities rather than the ones that are located in small and medium-sized towns and territories.

Finally, the introduction of new information systems in the health sector is not straightforward. First, there are some constraints related to the payment procedures either between the private and the public sector or between the different levels of the public sector. Second, some information related to the diagnosis can only be retrieved from the patient him/herself. Third, there are information procedures concerning the attendance stage of the health value chain where new information systems are becoming quite helpful. Summing up, probably some medium-sized towns can profit from the new information systems associated with health services and other public services due because these services are not easily tradable between distant places.

9.5. Conclusion

In this chapter we have looked into the information systems along value chains rooted in small and medium-sized towns and territories in order to understand their possible contribution for regional competitiveness and welfare. Looking at representative value chains associated with small and medium-sized towns and territories we showed that, for value chains linked with tradable products, small and medium-sized towns and territories are losing control, whereas for value chains connected with non tradable goods and services, medium towns can gain some benefit from the adoption of new information systems. This means that small and medium-sized towns and their surrounding territories are losing the capacity to explore the externalities associated with physical proximity because the new topology of the information space is hindering the former collective knowledge of small and medium-sized towns.

According to August Lösch (1954), the existence and development of towns depends on advantages related to transportation costs, production factors costs, production agglomeration economies and consumer agglomeration economies. As explained in the paper, the processes associated with the adoption of new information technologies by value chains rooted in small and medium-sized towns seems to be destroying the role of production agglomeration economies in those territories.

References

Akoy, A. 1990. Computers are not Dynamos: Frontiers in the Diffusion of Information Technologies. CURDS, Newcastle upon Tyne.

Arrow, K. 1979. The Economics of Information. The Computer Year View, in *A Twenty Year View*, edited by M. Dertouzos and J. Moses. Cambridge, Mass: MIT Press, 305-317.

Barabba, V. and Zaltman 1991. Hearing the Voice of the Market, Competitive Advantage through Creative Use of Market Information.

Basant, R. 2003. Knowledge Flows and Industrial Clusters. A background paper commissioned by the *International Development Research Centre (IDRC)*.

BIS Strategic Decisions 1992. *Telecommunications Industry in Portugal*, Lisbon: GATIE.

Boulding, K.E. 1966. The Economics of Knowledge and the Knowledge of Economics. *American Economic Review*, 56(2), 1-13.

Bruce, R., Cunard, J. and Director, M. (eds) 1988. The Telecom Mosaic; Assembling the New International Structure. Debevoise and Plamton, Washington DC., Brussels, 5.7.2005

COM 1989. The Economic Impact of Information and Communication Technologies. Economic Development and Employment Implications, Luxembourg: EEC.

Demac, D. and Rorrison, R. 1989. US Caribean Telecommunications. *Making Great Strides in Development*. Telecommunications Policy.

Frey, W.H. and Zimmer, Z. 2001. Defining the City, in *Handbook of Urban Studies*, edited by R. Paddison. London: Sage Publications.

Goddard, J. and Gillespie, A. 1988. Advanced Telecommunications and Regional Economic Development. *Information and Regional Development*, edited by M. Giaoutzi and P. Nijkamp. England: Avebury.

Gillespie, A., Goddard, J., Hepworth, M. and Williams, H. 1991. Information and Communication Technology and Regional Development. An Information Technology Perspective. *Science Technology and Industry Review*, 5, OECD, Paris.

Goddard, J. *et al.* 1990. *Annual Report: Program on Information and Communication Technologies*. PICT, CURDS, ERSC, UK.

Harchill, I. and Wynarczyzyk, P. 1990. A Research Note. *Information Technology and Company Performance in Textile Industry*. New technology, Work and Employment. UK.

Hepworth, M. 1986. The Geography of Economic Opportunity in the Information Society. *The Information Society*, 4(3).

Jussawalla, M. and Lamberton, D. 1989. Communication Economics and Development. An Economics of Information Perspective. *Communication Economics and Development*, edited by M. Jussawalla and D.M. Lamberton, London: Pergamon Press.

Jussawalla, M., Okrima, T. and Arali, T. 1989. Information Technology and Global Interdependence. London: Greenwood Press.

Keen, P. 1988. Competing in Time. *Using Telecommunications for Competitive Advantage*, Cambridge: Ballinger.

Lamberton, D. 1989. Current Developments in Australian Telecom Policy. *European Telecommunications Policy Research*, N. Ganham, Eds IOS, Amsterdam.

Lawson, C. 1999. Towards a Competence Theory of a Region. *Cambridge Journal of Economics*, 23(2), 151-166.

Lösch, A. 1954. The Economics of Location. Translation from the 2nd rev. edited by William H. Woglom, with the assistance of Wolfgang F. Stolper. Yale University. Press, New Haven.

Melody, W. 1986. Telecommunications Implications for the Structure of Development. *5th World Telecommunications Forum*. Geneva: ITU.

Nicol, L. 1985. Communication Technology: Economic and Spatial Impact, in *High Technology, Space and Society*, edited by M. Castells and P. Hall, Beverly Hills: Sage.

Nijkamp, P., Rietveld, D. and Salomon, I. 1990. Barriers in Communication, Conceptual issues. *NETCOM*, 4, 10-36.

Porter, M. 1990. *The Competitive Advantages of Nations*. London: Macmillan Press Ltd.

Porter, M. 1994. *Construir as Vantagens Competitivas de Portugal*, Lisboa: Cedintec.

Rietveld, P., van Nierop, J. and Ouwersloot, H. 1991. Barriers to International Telecommunication, What are your most frequently called countries?. *Regional Science Association*. 31st European Congress, Lisbon.

Rosenstein-Rodan, P.N. 1934. The Role of Time in Economic Theory. *Economica*, 77-97.

Sabbath, F. 1985. The New Media. *High Technology, Space and Society*, edited by M. Castells and P. Hall, Beverly Hills: Sage, 210-216.

Schmitz, H. 1999. Global Competition and Local Cooperation: Success and Failure in the Sinos Valley, Brazil. *World Development*, 27(9), 1627-1650.

Spence, A.M. 1974. An Economist's View of Information. *Annual Review of Informatio Science and Technology*, 9.

Stiglitz, J.E. 1988. Economic Organization, Information and Development, in *Handbook of Development Economics*, edited by H. Chenery and T.N. Srinivasan, 1, Ch. 5, North Holland: Elsevier Publisher. B.V.

Strassmann, P. 1990. Information Pay-Off. *The Transformation of Work in the Electronic Age*. London: Free Press.

Taylor, J. and Williams, H. 1990. The Scotish Highlands and Islands Initiative. An Alternative Model for Develeloment. *Telecommunications Policy*. 189-192.

Theil, H. 1967. *Economics of Information Theory*. Amsterdam: North Holland Publishing Company.

Thorngren, B. 1970. How do Contact Systems Affect Regional Development. *Environment and Planning: A*, 409-427.

Van Leeuwen, E.S. 2010. Urban-Rural Interactions: Towns as Focus Points in Rural Development, Contributions to Economics, Heidelberg: Physica Verlag.

Vanguard 1987. The Economic Effects of Value-Added Data Services. *Department of Trade and Industry*, London.

Vickers, G. 1955. Communication in Economic Systems. *Management Information Systems*, edited by T. McRae, Penguin, 1971.

Chapter 10

The Role of Universities for Economic Development in Urban Poles

Clive Winters, John Dodd and Keith Harrison

10.1. Introduction

Since the Lisbon European Union Spring Council of 2000 set a strategic goal for the European Union to become the most dynamic and competitive knowledge-based economy in the world by 2010, there has been significant research, policies and projects on how to stimulate the Knowledge Economy and, in particular, the importance of Universities within Triplex-Helix Structures.

In this context the Knowledge Economy relies on the transfer of knowledge from those who generate it to those who use it and can build on it. Research represents a key component of this approach and the role of universities is particularly important as actors in research, education and training. Universities account for 20 per cent of European Research, 80 per cent of fundamental research and employ one third of European researchers (European Commission, 2005a). They transmit knowledge through education and training and have an increasing role in innovation and economic development at the regional level. In support of this, the 2005 Lisbon mid-term review explicitly highlighted the importance of the role of universities in the creation, dissemination and transfer of knowledge (European Commission, 2005b).

In this innovation and economic development role it is recognized that links and synergies between universities and local society (e.g. Industry, Chambers of Commerce, and Local Government) should be enhanced (European Commission, 2005). Cities are widely recognized as playing a fundamental role in the promotion of the Knowledge Economy, but most research and policy has focused on large cities with World-class educational and research institutes and advanced clusters of economic activity.

There are clear and significant gaps in the knowledge of how smaller sized cities, with different levels and types of knowledge institutions and different levels of economic activity can compete within the Knowledge Economy. Yet such cities are recognized within European Union policy as playing a vital role in the implementation of the Lisbon agenda. In this regard, medium-sized cities with populations of between 50,000 and 200,000 people which have universities are at a considerable advantage and can gain from strong localization economies if they have a strong knowledge base and innovation culture.

10.2. Research Methodology

This chapter has been researched through the activities undertaken in the development phase of the URBACT II thematic network RUnUP (The Role of Universities for Economic Development in Urban Poles) between April and October 2008. The authors represent the Lead Partner of the network, Gateshead Council and an independent Lead Expert. The chapter has been created through a review of the state-of-the-art literature in the field and an individual Lead Expert visit to each of the 9 network partners. Each Lead Expert visit was undertaken over the course of 2 to 3 days with individual meetings with Triple-Helix stakeholders.

10.3. The Knowledge Economy and the Role of Universities

Defining the Knowledge Economy has been the subject of significant debate and, while a number of general definitions have been articulated, no single definition has been able to capture all aspects of the commodity that is knowledge (Brinkley, 2006). Given this confusion an alternative argument has emerged that the Knowledge Economy is not a new phenomenon, and that 'the economy has always been driven by knowledge leading to innovation and technological change and knowledge based institutions have helped store and share knowledge for centuries. What we see today is essentially more of the same but operating on a bigger scale and at a faster pace' (Brinkley, 2006).

For a local economy, engagement in knowledge-based industries (although they do not fully represent the scope of the Knowledge Economy) can have a significant impact: between 1995 and 2005 employment in knowledge-based industries in the European Union went up by 23.9 per cent, in contrast to 5.7 per cent for all other industries. In particular, while manufacturing employment overall in the period between 1995 to 2005 declined by 5.6 per cent on average across the EU, only 2.4 per cent of employment losses were from technology-based manufacturing. In comparison, knowledge-based services have seen a significant employment rise of 30.7 per cent across the decade much greater than the 13.5 per cent for less knowledge-intensive services.

For the partners in the RUnUP network, understanding the dimensions of the Knowledge Economy is critical as the profitable utilization of knowledge can have a significant impact on the modernization of existing industries through technology adoption, the diversification of existing industries into new economic sectors, the transplantation of industry (inward investment) and the creation of new economic sectors. In this regard Brinkley (2006) summarizes the key features of the Knowledge Economy and Knowledge Economy organizations as follows:

- The Knowledge Economy represents a 'soft discontinuity' from the past; it is not a 'new' economy operating to a new set of economic laws. Its characteristics are:

- A growing share of GDP devoted to knowledge intangibles compared with physical capital;
- Knowledge Economy organizations reorganize work to allow them to handle store and share information through knowledge management practices;
- The Knowledge Economy is present in all sectors of the Economy, not just the knowledge intensive industries;
- The Knowledge Economy has a high and growing intensity of ICT usage by well educated knowledge workers;
- The Knowledge Economy consists of innovating organizations using new technologies to introduce process, organizational and presentational innovation;

European policy approaches to the Knowledge Economy for the most part take universities as their point of reference regarding competitive research and their contribution to the European Research Area. In particular, the European Commission publication European Universities: Enhancing Europe's Research Base (European Commission, 2005a) identifies the entrepreneurial role of universities as a source of spin-offs and start-up companies and their role in knowledge and technology transfer. In this context, universities are seen as environments that are:

- The centre of the research and teaching systems;
- The training institutions for our future researchers;
- A point where frontier knowledge meets practical applications;
- The school and library of the knowledge society.

This has led to a view of the university's role in innovation and competiveness in the local economy driven by technology transfer. In this context, universities have seen the growth of standard models, e.g. external liaison offices, research and development offices, technology transfer offices, as central mechanisms for linking academia with industry, with a particular focus on (IRE Knowledge Transfer Working Group, 2008):

- Contributing to faster and better commercialisation of research results;
- Improving innovation performance and accelerate the dissemination of new technologies;
- Better management of intellectual property and research capacities of public research organizations;
- Identifying specific research requirements through dialogue with enterprises;
- Helping companies grow and become more competitive.

Despite the creation of technology and knowledge transfer support mechanisms, the strategic challenges and key issues regarding the knowledge transfer topic which are often underlined (IRE Knowledge Transfer Working Group, 2008) at a strategic level include:

- Little cooperation between firms and R&D Institutions;
- Low level of SMEs participating in knowledge transfer activities;
- Companies which are more focused on distribution and assembling than on R&D activities;
- Low technology transfer rates and a weak entrepreneurship culture;
- Low creation rate of spin-offs.

Such support mechanisms designed to raise R&D levels are likely to be most appropriate for and successful in, those economic areas where levels of innovation in product, process and service developments are already high. While such approaches are generally accepted and widely adopted there remain concerns regarding their long-term effectiveness.

10.4. Economic Development and the Role of Universities

To support the development of their local economy, the partners in the RUnUP network need to examine how knowledge is transferred into the economy in order to maximize productivity and employment. The RUnUP partners operate in urban areas with generally a large number of micro-sized companies and Small and Medium-Sized Enterprises (SMEs). In this context the 'absorptive capacity' of companies plays a key role in determining their capability to access and make use of external knowledge in particular through external collaboration with other companies (e.g. Suppliers, Customers and Partners) or with Universities and Technology Centres.

Absorptive capacity (Cohen and Leventhal, 1990) refers to the ability of the company to support problem solving and development using innovation processes. The knowledge to enable the company to do this is often 'provided' to the organization from the external environment rather than from within the company itself. Knowledge for innovation must be absorbed through interaction and cooperation with the networks available to the company.

Specific knowledge is required for the development and implementation of new business products, processes or services. Where this information cannot be found within the knowledge base of the company, the company can decide to either develop knowledge itself or obtain knowledge from the external environment. Generally, it is accepted that in most cases knowledge will be sought from the external environment when looking for solutions to problems. Through its absorptive capacity the organization learns from this external information.

To enhance the absorptive capacity of firms it is argued (IRE Science-Industry Sub group, 2006) that the range of 'innovation services' offered to SMEs should be extended to assist them with engaging with innovation support agencies and in developing longer-term relationships with the science base. Such services need to be translated through the work of "non-academic" business support specialists who can work with SMEs on a needs-driven basis within the framework of approved projects and programmes, integrating with academic staff as appropriate. However, the current role of many industrial liaison offices and technology transfer offices does not support the development of such activities.

To support growth in the Knowledge Economy the RUnUP partners need to develop with other partners mechanisms that support the capability of companies to acquire knowledge through connections with external organizations (including universities) in line with the transformation of the economy.

Seeking to address the performance issues of universities in supporting innovation and competitiveness in local economies in 2002, the Industrial Performance Centre of Massachusetts Institute of Technology began a research programme (Lester, 2005) examining the role of universities in supporting industrial development through participation in innovation projects and activities.

Their research adopted an 'outside-in' perspective of the role of the university describing and contextualizing the local economy as a set of industries that changes over time. This approach directly meets the requirements of the RUnUP partners, which are either local municipalities or councils, by providing a framework in which the economic activity of the urban area can be categorized. Such a model that recognizes the issue of enhancing the absorptive capacity of SMEs is vital if local companies are to continually adapt to new market and technology opportunities and introduce new products and processes. Significantly, the approach of the MIT research was driven by exploring the role of the local university in supporting local companies to take up technology and new knowledge and apply this profitably.

By adopting an industrial perspective, consideration is given to situations in which the university can contribute in additional ways to local economic development. Engagement is not limited solely to the creation of spin-out companies or licensing agreements, it addresses situations in which the University may not be a key economic player, and takes an external perspective by considering transformation of local economies over time.

This approach is central to the work in the implementation phase of the RUnUP thematic network, and provides a mechanism through which local authorities can become actively engaged in defining and delivering their local approach to engage business in the Knowledge Economy and in influencing the role of local and regional universities.

This aligns well with European Commission policy that seeks to support the engagement of universities with civil society; the uptake of innovation; the build up of concrete synergies between universities and surrounding society; and the recommendation that exchange of knowledge with industry and within society is not the responsibility of the universities alone, and that companies, national, regional and local authorities, business promotion agencies, private and public joint venture investors and other stakeholders must be active in creating the appropriate infrastructure and surrounding environment

A 'cultural change' is required to highlight the importance and value of SMEs working with universities and research centres and the impact on long-term company profitability. The focus of university expertise on the transfer of research to industry is distinctly different to many of the innovation requirements of SMEs which require basic support in marketing, sales and training. In this field, training and mentoring services for companies are critical, and existing tools for supporting companies need to be embedded within the offer to companies. At both the regional and the local level, support needs to be co-ordinated and activities clustered to facilitate easier access to companies.

Similarly, there is a requirement to 'Stimulate SMEs to innovate'. This means that SMEs nead to be challenged to extend their perspective of innovation and the development of innovation activities within the business. In the scope of science-industry linkages this can be improved through the adoption of business mentoring, continuous education and the utilization of schemes that place experienced academic staff and graduate students in industry, e.g. UK Knowledge Transfer Partnerships (IRE Science-Industry Subgroup, 2006).

10.5. Challenges for Medium-Sized Cities: Case Studies from the RUnUP Network

The URBACT I network STRIKE (van Winden, and van den Berg, 2004) identified that urban areas are focal points in the Knowledge Economy and that larger cities in particular are well placed as they are locations where knowledge is created, developed and commercialized, have higher levels of educated staff, have well-developed infrastructure, and are well-networked in the Global Economy.

In particular the large cities of Helsinki, Copenhagen, Stockholm, Lisbon and Madrid are well-recognized as cities which emphasize economic development and the development of processes and methods (The Union of Capitals of the European Union, 2002). These cities highlight the direct benefit of investing resources into co-operation with Universities. Helsinki, Copenhagen and Stockholm present a technology oriented cooperation model, where one of the main goals is to create new business enterprise, whereas Lisbon and Madrid present models for organizing cooperation and best practice in different fields of research and services. But, while medium-sizedcities and large cities face some common challenges, there are clear differences purely based on their size (The Work Foundation, 2006).

The STRIKE network (van Winden, and van den Berg, 2004) established a framework for analysis to understand the position of urban regions in the Knowledge Economy, with distinctions between knowledge foundations and knowledge activities. Utilizing this framework the distinctive challenges faced by medium-sized cities in the development of their Knowledge Economy can be articulated.

The quality, quantity and diversity of the universities, other education institutes and R&D activities determine to a large extent the starting position of a city in the Knowledge Economy and together are the first element of the STRIKE framework. The RUnUP network partners face two of the most common challenges in this context in having no university within the city (Gateshead, Barakaldo) or having a university whose potential for knowledge transfer and transfer of skills has not been developed to support economic development.

The second element, the economic base, determines for a large part the economic possibilities and restrictions, but also the difficulties, for an urban region within the Knowledge Economy. For medium-sized cities there are challenges in devising economic development strategies and a distinctive offer, in particular if they have reduced industry specialization. In this context, medium-sized cities need to identify what their core strengths are and actively work to these.

Geographically, the cities of the RUnUP network can be considered as either from within a 'city-region': namely, Newcastle-Gateshead; Bilbao-Barakaldo; Stockholm-Solna and Berlin-Potsdam, or from within a wider regional context as a principal or smaller town or city: namely, Leszno, Dunkirk, Campobasso, Patras and Águeda. Those partner cities and towns operating within a city-region are economically stronger performers, thus supporting the arguments in the literature that 'larger cities in particular are well placed as they are locations where knowledge is created, developed and commercialised, have higher levels of educated staff, have well developed infrastructure and are well networked in the Global Economy'. The key challenges for the nine Medium-Sized Cities of the RUnUP network are as follows:

Gateshead

Gateshead is the largest in area of five Tyneside local authorities that cover Gateshead, Newcastle, North Tyneside, South Tyneside and Sunderland, and occupies a central position in the Tyneside conurbation alongside the City of Newcastle on the South bank of the River Tyne.

As mentioned earlier, the quality, quantity and diversity of universities, other education institutes and R&D activities determine to a large extent the starting position of a city in the Knowledge Economy (van Winden and van den Berg, 2004). The challenge for Gateshead in promoting the Knowledge Economy is that, while it has no university located within its metropolitan borough, there is a clear need to work closely with the excellent range of nearby university institutions, and to ensure that their focus is increasingly aligned to the needs of the Gateshead economy. While it operates collaborative activity with its partner universities, the Council needs to fully understand how its knowledge-based partners deliver activity in support of economic transformation so that, as a result, it can deliver new knowledge-based collaboration activity in line with economic transformation requirements. In particular, it needs to articulate the state of transformation within its local economy, specifically its role within the creative industries and its support for the modernization and diversification of its manufacturing economy.

In delivering innovation-led growth for Gateshead the relationship between the Council and its knowledge-based partners needs to be redefined. Work to date has identified how European policy has taken the university as its point of reference for the Knowledge Economy. At a local level in Gateshead, while the Business Development Team of the Council has good relationships with its knowledge based partners, it is the needs of the economy and its transformation that must be taken as the point of reference, rather than the traditional approach of universities in technology transfer. In this context, the Council is the only actor with a fully exclusive focus on the needs of Gateshead and the motivation to mobilize universities and knowledge based partners to support its economic development.

Águeda

Águeda is located in the central region of Portugal, in the NUTS 3 Level area of Baixo Vouga. Its territory covers 335.2 km² and is therefore the largest municipality of the Aveiro district. The Municipality of Águeda is characterized by an industrial tradition and an endogenous entrepreneurial capability, which are the major factors that have contributed to the economic success of the city during the 20th century. However, changes in the demand patterns of international markets, as well the economic crisis that took place as a result of these changes, have affected Águeda's economic environment, forcing it to rethink its approach to economic development and innovation.

Within Águeda there is a requirement to focus on the development of entrepreneurship development. This is the basis on which the city of Águeda has grown, but it is now in need of revitalization to reduce unemployment and improve the social and economic prosperity of the city and its population. Factors, including entrepreneurial capability, the existence of a technical culture based on traditional knowledge, and a large variety of small and medium-sized enterprises in Águeda, provide a framework for sustained development and an improvement in competitiveness.

The focus of the Municipality of Águeda in its development is the requalification of human resources, including unemployed graduates, by developing new courses in essential areas for economic development, e.g. environmental management. The aim is to enhance skills, adapting them to market needs to act as a catalyst for process improvement and product development; and to create a new generation of entrepreneurs who have access university knowledge and expertise focusing on new market opportunities, related to state-of-the-art environmentally-sustainable technologies, creating a new local and regional cluster.

Barakaldo

Barakaldo with a population of 98,000 people is located in northern Spain, in the Autonomous Community of the Basque Country which is divided into three provinces (Álava, Bizkaia and Gipuzkoa). Barakaldo is situated in Bizkaia.

While Barakaldo has undergone significant economic transformation and economic regeneration, to date this has not included the development of knowledge based economy activities. In particular, Barakaldo has only a small campus location of the University of the Basque Country with no direct engagement with the technology transfer and spin-out activities of the University. This determines to a large extent the starting position of the city in the Knowledge Economy (van Winden and van den Berg, 2004).

The Municipality of Barakaldo, through its economic development agency Inguralde as the principle actor in economic development, needs to develop a strategy that supports both the creation of new economic sectors linked to the research activities of its university and technology centres and existing sectors of the economy: namely, business services and construction. In this context, Inguralde, for example, has some business infrastructures which could be used to deliver new activities which link research with the generation of spin-off companies and entrepreneurial activity and stimulate the local economy.

Campobasso

Campobasso with a population of 53,321 people is the capital of the central Italian region of Molise, bordered by the Sannio and Matese mountains and the Adriatic Sea.

The integration of services for enterprises and entrepreneurs linked to knowledge and technology transfer, in particular connections with universities and research centres, is seen as the key problematic for Campobasso. The Municipality of Campobasso is home to two universities, the public University of Molise and the private Catholic University of the Sacred Heart operating alongside other knowledge-based partners, including the Chamber of Commerce and Innovation Point located at the Cittadella dell' Economia in Campobasso.

The challenge facing Campobasso is that its existing economic structure is dominated by the agriculture sector. The Scientific and Technological Park of Molise (Molise Innovazione) is supporting businesses operating in this sector, but is limited in its current level of engagement and support for businesses. Its operations and approach to working with business need to be further developed and enhanced. Innovation, therefore, has a fundamental role in supporting the competitiveness of the entire economic system. Productive regional support must be developed through initiatives that promote the application of research and innovation. This will increase SMEs awareness of the central role of research and innovation as a competitive advantage to facilitate the paths of renewal and ensure the proper functioning of a unitary system of governance.

Dunkirk

The Greater Dunkirk Council consists of 18 towns with a total population of 210,000, located in the region of Nord Pas de Calais that stretches from the Belgian border to the Calais region. The Greater Dunkirk district is an industrial and seaport conurbation, marked by the establishment of an internationally-important iron and steel centre in the 1960s. During that period, the population doubled, mainly as a result of immigration. In the late 1980s, it went through a major economic crisis that resulted in a sharp increase in unemployment and that weakened the economic fabric with resultanting negative effects on social and urban life.

Economic diversification is seen as the kor Dunkirk, where the university's contribution to the economy is seen as insufficient, and the linkage of the local economy to the energy sector makes the future particularly uncertain, given the current global climate. The focus in this case is on the diversification of companies into new Knowledge Economy areas linked to the environmental sector and sustainability with particular links to the environmental research centre, and on the development of the entrepreneurial support services of the university.

- The development of an entrepreneurial and innovation culture is of particular importance. In this context the Council sees the importance of a strategy that targets:
- The development of emerging and potential new economic sectors;
- The creation of an entrepreneurial university campus;
- The attraction and retention of students, graduates, researchers and businesses;
- The establishment of an innovation culture and environment for SMEs;
- The development of Innovation and projects with large enterprises.

In particular, there is a requirement to enhance the level of innovation by developing partnership working between businesses in order to maintain and develop industrial employment. The potential impact of concentration on Large Enterprises for employment is well recognized, and there is a requirement to maximize the position of the Council's area as a transport and logistics hub. Specifically, the Greater Dunkirk Council sees the formation of a cluster of sustainable technology supported by the involvement of the university in technology transfer and logistics as key development.

Leszno

Leszno with a population of 63,955 people is located in Central West Poland, in the Wielkopolska region between the economic centres of Poznań and Wrocław. Leszno is a major commercial and industrial centre with a diverse range of companies operating in the industrial and service sectors and a mix of micro-companies through to large multinational companies. Employment is significantly (50 per cent) based in the industrial sectors of the economy: namely, machinery, furniture, metal, clothing and food production. Although it represents 50 per cent of employment, the industrial sector accounts for only 10 per cent of registered businesses.

The challenge facing Leszno is that its economy is based on traditional industries with low levels of productivity. In delivering innovation-led growth for Leszno through the modernization of its existing industrial base and the creation of new companies, a new relationship between the Municipality and business support organizations in Leszno needs to be established. Similarly, the role of higher education institutions in Leszno needs to be maximized to look beyond just their role of skills development through education to examining their potential for supporting businesses through consultancy, best practice scanning, technology/ foresight exercises, and in creating new areas of the economy by supporting the development of entrepreneurial services, e.g. incubation, to students, graduates and the wider community.

Patras

The City of Patras with a population of 171,616 people is the capital of the Peloponnese region of Western Greece and the Prefecture of Achaia. In line with the economy of Greece, international sea transportation and commerce are important elements of the economy of the Achaia prefecture, with transportation accounting for 7.2 per cent of gross value added, recognizing the importance of Patras as an important gateway to the markets of the European Union. Activities in agriculture and manufacturing remain of significant importance although activities in these primary and secondary sectors have declined by 2 per cent and 7.5 per cent, respectively, between 1995 and 2001.

The challenges facing Patras are that it has no focus on the transformation of its existing sectors of the economy (agriculture, food manufacturing) through either modernization or diversification, and that it has no economic strategy or economic development activity at the municipality level. A lack of data at the city level means that the identification of business need and the development and delivery of business support is being based on the needs of the prefecture and the region rather than on local demand. In addition, given the high level of unemployment of 16.1 per cent with business start-up rates below both the national average and that of the convergence regions of the European Union and the decline in economic activity within the primary and secondary sectors, it is particularly important to consider the development of new economic activities potentially in the fields of Informatics and Communications and Environmental Management and Protection.

Potsdam

Potsdam with a population of more than 150,000 people is the capital of the state of Brandenburg within the convergence region of Brandenburg South-West. In recent years Potsdam has experinced significant economic growth with the number of new business registrations per year more than doubling between 2001 and 2004 – from 720 to 1,824 companies, while there has been a corresponding reduction in business de-registrations per year from 823 in 2001 down to 388 in 2004. As a result of this business growth, Potsdam has created a profile for itself as a modern business centre with a rich tradition; one that is developing increasing autonomy, independent from Berlin, its immediate neighbour. The main activities in its economy take place within a widely diverse service sector encompassing the areas of media, information and communication, biotechnology, trade, banks, insurance and tourism.

The challenge facing Potsdam is that, while its existing economy is growing and developing in the areas of Media, Information and Communications and Biotechnology, the transfer of knowledge through students and graduates into the Knowledge Economy is limited given the predominance in the university of Research and Education and the significant number of students commuting from Berlin to Potsdam on a daily basis. While Potsdam is economically developing, it is disconnected from the university community, and its long-term prosperity is dependent upon the enhancement (European Commission, 2005) of links and synergies between the universities and their local community.

Solna

Solna with a population of 65,000 people is located in East Central Sweden, part of the capital Stockholm's metropolitan area. During the early 1990s Sweden suffered an economic crisis, during which Solna had high levels of unemployment. In 1997, politicians from all political parties in Solna agreed upon a strategy to become the most business-friendly municipality in Sweden. Since then, the number of companies has almost doubled to about 8,500 and there are slightly more jobs, 67,000, than inhabitants in Solna. The economy has been transformed into a service and knowledge-intensive economy; there is virtually no larger-scale manufacturing industry left in Solna. Expansion has intensified in recent years and will continue until the year 2025, when the population is expected to reach above 90,000, with an equal number of work places. Solna will then encompass five new city districts, including the "Arena City" with the new National Arena for football and Scandinavia's biggest shopping mall, the Mall of Scandinavia.

For Solna, with the world-class Karolinska Institute (KI) located in its municipality and existing activity already in place to support the establishment of Bio-Tech and Life Science companies through KI Science Park and KI Innovations, the focus of its engagement in the RUnUP network is specifically concerned with exploring options for supporting an additionaltier of spin-off companies through incubation and improvements to the referral process for potential spin-out and licensing opportunities, alongside the establishment of stronger relationships between the City of Solna and the Karolinska Institute. Solna's position within the Stockholm Metropolitan Area enables it to present a technology-oriented cooperation model (The Union of Capitals of the European Union, 2002), where one of the main goals is to create new business enterprises.

10.6. Outcomes and Results

The RUnUP network has identified that medium-sized urban areas often seek to work and integrate universities into their economic activities in line with the principles of the Knowledge Economy, but often take a classical perspective of universities focused solely on technology transfer and spin-off activity linked to research. The introduction of a model for mapping the transition of local economies with university roles provides a structure for debate between municipalities and universities on how to drive forward and support their local business community in line with the principle of the Triple Helix of university-business-government relations (Leydesdorff and Etzkowitz, 2001).

Utilizing this model as a framework for exploring the future activities of the RUnUP network, comparisons can be made between each of the partners' detailed problematic that will then be explored.

i) Creating New Economies

The creation of new economies based on Knowledge is a key focus and problematic in all of the partner cities with the exception of Dunkirk and to a lesser extent Leszno. This is not unrealistic as the partners are proactive in seeking to develop their economies around higher value-adding sectors in line with the principles of the Knowledge Economy.

For Águeda the Municipality has already identified the importance of establishing a business incubator linked to environmental technologies. Such an activity linked to the commercialization approach of the University of Aveiro and the School of Technology and Management in Águeda is essential to encourage entrepreneurial development among students, graduates, staff and the local community.

In Campobasso and Patras there is a particular requirement to define these new sector opportunities in partnership with their local universities, but it is considered that opportunities exist in the fields of: sustainable industries and bio-medical/biotech for Campobasso, and Informatics and Communications and Environmental Management and Protection in Patras. Similarly, Barakaldo needs to define its sector focus but is clear in its aim to develop a joint local initiative that links research with the generation of spin-off companies and entrepreneurial activity, enhancing linkages with local business.

In comparison, Gateshead Council is already examining the potential for the creation of new economic activity based on the cultural and creative sector, possibly focusing on a design-led economy linked to the Design Centre for the North, although the viability and impact of such a focus must be examined.

In Potsdam the University needs to articulate a strategy for enhancing its awareness of structures and processes for increasing its commercialization activities and how these can align, integrate and mutually support the education and research activities of the university. Additionally in implementing a strategy for knowledge-based transformation the university needs to encourage and develop business development skills and capabilities within their university staff to support longer-term strategy implementation.

For Solna the situation can be more precisely defined. With the world-class Karolinska Institute located in its Municipality and existing activity already in place to support the establishment of Bio-Tech and Life Science companies through KI Science Park and KI Innovations, the focus of their engagement in the RUnUP network is specifically around supporting an additionaltier of spin-off companies through incubation and improvements to the referral process for potential spin-off and licensing opportunities together with the establishment of stronger relationships between the Municipality of Solna and the Karolinska Institute.

ii) New Industry Transplantation

While new industry transplantation can be seen traditionally and more extensively in the lower wage economies of the European Union, this element of University interaction with the economy has not been identified as a problematic by the RUnUP Partners. While Leszno with a focus on the development of Special Economic Zones has a potential interest in this area, its main focus is seen as the modernization of its existing industry, firstly, in the design and manufacture of products; and, secondly, in the development of incubation activity in support of the development of new economic sectors.

iii) Diversification of the Economy

Economic diversification is seen as the key problematic in relation to Dunkirk, where the university contribution to the economy is seen as insufficient and the linkage of the local economy to the energy sector makes the future particularly uncertain given the current global climate. The focus in this case is on the diversification of companies into new Knowledge Economy areas linked to the environmental sector and sustainability, with particular links to the environmental research centre, and to the ment of developing the entrepreneurial support services of the university.

In addition, diversification within the manufacturing sector of Águeda is a priority as, with nearly 50 per cent of its employment within manufacturing and the increasing pressures of globalization in their traditional product markets, they are seeking to move into environmental technology-related economic activity areas.

Diversification is also related to modernization. In this context, however, is a secondary priority for Gateshead, Patras and Campobasso.

iv) Upgrading of Mature Economies

The Modernization of its industry is a primary goal of Leszno, whose economy is based on traditional industries with low levels of productivity. In delivering innovation-led growth for Leszno through the modernization of its existing economic base and the creation of new companies, a new relationship between the municipality and business support organizations in Leszno needs to be established.

Similarly, manufacturing remains a significant part of the Gateshead economy, and there is a particular requirement to develop a strategy that supports the modernization of its existing manufacturing and an upgrading of its skills base.

The challenge facing Campobasso within this context is that its existing economic structure is dominated by the agriculture sector. The Scientific and Technological Park of Molise is supporting businesses operating in this sector, but is limited in its current level of engagement and support for businesses. Its operations and approach to working with business need to be further developed and enhanced.

10.7. Conclusions

For medium-sized cities with populations of between 50,000 and 200,000 inhabitants the challenge of engaging in the Knowledge Economy is a critical one as these cities often lack the presence of a university, as is commonly found in large cities that are strong in research and integration with the local economy. As a result of their size, they also lack economic development strategies that have been fully articulated and debated and are unable to fully identify their economic strengths and distinctive offer.

In response to this challenge, such medium-sized urban areas seek to work and integrate universities into their economic activities, but often take a classic perspective of universities focused solely on technology transfer and spin-off activity linked to research. The introduction of a model for mapping the transition of local economies with university roles provides a structure for debate between municipalities and universities on how to drive forward and support their local business community in line with the principle of the Triple Helix of university-industry-government relations.

The URBACT II RUnUP network provides a unique opportunity to examine the role of universities in urban poles from the perspective of local government, given the constitution of the partners, rather than using a traditional model which takes Universities as the point of reference. In the development phase this unique perspective has provided valuable insights, namely:

Universities are positioned as mechanisms for R&D and subsequently licensing, patenting and spin-offs (and this is reinforced in European and National policies), although this may not be where their potential for supporting local economic development truly exists.

Local government organizations see universities primarily as vehicles for Education and expect them to support the development of their local economy by default, although universities operate in regional, national and international markets and are not entirely (if at all) aligned to local priorities.

An economic development perspective which examines the needs of the local economy, its modernization, transformation, transplantation and new sector creation establishes common ground where local priorities can be articulated, and, in this context, the role of the university can be openly explored and suitable knowledge transfer approaches defined in support of Triple-Helix development.

The RUnUP network provides a new framework for small and medium-sized local authorities and municipalities to engage with and support universities in encouraging innovation at the local level. The activities of RUnUP will extend and highlight the range of alternatives regarding the role of universities in such environments. As a result, the network will be able to highlight, through individual partner case studies and actions and through reference to other cities, the case for extending European policy regarding the role of universities, thereby demonstrating how local authorities and municipalities should adapt their local economic development policies to support a wider engagement of their local universities with their local economies.

Acknowledgements

The RUnUP network is funded through the European Commission URBACT II Operational Programme (2007 – 2013). Acknowledgement is also due to the City partners of RUnUP who provided detailed information for the development phase of the network.

References

Brinkley, I. 2006. *Defining the Knowledge Economy*, Knowledge Economy Programme report.

Cohen, W. and Leventhal, D. 1990. Absorptive Capacity: A New Perspective on Learning and Innovation, ASQ. 35.

European Commission 2005. European Universities: Enhancing Europe's Research Base.

European Commission 2005. Working Together for Growth and Jobs: A New Start for the Lisbon Strategy.

IRE Knowledge Transfer Working Group 2008. Knowledge Transfer Strategies for Regional Development and Competitiveness.

IRE Science-Industry Subgroup 2006. Co-operation and Partnerships between the World of Business and Science as an Instrument for Enhancing Innovation.

Lester, R. 2005. Universities, Innovation and the Competitiveness of Local Economies: A summary report from the Local Innovation Systems project – Phase 1. *MIT IPC Working Paper IPC-05-010*.

Leydesdorff, L. and Etzkowitz, H. 2001. The Transformation of University-Industry-Government Relations, *Journal of Sociology*.

Union of Capitals of the European Union, the, 2002. Co-operation and Local Partnerships between Cities and Universities: Experiences of European Union Capital Cities.

Winden, W. van, and van den Berg, L. 2004. Cities in the Knowledge Economy: New Governance Challenges, Ministry of the Interior and Kingdom Relations, Rotterdam.

Work Foundation, the, 2006. *Enabling Cities in the Knowledge Economy.*

Chapter 11

The Influence of the Urban-Rural Gap on the R&D and Innovation Potential in Romania

Anca Dachin, Daniela L. Constantin and Zizi Goschin

11.1. Introduction

The regional scale for the generation of new knowledge and its economic exploitation have become more and more important and policy actions have been adopted by central and regional authorities towards promoting integrative processes and innovation in regions. The formation of regional clusters and the development of partnerships between actors involved in production, R&D and innovation increase the regions' development potential. This issue is of a particular concern when the lagging regions are considered, and the main question which arises in such a case refers to the capacity of regional policy to support the creation of factors able to foster technological innovation in these regions (Frenkel, 2000). The effectiveness of regional policy in this respect is closely related to the regional innovation potential and innovativeness, which may display significant variations.

Both theory and empirical observations point out that in many cases the results are closely related to the presence and the quality of economic linkages between urban centres and their surrounding rural areas (Scottish Government, 2005), bearing in mind the higher share of rural population in most lagging regions. According to the current viewpoints on integrated and sustainable rural development, a living rurality requires a new policy based on packages of measures that aim to encourage the immigration of new population and activities and to provide a stronger support for the improvement of competitiveness and attractiveness of rural areas by developing essential services, infrastructure and technologies. Thus, synergies between territories based on solidarity and cooperation is encouraged (RURAN (2007), Gurria (2007)).

In the European Union, rural areas benefit from increased support to research and innovation as a result of complementarities established between rural development policy and cohesion policy. At the regional level better territorial cohesion can be ensured via rural-urban synergies created by integrated governance (Ruract, 2008). The urban centres located in predominantly rural areas are very attractive for rural development initiatives as a result of their institutional capacity necessary to manage regional, national or European initiatives in a reliable and accountable manner. Also, the concentration of rural development initiatives in small towns may allow the benefits to spread out into the surrounding countryside (Scottish Government, 2005).

For Romania these potential benefits are of a special interest, given the important allocations from the EU funds via the cohesion and common agricultural policy. Romania still has a big share of rural population, and the increase of the quality of life in rural areas is a must. This requirement is strongly related to the development of non-agricultural activities while the cooperation with the urban centres can be extremely helpful.

Our chapter proposes an inquiry into the capacity of urban centres to contribute to rural development in Romania from the R&D and innovation perspective. First, the rural-urban gap is discussed, pointing to the consequences of the delay in implementing the reform of the production system in agriculture in terms of employment and income. Then the positive influence of towns and cities on raising the share of employment in non-agricultural activities in rural areas is demonstrated by means of the available statistical data. Later on, the analysis of the regional dimension of R&D and innovation shows an increasing polarization both between and within the eight development regions. The main conclusion is that the regions or counties with predominantly agricultural activities which have developed in subsistence households are not enough prepared to access R&D and innovation results. This conclusion is also confirmed by the regression model presented in the next section, which analyses the influence of rural areas on regional growth. The above findings are examined in relation to the expected positive contribution of the current rural development programme, as well as of the regional operational programme and competitiveness sectoral programme funded by the EU.

11.2. The Rural-urban Gap in Romania

Of the EU countries, Romania has the highest share of rural population (45 per cent) and most of it is employed in agriculture. Romanian agriculture has radically changed its ownership structures. Private ownership has become dominant and has created the conditions for market competition. But the agricultural structures which can give an impulse to economic expansion by an efficient use of human, natural and financial resources still do not allow the normal functioning of the market.

In Romania the sector of small family subsistence production units in agriculture is very resistant and it has survived after 1990, based on the structure of the old rural households. Nevertheless, it has experienced some decline in recent years. The total number of agricultural holdings at the end of the year 2007 was 3.93 million, compared with 4.26 million in 2005 and 4.48 million in 2002 (NIS, 2007). In 2007 the share of holdings up to 5 hectares represented 89.6 per cent of the total number and 35.1 per cent of the total utilized agricultural area. However, in order to reach the competitive average size of 10 hectares per holding, the number of subsistence holdings should decrease by 2.4 million by 2013.

The delay in implementing a real reform of the production system in agriculture keeps a high level of employment in this branch. In the period 2002-2008 there was a significant reduction of employment in the rural areas while in the urban areas there was an opposite trend (Table 11.1).

Table 11.1 Employment by area of residence, 2002-2007

Year	Urban		Rural	
	Employment (in 1000 persons)	Employment rate[1] (%)	Employment (in 1000 persons)	Employment rate[1] (%)
2002	4607	53.7	4627	63.7
2003	4662	54.0	4561	62.9
2004	4906	55.9	4252	60.6
2005	4889	55.0	4258	61.6
2006	5115	57.2	4198	61.1
2007	5072	56.8	4281	61.5

Note: 1. Calculated for working age population (15-64 years).

Source: Romanian Statistical Yearbooks Time Series 1990-2007 and 2008, National Institute for Statistics.

The employment rate in Romania is higher in the rural areas compared with the urban areas for the working age population (15-64 years). In addition, in 2007 about 19 per cent of the farmers and skilled workers employed in agriculture forestry and fishery were elderly people of 64 years and over.

In Romania the labour force employed in agriculture, hunting and forestry reached a peak of 41.4 per cent of total employment in the year 2000. This process extended the subsistence economy. After 2000, the sustained economic growth created favourable conditions for the development of non-agricultural activities and determined the reduction of employment in agriculture down to 28.2 per cent in 2007. During the economic growth period (2000-2008), agriculture gradually lost its status of employment buffer specific to the transition period (Toma et al., 2009). This demonstrates the unsustainable economic development in the rural areas. However, it is expected that the prolonged period of economic crisis during 2009 could result in higher net migration flows from urban to rural areas.

Since subsistence agriculture is still a major option for people living in the rural areas, the rural households largely depend on income from agriculture. In 2008 the total income of households in the rural areas consisted of gross salaries (29.5 per cent), the equivalent value of consumption of agricultural products from their own farms (28.5 per cent), income from social security (24.4 per cent), money income from agriculture (6.3 per cent) and income from non-agricultural independent activities (3.8 per cent). This structure shows that most households are not connected to the labour market and are less prepared to develop market-oriented farms or other production units.

The rural population has lower income than the urban population because of the dominant employment in agriculture, which has low productivity. In 2008 the average income per household in the rural areas was only about 72.3 per cent of the average urban income. The expected increase of agricultural income as a result of the application of the Common Agricultural Policy could diminish these differences.

The potential of multifunctional agriculture and of the rural areas as a whole is a starting point for the development of non-agricultural activities. In recent years the share of gross salaries has increased in the rural areas, from 21 per cent in 2002 to 29.5 per cent in 2008. The alternative non-agricultural activities are attractive for the younger rural population. The possibility to work for a salary in a non-agricultural activity is a good reason for them to give up self-employment. The gradual increase of the total income on the basis of a higher share of salaries is already a trend in the rural areas that will continue after the recovery from the economic crisis.

11.3. The Role of Urban Centres in Rural Areas

The unequal distribution of rural population by region is correlated with the employment rates and the development disparities by region (Table 11.2). In the regions with the highest share of rural population, the main activity is agriculture, while the GDP per capita is the lowest.

Rural areas with higher employment in non-agricultural activities are under the influence of cities. The distribution of municipalities and towns in Romania has been determined by historical and geographical conditions, industrial development, as well as by the territorial policy aimed at balanced urban-rural development.

Towns are urban agglomerations with an administrative function and a lifestyle specific to the urban areas, where people are employed mainly in non-agricultural activities. Municipalities are towns with an important economic, social, political and cultural role, which usually also have an administrative function.

Most counties that have employment in agriculture under the national average of 28.2 per cent are in the sphere of influence of major municipalities, such as Bucharest for Ilfov county, Braşov for Braşov county and Covasna county, Sibiu for Sibiu county, Constanţa for Constanţa county, Ploieşti for Prahova county, Timişoara for Timiş county, Cluj for Cluj county, Arad for Arad county, Piteşti for Argeş county (Table 11.3). Hunedoara county has an industrial profile, dominated by activities in mining and metallurgy, while urban life is dispersed in several smaller municipalities (cities) and towns.

Table 11.2 Population, employment and development indicators in Romania, by NUTS 2 region

Development regions	Rural population 2007 (%)	Employment rate[1] 2007 (%)	Employment in agriculture[2], 2007 (% of civil employment)	GDP per capita 2006 (EUROSTAT estimation in PPS)
Romania	44.9	56.1	28.2	8800
North-West	46.6	57.0	31.1	8500
Centre	40.4	55.1	23.5	9100
North-East	56.6	61.3	39.5	5800
South-East	44.7	54.7	31.5	7700
Bucharest-Ilfov	7.6	62.4	3.5	19800
South – Muntenia	58.4	60.5	35.8	7600
South-West Oltenia	52.3	59.3	38.0	7200
West	36.6	59.6	23.7	10600

Notes: 1. Calculated for working age population (15-64 years).

2. Includes hunting and forestry.

Sources: Economic and Social Regional References: Territorial Statistics 2009, National Institute of Statistics (NIS) Romania, and EUROSTAT

Table 11.3 Rural population and urban centers in Romania in 2007, by county

	Employment in agriculture (%)	Rural population (%)	Number of towns	Number of municipalities
Teleorman	54.9	66.3	2	2
Giurgiu	53.1	68.8	2	1
Botoşani	48.8	58.3	5	2
Călăraşi	48.0	61.4	3	2
Vaslui	47.6	58.8	2	3
Ialomiţa	44.8	54.2	4	3
Olt	44.7	59.4	6	2
Suceava	44.3	57.1	11	5

	Employment in agriculture (%)	Rural population (%)	Number of towns	Number of municipalities
Vrancea	43.7	62.2	3	2
Mehedinţi	43.7	51.4	3	2
Neamţ	42.7	61.8	3	2
Buzău	40.7	58.6	3	2
Dolj	39.4	46.3	4	3
Satu Mare	37.3	52.3	4	2
Maramureş	37.2	41.2	11	2
Dâmboviţa	35.0	68.8	5	2
Tulcea	35.0	50.7	4	1
Bistriţa-Năsăud	34.7	63.3	3	1
Sălaj	34.5	59.1	3	1
Caraş-Severin	34.3	43.6	6	2
Vâlcea	33.0	54.6	9	2
Harghita	31.9	55.9	5	4
Iaşi	31.8	52.3	3	2
Bihor	31.2	49.7	6	4
Bacău	29.9	54.3	5	3
Mureş	29.7	47.5	7	4
Brăila	29.7	34.9	3	1
Galaţi	29.2	43.5	2	2
Alba	28.8	41.7	7	4
Gorj	28.4	53.0	7	2
Covasna	27.6	49.9	3	2
Argeş	27.3	52.1	4	3
Ilfov	22.9	57.8	8	0
Arad	22.4	44.6	9	1
Cluj	22.2	32.9	1	5
Timiş	22.1	37.2	8	2
Prahova	21.6	49.5	12	2
Constanţa	21.4	29.6	9	3
Hunedoara	21.2	23.2	7	7
Sibiu	15.7	32.6	9	2
Braşov	13.1	25.8	6	4

Source: Economic and Social Regional References: Territorial Statistics 2009, National Institute of Statistics (NIS) Romania.

The most obvious forms of relationship between towns and rural areas are trade, employment opportunities, migration and remittances, exchange of population and services to the rural area.

The rural areas around towns are the source of fresh food that farmers sell in the urban markets. Improvement in transport and the development of intermediate markets provide additional opportunities, since small shops can develop in villages, based on trade relations with towns. Many farm families are diversifying their sources of income by involvment in transport and commercial services.

The income gap between rural and urban areas causes people to look to the cities for a livelihood. Employment opportunities in small towns are most often in traditional industries, commerce and services. Younger people are more inclined to move to towns, while they still rely on social networks based on their place of origin. Some of these urban migrants support their extended rural family by remittances. At the same time, the rural family provides food. In Romania, the equivalent value of consumption of agricultural products from their own resources in urban families was about 6.4 per cent of the average total income per person in 2007. This share is much higher in small towns situated in predominantly rural areas.

In Romania after 1990 there was a trend of urban-rural migration. Since 1996 there has been a positive net migration flow into the rural areas, but this did not change the share of rural population. In 2007 the net migration flow to the rural areas was +38,002 persons representing only 0.39 per cent of the rural population. The migration trend shows rather an exchange of population, meaning that younger people move to the towns and elderly people move to villages, especially after retirement. Emigration is more and more selective in terms of age and level of education.

The international emigration of rural population has intensified in the last decade. Initially, migrants came mainly from the more developed Western regions of Romania, but recently there as been growing emigration flow from the Eastern and poorer regions. Many rural emigrants work only temporarily abroad. International migration from the rural areas has some particularities (UNDP, 2003-2005). On the one hand, some of the migrants for work who live in villages have had a long experience of mobility even before 1990, through commuting to large urban plants. That is why communities with large flows of migration are around the major cities of Romania, especially in Western and Eastern regions. On the other hand, villages with low international migration are concentrated in regions where there is the strong attraction of an urban centre (like Bucharest).

Urban centers, including small towns, also extend their influence into the surrounding rural areas by means of services. Firstly, there are the educational services. Village people prefer to send their children to school in town, even to the primary school if the town is close enough and provides good transport connections. Secondly, there are the communication services. In the last two decades in the rural areas there has been a dramatic expansion of mass media, especially television, and telecommunication services, especially mobile phones.

Access to specific services also depends on the proximity of towns. These service systems introduce the urban lifestyle and values in the rural areas.

The influence of small towns depends, however, on their economic, social and cultural strengths. Some counties in Romania have many urban centers, but with little polarization capacities. Examples are the North-East region, including the county of Suceava (5 municipalities and 11 towns) and the county of Botoşani (2 municipalities and 5 towns). These counties have a very high rural population, 44-49 per cent which is employed in agriculture. In a similar situation is the South-West Oltenia region, with the counties of Olt (2 municipalities and 6 towns) and Valcea (2 municipalities and 9 towns). Actually some of the towns are rural-type localities with additional functions in public services. They may gain the capacity to stimulate the rural settlements and stabilize the skilled labour force in the long run if they engage more in production activities by developing companies able to use the resources provided by the rural area.

Rural development is a key concept of the EU Common Agricultural Policy and refers to the restructuring of agriculture, diversification of activities, and innovation in rural areas. Besides agriculture, the environment and associated tourism are major opportunities for employment in rural areas, as well as potential fields of innovation. Small towns could play a complementary role, by extending the ICT infrastructure, developing the agro-food chain, cooperating in R&D in specific fields (agriculture, natural environment), etc.

11.4. The Regional Dimension of R&D and Innovation in Romania

In Romania, the research and experimental development potential is concentrated mainly in the Bucharest-Ilfov region and in other few counties established at NUTS 3 level (Table 11.2). The R&D activities in the selected counties have actually developed actually around large urban agglomerations which are also important higher education centers.

After 2000, the industrial restructuration in the context of economic growth, the increasing foreign direct investment, and the integration of Romanian research units in the European research networks resulted in an increasing *R&D polarization within regions*. Bucharest has an outstanding position regarding R&D personnel (Figure 11.1). In the period 2000-2007 the most dynamic counties were Iaşi, Cluj and Ilfov, while Bucharest moved part of its R&D activity to Ilfov county. Also the Argeş had county good dynamics, mainly connected to the inflow of foreign investment in the automobile industry. In the same period all other counties relevant for R&D activities had a decline in R&D.

The analysis of R&D expenditures as a synthetic indicator reveals about the same territorial distribution. The selected 13 counties and Bucharest cover together about 92 per cent from the total R&D expenditures in Romania. The largest share (57.6 per cent) is attracted to the Bucharest-Ilfov region (Figure 11.2). The capital city, which is the largest development pole in Romania, has an important influence

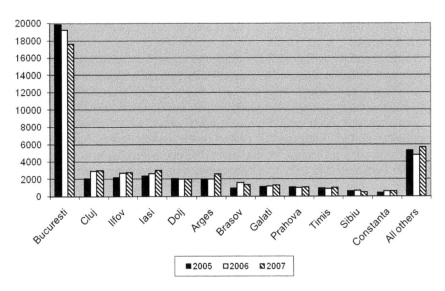

Figure 11.1   Number of employed in R&D (persons at the end of the year) in selected counties of Romania, 2005-2007

Source: Territorial Statistics 2009, National Institute of Statistics (NIS) Romania

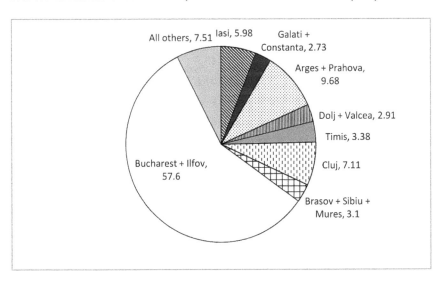

Figure 11.2   R&D expenditures in Romania, by selected counties, 2007 (% of total)

Source: Data from *Territorial Statistics 2009*, National Institute of Statistics (NIS) Romania

on its county Ilfov, which alone has R&D activity even higher than that of Cluj and Iasi counties.

These significant territorial R&D disparities are also connected to the uneven distribution of income measured by regional GDP per capita. This makes Bucharest the only region in Romania that is less vulnerable to globalization, according to the assessment of the European Commission over the medium term to 2020 (EC, 2008).

The economic development of some urban areas has contributed and also benefited from R&D. Only in a few comparatively developed areas have the R&D expenditures as a percentage of regional GDP exceedeed the national average in 2006: Bucharest and Ilfov (1.23 per cent), Argeş (0.88 per cent), Cluj (0.78 per cent) and Iaşi (0.79 per cent) (Table 11.4). Even though Iasi is located in the North East region, which is the poorest region in Romania and in the EU27, it nevertheless has a strong dynamic due to its position as a higher education and research centre.

It is obvious that the national average is hiding important regional disparities, even if the absolute R&D input effort is rather low.

Table 11.4   R&D input indicators in Romania, by region and by selected county

Development regions/ counties	Employed in R&D / 10000 civil employed		R&D expenditures / regional GDP (in %)
	2006	2007	2006
Romania	**49.9**	**48.7**	**0.63**
North-West	**30.2**	**33.1**	**0.28**
Cluj	92.7	91.2	0.78
Center	**28.0**	**25.2**	**0.15**
Braşov	68.2	58.1	0.23
Sibiu	37.6	26.8	0.21
Mureş	19.0	18.7	0.15
North-East	**31.9**	**32.9**	**0.28**
Iaşi	90.9	101.2	0.79
South-East	**20.1**	**20.8**	**0.14**
Galaţi	59.3	63.3	0.36
Constanţa	20.4	20.5	0.10
Bucharest-Ilfov	**194.1**	**168.0**	**1.23**
Bucharest, capital city	194.2	165.7	1.06
Ilfov	193.6	184.7	2.58
South – Muntenia	**32.0**	**36.0**	**0.33**

Development regions/ counties	Employed in R&D / 10000 civil employed		R&D expenditures / regional GDP (in %)
	2006	**2007**	**2006**
Argeş	79.8	100.4	0.88
Prahova	34.6	35.8	0.18
South-West Oltenia	**29.2**	**28.6**	**0.19**
Dolj	74.0	71.6	0.35
Vâlcea	12.1	12.9	0.31
West	**18.9**	**26.7**	**0.19**
Timiş	27.2	30.0	0.33

Source: Territorial Statistics 2009, National Institute of Statistics (NIS) Romania.

The innovation process is also strongly connected to the level of GDP/capita. Again Bucharest has the best position, much above the rest of the regions. The Innovation Score (IRECSON, 2008) for Romania, based on 64 criteria of analysis (including indicators from the European Innovation Scoreboard – EIS), shows the regional differences (Table 11.5). Considering the general score per region, there is a little difference between seven NUTS 2 regions, while the Bucharest-Ilfov region has a value at least double that of the other regions. However, some examples are relevant:

The South-East region (including Galaţi – Constanţa) has the lowest potential for knowledge creation, also in connection with comparatively low R&D efforts, but has a good score just lowest than that of Bucharest regarding the potential for innovation management and the efficiency of innovative activities.

The North-West region (including Cluj) has good potential for innovation and integration in a network system, considering also that the R&D expenditures /regional GDP in Cluj county reached 0.78 per cent, which is higher than the national average.

The North-East region (including Iasi) tries to overcome its economic disadvantages by the inclusion of people in permanent education programmes and by comparatively high efforts in marketing, promotion and R&D efforts. In Iasi county the number of companies with R&D and a high-tech profile had the highest dynamics in the business sector in the period 2000-2006.

The three examples given above show that a similar innovation score may be reached starting from various situations.

Table 11.5   Innovation indicators in Romania, by region

Development regions	Number of companies 2004-2006	Innovative enterprises, % of total 2004-2006 %	Innovation expenditures (per1000 lei of regional GDP in 2004) in lei	Innovation score
Romania	**28488**	**21.1**	**18.6**	-
North-West	4288	21.2	18.4	29.56
Centre	4026	20.1	19.7	28.90
North-East	3226	26.7	9.1	29.44
South-East	3026	43.2	25.0	31.73
Bucharest-Ilfov	6394	15.5	20.5	72.49
South – Muntenia	2883	19.9	25.4	28.04
South-West Oltenia	1686	13.9	23.7	21.35
West	2959	11.1	4.8	26.05

Source: Economic and Social Regional References: Territorial Statistics 2008, National Institute of Statistics (NIS) Romania, EUROSTAT and Inobarometru 2008, and own calculations.

The need for permanent links between the R&D system and business was the reason for the construction of the National Innovation Network and Technology Transfer (ReNITT, 2008) in Romania. This institution building is strongly supported from public financial sources and encourages partnership in this field. The network is composed of centres for technological information, centres for technological transfer, technological and business incubators and scientific and technological parks.

The distribution of the network shows the institutional efforts of the national authorities to construct a network for technological information centres covering all regions. All other forms of technological transfer need a strong partnership with the business sector, and these links could be established mainly in the Bucharest-Ilfov region and in a limited number of cities with universities and important industrial activity.

The creation of a stimulative environment for innovation-based development highly depends on the geographical proximity to industrial agglomerations, as well as on the R&D institutional structures. Regions or counties with predominantly agricultural activity in subsistence households are not prepared to access R&D results or to innovate. This conclusion is confirmed by the model presented in the next section, which analyses the influence of rural areas on regional growth.

11.5. The Determinants of Economic Growth from a Spatial Perspective

11.5.1. The model

This section aims to explore, by means of a regression model, the driving forces of Romanian economic growth from a spatial perspective, focusing on the influence of rural areas. Using the available territorial data regarding Romania's economy in 2007, we have built up a corresponding spatial data series (Table 11.6) for performing an analysis based on the linear multiple regression model. Our analysis can shed important light on critical dilemmas of development that are specific to rural areas in Romania.

Table 11.6 Main economic indicators by county, 2007

Regions Counties	Gross domestic product (in million lei, in current prices) 2007	Gross fixed capital formation (in million lei, in current prices) 2007	Employed population (persons) 2007	R&D total expenditures (in million lei, in current prices) 2007	R&D employees (persons) 2007	% rural population 2007	CDI* 2006
North – West							
Bihor	11355.36	2618.703	277901	6.757	503	49.704	0.359554
Bistriţa-Năsăud	4897.038	988.1226	126712	27.315	185	63.327	0.317787
Cluj	16248.68	5184.089	329825	154.812	3008	32.924	0.555759
Maramureş	7109.172	1235.153	198889	3.413	179	41.180	0.305956
Satu Mare	5632.139	918.8119	150000	1.161	48	52.307	0.287961
Sălaj	3659.926	632.6828	100000	1.415	17	59.140	0.307995
Center							
Alba	7159.385	1484.85	173826	3.801	259	41.734	0.344617
Braşov	13495.59	5516.426	237177	48.653	1378	25.825	0.375229
Covasna	3331.204	445.1883	87179	2.398	34	49.872	0.284523
Harghita	5350.275	1073.428	131250	0.392	42	55.924	0.280716
Mureş	9795.874	1998.46	238503	12.635	446	47.518	0.383864
Sibiu	9152.811	3363.349	179851	6.377	482	32.655	0.413467
North – East							
Bacău	10193.62	2016.232	225641	5.925	352	54.278	0.314137
Botoşani	4267.876	510.0561	154348	2.871	71	58.300	0.200203
Iaşi	12032.7	3697.462	297727	130.298	3013	52.322	0.369709

Regions Counties	Gross domestic product (in million lei, in current prices) 2007	Gross fixed capital formation (in million lei, in current prices) 2007	Employed population (persons) 2007	R&D total expenditures (in million lei, in current prices) 2007	R&D employees (persons) 2007	% rural population 2007	CDI* 2006
Neamț	7013.899	1323.125	196721	5.704	120	61.850	0.26486
Suceava	8454.141	1875.833	243810	14.199	512	57.089	0.288155
Vaslui	4092.31	446.0769	146667	4.564	88	58.781	0.118712
South – East							
Brăila	4980.567	868.1617	131429	3.305	92	34.928	0.302739
Buzău	6392.527	1572.821	182759	1.945	53	58.653	0.260105
Constanța	17560.57	4253.726	302439	19.764	620	29.568	0.422238
Galați	8579.734	2189.509	206477	39.678	1307	43.478	0.3006
Tulcea	3627.928	485.1753	88060	15.12	118	50.738	0.265761
Vrancea	5007.651	598.0274	137500	0.818	11	62.242	0.284095
Bucharest - Ilfov							
Ilfov	10422.04	6314.388	149432	288.781	2760	57.842	0.511339
Bucharest Municipality	82706.53	43877.26	1062161	965.503	17600	0.000	0.930337
South - Muntenia							
Argeș	14106.29	4355.915	259661	167.737	2607	52.083	0.397657
Călărași	3219.872	757.9754	101534	8.684	331	61.452	0.143224
Dâmbovița	7672.782	1353.337	202532	11.366	320	68.831	0.31466
Giurgiu	2969.166	579.3669	87500	0.178	7	68.827	0.244634
Ialomița	4004.227	507.3903	100000	0.056	1	54.162	0.234728
Prahova	16508.37	4270.609	303631	43.073	1087	49.468	0.392827

Regions Counties	Gross domestic product (in million lei, in current prices) 2007	Gross fixed capital formation (in million lei, in current prices) 2007	Employed population (persons) 2007	R&D total expenditures (in million lei, in current prices) 2007	R&D employees (persons) 2007	% rural population 2007	CDI* 2006
Teleorman	4610.26	516.2763	164286	0.676	23	66.356	0.205904
South - West Oltenia							
Dolj	10593.17	2496.076	276397	38.517	1979	46.347	0.345515
Gorj	7171.369	1052.102	139506	2.397	226	52.963	0.352766
Mehedinţi	3890.738	796.1851	113208	1.089	60	51.394	0.252298
Olt	5465.202	1157.845	172727	0.941	19	59.457	0.241774
Vâlcea	7140.93	1257.368	172093	24.849	222	54.604	0.372167
West							
Arad	10074.62	1973.579	211315	21.083	691	44.630	0.385476
Caraş-Severin	5327.146	1073.428	122857	2.579	129	43.619	0.255169
Hunedoara	8229.56	1692.782	199194	14.413	494	23.196	0.341769
Timiş	19258.23	6317.942	335667	73.508	1007	37.238	0.534898

*Composite Development Index.

Source: Authors' processing based on data provided by the Statistical Yearbook of Romania and Territorial Statistics Yearbook.

Variables of the linear multiple regression model. The following statistical data were used at the county level:

> The dependent variable is Gross Domestic Product - GDP as an expression of output; Gross fixed capital formation - K as an approximation of the capital production factor: even if these data do not reflect entirely the production factor capital, they represent currently the best available information in the Romanian official statistics;
> Employed population - L as the labour factor;
> R&D total expenditures - Kr: are used in this model as a measure of total investments (material and intangible) in the R&D sector;
> R&D employees - Lr;
> Percentage of rural population R;
> Composite territorial index of development (CDI) (ranging from 0-lowest performance to 1-top position) computed as weighted average of various indicators grouped in four blocks: economy, health, education, infrastructure and standard of living.

The model is specified by the following equation:

$$GDP_{ti} = aK_{ti} + bL_{ti} + cKr_{ti}, + dLr_{ti} + eR_{ti} + fCDI_{t-1,i} + \varepsilon_{ti}, \quad i=1,...,42, \quad t=2007 \quad (1)$$

The hypothesis to be tested is that territorial variation in GDP can be explained partly by the size of rural areas. To allow for other influences, the capital and labour production factors were included in the model, together with the number of R&D employees and the R&D total expenditures as a proxy for R&D investments. The estimation model in this chapter uses only information on R&D expenditure, not R&D stock, which brings about the advantage that there is no need for strong assumptions with regard to R&D activity, such as a fixed rate of depreciation and the linear and certain accumulation of knowledge.

The economic and social development of the counties was also included by means of a composite territorial index CDI, which is one-year lagged to capture persistence of the development level. The composite index had been computed as a weighted average of various indicators grouped in the following blocks: economy, health, education, infrastructure and standard of living (Box 11.1). The value of the index is at least 0 (if the same county has the lowest performance for all variables included in the index) and at most 1 (if one county is in top position for all variables). The computations undertaken for the year 2006 showed that the values of the composite index of development range from 0.930 for the capital city Bucharest to 0.119 for the least developed county – Vaslui, but most of the counties belong to the 0.2-0.4 interval.

Box 11.1   Methodology for the Composite Territorial Index of Development

The economic and social development of the counties and regions was estimated by means of a Composite Territorial Index of Development computed as an weighted average of various indicators grouped in the following blocks: economy, health, education, infrastructure and standard of living.

The components of the Composite Territorial Index of Development

	Indicators	Unit of measurement	Coefficient of variation (%)
Economy	GDP per capita	1000 RON/ inhabitant	35.10
	Average net monthly earnings	RON/employee	11.98
	Unemployment rate	%	36.14
Health	Hospital beds/1000 inhabitants	Beds/1000 inhabitants	26.32
	Number of physicians/1000 inhabitants	Physicians/1000 inhabitantss	55.35
	Infant deaths	Death under 1 year of age per 1000 new-borns	23.43
	Life expectancy	Years	1.28
Education	Drop rate in primary and secondary education	%	33.70
	Number of students per 1000 inhabitants	Students/1000 inhabitants	141.66
Infrastructure	Density of town streets	km/100 skm	406.11
	Density of public sewerage	km/100 skm	467.6
	Density of green spots in municipalities and towns	%	556.5
Standard of living	Residencial floor space	sqm/inhabitant	9.23
	Volume of natural gas distribution	cm/ inhabitant	225.49
	Volume of drinking water supplied to consumers	cm/ inhabitant	47.56
	Criminality rate	Persons convicted /100000 inhabitants	24.21

Source: Authors.

The value of this composite index is at least 0 (if the same county has the lowest performance for all variables included in the index) and at most 1 (if one county is in the top position for all variables).

11.5.2. The results

We ran the regression specified in equation (1). The parameters of the regression model were estimated using Ordinary Least Squares (OLS) and the regression coefficients are shown in Table 11.7.

The regression results indicate that regional GDP is positively related to changes in capital and labour production factors. As expected, the lagged development level CDI is also positively linked to GDP territorial variation, while the percentage of rural areas seems to negatively influence the GDP level, although the high standard error does not permit for definite results. The number of R&D employees and the R&D total expenditures also give inconclusive because of the unexpected sign indicating a lack of linkage to the GDP level. This territorial dissimilarity between R&D and GDP is consistent with their time-series dissimilarity: the persistent decline of R&D activity in Romania, in contrast to strong economic growth in Romania in recent years may be indicative of the lower contribution of national research to this economic growth, as most foreign companies investing in Romania rely on the research activities performed in their own countries.

Table 11.7   Determinants of territorial Gross Domestic Product, 2007

Coefficient/ Statistics	Estimate
K (coefficient) t-Statistic	1.318787 (10.25227)*
L (coefficient) t-Statistic	0.031496 (8.311334)*
Kr (coefficient) t-Statistic	-6.4763 (-0.86494)
Lr (coefficient) t-Statistic	-0.36704 (-0.8215)
R (coefficient) t-Statistic	-6.17816 (-0.37955)
CDI (coefficient) t-Statistic	6222.328 (2.413376)**
R-squared	0.9960
F-statistic and Prob (F)	1497.267 (0.0000)

Notes: *significant at the 99% level; **significant at the 95% level.

The R-squared and F-statistic are both very high indicating the good fit of the model. The correlation matrix is presented in Appendix A 11.1.

11.6. Concluding Remarks

In Romania the rural population is partly employed in small family subsistence households and highly depends on low productivity agriculture. The delay in implementing a real reform of the production system has kept the share of employment in agriculture at 28.2 per cent in 2007, which is an extremely high share compared with the other EU27 countries. The low performance in agriculture, connected to a less educated and ageing labour force, as well as the insufficient opportunities for non-agricultural activities are the main causes for the rural-urban income gap.

In the regions with the highest share of rural population, the main activity is agriculture, while the GDP per capita is the lowest. Most counties which have employment in agriculture below the national average of 28.2 per cent are in the area of influence of major municipalities. The towns, which are smaller urban agglomerations with an administrative function and a lifestyle specific to the urban areas, develop a relationship with rural areas mainly regarding trade, employment opportunities, migration and remittances, exchange of population and services to the rural area.

The influence of small towns depends, however, on their economic, social and cultural strengths. Some counties in Romania have many urban centers, but with little polarization capacities. However, some of the towns are rural-type localities with additional functions in public services. They may gain the capacity to stimulate the rural settlements and stabilize the skilled labour force in the long run if they engage more in production activities by developing companies able to use the resources provided by the rural area. Small towns could play a complementary role, by extending the ICT infrastructure, developing the agro-food chain, cooperating in R&D in specific fields (agriculture, natural environment), etc.

Romania is lagging behind most EU countries and other developed countries regarding research potential and innovation performance, owing to low input efforts for R&D and innovation, as well as to the rather low cooperation capacity of firms with knowledge-creating partners.

In Romania there is increasing R&D polarization within regions, while the innovation-based development depends highly on the geographical proximity to industrial agglomerations, as well as to the R&D institutional structures. The involvement of small towns in the innovation process is rather low, but the situation may change as a result of stimulative programmes for rural development, as well as for the increase of SMEs competitiveness, supported by EU funds. Thus, the current measures of the National Programme for Rural Development envisage, among other things, support to: settling young farmers; establishing producer groups; developing the food industry; improving and developing agriculture and forestry infrastructure; establishing and developing micro-firms; promoting village development, involving the improvement of basic services for the rural economy. (MAPDR, 2009). The operational programmes can enhance the results of the rural development programme implementation since they can contribute to overall regional development, by improving the business environment, the social and transportation infrastructure, the quality of labour force, economic competitiveness, etc. In this way, the coherence and complementarity of common agricultural policy-derived measures with those supported via Structural Instruments can be ensured and, on this basis, also the prerequisites for a significant presence of R&D and innovation in the predominantly rural areas.

The analysis of the driving forces of Romanian economic growth in 2007, based on a linear multiple regression model, shows that the regional GDP is postively related to changes in capital and labour production factors. The lagged development level Composite Development Index is also positively linked to GDP territorial variation, while the percentage of rural areas seems to negatively influence the GDP level.

References

EC 2008. Regions 2020. An Assessment of Future Challenges for EU Regions. *European Commission staff working document*, Brussels.

Frenkel, A. 2000. Can regional policy affect firm's innovation potential in lagging regions?. *The Annals of Regional Science*, 34(3), 315-341.

Gurria, A. 2007. Innovation in Rural Areas: An Exception or A Must?. Plenary presentation at *OECD Rural Conference*, Caceres, Spain.

IRECSON 2008. *Innobarometer 2008. Innovation at development region level*, Report of the IRECSON Institute – Center for Technological Information, Bucharest (in Romanian).

MAPDR 2009. *National Programme for Rural Development*. Available at: http://www.maap.ro/.

National Institute of Statistics (NIS) Romania. 2007. *Farm Structure Survey.*

National Institute of Statistics (NIS) Romania. 2009. *Territorial Statistics.*

National Institute of Statistics (NIS) Romania. *Romanian Statistical Yearbooks Time Series 1990-2007 and 2008.*

Ruract 2008. *Regional Policy at the Service of Territorial Rural Development*. Available at: http://www.ruract.eu/spip.php?rubrique41.

RURAN 2007. *Innovation at the service of integrated and sustainable rural development*. Available at: http://www.agr.unideb.hu/hvtk/doc/velemeny03.pdf.

Scottish Government 2005. *Economic Linkages Between Small Towns and Surrounding Rural Areas in Scotland*. Final Report. Available at: http://www.scotland.gov.uk/Publications/2005/03/20911/55372.

Toma, E., Dachin, A. and Alexandri, C. (eds) 2009. *Romania's Agriculture in the Process of European Integration*. Bucharest: Ars Academica Publishing House (in Romanian).

UNDP 2003-2005. *National Human Development Report for Romania*, United Nations Development Programme.

Appendix A 11.1 The results from the multiple regression model

*Correlation matrix**

	GDP	K	L	KR	LR	R	CDI
GDP	1						
K	0.986553	1					
L	0.979816	0.945945	1				
KR	0.938835	0.969402	0.890284	1			
LR	0.964198	0.981223	0.933774	0.984511	1		
R	-0.68619	-0.65134	-0.67022	-0.56186	-0.61342	1	
CDI	0.871108	0.843122	0.84971	0.833364	0.826794	-0.71122	1

Notes: *Variables: Gross domestic product GDP; Gross fixed capital formation K; Employed population L; R&D total expenditures KR; R&D employees LR; Percentage of rural population R; Composite territorial index of development CDI.

Chapter 12

Rural Tourism in Peripheral Areas: Evidence from the Portuguese Municipality of Almeida

Fernando P. Fonseca and Rui A.R. Ramos

12.1. Introduction

Constrained by remoteness and underdevelopment, rural areas have limited options for economic development. In Portugal, this affects more or less severely all the inland and mountain areas, where demographic erosion has already led to the partial (and, in some cases, to the complete) depopulation of several villages and small towns. The recognition of this trend has been generating growing concern over these territories, as manifested in communitarian, national and regional programmes and plans to promote alternative ways of development. To stimulate rural economies, it has become inevitable for rural regions to seek alternative uses for local resources. The two main driving forces are grounded in the diversification of these economies and in the enlargement of new territorial functions. Despite the top down orientation of the public policies, rural communities have a determinant role in the management of local resources. Although they approach it with a strong cooperative and entrepreneurial mind, this is usually insufficient in these territories. The reversal of this strongly rooted path is perhaps the biggest challenge that these vulnerable territories have to face, in order to establish internal networks and new patterns of governance and collective mobilization.

With comparatively advantageous effects in income and employment generation, tourism is an option for enhancing rural lifestyles and for inducing positive changes in the distribution of income in underprivileged regions (Liu, 2006). In fact, tourism has been presented as a key activity to achieve the economic diversification and the social regeneration of less-favoured territories. In particular, tourism has been widely promoted as an effective source of income and employment, particularly in peripheral rural areas where traditional agrarian industries and activities have declined (Sharpley, 2002). The integration of such alternative sources may help to equilibrate local economies and to encourage local development. On the other hand, more and more tourists are seeking rural destinations which are able to offer pleasant experiences combining heritage, nature, landscape, authenticity and quietness. This may explain the enthusiasm around the potential of tourism to stimulate the economy of the less favoured territories.

Similarly to what is happening in Europe and overseas, in Portugal rural tourism (RT) has become a recurrent and strategic subject in a wide range of public speeches, written documents and policies, often aimied at sustaining the economy of peripheral territories. The purpose of this chapter is to investigate the extent to which this role for RT represents a realistic tourism development strategy. Based upon research on the development of RT in the Portuguese rural municipality of Almeida, it highlights the challenges and problems encountered by RT entrepreneurs. At the same time, this chapter identifies a number of issues, which oppose the success of RT development, and analyses the true impact of RT in this border municipality. The selection of Almeida as a case study for this research is supported by four main reasons: (i) the chapter extends previous research undertaken by the authors in this municipality (Fonseca, 2006; Fonseca and Ramos, 2007; Fonseca and Ramos, 2008b); (ii) Almeida is located in peripheral and underprivileged region and shows a cycle of demographic and economic decline; (iii) the municipality has several important attractions to reinforce its position in the RT segment; and (iv) local actors classify tourism as the most promising activity to reverse Almeida's economic, social and cultural decline. These findings are supported by a survey from 2008 carried out with the owners of RT establishments located in Almeida.

In order to reach the aims outlined above, the chapter is organized as follows. In Section 12.2 we revisit the relevant literature about tourism benefits and constraints in the socio-economic regeneration of peripheral territories. Then, we trace the origins and evolution of RT, focusing the analysis on the Portuguese context. Finally, in Section 12.3 we present and discuss the results of the Almeida case study, comparing the findings extracted from RT entrepreneur's surveys with the principles derived in Section 12.2. Section 12.4 concludes.

12.2. The Relation between Tourism and Rural Development

12.2.1. The golden view of tourism as a development tool

Tourism as a strategy for economic growth has been on the international and Portuguese regional development agenda for some time and in different contexts. Peripheral rural areas in many countries have undergone economic restructuring since the early 1990s, as part of the transition from Fordist to Post-Fordist methods of production (Cawley and Gillmor, 2008). Sharpley (2002) emphasizes that a significant portion of the European structural funding has been invested in tourist development projects. This includes 1/3 of the funds provided by the LEADER (an EU Communitarian programme geared to the development of rural economies), which were invested in projects related to tourism. Furthermore, RT development programmes have become increasingly common elsewhere, such as those in the

USA, where 30 states have developed tourism policies specifically targeted at rural areas (Sharpley, 2002). Also Israel et al. (1997) show that, despite its recent origin, RT is a growing activity and an alternative way of obtaining supplements in the rural settlements (*kibbutzim*), where agriculture has declined. In Malaysia, tourism is largely seen as an economic tool of rural development and regional authorities anticipate a strong growth in the tourist industry (Liu, 2006). Also in many other countries, including Canada, Australia, New Zealand and in the Eastern Europe and Pacific regions, tourism is employed as a vehicle of economic growth and diversification for rural areas (Sharpley, 2002).

In Portugal, tourism is being considered as a tool for rural development by several policies, plans and authors. At the national scale, the National Strategic Plan for Rural Development (published in 2007) supports tourist investments in rural areas as a way to diversify rural economies. The National Programme for Territorial Planning Policy (Law number 58/2007, 4 September) highlights the development of tourist initiatives in the depressed rural areas through the exploitation of their heritage and natural values. Also the National Strategic Plan for Tourism (Resolution of the Council of Ministers number 53/2007, 4 April) classifies as *strategic* many products that are frequently located in rural areas: namely, nature tourism, health/wellness tourism and cultural touring. At the municipal scale, tourism also occupies a key position in development policies and in political speeches, and is often considered a priority sector. Moreira (2000) identifies tourism as having an important role in the peripheral municipalities due to the lack of other alternatives and sources of development. In these cases, tourism appears almost as the last opportunity to save the future of rural communities. Furthermore, there is a large number of publications focused on the experiences of tourism in the development of unfavoured areas (Buhalis, 1999; MacDonald and Jolliffe, 2003; Nash and Martin, 2003), as well as on the advantages of developing tourism initiatives in the Portuguese peripheral territories (Cristóvão, 1999; Ribeiro and Marques, 2000).

If there is such a strong agreement, what benefits can tourism actually bring to the development of peripheral areas? According to Sharpley (2002), the support given to tourism by public and private entities is expected in response to the downturn suffered by several rural economies, which has caused the decrease of employment and income levels of traditional agrarian activities. That may explain why tourism has been embraced as a potential tool to overcome the declining trend of these areas. In fact, the interest of tourism as a development strategy has grown in recent decades, partly in response to the changes in agricultural and rural policies and also to the changes in thinking and practice in the tourism market (Snowdon et al., 1997).

The benefits brought by tourism are interrelated and can be summarized in three great domains: economic, social and environmental/cultural. Tourism has been identified as one of the primary activities with the potential to assist local communities in developing economic diversity (Byrd et al., 2009), reducing reliance on agriculture and providing new economic opportunities. In this sense, tourism can contribute to economic growth and to the diversification of local economic resources. This can be achieved through the creation of jobs in both new (tourism-related) and existing businesses, trades and crafts, and by the emergence of new markets for agricultural products. In turn, this can support a wide range of services and activities related to tourism, e.g. commerce, dynamism, culture, and transport (EC, 1998; Fleischer, 1999; Cardoso, 2001). Hence, tourism has the potential to introduce new activities by reinforcing rural regions as places of leisure, as well as being residential areas and spaces with heritage value (Caffyn and Dahlström, 2005; Covas and Covas, 2007). At the same time, tourism is proposed as a vehicle to renew agriculture and other rural production by creating an added-value commercial channel for local produce (Liu, 2006) that is mostly demanded by tourists for its singularity and quality (Fleischer and Tchetchik, 2005). In the social domain, it is believed that tourism can also bring important contributions. According to Cànoves et al. (2004), tourism can contribute to the maintenance of public services (health care, public transport, equipment, etc.) and increases opportunities for social contacts and exchange, thus reducing the isolation of the communities. In some cases, tourism can also contribute to the repopulation of rural areas. With regard to the cultural domain, tourism should offer support for the preservation of landscapes and stimulate the protection, conservation and improvement of natural ecosystems (Garcia-Ramon et al., 1995; López-López, 2001; Cànoves et al. 2004). Furthermore, the built and intangible heritage is often included in these safeguard policies (Orbaşli, 2000). In fact, the quality and the uniqueness of natural and cultural heritage is incontestably the most powerful attraction for tourists who are searching for the appeal of rural areas (Fonseca and Ramos, 2008a).

Despite the benefits mentioned in the relevant literature, these advantages remain the subject of discussion, as the real impacts of tourism development in rural areas are very specific for each territory. The conclusions of research advise caution about the relevance given to tourism. In the next subsection we underline the main issues related to these constraints.

12.2.2. The dark side of tourism as a development tool

Without undermining the role of tourism as a tool of economic growth and diversification, both at the level of the individual farmers and more widely in the local economy, the practical results obtained are frequently far from the theoretical benefits claimed. According to several authors and researchers, the relation between tourism and development in rural regions is unbalanced. A lot of unsupported expectations have been ascribed to the role of tourism, mainly by public policies and rhetoric. Some authors (Cristóvão, 1999; Ribeiro and Marques, 2000; Sharpley and Vass, 2006) claim that this exaggerated attention given to tourism results from rhetoric which is excessive relative to the limited results actually achieved. Along this line of thinking, other authors argue that tourism should not be considered a panacea that can be successfully applied to all rural areas. For instance, Byrd et al. (2009) strongly argue that tourism is not a panacea for economic decline, as it can bring both positive and negative consequences to rural areas. In the same way, Sharpley (2002), notes that tourism must be treated with some caution when labelled as a vehicle of rural development. Furthermore, Gunn (1994) emphasizes that there is no other form of development that has so many far-reaching tentacles as tourism. This means that the extent to which tourism contributes effectively to rural development is uncertain in many cases. As Sharpley (2002) notes, a large number of factors (both local and exogenous) oppose the achievement of rural economic diversification and growth through tourism.

More support from these ideas comes from Fleischer and Felsenstein (2000), who argue that at the back of every reason for promoting tourism in rural areas, there is a counter-reason. Thus, while tourism is heralded as a job producer, it is also blamed for creating low wages, seasonal employment and a reduced number of jobs. These problems are related, respectively, to the lack of qualifications for some of the jobs created (Ribeiro and Marques, 2000), to the seasonality of the demand (Cadima et al., 2001) and to the reduced demand for rural amenities, known as non-massive or Post-Fordist tourism (Balabanian, 1999; Fonseca and Ramos, 2007). For instance, Ribeiro and Marques (2000) concluded that their case study (based on the inner region of Trás-os-Montes, Portugal), that rural tourism generated, on average, only two new jobs in each unit, only one of which is a paid job (the other is performed by the owner's relative).

Despite the tourists' origins (most come from socio-economically privileged strata), several researchers show that tourism incomes are particularly reduced when compared with the initial investment and are mainly absorbed by the accommodation sector (bed and breakfast). According to Fleischer and Pizam (1997) the small size of rural tourism firms contributes to this problem, as well as the high seasonality of demand. One of the most recurrent problems in this context is related to some weaknesses that characterize rural areas: namely, the lack of (cultural) animation and equipment that are responsible for the short tourist stays and for the small amount spent. This means that the weaknesses are associated with the rural areas themselves rather than with the tourists.

Another issue is related to the real impact of tourism in the rural development process. Several authors (Umbelino, 1998; Cristóvão, 1999; Barros, 2003) have concluded that a good portion of tourist incomes are captured by exogenous entities, mainly by travel agencies and other institutions that organize and explore tourist activities. Once again, the small scale of local firms and the lack of financial resources and skills are the main reasons that explain the interference of organizations from other territories in the exploitation of rural amenities. That interference extends to the offer of rural goods in the tourism establishments, which are usually replaced by products originating in other regions, contradicting the purpose of regenerating those traditional activities that are mostly attached to tourism (Cristóvão, 1999; Joaquim, 1999). Again, the origin of this problem is associated with the insufficient exploitation of resources by local organizations and to the lack of entrepreneurial behaviour. As Fleischer and Tchetchik (2005) note, in some cases there is almost a divorce between rural accommodation and agriculture, despite the demand for and the touristic value of rural goods. In the particular case of *agro-tourism* (a typology of rural accommodation described in the next section), some research shows that a large portion of tourist incomes are obtained by the farmers, but the other rural organizations benefit less (Fleischer and Pizam, 1997).

There can be other undesirable consequences of tourism development in rural areas. For instance, Fleischer and Felsenstein (2000) and Orbaşli (2000) emphasize the degradation of valuable and infinite resources (tangible heritage) that could be caused by tourist pressure. On the other hand, as Sharpley (2002) demystified the situation, not all rural areas are equally attractive to rural tourists, and the simple offer of accommodation facilities does not guarantee future demand. Only the places with better rural appeal and interesting product packages can expect larger expenditures by tourists. Related to this, the lack of quality of accommodation, services and resources is a common problem that frustrates rural tourists' expectations, as they normally seek products of high quality (Fleischer and Tchetchik, 2005). The lack of skills, the scarce resources, the small size of firms and the lack of coordination between organizations usually hamper the entrepreneurs' ability to provide products of better quality. At the same time, this affects the way rural amenities are packaged and promoted through marketing operations. Given all the prerequisites for success, as Fleischer and Felenstein (2000) remark, in such cases government subsidles may be required to maintain the social benefits promoted by tourism.

12.2.3. The tourist impact in review and further approaches

As we can conclude from the previous discussion, tourism is associated with both desirable and unfavourable impacts to rural areas, in an umbalanced relationship (see Table 12.1). Although not always evident, the magnitude of the constraints involved suggests that tourism is not the magic solution to the problems of rural areas. Furthermore, the limitations described and experienced in many places is evidence of the high expectations resting on tourism and the gap between rhetorical speeches and the practical results obtained. As argued by Sharpley (2002), tourism may not always represent the most suitable development path, whilst the costs and other weaknesses may restrict the potential economic returns. Hence, in many cases, tourism does not have the potential to underpin a sustained development process in the peripheral rural areas.

Considering the nature and the institutional limitations of rural areas positioned in inner regions, which changes (and challenges) can be presented to these territories to obtain more benefits from tourism? A critical issue emphasized by Fleischer and Tchetchik (2005) is related to the interconnectivity of tourism with other sectors, i.e., tourism is not footloose, but depends on several related activities. In the same way, to face efficiently the external competition and the rapid changes promoted by globalization, a great degree of involvement is needed from tourist entrepreneurs, as argued by Barros (2003) and Lordkipanidze et al. (2005). Nevertheless, in rural territories, awing to their specific nature and skills, institutional innovation and economic cooperation have greater difficulties of penetration.

The lack of an entrepreneurial mind constitutes another common barrier in the development of tourism in peripheral rural areas. Besides their economic unattractiveness and disinvestment in these areas (at least in the Portuguese case), other factors, such as the small market, the low and elderly skills, restrict the low level of entrepreneurship even more. On the other hand, in peripheral areas, tourism comprises mainly small entrepreneurs and family-centred firms (Fleischer and Felsenstein, 2000; Lordkipanidze et al., 2005). As emphasized by these authors, if, on the one hand small enterprises can respond more quickly to new demands, on the other hand, their small resources can limit the capacity to take the necessary actions to face competition. In this context, the development of tourism entrepreneurship is even more important because it strengthens the local culture and identity, diversifies rural tourist activities, avoids conflicts of interest, reduces the rivalry that exists among private businessmen and prevents the cannibalism phenomenon between small firms. Because of the financial restrictions and the limited competence of entrepreneurs, public support from central and municipal administrations is the main incentive to launch new projects and encourage entrepreneurship.

Finally, the governance pattern in the inner rural areas, shaped by the dominance of public entities and characterized by a low-level of collective cooperation, is also responsible for the current situation. In this context, the strengthening of proximity relations, help and encouragement are essential to mobilize and persuade entities to develop new projects (Rhodes, 1996). As defended by some policies and authors, finding innovative governance models is one of the best ways to encourage entrepreneurial behaviour and exploit new opportunities of local development. These can bring together the contributions of the most influential entities based on cooperation and the setting-up of partnerships (Fonseca and Ramos, 2008a).

Moreover, aligning and joining the action of local entities is essential to provide more critical mass to projects and to obtain local synergies and complementarities. This way, it is possible to overcome the fragmentation and the limited extent of individual initiatives. Particularly in the case of Portugal, the strongly-rooted tradition of public dirigisme and the inexperience of management structures of collective participation constitute obstacles to the adoption of these mechanisms. One of the motives for this, is the frequent friction that arises between organizations with different levels of influence and legitimacy.

Table 12.1 The impacts of tourism on rural development

Benefits	Constraints
Generation of jobs	Reduced number and seasonal jobs
Diversification of the economic bases	Reduced and funnelled incomes (bed and breakfast)
New territorial functions	Small interaction with rural activities and populations
Rehabilitation of traditional activities	External organizations positioned as the main beneficiaries of the new incomes
Reinforcement of heritage protection	Cultural and environmental pressure
Reinforcement of environmental protection	Financial and technical deficiencies of the rural actors/entrepreneurs
Improvement of the rural areas' own image and the external promotion to attract exogenous resources	The limitations of the rural supply (low quality, lack of dynamism, disinvestment, etc.)
Encouragement of entrepreneurship and cooperation between the rural actors	The remoteness and the distance to the main urban centres

In conclusion, the success of projects (tourist or other) in peripheral rural areas is constrained by a deep and linked range of deficiences that result from decades of wrong policies that tend to forget and ignore these territories, accentuating even more their peripheral and unattractive character. Reversing this trend presents an enormous challenge to rural entities and requires proportional (and real) support from the central administration.

12.2.4. Description and evolution of the rural tourism concept

The concept of rural tourism (RT) has different interpretations and is frequently used in diverse contexts. According to some authors (Sharpley and Sharpley, 1997; Umbelino, 1998; Cunha, 2006), RT should not be understood as a *tourist product*, but as a *tourist activity developed in rural areas* because it comprises several activities and different types of tourism and accommodation.

RT is not a recent phenomenon in the developed countries. According to Menezes (2000) people have been travelling to the countryside on holidays in significant numbers since, at least, the early part of the 19th century, inspired by fine landscapes and a desire for peace and recreation. Likewise, Yagüe (2002) argues that RT has been practised since the Industrial Revolution, with homecoming connotations (understood as tourism sought by those city dwellers, originating in rural zones, who usually spent their vacations in their *home town*). In the developed countries, the rapid urbanization seen in the last two centuries was nurtured by strong migration from the countryside to the city, giving rise to deep social and economic changes in societies. Concerning tourism, this phenomenon emphasized the countryside as a growing tourist destination for the new urban inhabitants, a pattern which has persisted to the present day (Sharpley and Sharpley, 1997).

However, the first rural tourists had a very different profile from those of today. Yagüe (2002) distinguishes the traditional RT, practised as a return to the origins, from the modern typology of RT. In the traditional pattern, homecoming was the main reason to spend holidays in rural areas. In the vacation period, usually in summertime, rural areas were visited by their former inhabitants, multiplying their population. Those visitors, would, however, be associated with a low level of expenditures and show reduced interest in complementary services. As a result, the positive impacts promoted by the first rural tourists were limited and occasional. The last three decades of the 20th century were characterized by the development of new RT modalities, which followed some behavioural and social changes operating in segments interested in the rural idyll: the Post-Fordism tourism. According to Salvà-Tomás (2000), Post-Fordist tourists pursue unique destinations that are expected to provide remarkable and richer experiences, as well as personal education through the contact with other cultures and places. In opposition to the conventional and still dominant tourist demand (the Fordist tourism guided by the triad *sun, sea, and sand*), this new framework defines a different profile where tourists, usually with more qualifications and social status, appreciate active holidays in authentic and relaxing destinations. In this context, rural spaces present a whole range of resources, compatible with the Post-Fordist expectations, offering cultural and recreational activities in inland areas not yet absorbed by the current way of urban life. Another contributing factor to Post-Fordism growth is the tendency towards splitting holiday periods, no longer concentrated entirely during the summer (short breaks), and the preference for small near destinations. According to several researchers (Hummelbrunner, 1993; Yagüe, 2002; Cànoves et al., 2006), RT is especially demanded by urban people, with high socio-cultural levels, medium-high purchasing power, aged between 25-45 years old. Post-Fordist tourists display a proactive attitude towards enjoying typical rural activities, including agriculture-related tasks, sports and landscape sightseeing, among others. Thus, as a result of the growth of demand, rural areas are offering more and more quality and diversified accommodation to attract tourists. Such tourism takes advantage of the existing supply in rural areas: namely, typical houses, and small living rooms and bedrooms farms. As emphasized by Yagüe (2002), the *new rural tourist* spends more than the first rural tourists, showing behaviour and consumption patterns that theoretically represent more value to rural development.

In Portugal, RT is mainly associated with culture and activities developed in peripheral regions, not yet absorbed by the modern urban lifestyle. The tourist demand for the rural idyll results from its persistence in the imagery of urban residents' memory. Or, as Menezes (2000) argues, it is based on the return to the origins, an attempt to re-establish the balance between man and nature, which was destroyed by urban and industrial development (a return to Nature as Rousseau wished). These principles are considered in the legislation which describes RT in terms of units located in appropriate and typical houses, currently country mansions that offer accommodation and conveniences (equipments, structures and services) so that tourists can enjoy a complete and diversified product.

The first tourist investments in the Portuguese rural areas occurred in the 1950s through the creation of inns, state hotels located in historic places or in areas with scenic interest (Menezes, 2000). The number of inns significantly increased over the years and these can still be found today in different areas of Portugal. Nevertheless, and according to Cadima et al. (2001), the first RT official experiences took place in the 1970s in the small towns of Ponte de Lima, Vouzela, Castelo de Vide e Vila Viçosa, where a significant built heritage evokes the opulent and aristocratic past of these areas. The first rural accommodation was known as *dwelling-house tourism* and owned for the tourist exploitation of the heritage and landscape values in these small towns. The support given by the governmental authorities to the rehabilitation of historic mansions and country houses, significantly increased the amount of RT accommodation and, consequently, forced the legal regulation of RT in 1986 (Decree-Law number 256/86, 27 August). Then, over the course of time, different categories of accommodation were allowed. Nowadays, however, the law in force (Decree-Law number 39/2008, 7 March), only takes three different categories of RT into consideration: cottages, rural hotels, and agro-tourism units. *Cottages* are private houses located in villages where the owners or the householders may be living or not. In terms of design, materials and other characteristics, cottages should always be compatible with the dominant regional architecture. On the other hand, *rural hotels* define a typology constituted by either old or new buildings (with respect to the regional architecture) positioned outside the urban limits and providing a larger capacity than cottages. *Agro-tourism* is described as the provision of family accommodation in typical farmhouses, whilst allowing the boarders to participate and learn about how to conduct agrarian activities or to participate in other activities within the premises of the farm, under the supervision of the owner/manager. With respect to the dwelling-house tourism, the Decree-Law number 39/2008, 7 March, maintained the typology but shifted the territorial occupancy that now embraces both the rural and urban areas. Dwelling-house tourism is a typology reserved for large country mansions, representative of a certain period, distinguished by their architectural, historical and artistic value, providing accommodation and services both to their owners and to rural tourists.

Concerning the recent evolution of RT in Portugal, several studies show strong growth (Cadima et al., 2001; Cardoso, 2001; Jesus, 2007). In the same way, the official statistics reveal significant progress both in the rural demand and supply. Thus, in 2007, according to the Portuguese Tourism Institute, 1,023 RT establishments were licensed (11 per cent more in relation to 2006), offering a total of 11,327 beds. Furthermore, in 2007, the demand (nights in RT establishments) increased by 11 per cent compared with 2006. Interestingly, in 1990, only 223 RT units were in operation, the lodging capacity was 1,811 beds, and the nights spent in RT reached a total of 60,979 (DGT, 2000). However, despite the significant growth observed, RT still attracts only a small fraction of the Portuguese tourists

(Umbelino, 1998). This clearly results from the reduced scale of this segment in Portugal and the lack of potential to regenerate rural economies, even though tourists have a high buying power and an inclination to spend money during their holidays (Cristóvão, 1999).

12.3. Rural Tourism in the Municipality of Almeida

12.3.1. Geographic description of Almeida

The Municipality of Almeida is located in the inland region of Beira Interior Norte (BIN) (Figure 12.1). The BIN has a low population density and is markedly characterized by rural features, with the city of Guarda standing out as the main polarized urban centre of the region. The Municipality is composed of 29 small villages where, according to the last Census (INE, 2002), 8,423 inhabitants live.

Like the surrounding region, Almeida is a territory that has aged and regressed demographically during the last decades. According to the 2001 Census (INE, 2002), Almeida had a population density of only 16persons/km², and the proportion of population aged over 65 years old was 29.8 per cent (13 per cent above the Portuguese average). The unattractive character of the Municipality is reflected in the loss of 19.2 per cent of the residents during the 1990s. The tendency for demographic emptiness appears as one of the main weaknesses of the municipality, which has lost half of its resident population over the last 40 years.

The municipal economic structure is also unbalanced. In 2001, the activity rate was low; the total population dependency rate (69 per cent) revealed that the active population was less than the inactive one. With 63 per cent of the population employed in activities belonging to the tertiary sector, the municipal economy demonstrated the importance of services and commercial activities in the small towns of Almeida and Vilar Formoso, the most important urban areas in the municipality. Together, they house 47.2 per cent of the entire population, clearly showing the municipal bipolarization. Overall, the manufacturing sector was one of the smallest in the entire region. The primary sector activities had considerable strength, employing 15 per cent of the active population (10 per cent above the Portuguese average, according to INE, 2002), which confirms the rural character of the municipality.

However, even agriculture seems to be affected by the depopulation and demographic aging. According to the INE (2001), the percentage of agricultural coverage and the total number of agricultural business decreased (by 30 per cent and 9 per cent, respectively) between 1989 and 1999. The loss of competitive capacity of local agriculture is confirmed by the fact that in 70 per cent of the agricultural business, most of the incomes had an origin external to the activity.

**Figure 12.1   Geographic location of Beira Interior Norte and the Municipality
of Almeida in Portugal**

12.3.2. Tourist potentialities of Almeida

Tourist resources include both physical and intangible elements liable to motivate people to travel or to represent free time occupations/activities (Albino et al., 2000). Offering a tourist package requires a reasonable coordination between tourist resources (that should offer quality and diversity), appropriate equipment and tourist services, and an integrated exploitation performed by the local organizations. Because of their specific limitations, rural areas usually do not display tourist products in a structured manner.

Instead, the initiatives promoted by some entities are not organized, as is the case in Almeida, where the most important attraction resides in several products related to the cultural heritage.

Cultural resources

Cultural heritage stands out as the most important tourist resource of the municipality. In Figure 12.2 the most valuable heritage resources are depicted according to their distribution in the Almeida's *freguesias,* a lower political and administrative subdivision of the Portuguese municipalities. Almeida's fortress is the noblest heritage element of the municipality, and has been classified as National Monument since 1928 and as a Historic Village. The fortress is one of the most emblematic and well-preserved examples of the military architecture of the 17th century, where several valuable elements can be found, such as: the extensive wall in a stellar shape (Vauban structure), the double-arched gates, and various architectural elements of original military use (prison building, powder room, casemates, ancient artillery train, ancient artillery headquarters, and the ruins of the medieval castle destroyed during the 3rd Napoleonic Invasion).

The Historic Village of Castelo Mendo (B) is also an outstanding example of heritage. Although the castle had already been classified as a National Monument in 1946, its interest was recognised again in 1984, when all the urban area enclosed by the walls was classified as being of Public Interest. Castelo Mendo is a medieval fortress that had an important defensive function till the establishment of a definite boundary line by the Alcañices Treaty (1297). Castelo Mendo has kept its medieval urban structure, with fine architectural features and many interesting civil (Manueline, Hispanic, Philipin, Judaic) and religious elements.

All around the Municipality of Almeida, there are other elements of architectural and historical interest, such as the walled village of Castelo Bom (C) with elements classified as National Monuments; the medieval pillory of Vale de Coelha (E); the St Miguel Church and megalithic monument of Malhada Sorda (G); and the archaeological site of Malpartida (D), among others.

In the intangible heritage domain, Almeida also has a rich and varied handcraft production, a traditional cuisine, regional products, folk groups and a very strong collective memory. Almeida is also known for its re-creation of the 3rd Napoleonic Invasion, which attracts different Napoleonic European Associations. Over the course of three days, the siege, the fighting and the capitulation of Almeida after the castle was destroyed in an explosion are revisited in an authentic re-enactment of the 3rd Napoleonic Invasion. This is the event that attracts more tourists and visitors to Almeida.

Figure 12.2   Distinctive heritage in the Municipality of Almeida

Natural resources
The natural resources of Almeida are equally rich and diverse. Nature and landscape reveal little impact from human activities on account of the low urbanization and industrialization in the Almeida area. As a result, Almeida has good environmental preservation, with large areas relatively unaffected by human activities. The inclusion of two sites of the National Natura 2000 Network (Figure 12.2) attests the important function of Almeida in nature conservation. The traditional prevalence of agriculture also plays an important role in the landscape and in habitat maintenance (with several species of cynegetic importance). The hot-spring of Almeida has also been known since ancient times for its medicinal and therapeutic properties. The morphological conditions, characterized by the

presence of a tableland, dissected by the Côa river valley, along which flows the main water course of the region, allow the practice of different types of nature activities (hiking, cycling, horse-riding, balloon flights, orientateering, canoeing, rafting, etc.).

12.3.3. Methodology

On the basis of previous research conducted by the authors in Almeida (Fonseca, 2006; Fonseca and Ramos, 2007), tourism was identified by the regional and the local entities surveyed as the most promising activity to reverse the negative tendencies affecting Almeida. Thus, the data used to achieve the purpose of this chapter, *i.e.* the analysis of the socio-economic impact of RT in the economic development, comes from a cross-sectional survey of RT operators in Almeida. The survey included a wide range of questions concerning the elements, the hospitality and the organization of each unit of rural accommodation. The survey questionnaires were subdivided into six parts. In the first part, the aim of the survey was to collect some general information about the individual RT establishments, such as their identification, location, typology and start of activity. The second part was related to the description of the entrepreneurs' profile: namely, their age, educational level, origin and business motivation. In the third part, the survey focused on the description of the supply of tourist accomodation, data of particular importance to analyse the lodging capacity, its characteristics and relation with the local economy and activities. These data included a description of the hospitality units, the garden, the view from the units and the tourist activities related to the accommodation. The fourth section was related to the demand characterization, including the guests' origins and occupations and their average stay during the year. This information was also very relevant in order to understand what attracts tourists to Almeida. The fifth part focused on organizational questions to understand, among other things, the marketing strategies undertaken by RT operators, as well as the level of cooperation maintained with other local or regional organizations. The questions included in the sixth and last part aimed to understand the impacts of RT on heritage regeneration and the rehabilitation of traditional activities. Also in this part, the owners with a working farm were asked about the agricultural elements relevant to the RT accommodation. Other kinds of questions included the capital and labour inputs of the owners. A general overview of tourism potentialities and deficiences was also requested, in order to assess the entrepreneurs' opinion.

The surveys questionnaires were structured in a closed answer format with a typology of multiple choice options. In some questions the Likert scale was used to evaluate the entrepreneurs' agreement/disagreement concerning their content. To gather other points previously not covered, an open-ended comments section was attached at the end of survey. The use of different question types to determine the nature and the quality of the data obtained is justified by the need to cover some relevant variables related to RT in a compact survey format. The surveys were undertaken between June and July 2008. The main findings will be described in the following subsections.

12.3.4. A general overview of tourism activity in Almeida

Considering the existing equipment and accommodation, Almeida's tourist supply is relatively reduced, both in quality and in lodging capacity and covers different categories that include conventional accommodation, RT accommodation, and one inn. In the conventional segment, and taking into account the establishments classified by the Directorate General for Tourism, Almeida has four units that represent 17 per cent of the BIN registered supply. In fact, only the main urban regional centre (Guarda) has a higher capacity. However, Almeida's accommodation capacity is even greater if the seven non-classified establishments located in the small town of Vilar Formoso are considered.

With respect to the evolution of the demand over recent years (from 2000 to 2006), the proportion of nights spent in Almeida's conventional accommodation was irregular with a tendency to decrease. In that period, the temporary stays had an average rate of 17,500/year (representing 20 per cent of the regional rate). Being the main receptor centre of the region, Guarda has a dominant position and in the period received 44 per cent of the temporary stays reported in the region. On the other hand, during that period, Almeida stands out as the BIN's municipality where the proportion of foreign guests was the highest, probably due to its position on the border which is crossed by the IP5, a motorway connection with Spain. In fact, the proportion of Portuguese tourist nights in Almeida's conventional accommodation (65 per cent) is less than that recorded in the remaining region. Besides, the Spanish tourists' temporary stays (17 per cent) are 11 per cent more than the regional values, while the French stays (7 per cent) also have a great significance. Nevertheless, the Almeida's tourist stays were shorter (1.1nights) than the regional average (1.3 nights). The lack of tourist activities and the border position could be the main reasons for that difference.

Another perspective of the municipal tourist demand is given by Almeida's tourist office statistics, concerning the number of tourists/visitors who search this service to get information. According to this source, and taking into consideration the period between 2000 and 2007, the number of visitors increased by 112 per cent. In 2007, the tourist office received 81,402 visitors, a number 8 times higher than the municipal population. However, despite the numbers, the real impact of this significant tourist flow is unclear, and the answers to questions such as: *How many visitors spent money in Almeida?* or *How many visitors plan to return to Almeida in the future?* are unknown.

12.3.5. Rural tourism impact in the development of the Municipality of Almeida

Almeida's rural tourism supply and entrepreneur's description

Compared with conventional establishments, the regional position of Almeida in the RT segment is less advantageous. In fact, the three RT units located in the municipality only represent 5.4 per cent of the regional supply, suggesting that Almeida's accommodation is oriented to other demands and specific markets. The prevalence of conventional accommodation with general low quality (such as boarding houses), mainly in the small town of Vilar Formoso, seems to be part of a strategy to attract the people passing over the border. The low rate of tourist stays corroborates this hypothesis.

According to the surveys, Almeida's establishments are mainly of the cottage type dexcribed above, although one unit is within a farm (not exploited by the owner as agro-tourism accommodation because of the investments and legal procedures required). As in many other Portuguese peripheral territories, the RT phenomenon in Almeida is relatively recent, with the first unit beginning its activity in 1998, and the last opened its doors in 2003. Two of the cottages are located inside the walls of Almeida's fortress and the other in the village of Freixo (20km from Almeida). Almeida's cottages occupy typical buildings (one of them was built in the 18th century) while the Freixo unit functions in a typical regional style house of 1720 which is located in a farm. All the three buildings were repaired according to the original architectural plan and respect the legal requirements for these establishments. Their furniture was made using local materials and hand crafted by local artisans. With no exception, all the operators surveyed complained about the insufficient financial support from the central administration to repair and convert the original buildings. In one case, the respondent said that the building renovation costs had reached €200,000, but the return on that investment is not expected in a short/medium term. In fact, only one entrepreneur had benefited from public subsidies to renovate an old building amounting to €25,000 provided by a programme managed by the Centre Regional Coordination and Development Commission. The finance needed for these operations and, as we will see, the low revenues generated with RT, restrict the survival of entrepreneurs with no other sources of income. To overcome these difficulties, all Almeida's RT entrepreneurs have other professional activities, for which they obtain most of their incomes. RT is therefore managed as a complementary activity and as a partial source of income. The pleasure of the activity and the motivation in rehabilitating the (family) legacy were highlighted by the entrepreneurs as the most important reasons to make the investments.

The lodging capacity is low (but still enough to meet the demand, as we will emphasize), offering together 12 rooms and 24 beds. RT units are occupied during the whole year and the prices charged do not oscillate in accordance with changes in demand during the high and low seasons. In Almeida, the average daily single-room price for bed and breakfast in traditional rural accommodation fluctuates between €60 and €80. These prices are significantly higher than those charged by the owners of conventional accommodation, where a stay can cost less than €30. The price gap between conventional and RT accommodation also demonstrates the different socio-economic status of the guests.

All Almeida's RT units provided common services (dining-room, sitting-room, games room), with one of them also having a swimming-pool (important due to the geographic position of Almeida, far from the sea and river beaches). Catering only included breakfast, which is justified by the respondents on account of the short average stays of the guests and the existence of restaurants in the vicinity.

Concerning the entrepreneur's profile, their ages range from 45-64 years old and only one of them has a university qualification (the others have secondary education). It is important to highlight that none of these operators has qualifications in tourism or in related domains.

All the RT units are organized as small businesses and are managed by the owners. Among other reasons, the low occupancy level of Almeida's RT units is explained by ineffective marketing policies. Rather than working together to promote the sector collectively, local entrepreneurs are working only for their own benefit without engaging other external services and support. Promotional material is published in different vehicles, mostly of local and regional origin, and include pamphlets, brochures, newspapers and magazines. Only one establishment had its own site on the Web, while others were promoted elsewhere, such as the web page of Serra da Estrela Tourism. However, online reservations were not available for any of the RT units, demonstrating the technological neglect of this important and useful tool.

12.3.6. Almeida's rural tourism demand

The demand analysis is more indicative of the attractiveness of Almeida in the RT segment. As we reported, over recent years Almeida has had a significant increase in the number of tourists/visitors. Despite this increase being frequently highlighted by local organizations (mainly by the Municipal Government) as a proof of tourism development and maturity, the local benefits of this rise in numbers are, in fact, unknown. Questions, such as how many visitors stay overnight in Almeida, or how many of them eat in the restaurants, or buy souvenirs in the local shops, are yet to be clarified. Moreover, the official statistics concerning the period between 2001/2006 (INE, 2007) show different trends, with a rise of the total number of guests (+3 per cent), but a decrease of the nights spent in the establishments (-0.8 per cent).

However, the data collected can suggest the answer to those questions. A significant problem faced by the RT entrepreneurs is related to the reduced occupancy level. According to the respondents, occupancy is always under 20 per cent all through the year, even in the summer, traditionally the busiest period for tourism in Portugal, when Almeida receives the highest number of visitors. At the same time, the stay period of guests in Almeida's RT units is really low (mostly 1 night, rarely 2 nights or more), restricting even more the income gained and the RT contribution to local economic development. Almeida's RT entrepreneurs expressed their disappointment with these levels, stating that they had expected much more business. Additionally, as we mentioned before, occupancy levels confirm that the low number of RT units is more than enough to satisfy the local demand.

The respondents advanced some specific reasons for the low level of business achieved. Repeated emphasis was given to the lack of facilities and tourist entertainment to strengthen the attractiveness and length of the guests' stays in Almeida. In spite of the public investments over recent years (for instance the construction of the new thermal centre and the Museum of Military Architecture), tourist equipment and services are still insufficient to retain tourists for longer periods. In Almeida, tourism is still very attached to the main visitor attraction (the fortress), as if no other efforts were needed to attract tourists.

However, the lack of cultural activities and equipment restricts the possibility of local culture and heritage being absorbed and perceived by tourists. This problem is exacerbated in the small villages where the more elementary services (like bars, restaurants, craft shops, etc.) are almost totally absent and, when they do exist, they have a quality incompatible with the RT requirements. In these cases, tourists are left to observe and explore (without tourist guidance) rural amenities, and particularly the built heritage, in visits that go on for only a few hours.

In these conditions, even considering the financial capacity and the predisposition to spend, rural tourists have no way of generating incomes for the local population. A second reason highlighted by respondents is related to the lack of local entrepreneurship. RT entrepreneurs considered the other local organizations (public and private) indifferent and lethargic concerning the risk of investment in a territory with the characteristics of Almeida. According to the respondents, the regional disinvestment, the reduced skills, the elderly entrepreneurs, and the wrong idea that all investments should be promoted by public bodies, are the main factors that have contributed to the insufficient entrepreneurship. While recognizing their own responsibilities, RT entrepreneurs also considered the lack of cooperation as a reason for the insufficient tourist activities, caused by the dominance of an individualist behaviour in managing each entity. The remoteness and the distance to the West coast, where the greatest proportion of the Portuguese population lives, were also mentioned by two respondents as a cause for the reduced tourist demand of Almeida.

Finally, entrepreneurs were asked to describe some general characteristics of their guests, to understand the profile of rural tourists attracted to Almeida. Thus, rural tourists can be male or female, mostly middle-aged adults (45 years old and above). The majority of the guests are entrepreneurs, independent workers, qualified workers and retired people, all of whom mainly have a university degree or a high school education. The very young and less-educated people do not tend to select Almeida's rural accommodation. These conclusions are in line with those of other studies undertaken in other rural destinations in Portugal (Silva, 2007) and abroad (Cànoves et al., 2006; Vela, 2009). Concerning the guests' origins, respondents declared that most of them come from other Portuguese regions, and Spain was the most represented country among the foreign tourists. This representation is also in accordance with the official statistics described previously. When asked about their perception of tourists' motivations, respondents emphasize that rural tourists in Almeida are captivated by the heritage and the historic past of the fortress, by the quietness of the place (making it possible to rest and relax), by the desire to discover a new type of vacation and by the hospitality of the place.

12.3.7. Rural tourism's impact in the development of Almeida

The analysis focused on the supply and demand revealed several constraints (related to the specific market segment and including municipal and regional deficiencies) which suggests that RT does not make a strong contribution to local development, thus refuting several of the advantages attached to rural tourism previously described in Section 12.2.1.

In the socio-economic domain, the role played by RT is far from that expected. Firstly, and regarding employment, the RT units of Almeida did not create any paid jobs, since all accommodation is managed and exploited by the owners or by close relatives (usually the housewife). Entrepreneurs justified this by referring to the irregularity and low occupancy of accommodation that generates insufficient income to justify recruiting external workers. As Cànoves et al. (2004) mentioned in their study, rural tourism is frequently not considered as a *real job* because the incomes obtained are limited and are just intended to increase the family budget. Also, because RT is practised as a part-time activity, the owner can carry out other regular domestic tasks and work. Hence, the RT impacts identified in Almeida contradict one of the most defended positive impacts in rural economies. At the same time, this corroborates other national and international researches (Ribeiro and Marques, 2000; Fleischer and Felsenstein, 2000; Cànoves et al., 2004), thus confirming some excessive optimism around RT and its favourable contribution to employment. The lack of skilled professionals who can fulfil the requirements of a job related to RT was underlined as an additional problem.

Secondly, the impact of RT in the regeneration of traditional activities in the municipality is also very weak. In the three rural accommodation units analysed, the average amount of local goods consumed by tourists (handcraft and agricultural products, for instance) is less than 20 per cent of the total. This means that the great portion of products provided to tourists come from other regions. Again the critical problem is related to the small scale of RT activity and to the lack of entrepreneurial vision that provides an opportunity to external entities. For example, in the only accommodation unit based within a farm (in Freixo), the lack of tourist exploitation of farmers' services and products, demonstrates the absence of strategic vision and the deficiencies of local entrepreneurs. These findings show that RT can have only a limited role in economic diversification and in the regeneration of rural activities, contrary to earlier theoretical claims. Moreover, Joaquim (1999) came to identical conclusions in his research, arguing that RT is frequently not connected to rural development, but, instead, is sustained by exogenous resources and produces more profitable benefits for outsider entities.

Due to the low tourist exploitation of other local resources (nature, handcraft, intangible heritage, etc.), the contribution of RT to the regeneration of these elements is even more restricted. As far as nature tourism is concerned, there is a remarkable lack of equipment and some activities are very irregularly organized. As a result of this, the range of nature activities promoted by RT entrepreneurs is limited, and only one unit provides regular rides on horsesback and donkeys. The lack of public investments in the touristic exploitation of natural resources was highlighted by the respondents as the main cause of the stagnation observed in this segment. In fact, it is the unexploited character of Almeida's natural resources which is the most unique feature that tourists most appreciate. An identical situation was observed with respect to handcraft. In spite of their old age, the number of Almeida's artisans is high and their handcraft shows quality and diversity, including basketry, tapestry, lace, saddlebags and woodwork, among other products. However, the proportion of crafts provided to tourists in the RT accommodation is extremely low. The lack of cooperation among organizations emerges again as the dominant failing, exacerbated by the problems faced by artisans to control the distribution channels and to sell their products.

Thirdly, the direct impact of RT in the rehabilitation of the local houses is mainly restricted to the buildings where the units are installed. Therefore, most of buildings do not benefit from RT, and physical deterioration and abandonment is becoming more and more evident, especially in the more peripheral villages of Almeida. When asked about future investments in the conversion of buildings into RT accommodation, entrepreneurs were evasive and refuted the idea, on the grounds of the low return obtained and the legal procedures required. Indirectly some important measures have been taken by the municipality to protect and regenerate the built heritage, as a strategy to reinforce the tourist attractiveness of Almeida. The municipal government makes conservation plans for those urban cores with more value (Almeida, Castelo Mendo, Castelo Bom and Vilar Formoso) in order to impose rule physical constraints and protect the historic, picturesque, architectural and aesthetic elements presented in those cores. With the same aim, these urban cores have benefited from public programmes (provided by the Centre Regional Coordination and Development Commission) to rehabilitate buildings façades and roofs according to the regional architectural style, in order to strengthen their urban cohesion.

Finally, at the organizational and institutional levels, RT has been incapable of stimulating a great dynamic of cooperation and involvement between local (and regional) public and private organizations. The lack of cooperation identified reflects not only the insufficient dialogue but also the conflicting interests, the rivalry and the competition between local entrepreneurs in attracting the scarce resources (tourists). Even in apparently simple domains, such as marketing, the cooperation between entities has been complex. In fact, the three RT operators work individually and no activity is put into practice jointly. The only exception is Casa do Cantinho (Almeida), which cooperates with Almeida's only inn in the promotion and tourist animation of different cultural and nature activities, because of the common management of both units.

Despite local cooperation being clearly more difficult in territories with characteristics like Almeida's (Barros, 2003), it is essential to overcome the selfishness, the lack of dimension, and the fragmentation of the individual action of local entities. In fact, the implementation of a new pattern of involvement and governance could be the key to adopting a more efficient and sustainable exploitation of tourism (and of local development). This strategy would also support and stimulate the entrepreneurial behaviour, defining actions shared by all the organizations and adopting structural and complementary policies focused on the future.

12.4. Conclusions

The exploitation of tourism resources in rural territories has generated great enthusiasm, and still continues to do so, as we can conclude by the volume of research, policies and actions undertaken. In peripheral territories, great hopes have been put into tourism, as a way to renew the economy, to promote the cultural values, and to improve the social conditions of rural areas. However, the results obtained in several rural territories advise some caution in the evaluation of the real impact of RT. That is why some authors (Cristóvão, 1999; Ribeiro and Marques, 2000) argue that tourism should not be considered as a panacea to solve all the rooted deficiencies of these areas.

The case of Almeida represents a paradigmatic example of this. Anchored in distinctive cultural and natural resources, the municipal organizations surveyed considered tourism as the most promising activity to reverse the declining trend experienced by Almeida in the last decades. Focusing on RT, we concluded that very many of its benefits can have a positive know-on effect in municipal development, when taking into consideration the creation of jobs, the rehabilitation of the urban heritage, and the economic diversification.

This research highlights several internal and external constraints that are explained by the analysis undertaken in this chapter. Considering tourism in its national dimension, we can verify that, with the exception of some policies and (scarce) resources oriented to this segment, the strongest investments are directed to the most important tourism regions and to massive tourism products, simply because they are more demanded and generate higher volume of incomes. In fact, the insufficient public financial support was identified by entrepreneurs as a huge obstacle to the sector's growth. Therefore, there are several inherent to the municipality itself which hold back the development of tourism activity and RT in particular. As the entrepreneurs recognized, the most important of these reasons is the lack of cooperation among local organizations, due to the absence of new models of governance that encourage the implementation of integrated strategies to raise the local critical mass. At the same time, the current divisions reflect the individualism, the rivalry and the competitive attitude of local entrepreneurs. As Brunori and Rossi (2007) argue, this kind of entrepreneurial behaviour is common in rural areas, attesting to the failure of the strategies in place, and requires a deep change in the rooted and traditional way of governance. The lack of cooperation is present in two forms. Horizontally, in Almeida, the dialogue and cooperation is at a very low level (or nil if we consider only the entrepreneurs' activity), and has been driven by the municipal government. Vertically, the cooperation with other regional and border organizations is also limited and demonstrates the dominant pattern of public and individualist government. That position results from the focus on the Municipality's own territory, ignoring the potential located in the adjacent areas. Consequently, Almeida needs a new pattern of territorial organization, one that stimulates the dialogue between local organizations, encourages investments, makes the territory more attractive to exogenous resources, and defines a new and global policy of development that should answer the question: *What future do we want for Almeida?*

However, while perceiving the nature of these problems, some promising steps have been undertaken by the municipal government in order to reverse the state of things. In the recent past, several actions have been undertaken. One example of this is the creation of Almeida's Promotion Agency, a structure to coordinate actions among tourist operators who have been sponsored both by municipal and regional entities. There is the reinforcement of regional and border cooperation, with a partnership established with the Spanish city of Ciudad Rodrigo, in order to share experiences and develop common tourist actions. In addition, there has been growing investment in external promotion, with a presence in recent publications of the International Tourism Trade Fair of Madrid, the Lisbon Travel Market and the International Interior Tourism Trade Fair of Valladolid. These measures undertaken by the municipal government reveal a new concern for tourism promotion and organization and could constitute the first steps of broader and more effective territorial governance. At the same time, it suggests that the municipal government performs the leading role in the socio-economic animation, because of its greater capacity for local dialogue and mobilization. In fact, private organizations and particularly the local entrepreneurs are significantly more passive (although they should not be) and highly positioned as beneficiaries of public funds and supports.

The regional context of disinvestment and the socio-economic abandonment observed in rural areas located in peripheral regions also contributes to the low innovative and entrepreneurial spirit in tourism (as well as in other economic activities). This fact was also considered by the entrepreneurs as an impediment to tourism growth in Almeida. Additionally, this context repels investments and promotes an atmosphere of discredit and doubt about the future. The entrepreneurs' low levels of qualification, as well as their advanced age, are additional obstacles which discourage investments in RT. And these dominant characteristics of local entities will continue to discourage more investments in tourism in the future. The distance to (but not the isolation from) the main urban centres located on the west

Portuguese coast and to some Spanish towns, associated with the absence of an integrated and solid policy of tourist exploitation, also contributes to the feeble impact that RT has had in the socio-economic development of Almeida. Thus, RT weaknesses are much more due to the inability and incapacity of Almeida to induce tourists' expenditures, rather than to the tourists' own unwillingness to spend.

In conclusion, the Municipality of Almeida has a long way to go before tourism is in a position to better sustain its local development. For this purpose, tourism should be inserted in a global and integrated perspective. The two recommendations are: (i) the policies should favour and stimulate the participation and the involvement of the most representative organizations in the planning process, integrating the other policies and dimensions with tourism. This institutional solidarity is essential to obtain more critical mass, to encourage the entrepreneurial spirit and to concentrate resources in strategic and mobilizing actions; (ii) even though it transcends the municipal action and competence, Almeida should strengthen the touristic cohesion on a regional scale, preferably through the establishment of a common platform, where actions related to the planning activities and marketing should be undertaken. The global vision described is essential to reinforce tourism in Almeida, to ensure that RT can effectively contribute to renew the local economy, rather than just being a stereotypical idea of rural development.

Because of the common nature of the constraints involved, we also believe that the problems diagnosed in Almeida could be extrapolated to the BIN region as a whole. Enlarging the sample and the case study to the regional scale is proposed as future work, and we expect to report these findings in future publications.

Acknowledgements

The authors would like to express their gratitude to Almeida's entrepreneurs who participated and have been involved in this study. The authors would also like to thank the Centre of Iberian Studies for the financial support given to this research.

References

Albino, J., Mergulhão, L., Bigares, J., Magalhães, A., Rato, B. and Gonçalves, J. 2000. *Turismo e desenvolvimento no Norte Alentejo*, Edições Colibri, Lisboa.
Balabanian, O. 1999. Le tourism vert: défie ou utopie?, in *Desenvolvimento Rural: Desafio e Utopia*, coordinated by C. Cavaco, Lisboa: Centro de Estudos Geográficos, 255-262.
Barros, V. 2003. *Desenvolvimento rural, intervenção pública 1996-2002*. Lisboa: Terramar.
Brunori, G. and Rossi, A. 2007. Differentiating countryside: social representations and governance patterns in rural areas with high social density: the case of Chianti, Italy. *Journal of Rural Studies*, 23, 183-205.

Buhalis, D. 1999. Tourism on the Greek Islands: issues of peripherality, competitiveness and development. *International Journal of Tourism Research*, 1, 341-358.

Byrd, E., Bosley, H. and Dronberger, M. 2009. Comparisons of stakeholder perceptions of tourism impacts in rural eastern North Carolina. *Tourism Management*, 30, 693-703.

Cadima, J., Freitas, M. and Mendes, R. 2001. *O turismo no espaço rural: uma digressão pelo tema a pretexto da situação e evolução do fenómeno em Portugal*. Núcleo de Investigação em Políticas Económicas, Universidade do Minho, Braga.

Caffyn, A. and Dahlström, M. 2005. Urban–Rural interdependencies: joining up policy in practice. *Regional Studies*, 39(3), 283-296.

Cànoves, G., Villarino, M., Priestley, G. and Blanco, A. 2004. Rural tourism in Spain: an analysis of recent evolution. *Geoforum*, 35, 755-769.

Cànoves, G., Herrera, L. and Cuesta, L. 2006. *El turisme rural a Catalunya: una aposta mediambiental i de qualitat*. Barcelona: Fundació Abertis.

Cardoso, A. 2001. Turismo, Ambiente e Desenvolvimento Sustentável em áreas rurais. *1º Congresso de Estudos Rurais*, Vila Real, 16-18 Setembro.

Cawley, M. and Gilmor, D. 2008. Integrated rural tourism: concepts and practice. *Annals of Tourism Research*, 35(2), 316-337.

Covas, A. and Covas, M. 2007. Da razão sustentável à gestão multifuncional dos espaços rurais. *5º Congresso da Associação Portuguesa de Economia Agrária*, Vila Real.

Cristóvão, A. 1999. Ambiente e desenvolvimento de áreas marginais: o caminho tortuoso para uma relação potencialmente frutuosa. Actas do *1º Encontro Galiza-Portugal de Estudos Rurais*, Bragança, 12 e 13 de Novembro.

Cunha, L. 2006. *Economia e política do turismo*, Lisboa: Edições Verbo.

DGT – Direcção-Geral do Turismo 2000. *O turismo no espaço rural (1984/1999)*. Divisão de Recolha e Informação Estatística, Lisboa.

EC – European Commission 1998. *Report of the High Level Group on Tourism and Employment*, EC, Brussels.

Fleischer, A. 1999. Incentive programs for rural tourism, in *Israel: A Tool for Promoting Rural Development*, edited by P. Rietveld and D. Shefer, *Regional Development in an Age of Structural Economic Change*, 97-110, Aldershot: Ashgate.

Fleischer, A. and Felsenstein, D. 2000. Support for rural tourism, does it make a difference?. *Annals of Tourism Research*, 27(4), 1007-1024.

Fleischer, A. and Pizam, A. 1997. Rural tourism in Israel. *Tourism Management*, 18(6), 367-372.

Fleischer, A. and Tchetchik, A. 2005. Does rural tourism benefit from agriculture?. *Tourism Management*, 26, 493-501.

Fonseca, F. 2006. *O planeamento estratégico em busca de potenciar o território: o caso de Almeida*. MSc Thesis, Universidade do Minho, Braga.

Fonseca, F. and Ramos, R. 2007. Potenciar o desenvolvimento turístico a partir de um processo de planeamento estratégico de marketing: o caso de Almeida. *Revista Portuguesa de Estudos Regionais*, 15, 41-64.

Fonseca, F. and Ramos R. 2008a. Almeida's heritage as factor for local and sustainable development, in *Heritage 2008 – World Heritage and Sustainable Development*, edited by Amoêda et al., 1, 129-138.

Fonseca, F. and Ramos R. 2008b. *The entrepreneurship dynamic in rural tourism: the case of Almeida municipality, Portugal.* Paper presented at the International Conference on Knowledge in Small and Medium Sized Towns: Towns as a Place of Knowledge and Diffusion, Faro, 4 and 5 of December.

Garcia-Ramon, M., Cànoves, G. and Valdovinos 1995. Farm tourism, gender and the environment in Spain. *Annals of Tourism Research*, 22(2), 267-282.

Gunn, C. 1994. *Tourism planning: Basic concepts cases*. 3rd Edition. Washington D.C.: Taylor and Francis.

Hummelbrunner, R. 1993. *Touristic promotion and potentials in peripheral areas, the Austrian case.* Paper presented at the Social Exclusion and Rural Tourism Conference, Almeida, 7 to 9 May.

INE – Instituto Nacional de Estatística 2001. *Dados comparativos dos Recenseamentos da Agricultura de 1989 e de 1999*. Lisboa.

INE – Instituto Nacional de Estatística 2002. *XIV Recenseamento Geral da População*, Lisboa.

INE – Instituto Nacional de Estatística 2007. *Anuário Estatístico da Região Centro de 2006*, Lisboa.

Jesus, L. 2007. *Génese, evolução e distribuição do TER*. 5º Congresso da Associação Portuguesa de Economia Agrária, Vila Real, 4 a 6 de Outubro.

Joaquim, G. 1999. Turismo e mundo rural: que sustentabilidade?, in *Desenvolvimento Rural: Desafio e Utopia*, edited by C. Cavaco, C., Centro de Estudos Geográficos, 305-312.

Liu, A. 2006. Tourism in rural areas: Kedah, Malaysia, *Tourism Management*, 27, 878-889.

López-López, A. 2001. Turismo y desarrollo sostenible. *Sistema*, 162/163, 189-202.

Lordkipanidze, M., Brezet, H. and Backman, M. 2005. The entrepreneurship factor in sustainable tourism development. *Journal of Cleaner Production*, 13, 787-798.

MacDonald, R. and Jolliffe, L. 2003. Cultural rural tourism: evidence from Canada. *Annals of Tourism Research*, 30(2), 307-322.

Menezes, F. 2000. *Tourism as an agent of rural development construction of programmes and institutional forms of implementation, a case study of Leader I in Vale do Lima (in NW Portugal)*. MSc Thesis, Bournemouth University, Bournemouth, UK.

Moreira, A. 2000. *Planeamento estratégico municipal para o Turismo*. MSc Thesis, Universidade do Minho, Braga.

Nash, R. and Martin, A. 2003. Tourism in peripheral areas, the challenges for Northeast Scotland. *International Journal of Tourism Research*, 5, 161-181.

Orbaşli A. 2000. *Tourists in historic towns, urban conservation and heritage management*. London and New York: EandFN Spon.

Rhodes, R. 1996. The New Governance: Governing Without Government. *Political Science*, 44, 652-667.

Ribeiro, M. and Marques, C. 2000. Rural tourism and the development of less favoured areas between rhetoric and practice. *Tourism Sustainability and Territorial Organization*, Coimbra: APDR, 531-544.

Salvà-Tomàs, P. 2000. Tourism sector restructure sustainability and territorial perspectives at the beginning of 21st century. *Tourism Sustainability and Territorial Organization*, Coimbra: APDR, 97-112.

Sharpley, R. 2002. Rural tourism and the challenge of tourism diversification: the case of Cyprus, in *Tourism Management*, 23, 233-244.

Sharpley, R. and Sharpley, J. 1997. *Rural Tourism: An Introduction*. London: International Thomson Business Press.

Sharpley, R. and Vass, A. 2006. Tourism, farming and diversification: an attitudinal study. *Tourism Management,* 27, 1040-1052.

Silva, L. 2007. A procura do turismo em espaço rural. *Etnográfica*, 11(1), 141-163.

Snowdon, P., Farr, H. and Slee, B. 1997. The Economic Impact of Alternative Types of Rural Tourism. *Journal of Agricultural Economics*, 48(2), 179-192.

Umbelino, J. 1998. Turismo em espaço rural: da utopia à realidade, in *Turismo Horizontes Alternativos*, edited by J. Pintassilgo and M. Teixeira, Lisboa: Edições Colibri, 175-188.

Vela, M. 2009. Rural-cultural excursion conceptualization: A local tourism marketing management model based on tourist destination image measurement. *Tourism Management*, 30, 419-428.

Yagüe, R. 2002. Rural tourism in Spain. *Annals of Tourism Research*, 29(4), 1101-1110.

PART IV
Urban-Rural Interdependencies

Chapter 13

How Knowledge on Land Values Influences Rural-Urban Development Processes

Emília Malcata Rebelo

13.1. Introduction

Questions concerning territorial planning – availability of land for different uses at reasonable prices, quality of development projects, optimal plans, network exploration, scheduling of decisions, and confidence – are very important for regional and local economies. But currently in Portugal an immoderate greed has emerged (Talixa, 2008) in the form of land changes from rural to urban use, and in the intensification of land use. There have been inevitable consequences at the regional and urban levels, as far as the following issues are concerned: (i) municipal policies and planning decisions have not succeeded in reaching a sustained balance between public and private land interests (planning has failed to properly stimulate private initiatives, and land has not been able to accomplish its social function); (ii) city centres have been progressively shrinking as a counterpart of the sprawl of the urban peripheries; and, finally, (iii) the lack of control over land and real estate prices has been nourishing speculative processes.

Thus, regional and urban planning requires a monitoring system and decision tools in order to control and distribute the surplus-values that result from planning decisions and administrative interventions on the territory. It is also important to exert control on real estate final prices, preventing surplus-values from opportunistically resulting in exaggerated and undue profits.

Better monitoring and control of surplus-values that will strengthen the operation of planning bodies in pursuing their strategic goals refers, mainly, to: (i) the provision of land for different functional uses at acceptable prices; (ii) the enhancement of private initiatives of promoters, builders and sellers, by asserting the neutrality of landowner's interests in the face of changes in use and in intensities of use anticipated by planning; and (iii) the application of surplus-values taxes on behalf of the population's interests, avoiding excessive profits upstream and downstream the supply and demand chain of development land. Thus regional and urban planning needs to intervene by means of plans and regulations, and property taxation, on the one hand, and develop property appraisal tools suited to location, uses and intensities of use, on the other. This chapter proposes a methodology for the monitoring, evaluation and computation of surplus-values generated by planning and administrative decisions on the territory, thus supporting more efficient interventions of regional and local planning with taxation devices. Section 13.2 begins with a brief analysis of the concepts of land rent and surplus-values and respective underlying variables. Then, in Section 13.3, the consequences of different kinds of public interventions with regard to the control of property values are assessed in terms of the surplus-values they generate. In Section 13.4 the behaviour of the different agents involved in property markets (including public administration bodies) is analysed. In Section 13.5 a model (composed of a set of tools) is proposed for the computation of land rent and surplus-values (applied to the office market in Oporto city). Finally in Section 13.6 some critical reflections are enlarged with respect to the impact of the proposed regional and urban management information system and methodology on the control of the distribution of surplus-values generated by administrative planning decisions, taking into consideration the different agents involved in property markets.

13.2. Literature Review

13.2.1. Urban land rent and its respective underlying variables

Land and real estate prices have a marked cause-and-effect relation (Clark, 1995; Granelle, 1970; LeFeber, 1958; Thoman et al., 1968). The cost of land is a component of real estate prices, mainly due to: (i) the heterogeneous characteristics of the different plots of land;(ii) competition for land uses; (iii) planning regulations; and (iv) location choices of firms and families (Dunn, 1954; LaFountain, 2005; Needham, 1981). In addition, retention strategies, often adopted by landowners, block land supply and, as a result, generate absolute and monopoly rents that add to real estate production costs (Harvey, 1985). In Portugal, within the framework of a proper land use policy, land value should represent, at most, 15 per cent of the final real estate product value (however, in cases of exceptional centrality or attractiveness it may reach 25 per cent (Pardal, 2006a)). On the other hand, whenever there is competition for land use, the expected prices of real estate assets influence the prices of land plots (George, 1960; Ricardo, 1962; Smith, 1843).

According to these interconnections, land costs can be split into two parts: (i) the transference cost that corresponds to the capitalized income that results from land's productive use; and (ii) the economic rent. Whereas the transference cost is a part of real estate costs (and, thus, it enters into their prices), the economic rent is given by the difference between the market price of land and its transference cost (Chacholíades, 1986). Economic land rent includes, therefore, a surplus rent (in relation to the transference cost), and an additional profit margin, and, in practice, it is very difficult to make an objective distinction between rent and profit. That is why planning should control land profit generation, taking into account the land social function, on the one hand, and the need to stimulate initiatives and investments performed by promoters, builders and sellers, on the other (Pardal, 2006a; Rebelo, 2009).

Land values depend on the land's territorial structure, on the one hand, and on the land policy pursued by central and local authorities (Pardal, 2006a), on the other. The discipline of inter-territorial relations and the respect for private property rights is established within this framework (Pardal, 2004, 2006a). Land values are modelled by various factors, namely: (i) private property laws; (ii) taxation over land and real estate; (iii) land uses permitted by territorial plans; (iv) rules for the production of urban land; (v) public and/or private real estate promotion; (vi) renting laws; (vii) credit systems in real estate acquisition; (viii) subsidies for home-ownership purchase; (ix) legislation to support property acquisition; (x) the woodland regime; and (xi) agricultural land structure (Pardal, 2006a).

The main costs underlying real estate price formation, in their turn, relate to: land, development, technical building, management, administrative and marketing costs, financial charges, and property taxes. These costs refer specifically to (Pardal, 2006a): (i) the land's gross residual value (controlled by demand); (ii) the land's geomorphological characteristics; (iii) forested or agricultural land value (regulated by exploration rents, but often modelled by psychological factors); (iv) the plot's location in relation to the main centres and subcentres; (v) the plot's dimension; (vi) property division (that usually involves a rise in land prices); (vii) the licensed use (that depends on a political or administrative decision); (viii) changes in land use and/or in intensity of use (the administrative decision to change agricultural into urban land, or to alter the urban parameters potentially generate surplus-values); (ix) indirect surplus-values (that result from infrastructures, equipment, public services, or other undertakings), (x) demand (split into useful and speculative demand); (xi) land and real estate taxation; and (xii) private investment in building and in other improvements.

13.2.2. Surplus-values and their respective underlying variables

The increased value of property (usually called surplus-values) may be considered from the legal, the urbanist and the urban economics perspective. From the legal point of view, surplus-values are assimilated to capital gains, in order to include them in total income for taxation purposes. In urbanist terms, surplus-values refer to property's increased worth that accrues from public works or from planning decisions, such as: (i) changes from agricultural to urban land uses; (ii) the definition of urban perimeters; (iii) division of land property; (iv) the expansion of the building capabilities; and/or (v) expansion of autonomous land plots (Pardal et al., 1996). According to this point of view, surplus-values can be subdivided into: pure surplus-values (that results from the increase in property worth as a result of a strictly administrative decision), and non-pure surplus-values (that correspond to increased land worth that results from public works).

The state and municipal authorities are the entities theoretically responsible for the control over surplus-values, either through fiscal devices, or through a suitable land use policy, and respective urban management (Correia, 1993). If the public administration is in charge of the production of development land, the sale in public auction of these urbanized land plots allows the retention of surplus-values that accrue from their own decisions on behalf of society in general. (Gwin et al., 2005; Hong, 1998; Peto, 1997; RICS, 1996). This strengthens their possibilities to dictate the rules of urban growth, and to balance the operation of property markets, thus preventing conflicts with other involved agents (Pardal et al., 1996). But if the production of urban land is granted to private agents, the surplus-values include the costs of infrastructures, and the profits and losses of promoters, builders and sellers. Under these circumstances, the public administration will only manage to levy part of the surplus-values, and only indefinitely and indirectly, because taxation settles on presumed values. Thus public administration looses a basic policy tool to regulate the use of land plots' and urban growth (Correia and Silva, 1987; Pardal, 2006a).

Within the scope of the law, surplus-values, by definition, should belong to public administration. However, both overprofits and land use changes or intensification that result from urbanist undertakings will impact on the evolution of land value. Both these aspects enter in the urban economics understanding of surplus-values (this concept parallels the concept of economic land rent). In practical terms, the increase in property worth has two component parts: (i) one depends on its territorial-based value (the plot's location, dimensions and authorized use), results from social and territorial dynamics, and is independent of landowner's investment or worth and of market behaviour, and thus it can be controlled by territorial plans and other land policy tools; and (ii) the other proceeds from trade profit goals, and from current market operation, as well as from improvements in property undertaken by the owner or leaseholder (Pardal et al., 1996). This implies that, besides the difficult determination of urban surplus-values (due to practical problems in computing the effects of certain decisions), it is almost impossible to dissociate them from profits. This consequently shapes the effects of property taxation on urban economics: namely, through the subsequent behaviours and initiatives of private agents (Correia, 1993; Lichfield and Darin-Drabkin, 1980; Smolka and Amborski, 2003). As surplus-values are, by definition, publicly-due, the taxation system needs to ensure that, at least part of their value should be recovered by the public sector whenever they turn up in privately-owned property (Rebelo, 2003), while respecting the private initiative. Thus, within the current framework of territorial economies, taxes should exclusively fall upon the territorial-based value, with proper landmarks, in light of an informed land use policy (Pardal, 2006a). In the United States of America, Canada and the Latin American countries, different surplus-values appropriation tools are used that range from conventional taxes and urbanization rates (with varying tax basis and percentages, according to countries) to different urban policy contol tools, with diverse characteristics (Smolka and Amborski, 2003). In Portugal, the tax on the land's accrued worth (currently called surplus-values tax) falls on profits, urban surplus-values, and other increases in property worth, generated during a period of time prior to the transaction (Pardal et al., 1996). In the computation of surplus-values, property values are appraised according to the parameters of the municipal tax on real estate I. M. I. (Decree-Law n° 287/2003, of 12th November). Even though these parameters are clear and objective, the identification and distinction of the increased values that proceed from municipal interventions, and those that result from the initiative of promoters, builders and sellers are neither simple nor clear (Pardal et al., 1996).

The fiscal reform that has been currently undertaken in Portugal is based on the English system, where the measurable tax unit (called 'rateable value in the pound') indicates the contribution that each unit value of property should pay and, consequently, surplus-values taxation is perfectly under control (Rebelo, 2003). Event hough the Portuguese fiscal management information system already has concrete indicators concerning property prices, use, typology, location, age, and state of preservation (the latter, in its turn, defined as a function of building's age, and dependent on repairs carried out), it would be valuable to have a complementary database with data that enabled the ongoing monitoring and evaluation of real or potential property market prices, for the different kinds of functional land uses, according to the location concerned and characteristics. The combination of data from these two databases should allow, at each moment in time, the evaluation and quantification of the respective surplus-values.

13.2.3. Behaviour of the development agents

The production, allocation and prices of urban land are shaped by rules, opportunities and expectations concerning their expected uses (Aydalot, 1985). Thus, they depend on a complex set of interrelated decisions taken by different economic agents: landowners, promoters/developers/builders, real estate mediators, final buyers or tenants, credit institutions and public authorities. But, because of the main imperfections of property markets (few participants in transactions, lack of transparency, and monopolistic features), part of the surplus-values generated by development processes nourish speculative behaviour, escape authorities, and fail to be used on behalf of society in general.

When pursuing their profit goals, landowners try to appropriate as much surplus-value as they can, and they even try to take a slice of the promoters' profit margin, which increases the risk with which the latter will be faced (Pardal et al., 1996). If a market discipline able to stress property's useful sense and social value does not exist, landowners will pursue passive retention strategies, and other appropriation forms designated to planning uses, which frequently leads to vacant property, ruin and dereliction. This land abandonment maximizes its speculative value, and provides prompt availability of property when the opportunity to sell arises (Pardal, 2006a).

Promoters, builders and sellers play important roles in shaping property markets. They intervene on the production/supply side, and try to increase their profit levels not only through urban development activities, but also through the inclusion of surplus-values in their own profits, often escaping the payment of the tax concerned. In order to maximize the surplus-values within their reach, they often exert pressures on the public administration in order to: (i) change plans, regulations, building permits or licences to more profitable uses; or (ii) intensify land uses (especially in central urban areas, where the profit margins they may keep from surplus-values are already squeezed, because they were appropriated by a series of mediators and land speculators in search of a quick profit).

Real estate agents (including valuers, consultants and other real estate professionals) are an important source of information concerning real estate location, characteristics, and availability, connecting buyers and sellers and, thus, encouraging property market transactions. They also try to hold part of the surplus-values, especially though percentage commissions on transactions (Rebelo, 2003).

Final consumers are mainly guided by use values and not as much by trade values. The main function of the credit institutions, in their turn, consists in the regulation of the cash flows within the property markets. Usually banks and insurance companies are able to reach higher profit levels through their lending activities, and thus they leverage surplus-values and property inflation.

Finally, the role of local authorities in land use management and control is mainly expressed through: (i) the provision of real estate assets; (ii) zoning regulations; (iii) laws; (iv) taxes; (v) permits for land use changes; and (vi) decisions on investments in infrastructure, equipment and public spaces. The state, autarchies and the proper credit institutions also try, through resort to different processes, to take a share of surplus-values, either through tax collection, or throught negotiations involved in development processes (Lichfield and Darin-Drabkin, 1980; Pardal et al., 1996; Smolka and Amborski, 2003).

13.3. Methodology for the Computation of Economic Rents and of Surplus-values

The powers retained by planning and local authorities to generate surplus-values and minus-values draw attention to the urgent need to frame the political and administrative act of land use changes. In order to (i) ensure the availability of land for different functional uses at acceptable prices; (ii) avoid the generation of excessive profits in land and real estate markets; and (iii) assure the neutrality of the landowners interests confronted with planning decisions, urban planning shall, on the one hand, intervene in plans and regulations and, on the other, develop property appraisal tools that are suitable for locations, uses and intensities of use. This chapter proposes a methodology for the evaluation and computation of surplus-values more connected to sites that, consequently, supports more efficient interventions of regional and local planning in taxation, and in the monitoring and control of: (i) the evolution of the variables that underlie property prices and surplus-values; and (ii) the distribution of surplus-values generated by territorial plans and regulations. It is applied, as a case study, to the office market in Oporto city (Portugal) (Figure 13.1).

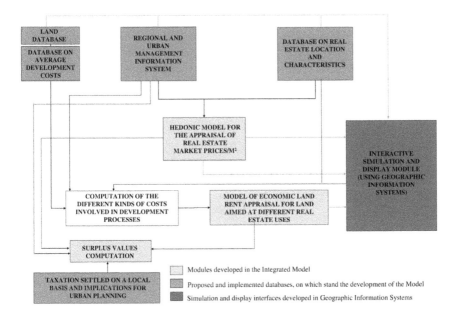

Figure 13.1   Integrated and interactive model to support municipal decisions concerning property markets

A management information system (with ongoing monitoring functionalities) was first developed. Subsequently an integrated and interactive model was implemented in order to compute surplus-values of land designated for office uses, based on a hedonic model of market prices, on average development costs, and on tributary patrimonial values (Rebelo, 2009).

13.3.1. Development of a management information system

The main office areas in Oporto city are located in the Boavista district, the Constituição/Marquês district and the old downtown centre (Figure 13.2).

A management information system (with monitoring purposes) was developed and implemented for Oporto city. It is comprised of databases on (i) land parcels; (ii) regional and urban indicators; (iii) average development costs; and (iv) real estate location and characteristics (Rebelo, 2009).

The database on land parcels supports the monitoring of most characteristics of the plots, as well as of their uses (enabled by territorial plans and other land-use policy tools). The included variables are: (i) the plot's dimensions; (ii) geo-morphological characteristics; (iii) absolute and relative location (in relation to the main centre and sub-centres); (iv) value of the agricultural land or woodland (computed using the exploration rents); (v) current or anticipated property

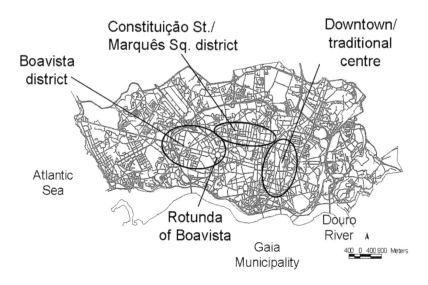

Figure 13.2   Main office areas in the city of Oporto

division; (vi) licensed use; (vii) real or anticipated taxes; and (viii) surplus-values that result from infrastructure, equipment, public services and other undertakings (indirect surplus-values).

The database on regional and urban indicators contains the variables that exert influence on office demand, supply and prices – some proceeding from market operation, and others under the control of local authorities (Rebelo, 2009). These variables refer to: (i) spatial/geo-referenced location of offices; (ii) planning regulations (including zoning regulations and land use coefficients); (iii) location indexes of different kinds of office activities (that show relative spatial concentration in relation to the overall territory); (iv) weighted distance to urban centres and sub-centres; (v) inertia exhibited by offices to remain in the same location; (vi) public investments in communications and transports, culture, sports and leisure time; public health utilities, environment; education; housing; economic development and tourism; civil protection; social action and urban (re) generation; (vii) number or density of inhabitants in each block; and (viii) date.

The database on average development costs includes: (i) land and land-related costs; (ii) development costs; (iii) building costs; (iv) management, administrative and marketing costs; (v) financial charges; and (vi) property taxes: The costs of land plots per square metre of building area correspond to the economic capitalized return from land use (it reflects its transference costs). They are considered to match the prices of the housing construction plots sold at public auction (that approach the prices of land for social uses). The computation of land costs for office uses takes account of those prices according to the average percentage that office prices represent over them. Land acquisition costs also include other elements, which are expressed as a percentage of the land acquisition costs/m²: (i) municipal transfer tax (10 per cent); (ii) stamp duty (0.4 per cent); (iii) property registration costs (0.5 per cent); (iv) notarized costs (0.5 per cent); and (v) legal fees (0.5 per cent). The development costs represent the costs of land infrastructures and participation in public investments. They are computed according to the municipal tax for urban infrastructures. The building costs include: (i) construction costs properly so called (that approach the selling prices/m² of common housing, annually published as a decree in the government diary); (ii) costs of equipment (namely, heating systems, lifts and special foundations); and (iii) building honoraries. This category of costs also includes different contingent costs (that generally go up to 5 per cent of the total costs), as well as the building inflation. It was assumed in this research that management, administrative and marketing costs amounted to 0.8 per cent of total construction costs/m². Additionally a 20 per cent added-value rate was imposed on those costs. In what concerns the financial costs, it was considered a 6.2 per cent rate of annual capital costs, and 50 per cent of borrowed capital for land acquisition purposes, and 50 per cent of borrowed capital for commercialization purposes (commercialization costs were assumed to represent 0.5 per cent of total building costs). Finally the municipal tax on property was applied, according to the kind of use.[1]

The database on real estate location and characteristics contains a set of indicators concerning the characteristics, location, morphology and typology of buildings and real estate units, and respective kinds of uses.

13.3.2. Methodology for surplus-values computation

The computation of surplus-values of land for office uses is undertaken in two steps: first the economic land rent is computed, and then the surplus-values are calculated.

The economic land rent/m² is given by the difference, per square metre, between the expected income and a set of anticipated land, development, technical building, management, administrative and marketing, and financial costs, property taxes and a normal profit rate (expressed as a multiple of those overall costs) (Rebelo, 2003, 2009). Office floor space selling price/m² according to the functional use concerned, its characteristics and location can be anticipated by a hedonic model that expresses it as a function of the indicators systematized in the urban management information system[2] (Rebelo, 2009). Each building site is assigned a certain licensed area or volume, according to planning regulations and restrictions. The total expected income is computed as 60 per cent of the product

---

1   The alternative uses may be housing, trade, industry and equipment.

2   This model provides ongoing monitoring functionalities, as it can be fitted to updated information introduced in the urban management information system.

of the licensed building area (according to the land use coefficient or index), and the office selling price/m² anticipated by the hedonic model.[3]

The surplus-values of land for office uses are then computed by the difference between the land market values and respective tributary patrimonial values (computed according to the municipal tax on property[4]) (Rebelo, 2009). The land market values are reckoned by the sum of the land rent (that corresponds to the economic return on land use, previously computed) and the economic land rent. The tributary patrimonial-value of building land is given by the sum of the value of the building implantation surface and the value of land adjacent to the construction (38th, 40th, 41st, 42nd and 45th articles). The value of the implantation surface of buildings varies between 15 per cent and 45 per cent of the building costs (this percentage already considers location characteristics). The taxable value of urban buildings targeted at housing, trade, industry and services is computed as the product of: (i) the property's territorial-based value; (ii) the gross construction area plus the area that is adjacent to the implantation surface; (iii) the use coefficient; (iv) the location coefficient; (v) the comfort and quality coefficient; and (vi) the building age coefficient. The use coefficient (41st article) depends on the kind of use: trade, services, housing, social housing, warehouses and industrial activities, or parking. The location coefficient (42nd article) considers accessibilities, such as nearness to social provisions, public transportation services, and location in expensive real estate areas.[5] The comfort and quality coefficient (43rd article) of urban property for trade, industry and services purposes is positively weighted by the location in trade centres or in office buildings, by the existence of central heating, by the building quality and the existence of lifts or escalators, and negatively weighted by the lack of sanitary installations, water and electricity nets, sewerage system, paved streets, lifts in buildings with more than three floors and low maintenance conditions. The building age coefficient (44th article) expresses the influence that building age exerts on prices.

According to the proposed methodology, and considering that the developed hedonic model (that accounts for 67.8 per cent of the explained variance) expresses office prices/m² as a function of variables with urban content, it becomes possible to observe the dissociation between the urban surplus-values (that accrue from variables mainly controlled by municipalities), and the profits (that result from

---

3   In the Oporto office areas, it was assumed that 60 per cent of each square metre is devoted to office uses, and the remaining 40 per cent to other uses (including public spaces). The total expected income was, thus, empirically computed as 60 per cent of the product of the average licensed number of floors, considering an average height of 2.7 metres (according to the general regulation of urban buildings R.G.E.U. and the selling price/m² anticipated by the hedonic mode)l.

4   The patrimonial value is computed according to the official valuation code (DL nº 287/2003) that sets the parameters for the computation of real estate reasonable prices/m², based on the application of socially-oriented land policy principles (Pardal, 2006b).

5   However subjective this judgement may be.

variables mainly regulated by the market[6]). The taxation of these two components can, therefore, assume different rates, so that surplus-values are recovered without discouraging private investments and initiatives (Arnott and Petrova, 2006; Rebelo, 2009).

The interactive model developed in this paper can be redefined by the inclusion of new and updated information. Furthermore, its simulation and display interfaces allows: (i) ongoing monitoring and control of factors that influence property prices; (ii) computation and cartographic display of economic land rent and surplus-values patterns and their respective evolution; (iii) analysis of changes in surplus-values that result from spatial and economic variations in planning variables; and (iv) simulation of alternative scenarios to support local authorities' decisions.[7] Because of its structure and flexibility, this model easily adjusts to other urban realities, and to other property markets.

13.3.3. Results

The developed hedonic model expresses office floor space selling prices/m² as a function of different urban variables (Rebelo, 2009): (i) offices' spatial location; (ii) urban planning regulations (zoning restrictions and land use coefficients); (iii) location indexes of different office activities; (iv) weighted distance to the most recent business centre (Rotunda of Boavista); (v) temporal inertia of office activities, (vi) different kinds of public investments; (vii) number of people working in the upper tertiary sector; and (viii) date. Table 13.1 below presents an excerpt from the database on the different kinds of costs involved in office development processes in Oporto city:[8]

The outputs of the integrated and interactive model that refer to the economic land rent and to the surplus-values of land aimed at office uses, according to respective characteristics and location, are detailed in Table 13.2 below.

Using the module of cartographic visualization leads to the distribution of surplus-values presented in Figure 13.3:

---

6   Considering the respective percentage in total land economic rent.
7   Namely, concerning the location of certain activities in certain areas.
8   The collected information refers to the year 2000.

Table 13.1 Different kinds of costs/m² involved in office development processes, in land acquisition and office building, according to their location in Oporto city (excerpt from the database)

Address	Zone in Oporto city	Land acquisition costs/m²									Building costs/m²				Financial costs/m²			Municipal tax on property/m²	Total costs/m²
		Land cost/m² of office buildings	Municipal transfer tax	Stamp duty	Property registration costs	Notarized costs	Lawyer honoraries (0,5%)	VAT on lawyer honoraries	Development costs	Total land costs/m²	Average office building costs (and specialised works)	Average costs of building garages/m² of office buildings	Total office building costs/m²	Management, administrative and marketing costs/m²	Financial costs of land acquisition/m²	Financial costs of commercialization/m²	Total financial costs/m²		
646 Rua Prof Correia Araujo R	Antas	211,5	21,2	0,8	1,1	1,1	1,1	0,2	31,5	268,4	415,0	43,8	458,8	3,7	8,3	0,1	8,4	0,770	740,0
94 Alameda Eca Queiros Al	Antas	211,5	21,2	0,8	1,1	1,1	1,1	0,2	31,5	268,4	415,0	43,8	458,8	3,7	8,3	0,1	8,4	0,770	740,0
130 Alameda Eca Queiros Al	Antas	211,5	21,2	0,8	1,1	1,1	1,1	0,2	31,5	268,4	415,0	43,8	458,8	3,7	8,3	0,1	8,4	0,770	740,0
194 Alameda Eca Queiros Al	Antas	211,5	21,2	0,8	1,1	1,1	1,1	0,2	31,5	268,4	415,0	43,8	458,8	3,7	8,3	0,1	8,4	0,770	740,0
256 Alameda Eca Queiros Al	Antas	211,5	21,2	0,8	1,1	1,1	1,1	0,2	31,5	268,4	415,0	43,8	458,8	3,7	8,3	0,1	8,4	0,770	740,0
191 Praca Pedra Verde Pc	Aldoar/ Antunes Guimarães/ Vilarinho	205,0	20,5	0,8	1,0	1,0	1,0	0,2	31,5	261,1	415,0	43,8	458,8	3,7	8,1	0,1	8,2	0,770	732,5

		205,0	20,5	0,8	1,0	1,0	0,2	31,5	261,1	415,0	43,8	458,8	3,7	8,1	0,1	8,2	0,770	732,5
216 Praca Pedra Verde Pc	Aldoar/ Antunes Guimarães/ Vilarinho	205,0	20,5	0,8	1,0	1,0	0,2	31,5	261,1	415,0	43,8	458,8	3,7	8,1	0,1	8,2	0,770	732,5
250 Rua Soeiro Mendes R	Aldoar/ Antunes Guimarães/ Vilarinho	205,0	20,5	0,8	1,0	1,0	0,2	31,5	261,1	415,0	43,8	458,8	3,7	8,1	0,1	8,2	0,770	732,5
305 Praca Pedra Verde Pc	Aldoar/ Antunes Guimarães/ Vilarinho	205,0	20,5	0,8	1,0	1,0	0,2	31,5	261,1	415,0	43,8	458,8	3,7	8,1	0,1	8,2	0,770	732,5
280 Rua Eugenio Castro R	Boavista/ Rotunda	290,0	29,0	1,2	1,5	1,5	0,2	31,5	356,3	415,0	43,8	458,8	3,7	11,0	0,1	11,1	0,770	830,6
300 Rua Eugenio Castro R	Boavista/ Rotunda	290,0	29,0	1,2	1,5	1,5	0,2	31,5	356,3	415,0	43,8	458,8	3,7	11,0	0,1	11,1	0,770	830,6
352 Rua Eugenio Castro R	Boavista/ Rotunda	290,0	29,0	1,2	1,5	1,5	0,2	31,5	356,3	415,0	43,8	458,8	3,7	11,0	0,1	11,1	0,770	830,6
370 Rua Eugenio Castro R	Boavista/ Rotunda	290,0	29,0	1,2	1,5	1,5	0,2	31,5	356,3	415,0	43,8	458,8	3,7	11,0	0,1	11,1	0,770	830,6
686 Rua Tenente Valadim R	Boavista/ Rotunda	290,0	29,0	1,2	1,5	1,5	0,2	31,5	356,3	415,0	43,8	458,8	3,7	11,0	0,1	11,1	0,770	830,6
174 Campo Martires Patria Cpo	Gonçalo Cristóvão/ Baixa	281,5	28,2	1,1	1,4	1,4	0,2	31,5	346,8	415,0	43,8	458,8	3,7	10,7	0,1	10,8	0,770	820,8
46 Campo Martires Patria Cpo	Gonçalo Cristóvão/ Baixa	281,5	28,2	1,1	1,4	1,4	0,2	31,5	346,8	415,0	43,8	458,8	3,7	10,7	0,1	10,8	0,770	820,8
9 Largo Adro Lg	Gonçalo Cristóvão/ Baixa	281,5	28,2	1,1	1,4	1,4	0,2	31,5	346,8	415,0	43,8	458,8	3,7	10,7	0,1	10,8	0,770	820,8
48 Largo Fontinha Lg	Gonçalo Cristóvão/ Baixa	281,5	28,2	1,1	1,4	1,4	0,2	31,5	346,8	415,0	43,8	458,8	3,7	10,7	0,1	10,8	0,770	820,8
26 Largo Prof Abel Salazar Lg	Gonçalo Cristóvão/ Baixa	281,5	28,2	1,1	1,4	1,4	0,2	31,5	346,8	415,0	43,8	458,8	3,7	10,7	0,1	10,8	0,770	820,8

Local	Zona																		
54 Praca Flores Pc	Gonçalo Cristóvão/ Baixa	281,5	28,2	1,1	1,4	1,4	1,4	0,2	31,5	346,8	415,0	43,8	458,8	3,7	10,7	0,1	10,8	0,8	820,8
95 Rua Joao Baptista Lavanha R	Foz/Gomes da Costa	241,5	24,2	1,0	1,2	1,2	1,2	0,2	31,5	302,0	415,0	43,8	458,8	3,7	9,4	0,1	9,4	0,8	774,6
67 Rua Infante Santo R	Foz/Gomes da Costa	241,5	24,2	1,0	1,2	1,2	1,2	0,2	31,5	302,0	415,0	43,8	458,8	3,7	9,4	0,1	9,4	0,770	774,6
399 Rua Alegria R	Marquês/ Constituição	226,0	22,6	0,9	1,1	1,1	1,1	0,2	31,5	284,6	415,0	43,8	458,8	3,7	8,8	0,1	8,9	0,770	756,7
582 Rua Alegria R	Marquês/ Constituição	226,0	22,6	0,9	1,1	1,1	1,1	0,2	31,5	284,6	415,0	43,8	458,8	3,7	8,8	0,1	8,9	0,770	756,7
7742 Estrada Circunvalacao Est	Bonfim/ Campo 24 Agosto	226,0	22,6	0,9	1,1	1,1	1,1	0,2	31,5	284,6	415,0	43,8	458,8	3,7	8,8	0,1	8,9	0,770	756,7
7762 Estrada Circunvalacao Est	Bonfim/ Campo 24 Agosto	226,0	22,6	0,9	1,1	1,1	1,1	0,2	31,5	284,6	415,0	43,8	458,8	3,7	8,8	0,1	8,9	0,770	756,7
11 Largo Jose Moreira Silva Lg	Bonfim/ Campo 24 Agosto	226,0	22,6	0,9	1,1	1,1	1,1	0,2	31,5	284,6	415,0	43,8	458,8	3,7	8,8	0,1	8,9	0,770	756,7
116 Praca Marques Pombal Pc	Marquês/ Constituição	226,0	22,6	0,9	1,1	1,1	1,1	0,2	31,5	284,6	415,0	43,8	458,8	3,7	8,8	0,1	8,9	0,770	756,7

Table 13.2 Estimate of economic land rent and surplus-values of land aimed at office uses in Oporto city (excerpt from the database)

Address	Zone in Oporto city	Land use coefficient	Average number of floors	Anticipated office selling prices/m²	60% of income/m²	Land, development, building, management, administrative, marketing, and financial costs, property taxes/m², and normal profit rate/m²	Economic land rent/m² [1]	Land rent/m² [2]	Land market value/m² [3]=[1]+[2]	Land patrimonial value/m² [4]	Surplus-values [3]-[4]
203 RUA GUEDES AZEVEDO R	Gonçalo Cristóvão/Baixa	5	1.85	1554,3	1726,9	543,4	1183,6	281,5	1465,1	645,2	819,9
227 RUA PINTO BESSA R	Corujeira/S. Roque da Lameira	5	1.85	1260,8	1400,9	515,4	885,5	173,5	1059,0	745	314,0
242 RUA S BRAS R	Gonçalo Cristóvão/Baixa	5	1.85	1504,2	1671,3	543,4	1128,0	281,5	1409,5	649	760,5
2533 FERNAO MAGALHAES AVE	Paranhos/Costa Cabral	5	1.85	935,3	1039,2	511,7	527,5	159,0	686,5	758,4	-71,9
35 RUA LIMA JUNIOR R	Paranhos/Costa Cabral	5	1.85	1284,0	1426,7	511,7	915,0	159,0	1074,0	756,2	317,8

411 RUA CASTELOS R	Ramalde/Monte dos Burgos	5	1.85	1362,1	1513,5	513,0	1000,5	290,0	1290,5	753,8	536,7
433 RUA NOSSA SENHORA FATIMA R	Boavista/Rotunda	5	1.85	1436,0	1595,6	545,6	1050,0	290,0	1340,0	637,4	702,6
49 RUA FORMOSA R	Bonfim/Campo 24 Agosto	5	1.85	1429,5	1588,3	528,9	1059,4	226,0	1285,4	659,5	625,9
55 RUA DR RICARDO JORGE R	Gonçalo Cristóvão/Baixa	5	1.85	1377,0	1530,0	543,4	986,6	281,5	1268,1	659,2	608,9
57 RUA FLORES R	Gonçalo Cristóvão/Baixa	5	1.85	858,0	953,3	543,4	409,9	281,5	691,4	653,1	38,3
393 RUA ALEGRIA R	Marquês/Constituição	5	1.85	1472,4	1636,0	529,0	1106,9	226,0	1332,9	696,5	636,4
1395 RUA CONSTITUICAO R	Marquês/Constituição	5	1.85	1304,9	1449,9	529,0	920,9	226,0	1146,9	694,3	452,6
455 COMBATENTES GRANDE GUERRA AVE	Antas	5	1.85	1160,3	1289,2	525,3	764,0	211,5	975,5	705,8	269,7
8 RUA BRAS CUBAS R	Antas	5	1.85	1052,4	1169,3	525,3	644,0	211,5	855,5	705,1	150,4

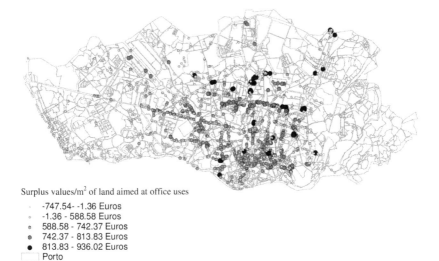

Surplus values/m^2 of land aimed at office uses
- -747.54- -1.36 Euros
- -1.36 - 588.58 Euros
- 588.58 - 742.37 Euros
- 742.37 - 813.83 Euros
- 813.83 - 936.02 Euros
- Porto

Figure 13.3   Expected distribution of surplus-values of land aimed at office uses in Oporto city, according to the proposed methodology

13.4 Conclusions and Recommendations

All participants in the development process should be encouraged to bring in to use their factors of production the socially-best way, in order to reach acceptable profit margins, while observing market rules, urban regulations, and land use policy principles (Clark, 1995; Correia, 1993; Pardal, 2006a,b). In the absence of a clear and objective assessement of surplus-values (including their generation, quantification and distribution), urban development or recovery processes risk being blocked either by supply or by demand.

A better awareness of the underlying conditions and ways to assess surplus-values will probably exert impacts on property agents' behaviour that results from these values. Landowners can still continue to search for profits, and have their own initiatives encouraged and rewarded. However, they are prevented from taking advantage of their extended prerogatives in land policy and cease to take advantage of their monopolistic/oligopolistic power. Promoters/developers/builders are becoming able to develop their activities in a more informed way, because their decisions are being better guided by the variables that underlie demand, and by the variables that underlie other suppliers' decisions, and are thus becoming more aware of legal, planning and market restrictions that they have to face. Property mediators, in their professional activities, can also take advantage of these analysis and intervention tools that may potentially induce a better efficiency in their decisions; namely, through a reduction in time adjustment mismatches between supply and demand. Through making it easy for final consumers (buyers or tenants) to have access to real estate products that fulfil their needs, and to a wider range of choices of characteristics and location, they will probably contribute to lower transaction prices, and still maintain reasonable profit levels. Credit institutions will have landmark cases settled on the assumptions for credit concession, thus using more realistic and socially-oriented criteria. Finally, this knowledge and these proposed tools allow regional and local public authorities: (i) the enhancement of the private initiative of promoters, builders and sellers, ensuring the neutrality of the landowners' interests in the face of land use dynamics and changes in intensity of use anticipated by planning decisions, and a more effective, balanced and informed intervention on property markets; (ii) the real-time provision of land and real estate products for the different needs; (iii) a better monitoring and control of property prices; (iv) prevention of speculative processes upstream and downstream the land development chain; and (v) a better control of taxation mechanisms, and of the collection of property taxes (namely, through parameter setting, and control over the distribution of the surplus-values).

Decision makers should implement planning strategic priorities in order to foster urban and socio-economic development, ensuring useful land purposes and social functions, through surplus-values control. Within this scope, the model to evaluate, compute and quantify surplus-values proposed in the research reported in this chapter seeks to reinforce strategic planning priorities in an effective and efficient manner, through fighting and preventing the speculation problem. As such, it should be considered in territorial plans and other land use policy tools, in order to appraise the economic and social impacts of administrative decisions and public investments concerning land uses or intensities of use.

It is hoped that this proposed methodology and developed model contributes to improve regional and urban strategies and policies in order to assure a better balanced rural-urban development, and the stronger sustainability of rural regions. Indeed, a better knowledge of: (i) land and real estate price formation mechanisms; (ii) the mutual cause-and-effect relations between them; (iii) the relations between rural and urban land; (iv) the land economic rent; (v) the surplus-values; (vi) the property taxation system; and (vii) the behaviour of property market agents, reinforces the role of planners and decision makers in regulation, guidance, coordination and control of land uses. In operational settings, this role will translate into more direct intervention on property markets: namely, through the use of these tools to assess, monitor, visualize and simulate the results of alternative regional and urban policies, and through a more effective application of taxation tools (in order to fasten them more to local realities, and to differentiate taxes on urban surplus-values and on private improvements). This more fair taxation of surplus-values would contribute to ensuring that they are used on behalf of populations, to control property prices, and to prevent/control property speculation.

References

Aydalot, P. 1985. *Économie Régionale et Urbaine*. Paris: Economica.

Arnott, R. and Petrova, P. 2006. The property tax as a tax on value: deadweight loss. *International Tax and Public Finance*, 13, 241-266.

Chacholiades, M. 1986. *Microeconomics*. New York: MacMillan Publishing Company.

Clark, E. 1995. The rent gap re-examined. *Urban Studies*, 32, 1489-1504.

Correia, P. 1993. *Políticas de Solos no Planeamento Municipal*. Lisboa: Fundação Calouste Gulbenkian.

Correia, P.V.D. and Silva, F.N. 1987. The peripheral city – urban development in Lisbon. *The Planner*, 25-27.

Dunn, E.S. 1954. *The Location of Agricultural Production*. Gainesville: University of Florida Press.

George, H. 1960. *Progress and Poverty*. 1st Edition (1879), New York: Schalkenbach Foundation.

Granelle, J.J. 1970. *Éspace Urbain et Prix du Sol*. Recherches Économiques et Financières, 14, Paris: Editons Sirey.

Gwin, C.R., Ong, S.E. and Spieler, A.C. 2005. Auctions and land values: an experimental analysis. *Urban Studies*, 42, 2245- 2259.

Harvey, D. 1985.*The Urbanization of Capital. Studies in the History and Theory of Capitalist Urbanization*. Baltimore: Johns Hopkins University Press.

Hong, Y. 1998. Transaction costs of allocating increased land value under public leasehold systems: Hong Kong. *Urban Studies*. 35, 1577- 1595.

LaFountain, C. 2005. Where do firms locate? Testing competing models of agglomeration. *Journal of Urban Economics*, 58, 338-366.

LeFeber, 1958. *Allocation in Space: Production, Transport, and Industrial Location*. Amsterdam: North Holland Publishers.

Lichfield, N. and Darin-Drabkin, H. 1980. *Land Policy in Planning*. London: HarperCollins Publishers Ltd.

Needham, B. 1981. A neo-classical supply-based approach to land prices. *Urban Studies*, 18, 91- 104.

Pardal, S. 2004. *A Fiscalidade e o Ordenamento do Território*. Paper presented at Jornadas Comemorativas dos 15 Anos da Reforma Fiscal, Faculdade de Direito de Lisboa, http://www.sidoniopardal.com/7_ afiscalidadeeoordenamentodoterritorio.pdf.

Pardal, S. 2006a. *A apropriação do território. Crítica aos diplomas da RAN e da REN*. Lisboa: Ingenium Edições, Lda., Ordem dos Engenheiros.

Pardal, S. 2006b. *Os Planos Territoriais e o Mercado Fundiário*. Paper presented at XVI Congresso da Ordem dos Engenheiros, Ponta Delgada, Açores, Available at: http://www.sidoniopardal.com/3_xvicongressodaoe.pdf.

Pardal, S., Vaz, A., Aubyn, A., Natário, I., Leitão, J., Costa, J., Lilaia, J., Reynolds, M., Lobo, M., Tomé, M., Fallen, P., Costa, P., Fernandes, R., Galvão, S. and Oliveira, V. 1996. *Contribuição Autárquica: Impostos de Sisa, Sucessões e*

Doações e Mais Valias. Lisboa Ministério das Finanças – Secretaria de Estado dos Assuntos Fiscais; Universidade Técnica de Lisboa – G.A.P.T.E.C.

Peto, R. 1997. Market information management for better valuations. Part II. Data availability and application. *Journal of Property Valuation and Investment*, 15, 411-422.

Rebelo, E.M. 2003. *Mercado Imobiliário e Transformações Urbanas*. PhD dissertation, Faculdade de Engenharia da Universidade do Porto, Porto, Portugal.

Rebelo, E.M. 2009. Land Economic Rent Computation for Urban Planning and Fiscal Purposes. *Land Use Policy*, 26, 521-534.

Ricardo, D. 1962. *On the Principles of Political Economy and Taxation*. 1st Edition (1817). Cambridge: Cambridge University Press.

Royal Institution of Chartered Surveyors (RICS) 1996. *RICS Appraisal and Valuation Manual*. London: Royal Institution of Chartered Surveyors.

Smith, A. 1843. *Recherches Sur la Nature des Causes de la Richesse des Nations*. 1re. Edition (1776), Paris: Guillaumin.

Smolka, M. and Amborski, D. 2003. Recuperación de plusvalías para el desarrollo urbano: una comparación inter-americana. *EURE – Revista Latino Americana de Estudios Urbanos*, Regionales, 29, 55- 77.

Talixa, J. 2008. Governo hesita sobre alterações à lei dos solos. *Público*, 22 August.

Thoman, R., Conkling, E. and Yeates, M. 1968. *The Geography of Economic Activity*. New York: McGraw-Hill.

Chapter 14

From Depreciation to Appreciation of Rural Areas: 'Beauty Idols' in Europe

Aliye Ahu Akgün, Tüzin Baycan and Peter Nijkamp

14.1. Depreciation of Rural Areas: Traditional Perspective

Geographic mobility is an indispensable factor in shaping human settlements in our era. Although mobility seems to be today's intrinsic need, the dominant type of population mobility in the 19th century, known as rural-urban migration, has stimulated the depreciation of rural areas and has emphasized the existence of rural areas with their specific problems, i.e. depopulation, lack of employment and other socio-economic deficiencies.

The term 'rural area' was used originally to mean the home of agricultural activities, in order to identify the areas which were not urban. In other words, rural areas were defined as the places where employment opportunities, infrastructure, and quality of life were missing, while, on the contrary, urbanized settlements were seen as the cradle of diverse activities, employment and a good life. The consequences of this point of view were observed first around 1850 in the UK, and then spread all around the world as rural-urban migration (Lewis, 1998; Lucas, 2007). The main reason for this one-way flow was the pursuit of employment opportunities (Harris and Todaro, 1970) that forced the rural population to move out of their settlements of origin towards surrounding towns or even further (Schucksmith, 2001). An increasing urbanization rate, due to immense mobility flows from poor rural areas, became the main concern of planners in the 19th century, which led them to find solutions for the associated problems (Gülümser et al., 2008). One of the planners' solutions was the suburbanization process which eased the flow to urban centres, this time, however, generating new settlements at locations close to and well-connected to urban areas (Woods, 2005). While this attempt was successful on the beginning, social life and employment remained the key concerns in rural areas at the end of 19th century. Thus, the depopulation and the depreciation of rural areas have continued.

Although this was the situation in 19th century, because of increased mobility the perception and cognition of people have been transformed in the late 20th and early 21st century. The impacts of this change can be cited as a reversal in demographic trends, a search for new lifestyles, and flexible production and work (van Geenhuizen et al., 2002: p. 3). Therefore, people and also policy makers no longer regarded rural areas as depressive, problematic and poor areas, but rather as diverse, attractive, and high-potential areas.

In recent years, as a result of the diversified characteristics and the changing perception of rurality including the reversal in mobility – called counterurbanization – rural areas have become some of the most attractive visiting and living places in Europe. Although they are sometimes seen, superficially by many visitors, as abandoned, underprivileged or poor places, we observe that creative and entrepreneurially-oriented visitors have not only passed through but have even developed business ideas and invested in these rural areas. Nevertheless, such newcomers are unaware of the need to change closed cultural and social systems which sometimes tend to have a very defensive sense of community and locality. In these circumstances, how can rural areas keep their existing assets and traditions while exploiting their increasing attractiveness? How can socially undesirable changes be kept under control? How can the transformation of rural areas from being depreciated to being appreciated be sustained? And can all rural areas become appreciated or attractive places?

One of the successful attempts to answer these challenging questions has come from France with the establishment of the Association 'Les Plus Beaux Villages de France', which later became the archetype for the Associations 'Les Plus Beaux Villages de Wallonie, Belgium', 'I Borghi più Belli d' Italia', 'Les Plus Beaux Villages de Quebec, Canada', and 'The Most Beautiful Villages of Japan'. Although the idea seems as simple as labelling particular villages as the most beautiful villages in order to turn them into sustainable trademarks which can compete in a modern global economic arena, the process of membership is complicated, strict and very selective, so that not all candidates succeed in becoming members. Therefore, these attempts may be seen as a rural success story which protects the local cultural heritage and the existing membership, while attracting much attention from diverse groups. Against this background, the present chapter aims to identify the most important factors associated with the attractiveness of villages, while comparing them using a newly-generated statistical attractiveness index. The data and information used for the comparison and investigation are based on extensive survey questionnaires filled in by relevant experts, i.e. 51 members of the above mentioned European Associations of the Most Beautiful Villages. Most data are qualitative in nature and call for a specific statistical treatment. Therefore, a recently developed artificial intelligence method, Rough Set Data Analysis, is applied to identify the most important factors which determine the attractiveness of these rural localities. The study will provide a list of the most important characteristics of such settlements in order to promote the attractiveness image of villages, while maintaining a sense of locality and community.

Next, Section 14.2 gives insight into the appreciation of rural areas and the modern perspective of rural areas, while Section 14.3 describes the sample and methodology used in this study, and applies the methodology. The study concludes with an evaluation of the important factors which have led rural areas to be appreciated rather than depreciated.

14.2. Appreciation of Rural Areas: Modern Perspective

Rural areas used to be isolated, traditional and less-developed regions in a country, and were usually seen as the opposite of, and dependent on, urban areas (Jacobs, 1969). But, in our modern age, they have enjoyed the benefits of the ICT era and can be distinguished less than in the past from urban areas and cities, apart from with respect to their demographic and natural characteristics (Gülümser et al., 2008). In urban regions, the structure of life is usually based on the pursuit of jobs and opportunities, but in rural regions, jobs come second to the pursuit of quality of life and the kind of lifestyles that people desire (Vias, 1999; Malecki, 2003; Labrianidis and Kalogeresis, 2006). From being traditional sources of socio-economic concern, many towns and villages have become high-potential areas where a good quality of life can be combined with creative and often flourishing economic activities.

The search for a new lifestyle and quality of life considerations rather than employment concerns were the keystones of the appreciation of rural areas which possess characteristics such as nature and landscape beauty that are missing in the urban settlements (Jones et al., 2003; Sofranko and Williams, 1980). Thus, the old and unattractive image of rural areas which represents traditional locality, has changed into an attractive image, so that both the local population and newcomers can experience the rural idyll. This new image of rural areas closely related to the dynamics of locality, especially to the cultural heritage and quality of life, is explained in the literature by many factors such as counterurbanization (Berry, 1976), the back-to-the-land movement, land-based lifestyles (Halfacree, 2007), eco-towns, and also green tourism.

In recent years, the maintenance and revitalization of locality have attracted much attention as critical success factors in order to obtain sustainable economic development in our modern age. The dynamics of localities, i.e. cultural heritage, social and physical environment, and economic opportunities, are related to the image and identity of an area. From an economic perspective, the relationship between locality and economic development is represented by the tourism sector, but the attractive image of an area shapes the vision not only of tourists but also of people who live and invest in the area (Forte et al., 2005).

Contemporary theories are based on the idea that the success of an area depends on quality-of-life issues, creativity, diversity of lifestyles, and local decisions, in tandem with regenerating the existing locality in all areas. On this basis, rural areas, which can, more than urban areas, offer quality of life and beautiful landscapes with their diversified uniqueness and preserved resources, play a crucial role in achieving sustainability and competitiveness in the complex world system. To sum up, the attractiveness of rural areas depends on their creative capacity, depending on the openness of the village and the use of technology in the village, locality, promotion, cultural heritage, and quality of life in the settlement. On the other hand, it is increasingly recognized that a mobile society incurs high social costs and generates a variety of negative externalities, including traffic congestion, accidents and fatalities, pollution and noise nuisance, destruction of visual landscape beauty, waste in the use of resources, raw materials and energy, and so forth (Van Geenhuizen et al., 2002). This new awareness and the influence of the mobile society have prompted a discussion on the future continuity and discontinuity of rural areas.

14.3. From Depreciation to Appreciation: The Associations of the Most Beautiful Villages

The quality of settlements is at stake in many countries. This negative development has led local authorities and individuals to develop innovative and creative ideas in order to ensure sustainable development at the local level and to promote it in the global scene. It is especially rural settlements with more local, traditional and natural values, which are being developed in an uncontrolled way because of the lack of administrative restrictions, that are in need of creative ideas in order to control and decide about the discontinuity or sustainability of their increasing attractiveness and cultural heritage. From the perspective of visitors and newcomers, creative practices are usually seen as related to the tourism sector, as they have contributed to diversifying leisure activities. On the other hand, from the perspective of the local population, these ideas have contributed to the protection and promotion of the locality, particularly its cultural heritage and traditions, while obtaining sustainable economic development.

Having aimed to control changes in rural areas and to expose and also transform their existing potential into a trademark in the global market, in 1982, Charles Ceyrac, the mayor of the French village Collognes-la-Rouge decided to bring together villages in his country, and established the Association of the Most Beautiful Villages of France with the collaboration of 18 mayors. The same year, in the first General Assembly of the Association, its President Ceyrac approved the strategy and the status of the Association (MBVF, 2008a, b). The strategy of the Association has three main dimensions, viz. (i) quality; (ii) *notoriété*[1]/ reputation; (iii) development, while aiming to develop, promote and protect the most beautiful French villages. The idea was to construct a form of national and thematic intercommunality/network which would help to make rural France attractive again, as it was lacking an image and misidentified by the consumers.

In order to achieve its aims and fulfil its strategy, the Association follows a strict and selective membership process. Villages having a rural character, with at least two historic monuments or sites registered, and the approval of the town

---

1   Note that in the literature the French word 'notoriété' is sometimes translated into English as 'notoriety' (Norman, 2006). However, in French 'notoriété' has only a positive connotation (fame for some good quality), whereas in English 'notoriety' always has a negative connotation (fame for some bad quality). The words 'reputation' or 'popularity' are closer translations of 'notoriété'.

council, may apply for membership. However, membership depends on whether the village concerned satisfies the criteria defined by the quality chart of the Association. If a village satisfies this quality chart, its mayor will become the active member. Besides villages, there are two other types of members that are honorary members. These are the founder mayors, and associated members. The latter are the partner enterprises which provide technical and financial support for the realization of the strategy of the Association. Usually, the Association sends an invitation to the villages to become candidates for membership, but some villages apply on their own initiative.

The idea of Ceyrac to bring together similar villages from different regions of the country in order to improve their quality, to boost their reputation, and to control their development has inspired municipalities and individuals all around the world, i.e. Belgium, Italy, Canada and Japan (Norman, 2006; MBVF, 2008a,b; MBVQ, 2008; MBVI, 2008; MBVW, 2008). Although each of the five Associations applied the French model, the Belgian and Canadian Associations cover only villages in one specific region, while the Italian and Japanese villages are established at a national level (Table 14.1). However, even though, their coverage area or type are different, the strategy of these Associations are the same.

Starting as a creative local thought in a French village, this movement has turned into an international federation called 'The Most Beautiful Villages on Earth' founded by the French, Belgian and Italian Associations in 2002, while the other Associations are just observers rather than members. So far, they have not been very active in the global scene, and therefore their future challenge is to represent their members in the policy circles.

Table 14.1 **List of the Associations of the Most Beautiful Villages in the world**

Association	Coverage area	Type of founder	Year of foundation	Number of member villages
Les Plus Beaux Villages de France	National	Municipalities	1982	152
Les Plus Beaux Villages de Wallonie	Regional	Individuals	1994	23
Les Plus Beaux Villages de Québec	Regional	Individuals	1997	36
I Borghi più Belli d'Italia	National	Municipalities	2001	178
Les Plus Beaux Villages de Japan	National	Municipalities	2005	11

Researchers and even the Associations themselves, forgetting the starting point and future challenges of these organizations, have evaluated them as a touristic action. However, tourism plays a crucial role in local economic development in many countries (Giaoutzi and Nijkamp, 2006) and in the representation of the local in the global scene (Gotham, 2005). Therefore, each action, which, achieves the representation of the local in the global scene cannot be claimed only as a tourism action but rather as an action to increase the general attractiveness of the space.

14.4. Attractiveness of Rural Areas

14.4.1. Sample

The data and the information used for evaluation are based on the extensive survey questionnaires filled out by relevant experts from 51 villages in Belgium (2), France (16) and Italy (33). The survey began in June 2008 by sending emails to the Associations' websites asking them: (1) to send the questionnaire for the village together with the invitation letter directly to their members, or (2) to provide the contact details of the responsible person in their member villages. The questionnaires were translated into French and Italian in order to avoid any language problems.

The French Association immediately replied to our email, while the Italian Association replied late as they were delayed by their General Assembly. Only the Italian Association helped with sending the questionnaire to its members. For the French case, via the website of the Association, we reached 81 French villages out of 152 members, and 16 villages replied by posting the completed questionnaire, while in the Italian case we were able to reach 113 members of which 33 villages replied either by fax or by email. The hardest case concerned the Belgian Association: the different structure and limited profile of the Belgian Association caused difficulties in collecting data. We were able to reach only 10 members and just 2 of them returned the questionnaire. Therefore, in total we obtained a total of 51 returned questionnaires. Our questionnaire process is still ongoing. The questionnaire has four main parts: (1) general information; (2) environmental characteristics; (3) relations and connections with the outside; and (4) membership. These four parts were designed for specific purposes: Part 1 and Part 2 to reveal the similarities and the differences of the characteristics of the villages; Part 3 to measure the attractiveness of the villages; and Part 4 to evaluate the impacts of the Associations on the villages.

When preparing the questionnaire, the aim was to highlight the perception of relevant experts, with a special focus on three main concerns of the Associations, viz. quality, promotion and protection. In Part 1 of the questionnaire, we investigated the perception of the responsible person when describing their villages. Even though each village needs to have at least one registered site to be a member, not all of them describe themselves as historic sites. Only 94 per cent, of the villages describe themselves as 'historic' while 45 per cent describe themselves as villages, which are dependent only on natural resources (Table 14.2). In Part 2, we asked questions about the natural, physical and social environment. Therefore, we focused on another membership criterion, which is to satisfy the quality chart related to the adequacy of the local infrastructure. However, although the villages in our sample did satisfy the chart and became members, 71 per cent of the villages claimed that their infrastructure was not adequate. This is because, although each house had electricity and water, and 90 per cent had a phone connection, today's indispensable urban infrastructures, cable TV and the Internet, exist in only 71 per cent and 37 per cent of the houses, respectively. Thus, infrastructure is still a differentiation criterion among villages.

Table 14.2   Four main factors of attractiveness

Description		%	#	Promotion		%	#
	Historic	94	48		Local events	92	47
	Dependent on nature	45	23		National Events	41	21
Quality					International Events	39	20
	Infrastructure	71	36		Outside Product Sell	84	43
	Cable TV	71	36	**Creativity**			
	Phone	90	46		Uniqueness	63	32
	Water	100	51		Technology use	90	46
	Electricity	100	51		Openness	27	14
	Internet	37	19				

The description and infrastructure of the villages show that they already have both cultural heritage and quality. In other words, they are ready to be exposed in the global scene by having local pull factors. But, these are not yet enough for them to be actually in the global scene: they need to have some products which can be promoted and some level of creative capacity to attract people. The product of the villages is one of the tools to attract people and all of the villages have their own particular product, i.e. cuisine, handicrafts, agricultural products, wine, and especially their landscape. However, the product itself is not enough if it is not promoted in the global market. Thus, villages use two types of promotion, viz. promotion in the village; and promotion outside the village. In the village, they organize different types of events, i.e. local, national, and international, while, in the outside world, the promotion of villages is done by selling the products. 92 per cent of the villages organize local events, while 41 per cent and 39 per cent of the villages organize national and international events, respectively. In the outside world, only 84 per cent of the villages are selling their products on their own or with the help of the Association (Table 14.2).

The description, quality, and promotion of the villages have accelerated the number of visitors. But the most important thing in order to obtain continuity not only of their attractiveness but also of their locality and rurality depends on the creative capacity of the villages. The creative capacity of the village is measured here by the uniqueness of the villages, the use of technology, and the openness of their inhabitants. 32 of the villages claimed that they have uniqueness, and 90 per cent use technology, but only 27 per cent said that their inhabitants are open to new ideas (Table 14.2). It is a well-known reality that villages usually have a defensive localism, and acceptance of novelty takes a long time in the village. This situation also affects the acceptance of visitors.

The attractiveness of a region is usually related to the tourism sector which plays a crucial role in local economic development in many countries (Giaoutzi and Nijkamp, 2006) and in the representation of local pull factors in the global scene (Gotham, 2005). The presence of tourists from nearby cities and from other countries shows that villages can attract people flows. Rural areas are seen as the leisure places of day trippers or short-stay tourists, although the attractive image of an area depends not only on the leisure activities but also on its other dynamics and economic opportunities mentioned above. In order to identify factors behind these extensive differences of attractiveness, we used Rough Set Data Analysis (RSDA), which is a particular tool for analysing qualitative data on the basis of an artificial intelligence (AI) method. RSDA is described below in Section 14.3.2. Then in Section 14.3.3, the methodology used in this study will be explained and applied.

14.4.2. Methodology: Rough Set Data Analysis

Rough Set Data Analysis (RSDA) serves to pinpoint regularities in classified data, in order to identify the relative importance of some specific data attributes and to eliminate less relevant ones, and to discover possible cause-effect relationships by logical deterministic inference rules (van den Bergh et al., 1997). In principle, RSDA is a non-parametric classification technique (Nijkamp and Rietveld, 1999), which has been developed as an AI method for the multidimensional classification of categorical data. It was introduced by Pawlak (1982) in the early 1980s and developed by Pawlak (1991) and Slowinski (1992). In recent years, RSDA has become popular in the social and economic sciences not only because of the advantage arising from its non-parametric character but also because of its ability to handle imprecise and qualitative data (Baaijens and Nijkamp, 2000; Dalhuisen, 2002; Vollet and Bousset, 2002; Nijkamp and Pepping, 1998a,b; Oltmer, 2003; Wu et al., 2004).

Therefore, we formed our data set by using 8 attributes and one decision attribute called 'attractiveness' (Table 14.3). Although we obtained condition attributes coded by the letter 'A' from the results of the questionnaire, the decision attribute coded by the letter 'D' is obtained by the generation of an attractiveness index.

In order to identify different attractiveness levels, we generated an attractiveness index by the ratio of the number of tourists to the number of inhabitants. Therefore, the attractiveness index ranges from 0.47 to 2228 (Appendix A14.1). Moreover, we classified these different attractiveness indexes into three levels, viz. less attractive, attractive, and very attractive.

Table 14.3   Attributes used in the analysis

Code	Variable	Explanation	Type
A1	Uniqueness	1=there is a uniqueness, 0=no uniqueness	Dummy
A2	Local Events	Number of local events	Numerical
A3	National Events	Number of national events	Numerical
A4	International Events	Number of international events	Numerical
A5	Use Of Technology	1= there is use of technology in the village; 0=no technology use	Dummy
A6	Openness	1= inhabitants accept new ideas; 0=no acceptance of new ideas	Dummy
A7	Infrastructure	1= infrastructure of the village is adequate; 0=infrastructure is not adequate	Dummy
A8	Product Sell	0=there is no outside product sell; 1= very low; 2=low; 3=average; 4=high; 5=very high	Categorical
D	Attractiveness Level	1= less attractive; 2=attractive; 3=very attractive	Categorical

Consequently, we obtained a data table. After obtaining the required table, RSDA can be performed. In order to perform RSDA, a modular software system Rough Set Data Explorer (ROSE) is used in order to implement the basic elements of rough set theory and rule discovery techniques. This software was created at the Laboratory of Intelligent Decision Support Systems of the Institute of Computing Science in Poznan by Predki, Slowinski and Stefanowski in 1998 (Predki et al., 1998; Wu et al., 2004). There are also other attempts to create software for the application of RSDA, *e.g.* ROSETTA, but ROSE is the most user-friendly software to apply RSDA. Therefore, the steps of the analysis are explained when applying RSDA in Section 14.3.3 below.

14.4.3. The Analysis: Important Factors of Rural Attractiveness

The basic idea in RSDA is to describe the data with rough sets (Rupp, 2005). A rough set can be characterized as a set for which the classification of a group of certain objects is uncertain (Dalhuisen, 2002). In our study, we defined important factors that are often associated with different attractiveness levels of rural areas. In the application of RSDA, three main steps based on rough set theory must be carried out, viz. pre-processing, attribute reduction, and rule induction.

The first step is pre-processing. This step enables the researcher to see the quality of classification and the accuracy of each of the categories of the decision attribute. This is done by dividing the lower approximation by the upper approximation of each category. In other words, if the quality and the accuracy of classification is lower than 1, then the chosen data and examples in the sample are not fully unambiguous concerning their allocation to the categories of decision attribute. This step strengthens the conclusions made on the basis of the other steps of the RSDA. The results of the first step show that the villages in our sample are fully discernible regarding the three levels of attractiveness (Table 14.4).

Table 14.4   Approximations

Approximations		Accuracy	Upper level	Lower level
1	Less attractive	1	25	25
2	Attractive	1	14	14
3	Very attractive	1	12	12
Accuracy of classification				1
Quality of classification				1

The second step of RSDA – the reduction – is used to form all combinations of condition attributes that can completely determine the variation in the decision attribute without needing another condition. In other words, in this step, minimal sets of attributes are found and these are called reducts. While finding reducts, RSDA can also find the frequency of appearance of all condition attributes in the reducts. If, among them, one or more attributes has a frequency of 100 per cent this is called the core. The result of the second step is that there are four combinations of condition attributes, which determine the variation in the different attractiveness levels (Table 14.5). In addition, two condition attributes, viz. local events (A2), and product sell (A8) are the core elements which are included in each reduct. This step shows that the cores are the most important attributes to determine the different attractiveness levels, while use of technology and infrastructure are relatively less important.

Table 14.5   Frequency of attributes, reducts and core

		1	2	3	4	Frequency
A1:	Uniqueness	+	+	+		75%
A2:	Local Events	+	+	+	+	100%
A3:	National Events		+	+	+	75%
A4:	International Events	+			+	50%
A5:	Use of Technology		+			25%
A6:	Openness	+		+	+	75%
A7:	Infrastructure	+				25%
A8:	Product Sell	+	+	+	+	100%

The third and last step is rule induction. This provides rules, which explain both the exact and the approximate relations between the decision and the condition attributes. An exact rule guarantees that the values of the decision attributes correspond to the same values of the condition attributes. Therefore, only in that case is it always possible to state with certainty if an object belongs to a certain class of the decision attribute. In addition, if a rule is supported by more objects, then it is more important, for instance, in classifying the different villages. In our RSDA application, we excluded those rules which are supported by less than three cases. Therefore, we have five exact rules, which are supported by more than 3 cases (Table 14.6). According to the rules, 27 per cent of the whole sample belongs to one of the three levels of attractiveness with certainty. Therefore, the rules are as follows: Rule 1. If there are no national events with a high level of product sell and defensive localism, then the village is less attractive; Rule 2. If there are no local events, then the village is less attractive; Rule 3. If there is a low product sell with open localism, then the village is attractive; Rule 4. If the infrastructure is adequate and there is no international event and the product sell is on average, then the village is very attractive; Rule 5. If the village has no uniqueness but it is open and uses technology, then it is very attractive.

Table 14.6 Rules

Factors	Rule 1	Rule 2	Rule 3	Rule 4	Rule 5
Quality					
Infrastructure				Adequate	
Promotion					
Local events		None			
National events	None				
International events				None	
Product sell	High		Low	Average	
Creative capacity					
Uniqueness					None
Openness	Close-defensive		Open		Open
Technology					Used
Attractiveness	**Less attractive**	**Less attractive**	**Attractive**	**Very attractive**	**Very attractive**
Strength	6 (24%)	4 (16%)	3(25%)	3(21%)	3(21%)
Name	Geraci Siculo(IT); Brisighella(IT); Pettorano sul Gizio L'Aqu(IT); Ars en Re (FR); Volpedo(IT)	La Flotte-en-Re(FR); Saint Quirin(FR); Orvinio(IT); Chiusa(IT)	Chardeneux (BE); Novara di Sicilia (IT); Crupet (BE)	Bova (IT); Giglio Castello (IT); Fources (FR)	Roussillon (FR); Vernazza (IT); Gourdon (FR)

The results of the analysis show that promotion of the dynamics of locality and openness of the inhabitants are the two most important factors of attractiveness of villages. On the other hand, the results also show that the quality of life is also an important factor, and the creative capacity of a village is becoming more important to attract diverse people and to sustain their arrival and relations with the villages.

14.5. 'Beauty Idols' in Europe: Retrospect and Prospect

In our times, globalization has changed the economy from being capital-based to information based. This has been reflected in the direction of population flows, and thus in the perception of people. Today, people are moving in all directions from less developed to developed or from developed to less developed settlements. This change has led to an immense reversal in the perception of rural areas. Therefore, rural areas are no longer places from which people are running away, and which then depreciate, but rather they are the places that people appreciate in experiencing their rural idyll.

Of course, it is not possible to say that all the rural areas in the world are appreciated, but in Europe many of the rural areas have become some of the most attractive visiting and living places. Although this new flow has helped the development and growth of rural regions, this increasing mobility towards rural Europe has also caused a number of problems, i.e. air pollution or the degradation of natural areas. Thus, with the aim of controlling these problems and sustaining the continuity of the villages and their attractiveness, Associations of The Most Beautiful Villages have been established, first in France, which then influenced other countries such as Belgium and Italy in Europe and Japan and Quebec in the rest of the world. But there are still unanswered questions, viz. How can rural areas keep their existing assets and traditions, while exploiting their increasing attractiveness? How can the transformation of rural areas from being depreciated to being appreciated be sustained? In order to answer these questions and to determine causes of different levels of appreciation, this study focuses on the member villages of the European Associations, and compares them with a newly-generated attractiveness index. In addition, in order to identify the most important factors associated with the attractiveness of villages, we used an artificial intelligence method called Rough Set Data Analysis (RSDA).

According to the results of the RSDA, the most important factors are: the reputation of the villages in the outside world and their creative capacity. Hence, although the appreciation of villages began with the pursuit of quality of life, today what makes a village attractive depends on its will to be a part of the global system and being known by outsiders and its will to accept novelty in the village. In other words, the 'idolization' of villages depends not only on their quality but also on their creative capacity and openness in our mobile network society.

However, focusing mainly on already attractive and known villages prevents us from developing an overall picture for all rural areas. Nevertheless, this study provides insights at least into why certain villages have become 'beauty idols' in Europe. On the other hand, this study also highlights the unknown hidden knowledge in traditions existing in rural areas, and moreover, the knowledge-based mobile network era of today's world needs to expose this knowledge in order to obtain a diverse creative and sustainable system. Therefore, subsequent research may focus on modelling a system that can indicate how to increase the appreciation and the continuity of rural areas, while developing strategies to turn defensive localism into open localism.

References

Baaijens, S. and Nijkamp, P. 2000. Meta-Analytic Methods for Comparative and Exploratory Policy Research: An Application to the Assessment of Regional Tourist Multipliers. *Journal of Policy Modelling*, 22(7), 821-858.

Berry, B.J.L. 1976. The counterurbanization process: urban America since 1970, in *Urbanization and Counterurbanization*, editeb by B.J.L. Berry. Beverly Hills, CA: Sage Publications, 17-30.

Dalhuisen, J. 2002. *The Economics of Sustainable Water Use: Comparisons and Lessons From Urban Areas*. PhD Thesis, Amsterdam: Vrije Universiteit.

Forte, F., Fusco Girard, L. and Nijkamp, P. 2005. Smart policy, creative strategy and urban development, *Studies in Regional Science*, 35(4), 497-963.

Geenhuizen, M. van, Nijkamp P. and Black W. 2002. Social Change and Sustainable Transport: A Manifesto on Transatlantic Research Opportunities in *Social Change and Sustainable Transport*, edited by W. Black and P. Nijkamp. Indiana University Press.

Giaoutzi, M. and Nijkamp, P. 2006. Emerging Trends in Tourism Development in an Open World, in *Tourism and Regional Development: New Pathways*, edited by M. Giaoutzi and P. Nijkamp. Aldershot: Ashgate, 1-12.

Gotham, K.F. 2005. Tourism from Above and Below: Globalization, Localization and New Orleans's Mardi Gras. *International Journal of Urban and Regional Research*, 29(2), 309–26.

Gülümser, A.A., Baycan-Levent, T., Nijkamp, P. and Poot, J. de 2008. *Indigenous and Newcomer rural entrepreneurs: a comparative study*. Paper presented at Regional Studies Association Conference. Regions: The Dilemmas of Integration and Competition?, Prague, Czech Republic, 27 – 29 May 2008.

Halfacree, K.H. 2007. Back-to-the-land in the twenty first century making connections with rurality, *Tijdschrift voor economische en sociale geografie*, 98(1), 3-8.

Harris, J.R. and Todaro, M.P. 1970. Migration, Unemployment and Development: A Two-Sector Analysis, *The American Economic Review*, 60(1), 126-142.

Jacobs, J. 1969. *The Economy of Cities*. New York: Vintage Books.

Jones, R.E., Fly, J.M., Talley, J. and Cordell, H.K. 2003. Green Migration into Rural America: The New Frontier of Environmentalism?, *Society and Natural Resources*, 16(3), 221-238.

Labrianidis, L. and Kalogeresis, T. 2006. The digital divide in Europe's rural enterprises. *European Planning Studies*, 14(1). 23-39.

Lewis, G. 1998. Rural migration and demographic change, in *The Geography of Rural Change*, edited by B. Ilbery. Harlow: Longman, 131-160.

Lucas, R.E.B. 2007. *Migration and Rural Development*, Electronic Journal of Agricultural and Development Economics, 4(1), 99-122. Available at: www.fao.org/es/esa/eJADE.

Malecki, E.J. 2003. Digital development in rural areas: Potentials and pitfalls. *Journal of Rural Studies*, 19, 201–214.

MBVF, 2008a. *Vivons L'exception!*. Document provided by L' Association des Plus Beaux Villages de France.

MBVF, 2008b. Available at: http://www.les-plus-beaux-villages-de-france.org/

MBVI, 2008. Available at: http://www.borghitalia.it/

MBVQ, 2008. Available at: http://www.beauxvillages.qc.ca/

MBVW, 2008. Available at: http://www.beauxvillages.be/

Nijkamp, P. and Pepping, G. 1998a. A Meta-Analytic Exploration of the Effectiveness of Pesticide Price Policies in Agriculture. *Journal of Environmental Systems*, 26(1), 1-25.

Nijkamp, P. and Pepping, G. 1998b. A Meta-analytical Evaluation of Sustainable City Initiatives. *Urban Studies*, 35(9), 1481-1500.

Nijkamp, P. and Rietveld, P. 1999. Classification techniques in quantitative comparative research: a meta-comparison. *Research Memorandum*, Amsterdam: Vrije Universiteit.

Norman, J. 2006. The strategy of cultivating Lifestyle entrepreneurs and amenity movers through most beautiful village associations. *Kumamto University studies in social and cultural sciences*, 4, 357-377.

Oltmer, K. 2003. *Agriculture Policy Land Use and Environment Effects: Studies in Quantitative Research Synthesis*. PhD Thesis, Amsterdam: Vrije Universiteit.

Pawlak, Z. 1982. Rough Sets [J]. *International Journal of Computer and Information Sciences*, 11(5), 341-356.

Pawlak, Z. 1991. *Rough Sets: Theoretical Aspects of Reasoning about Data*. Dordrecht: Kluwer Academic Publishers.

Predki, B., Slowinski, R., Stefanowski, J., Susmaga, R. and Wilk, S. 1998. ROSE: Software Implementation of the Rough Set Theory, Rough Sets and Current Trends in Computing, Lecture Notes in Artificial Intelligence, 1424, 605-608.

Rupp, T. 2005. Rough set methodology in meta-analysis-a comparative and exploratory analysis. *Discussion Papers in Economics*, Instituts fur Volkswirthschaftslehre, Technische Universitat Dramstadt, Darmstadt.

Shucksmith, M. 2001. *Development and ruralities in Europe: processes of change and social exclusion in rural areas*. Paper presented at the National Meeting of the Portuguese Association for Regional Development, Vila Real, June.

Slowinski, R. 1992. *Intelligent Decision Support: Handbook of Applications and Advances of the Rough Sets Theory*. Dordrecht: Kluwer Academic Publishers.

Sofranko, A.J. and Williams, J.D. 1980. Characteristics of migrants and residents, in *Rebirth of rural America: Rural migration in the Midwest, Ames, Iowa*. Iowa State University, North Central Regional Center for Rural Development, 19-31.

van den Bergh, J.C.J.M., Button, K., Nijkamp, P. and Pepping, G. 1997. *Meta-Analysis in Environmental Economics*. Dordrecht: Kluwer Academic Publishers.

Vias, A. 1999. Jobs follow people in the rural Rocky Mountain West. *Rural Development Perspectives*, 14(2), 14-23.

Vollet, D. and Bousset, J.P. 2002 Use of Meta-analysis for the Comparison and Transfer of Economic Base Multipliers. *Regional Studies*, 36(5), 481-494.

Woods, M. 2005. *Rural Geography: Processes, Responses and Experiences in Rural Restructuring*, Sage Publications.

Wu, C., Yue, Y., Li, M. and Adjei, O. 2004. The rough set theory and applications. *Engineering Computations*, 21(5), 488-511.

Appendix A14.1 List of Villages in the Sample

Name of the Village	Country	Number of Inhabitants	Number of Tourists	Attractiveness Index	Attractiveness Level
Geraci Siculo	IT	2150	1000	0.47	1
Saint Quirin	FR	965	700	0.73	1
Fagagna	IT	6080	7225	1.19	1
Neive	IT	2930	4000	1.37	1
Campo Ligure	IT	3170	4500	1.42	1
Brisighella	IT	7490	15000	2.00	1
Morano Calabro	IT	4966	10000	2.01	1
Buonconvento	IT	3234	6516	2.01	1
Orvinio	IT	457	1000	2.19	1
Oramala	IT	680	2000	2.94	1
Pettorano sul Gizio L'Aqu	IT	1323	5000	3.78	1
La Flotte-en-Re	FR	2900	12000	4.14	1
Moresco	IT	604	2500	4.14	1
Ricetto di Candelo	IT	7850	45000	5.73	1
Zavattarello	IT	1130	7000	6.19	1
Ars en Re	FR	1371	10000	7.29	1
Mombaldone	IT	235	2000	8.51	1
Chiusa	IT	5090	46000	9.04	1
Montsoreau	FR	503	4800	9.54	1

Name of the Village	Country	Number of Inhabitants	Number of Tourists	Attractiveness Index	Attractiveness Level
Pietracamela	IT	308	3000	9.74	1
Asolo	IT	9107	97700	10.73	2
San Donato Val di Comino	IT	2160	25000	11.57	2
Le Bec Hellouin	FR	417	5000	11.99	2
Volpedo	IT	1240	14986	12.09	2
Belves	FR	1431	21000	14.68	2
Chardeneux	BE	160	2500	15.63	2
La Bastide Clairence	FR	950	15000	15.79	2
Castel di Tora	IT	305	5000	16.39	2
Tourtour	FR	606	10000	16.50	2
Novara di Sicilia	IT	1753	30000	17.11	2
Crupet	BE	483	10000	20.70	2
Civita di Bagnoregio	IT	860	20000	23.26	2
Cutigliano	IT	1623	50936	31.38	2
Stilo	IT	2968	100000	33.69	2
Offida	IT	800	30000	37.50	2
Saint Lizier	FR	1659	65000	39.18	2
Furore	IT	810	35000	43.21	2
Borgio Verezzi	IT	182	12000	65.93	2
Castel del Monte	IT	500	40000	80.00	2
Gradara	IT	4300	400000	93.02	3

Name of the Village	Country	Number of Inhabitants	Number of Tourists	Attractiveness Index	Attractiveness Level
Cusano Mutri	IT	1500	150000	100.00	3
Bova	IT	462	50000	108.23	3
Giglio Castello	IT	750	100000	133.33	3
La Roche-Guyon	FR	516	80000	155.04	3
Lagrasse	FR	600	100000	166.67	3
Gordes	FR	2100	650000	309.52	3
Sauveterre de Rouergue	FR	830	270000	325.30	3
Fources	FR	291	100000	343.64	3
Roussillon	FR	1120	450000	401.79	3
Vernazza	IT	1035	2000000	1932.37	3
Gourdon	FR	437	1000000	2288.33	3

Chapter 15

ICT'S Role in Rural Areas Neighbouring Towns – Stakeholders' Perception

Zbigniew Florianczyk, Adam Wasilewski and Claudia Chlebek

15.1. Introduction

Numerous models and studies have indicated that economic development and ICT utilization are closely related processes. The EU development policies directly aim to stimulate ICT in order to the improve economy, society and the personal quality of life (Commission of the EC, 2005).

These policies promote the development of internal markets for ICT and support inclusion of these technologies in public and commercial services. Taking into account the differences in ICT utilization between urban and non-urban areas, a critical question, currently being debated, is how to support ICT investment, with the intent of increasing economic development in lagging regions. In this case the role of demand stimulation measures are stressed (Commission to the Council and the European Parliament, 2009). Among the rural actors that suffer from missing opportunities connected with ICT utilization are farms, small and medium-sized enterprises, and micro-businesses. The basically unsatisfactory access to modern communication technologies limits their commercial opportunities on local markets and participation in the decision-making process.

Prior to this, the dominant is philosophy of ICT focused on the adoption of ICT, in the belief that the poor "must gain eventually from adopting the technology because the technology is development" (Heeks, 1999, p. 12), and often regarded the use of ICT within development as an end in itself rather than a means of achieving other development goals (Heeks, 1999, p. 15). Simultaneously with this, other studies were concerned with whether ICT usage stimulates economic development, or whether the increase in ICT usage follows economic growth (Talbot et al., 2007). It has also been stressed that the engagement of local actors in the process of ICT implementation is the key factor to ensure its sustainability. However, among the most significant impacts of information technology the strengthening of social networking is listed (Lillrank, 2005).

These conflictual opinions reflect the complex nature of relation between ICT and economic and social development. Therefore, the authors of this chapter, in an effort to be more pragmatic, focus on answering the question how to support the overall process in order to stimulate economic and social development with respect to different functional types of rural areas.

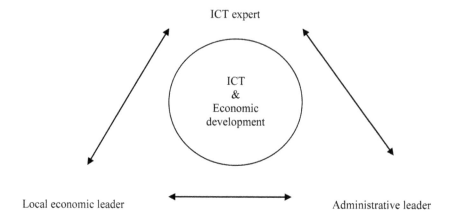

Figure 15.1   Interactive model of stakeholders on a local level

15.2. The Goals and the Methodology of the Study

15.2.1. Investigated relationships

The complex nature of the relation between ICT and economic development concerning rural areas can be described as a dynamic multidimensional process, as proposed by Gigler (2004). He postulates that the dynamics of this process results from interrelationship between technology and innovation, both in the social context.

Similarly, Mitchell and Gillis (2002) describe "the relationship between ICT and development [as a] multi-dimensional system" and propose an analysis of this relationship focused on three types of stakeholders. This model stresses the balance between:

- Development and deployment of ICT;
- Development of viable and sustainable economies; and
- Equitable access to the economic and broader social capital benefits of ICT.

On the basis of this work, the authors propose a simplified model to investigate the balance of local actors' perception of the role of ICT in economic development, and argue for its critical role in the stimulation of local development. The model consists of three stakeholder types: 1) ICT expert – the specialist most familiar with actual ICT issues in the community; 2) Local economic leader – the expert with an economic orientation; and 3) Administrative leader – the expert formally representing the interests of the community. It is assumed that those stakeholders are most influential at the local level regarding ICT development. Using the model, the authors seek to verify the critical role of a balanced perception of ICT potential between these stakeholders in local development stimulation based on a study conducted on the commune level.

15.2.2. Basic characteristics of investigated communes

The questionnaire-based survey study was carried out in 12 selected communes from the Province of Masovia, representing various economic functions and different locations with respect to urban agglomerations. Despite the formal classification of communes in three categories: 1 – urban; 2 – rural; and 3 – urban-rural, existing in Poland, the authors follow the concept of classification of the municipalities based on their functional characteristics (Bański, 2004). It is assumed that functionality shapes the possibilities and directions of the further socio-economic development of communes. In this article four functional types of communes are investigated i.e. (1) residential-industrial; (2) tourism-recreational; (3) agricultural; and (4) peripheral. In the functional approach, the small and medium sized towns are distributed among all types of communes.

Within the sample considered in the study, the farming function is represented by the communes of Belsk Duży, Grudusk, Sanniki, Korczew, Ceranów and Rzekuń; the housing and service function by the communes of Nieporęt, Zakrzew and Stara Biała; and the recreational and forestry function by Leoncin, Łąck and Łochów. The suburban communes are Stara Biała, Łąck, Nieporęt, Rzekuń and Zakrzew, with the remaining communes having a typically rural character. Of the latter, the communes of Ceranów, Korczew and Grudusk have a clearly peripheral location with respect to bigger towns and main transport routes.

The sample of communes, used in this and the parallel studies, was selected with the following main prerequisites in mind:

- It is at the level of communes that the character of a given area can be correctly defined, with the necessary differentiation, not just into 'more rural' or 'more urban', but also by taking into consideration its diverse functionalities and resource characteristics;
- The particular communes selected represent diverse functionality and endowment patterns, the latter in terms of both natural resources and man-made ones, including the opportunities offered by the particular location;
- All of the communes belong to just one province in Poland (Masovia, with the capital in Warsaw, which is also the capital of Poland), being both the largest of the provinces in Poland and the most differentiated one;
- The communes can be seen against the background of their respective counties, which is important, insofar as the counties themselves represent quite a diversified image across the province of Masovia; in fact, the counties represented in the sample span quite a variety of conditions, on which, however, we shall not be commenting here in any detail.

15.2.3 Synthetic measure of socio-economic development

Socio-economic potential is characterized with the synthetic indicator proposed by Hellwig (1968). The Socio-Economic Potential (S-EP) synthetic indicator aggregates the values of selected variables for each commune as follows:

$$\text{S-EP}_i(x) \quad x = (x_{ij})_{ij} \qquad (i = 1,2,...,12; j = 1,2,...,n),$$
where:
i = commune; j = variable; n = number of variables.

To facilitate summarizing different measures, the variables were standardized:

$$z_{ij} = \frac{x_{ij} - \overline{x}_j}{s_j},$$

where:

z_{ij} = standardized value in commune i for variable j;
x_{ij} = observed value in commune i for variable j;
x_i = average value of variable i in all communes;
s_j = standard deviation of variable j.

In this analysis, the development model reference value is represented by point P_0 with coordinates:

$z_{01}, z_{02},...,z_{0n},$
where:
$z_{0j} = \max(z_{ij})$ – for stimulators (positively perceived variables)
   or
$z_{0j} = \min(z_{ij})$ – for de-stimulators (variables with a negative significance).

The extreme values of coordinates for the development model reference value are the maximum of the standardized value for the stimulating variables and the minimum value for the de-stimulating variables. The S-EP indicator of development is based on the distance (c_{i0}) between the development model reference value (P_0) and commune (P_i), and is calculated as:

$$c_{i0} = \sqrt{\sum_{j=1}^{n} (z_{ij} - z_{0j})^2}.$$

The S-EP (d_i) for each commune is calculated as:

$$d_i = 1 - \frac{c_{i0}}{c_0},$$

where:

$$c_0 = \bar{c} + 2s_0,$$

and where:

$\bar{c} =$ arithmetic mean of distance between values for communes and the model's reference value;

$s_0 =$ standard deviation of distance between values for communes and the model's reference value.

In this analysis, the synthetic indicator of development factors refers to:

- Communal budget revenue per capita;
- Ratio of the number of physical persons owning business to the number of people in working age;
- Ratio of the number of enterprises with foreign capital to the number of people in working age;
- Percentage of the unemployed in working age population,
- Social dependency indicator: ratio of the post working age population to the working population;
- Ratio of the pre-working population to total population;
- Sewage network density; and
- Water supply network density.

Those characteristics are statistically important for the classification of the communes in Poland according to their development level. The de-stimulating variables are the percentage of the unemployed in the working age population and the indicator of social dependency, while all the others are stimulating ones. The socio-economic development reference value in this chapter is characterized with the highest values for the stimulators and the lowest value for the de-stimulators. Therefore, the socio-economic potential for the commune is between 0 and 1, with higher values corresponding to a higher development level.

15.3 Study results

15.3.1 ICT technologies and socio-economic development

Research was conducted in the Province of Masovia (NUTS 2: Mazowieckie voivodship) in central Poland. The area is characterized by high socio-economic development disparities on the commune level (NUTS 5). Disparities in the development levels of the communes are associated with different accessibility to ICT technologies (Figure 15.2). This differentiation mainly reflects the access of households to the Internet technologies, while almost all of them have mobile phone and traditional mass communication media like radio and TV. Therefore the following analysis concentrates on the Internet technology that is most promising from the point of view of development.

The shares of households with access to the Internet in the communes investigated were between 6 per cent and 46 per cent. Characteristically, the level of Internet accessibility did not correspond to the level of socio-economic development. Significant disparities between communes and low levels of Internet accessibility in relatively more developed communes (high S-EP values) seem to indicate that the Internet technology is in the first stage of implementation.

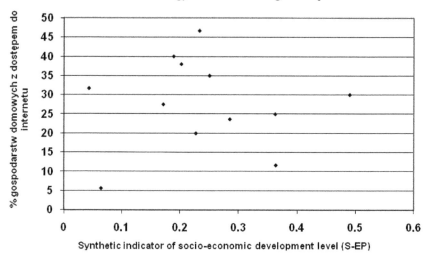

Figure 15. 2 Internet accessibility vs. socio-economic development potential in selected communes of the Province of Masovia

The differences in the level of Internet accessibility can be better explained by the differences in the municipality functionality type (Figure 15.3). The lowest share of households (18.7 per cent on the average) by Internet access was observed in peripheral communes. These communes were also characterized with the lowest level of socio-economic development. In tourism-recreational functional

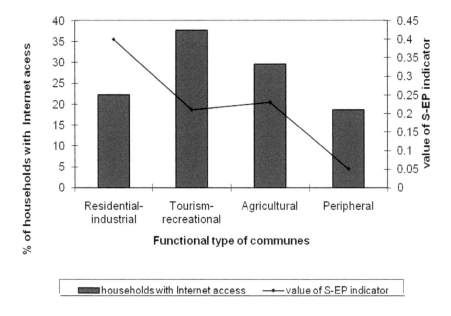

Figure 15.3 **Internet accessibility and socio-economic development potential in different functional types of communes in the Province of Masovia**

type communes, almost 40 per cent of households had Internet access. Communes of the agricultural functionality type had 29.5 per cent of households with Internet access. The residential-industrial communes, with the highest socio-economic development level, had, on the other hand, a relatively low (22.2 per cent) share of households with Internet access.

The relation between Internet accessibility and socio-economic development confirms the difficult situation of the peripheral type of communes. Given the multidimensional character of the process of ICT and socio-economic development in these communes, the implementation of Internet technology would have a minor influence on their development. Analysis of the socio-economic development potential of the communes also indicates that the Internet technologies are unlikely to intensify in use without external support. Therefore, the Internet cannot be recognized in these areas as a main driver of their development. In other words, the stimulation of development in these cases can be effectively achieved through the implementation of multidimensional strategies which combine different aspects of development.

Residential-industrial functional type of communes with relatively low levels of households with Internet access can also be described as relatively better positioned for development because of their relative proximity to urban centres. Thus, most of the inhabitants of these communes take advantage of the Internet in schools or at their workplaces. This hypothesis should be proved with the analysis of communal structure of businesses. In the communes of the residential-industrial functional type, businesses which heavily depend on Internet technologies were among the most important ones. Therefore, the high socio-economic development potential in these communes suggests that Internet technologies are likely to become an important driving factor for further development. Close proximity to urban centres would be a factor of stimulation for the Internet, in these types of rural communes, without external support.

Other development paths can be observed in communes of a tourism-recreational type with a relatively high share of households with Internet access. The Internet is more intensively used in these municipalities by households for commercial and home activities. For farms offering agro-tourist services, the Internet is a less expensive, and in some cases, the only affordable means of promotion and communication with potential customers. The Internet enables the promotion of locally-offered special services based on natural resources. In such cases, the traditional channels of mass promotion are not economically justified because of the relatively narrow group of clientele.

Growing numbers of farmers also recognize the advantages of the Internet. In communes of the agricultural functional type, the most advanced farmers are directly searching for new possibilities to improve their farming activities and for business communication.

It can be assumed that in communes of the agricultural and tourism-recreational functional type, the Internet can be recognized as an important development stimulating factor. However, their lower socio-economic development level could be an obstacle for further and faster development. Therefore, external support for improvements in Internet technology access would be necessary for the process to be effective.

This analysis clearly presents the differences in the potential capacity of Internet technology in stimulating local development with respect to the functional types of communes. This relation is explained by determining the different communication patterns of functional type of commune and, therefore, their utilization of the Internet. These relations influence the governance model on a local level: namely, through the participation of local society in the decision-making process. Concerning the stimulation of the overall process of investment ICT and socio-economic development, participation of the local society in the decision-making process is of critical importance. In particular, the elaboration of an effective strategy for Internet development needs to account for the local stakeholders' opinions. In this case, the most important opinions are those of local ICT experts and economic and administrative leaders.

The ability to formulate an effective strategy regarding Internet development can be demonstrated by comparing the representative stakeholders' opinions on the Internet's ability to improve local economic and living conditions. It is assumed that harmonized opinions of the above-mentioned three parties are the best for local development. The research conducted in the communes of the Province of Masovia proved that in most cases opinions of the ICT expert, and the local economic and administrative leaders regarding Internet potential are in agreement (Table 15.1). However, the differences observed were significant. In the case of residential-industrial type communes, the administrative leader's opinion on the positive impact of the Internet on local development exceeded that of the ICT expert's and the economic leader's judgment. These differences in opinions can be explained by the mentioned access to the Internet at the workplace and easy, direct access to services offered by neighbouring urban centres.

Table 15.1   Opinions of local ICT experts, administrative and economic leaders on the Internet' ability to improve local development

Commune type	Number of positive responses regarding the ability of the Internet to stimulate local development (out of 12 responses)		
	Administrative leaders	Economic leaders	ICT experts
Residential-industrial	11	9	9
Tourism-recreational	8	9	11
Agricultural	11	11	10
Peripheral	12	10	12
Total	10	10	10

Communes of the tourism-recreational type were characterized by very positive opinions on the Internet potential from the ICT expert representatives as compared with other stakeholders. However, the following analysis indicates that this opinion was connected rather to the weak promotion of the Internet technologies than to lack of administrative leader interest in their development. Therefore, in that type of communes, relatively the lowest level of harmonization of stakeholders' opinions regarding Internet potential was observed. Ensuring the integration of stakeholders in ICT development strategy formulation in tourism-recreational communes is critical to achieve the developmental goals with respect to ICT.

In agricultural communes, the driving Internet development parties were the local economic and administrative leaders. Surprisingly, these stakeholders' expectations regarding the ability of the Internet to stimulate local development were higher than those of the ICT experts.

The highest confidence in the ability of the Internet to stimulate local development among ICT experts and the administrative leader was observed in the peripheral communes. The relatively lower perception of ICT potential by economic leaders reflects in this case low access to these techniques and lack of capacity of local business to adopt modern technologies.

15.3.2 Strategic planning

Strategic planning is defined in this chapter as a process of formulating specific actions to fully utilize local endowments and minimize potential barriers to development. One of the major fields of strategic planning is concerned with infrastructure development. In practice, actions aiming at infrastructure development are defined by their variety in nature and scale. Definitely, Internet is potentially a part of local infrastructure development strategy.

Despite common opinion on Internet importance in local development, in some communes these opinions were not included in strategic plans, as shown in Table 15.2. In only five out of twelve strategic plans of the communes studied included actions aiming at development of Internet infrastructure and possible results of them.

At the functional type level, two out of three tourism-recreational communes had Internet development included in their strategic plans. However, both the local economic leaders and the Internet experts were not aware of Internet development actions present in the strategic plans for these communes. This contradicts the earlier statements about the relatively low potential of the Internet for local development in these communes expressed by administrative leaders. This paradox can be explained by the lack of importance of strategic plans or low participation of local stakeholders in strategic planning.

Table 15.2 Strategic planning of Internet development in the communes of the Province of Masovia and information transfer between their stakeholders

Type of communes	Number of communes			
	(a)	(b)	(c)	(d)
Residential-industrial	3	1	1	0
Tourism-recreational	3	2	0	0
Agricultural	4	2	1	0
Peripheral	2	0	0	0
Total	12	5	2	0

Explanation:

(a) – number of communes studied;
(b)– number of communes with the Internet issues included in local strategy development;
(c) – number of communes with the Internet expert aware of the inclusion of Internet technology in strategic planning;

(d) - number of communes with the local economic leaders being aware that Internet technology was included in strategic planning.

Concerning the peripheral communes, local government representatives, who placed strong emphasis on the development of Internet technologies, nevertheless, did not include them in the local strategy. This can be interpreted as a drastic disharmony between declarations and action. A total lack of actions regarding Internet development in strategic plans reflects a passive position of the local authority in this respect. The difficult financial situation of these communes creates psychological obstacles in considering new technologies as potential solutions to their development problems.

The research results confirm low participation of local economic leaders and Internet experts in the strategy planning process. This is partly associated with the ineffectiveness of the system of public information transfer and with the stakeholders' lack of interest in monitoring governmental activities on a local level. The low effectiveness of information transfer is the main factor impeding local development. Any missing information about the local society's expectations would directly result in a rejection of the proposed local government action. In other words, wider inclusion of stakeholders in the strategic planning process is the most desired way of putting forward development of Internet technologies. This recommendation should be of special interest for peripheral and tourism-recreational communes, which are characterized by relatively promising Internet utilization and a high degree of interference in the information transfer process. Improvement in collaboration between stakeholders would be helpful in diminishing the socio-economic development gap between these and residential-industrial type of communes.

In the majority of the communes, Internet development actions took place and in half of the instances this was recognized by local development stakeholders, as shown in Table 15.3. In most cases, implementation of Internet technology was based on the private sector. However, in none of the communes investigated was the administrative leader aware of such actions. In contrast, the local economic leaders and Internet experts did have the respective knowledge and were engaged in the process. The question then arises whether in such circumstances the actions proposed by administrative leader would perhaps overlap with the already undertaken initiatives. That would lead in most cases to certain economic ineffectiveness.

Table 15.3   Information transfer on Internet related actions in the communes of the Province of Masovia

Commune type	Number of investigated communes	Number of communes in which Internet related actions were known by:		
		ICT experts	Economic leaders	Administrative leader
Residential-industrial	3	1	1	0
Tourism-recreational	3	2	1	0
Agricultural	4	1	1	0
Peripheral	2	2	1	0
Total	12	6	4	0

An investigation into what motivates experts and leaders to undertake Internet development actions points out the self-initiative of local administrative leaders, as shown in Table 15.4. Particularly in peripheral communes, the local authority is recognized by other development stakeholders as a key actor in the process of undertaking ICT initiatives. To start with this can be assumed as desired and positive with a view to meet the local community's demand. Local authorities prove their willingness to be active in development-oriented bodies through these initiatives. However, as has been already noted, these administrative leaders' opinions are not reflected in the strategic development plans. In this respect, it is possible that problems with information transfer are likely to negatively influence the local authority's Internet development initiatives. Lack of the local society's control over the strategic planning results in 'empty' promises" of the local authority.

Table 15.4 Reasons for undertaking Internet development initiatives by communes in the Province of Masovia

Commune type	Reasons according to:		
	ICT experts	Economic leaders	Administrative leader
Residential-industrial	External private business initiative	Administrative leader's initiative	Administrative leader's initiative
Tourism-recreational	Administrative leader's initiative	Regional programmes	Administrative leader and regional programmes

Agricultural	Administrative leader's initiative	External private business and regional programmes	Administrative leader and external private business initiative
Peripheral	Administrative leader and regional programmes	Administrative leader and regional programmes	Administrative leader's initiative

The research results demonstrate the important role of national and regional programmes in stimulating local authorities in developing Internet infrastructures. This was observed in tourism-recreational and peripheral types of communes, which are characterized by relatively high levels of Internet utilization and moderate socio-economic development levels. This also suggests that national and regional programmes are important in stimulating development of regions with low economic development which are struggling with the local authority 'empty promises' phenomenon. It forces the local authority to effectively look for public financing for Internet infrastructure. In this light, it could be assumed that it will be also more effective in the mobilization of the private sector.

15.4 Discussion

This research has demonstrated the local authority's capacity to accelerate Internet utilization by improving the communication between different stakeholders. Therefore, the overall process of Internet and socio-economic development should be supported by an intensification of community participation in the process of local development programming.

The effectiveness of specific actions regarding Internet technologies development on a local level should take into account the functional type of communes. In this way it would be easier to ensure that stimulating or de-stimulating factors of local information transfer process are dealt with in a proper manner.

The present research results support the role of planning and the implementation of national and regional policies aimed at stimulating Internet infrastructure development in the different types of communes. In particular, improvement of the ICT utilization would lead to:

* Orientation of labour force and local business in the peripheral territories towards opportunities in urban centres;
* Increase of self-employment in tourism-recreational communes, with further development of communication with urban centres;
* Support of city centres with information on the possibilities offered in the surroundings territories;
* Increase of access to information in rural communes, both for farmers who are searching for new technologies and markets and farmers who are

willing to up take non-agricultural activities or are searching for seasonal non-agricultural jobs;

- Support of the uptake of home-based work in residential-industrial communes.
- The scale of the above listed positive effects of ICT development could, however, be reduced, if there is no coordination between ICT stakeholders on a local level, as well as on the national and regional levels. In particular, there is little evidence of self-assessment of the administrative leaders' role in local ICT development in local development plans. This is the case of peripheral communes where other stakeholders strongly depend on administrative actions. The study pointed out the weak perception of the role of private business in stimulating ICT development in rural areas, especially by local administrative leaders. This would lead to the economic ineffectiveness of ICT administrative projects, when overlapping with those of private business. The study confirms the need to further investigate whether and how communication from the masses needs to be improved. This approach would guarantee that the proper construction of top level development plans would be effective in all the different types of communes.

References

Bański, J. 2004. The development of non-agricultral economic activity in Poland's rural areas in Changing functions of rura areas in the Baltic Sea Region. *Rural Development Studies*, 2, 32.

Commission of the EC 2005. *A European Information Society for growth and employment*. Brussels: EC.

Commission to the Council and the European Parliament 2009. *Better access for rural areas to modern ICT*. Brussels: EC.

Gigler, B.-S. 2004. *Including the Excluded- Can ICTs empower poor communities?*. Paper presented at the 4th International Conference on the Capability Approach, Pavia, Italy, 5-7 September.

Heeks, R. 1999. *Information and Communication Technologies, Poverty and Development*. Institute for Development Policy and Management. Available at: http://www.man.ac.uk, 12-15.

Hellwig, Z. 1968. Application of taxonometric method for typology of country stratification according to level of development and structure of labour qualifications. *Statistical Review*, 4, Warsaw.

Lillrank, P. 2005. The Evolution of Organizational Structures in a Networked Society: The Case of Finland in Osamu Sudoh, in *Digital Economy and Social Design*. Tokyo: Springer-Veriag.

Mitchell, M. and Gillis, B. 2002. Making Sense of the Relationship between Information Communication Technologies and Economic Development. WSU Center to Bridge the Digital Divide, http://cbdd.wsu.edu

Talbot, H., Richardson, R. and Ward, N. 2007. Information and communications technologies in rural Europe: a literature review. *FARO EU project deliverable*, 31-37.

Chapter 16

Land-Use Conflicts and the Sharing of Resources between Urban and Agricultural Activities in the Greater Paris Region: Results Based on Information Provided by the Daily Regional Press

Ségolène Darly and André Torre

16.1. Introduction: The Specificity of Peri-urban Agricultural Areas: A Context of Extreme Competition for Access to Resources

Empirical observation of the forms of agriculture developing on the periphery of cities reveals the generalized presence of particular types of production or commercialization, which explains why certain sectors, such as the vegetable growing industry or the associated agricultural production, are sometimes called "peri-urban agro-industries".

However, two factors make it difficult to identify the production sectors that are specifically peri-urban: the first is the existence of a large variety of localized agricultural systems in peri-urban areas (see the high concentration of cereal growing on the periphery of Paris); and the second is the presence, in rural areas, of the same forms of food agriculture. Given this finding, most of the scientific community agrees that the specificity of the peri-urban sectors of agricultural production remains to be demonstrated, but that the specific nature of peri-urban land itself is undeniable. Its specificity lies in the fact that an increasing number of users compete for access to resources and land that have been traditionally reserved for agriculture.

The idea that peri-urban agriculture is above all defined by the state and location of the exploited resources is expressed by the concept of 'urban agriculture', proposed by Mougeot (2000):

> Urban agriculture is an industry located within (intra-urban agriculture) or in the fringe (peri-urban agriculture) of a town, a city or a metropolis, which grows and raises, processes and distributes a diversity of food and non-food products, (re-) using largely human and material resources, products and services found in

and around that urban area, and in turn supplying human and material resources, products and services mainly to that urban area.

Moustier and Salam Fall (2004) use and add to this definition by specifying that all agricultural systems located in an urban area (therefore peri-urban area) are at the heart of resources that are used for both agricultural production activities and industrial and other urban activities. This common need for and use of these resources can generate valuable productive synergies, but might also be at the origin of competition between the various systems of production for the consumption of territorial resources.

The territorial dimension of the peri-urban agricultural systems therefore lies in the existence of localized resources that are shared between an agricultural system and the closest urban centre, within what can be called an *agri-urban ecosystem.* At the scale of a territory, the urban productive systems consume, at the starting point, flows of primary raw materials (water, air, soil) or transformed materials (products from the primary sector, among which agriculture) produced from a stock of natural resources. As an output, they accumulate waste materials that must be exported to other territories, stored on site, or recycled so as to replace the stock of raw materials. Agricultural production systems are doubly connected to this network of material flows. On the one hand, they supply food and raw materials to the city. And on the other, they absorb part of the waste generated by the city (horse manure, wastewater, and nowadays bio-solids and composting products) by reincorporating it into the cycle of the agri-urban ecosystem (see Figure 16.1).

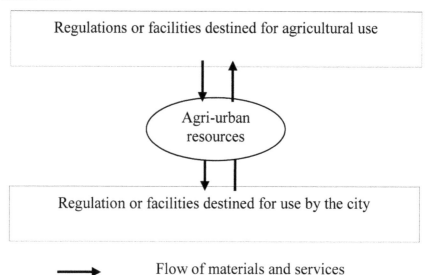

Figure 16.1   Graphic representation of the agri-urban ecosystem

By extension, we call 'agri-urban resources' the resources that circulate between the agricultural and the urban systems and which are usable for both agricultural production and for urban consumption. These resources include unbuilt-up land, water, air, and certain 'produced' resources such as landscape resources, food products or urban waste, all resources that can be incorporated into the agricultural production cycle.

16.1.1. A competitive system that generates conflicts

In areas where available resources are limited, the strong competition between the uses that consume these resources causes increasing conflicts and tensions. This is true in the case of agri-urban resources, which in peri-urban areas, are coveted by a diversity of users who perform different, often antagonistic activities (Bryant, 1992). The spatial expansion of cities is, indeed, a process that consumes natural, agricultural or forestland and that generates nuisances and pollutants transmitted through certain 'mobile' resources such as water or air. This universal finding conceals the fact that there is a diversity of ways in which built land expansion takes place, ways that do not always have the same impacts on the functioning of agricultural territories.

For a long time, this expansion took place through the progressive occupation of the closest land to the urban area. Bryant shows, at the end of the 1970s, that the ways in which land was appropriated when the large-scale projects of development of the suburban areas around Paris were realized have in some cases helped to improve the conditions of exploitation of agricultural land, thanks to the re-investment of the sale proceeds into the productive sectors (Bryant, 1973a). Furthermore, the growth of the urban market can provide an interesting opportunity for business expansion; indeed, during that period a number of fruit farmers expanded their acreage so as to be able to meet the demand of the urban population (Bryant, 1973b).

In the more recent model of urban sprawl, that of the dispersed city and of increasingly uncontrolled and fragmented urban expansion, agricultural land use has become durably 'interstitial', despite the fact that most of the land is still used for agriculture. Indeed, only 10 to 15 per cent of the land area in today's peri-urban belts is 'artificialized' (i.e. built or developed by man) (Boisson 2005); which means that over 80 per cent of the remaining space consists of open land, most of which is used for agriculture. At the scale of France, 40 per cent of all agricultural land is located within urban areas (see Figure 16.2).

Even though their consumption of agricultural land has been controlled or at least slowed down (IAURIF, 2005), these rural areas under metropolitan influence serve as support for the increasingly complex intermingling of the functional farmland and city. Moreover, the discontinuation of public investment in the large-scale programmes of urban development has reduced the margins

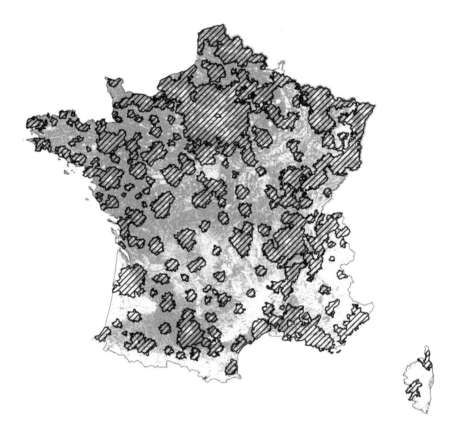

Figure 16.2   Location of agricultural land within urban areas

Notes
Striped area = Urban areas (urban poles, peri-urban, mono or multi-polarizedm municipalities)
*Remai*ning = Agricultural space (Data Corine Land Cover 2000)

of negotiations based on the expropriation indemnities received by the farmers. Neighbourhood tensions and conflicts are therefore fostered by this new peri-urban environment, and land exchanges do not lead to the investments that are necessary to reorganize the systems of exploitation. Conflicts are often considered as signs of the dysfunction of the social structures within peri-urban territories that must be resolved (Owen et al., 2000). Our research hypothesis, however, takes an opposite approach and supports the idea that conflicts contribute to the social control of the use of agri-urban resources.

- The analyses presented in this article are geared to three research objectives:
- Identify the objects and resources, the uses of which are regulated through

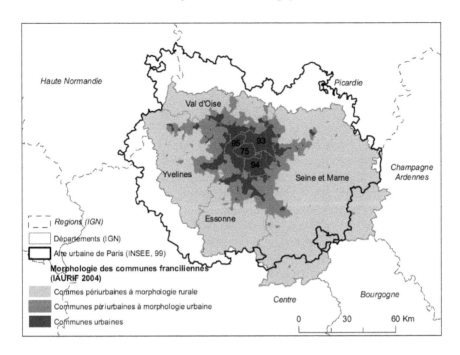

**Figure 16.3   The various spatial and political-administrative discontinuities
in the Greater Paris Region**

conflictual processes;
- Evaluate the scales of action implemented by the local actors according to
  the space-related issues from which conflict arises;
- Highlight the socio-economic situations that combine the spatial and social
  conditions that are conducive to the actors' engaging in conflict.

For this purpose, we have performed a quantitative inventory of the conflicts
related to the use of agri-urban resources, located within the Greater Paris Region.
Section 16.1 of this chapter presents the geographical context, the conceptual
framework, and the inventory method we have used. The results of the inventory
and the analysis of the data are detailed in Section 16.2, in which they are presented
according to the three research objectives we have set for ourselves.

16.2. Conflicts Related to the Use of Agri-urban Resources: Context, Concepts and Research Methods

16.2.1. The Greater Paris Region, a region representative of the diversity of peri-urban dynamics

The Greater Paris Region is by far the largest metropolitan area in France and can only be compared to two or three other metropolises of similar sizes in Europe. The national capital region is: the country's financial and industrial centre; the region with the highest number of tourists; and, in terms of its layout, the archetype of a radial-concentric city in spite of the urban outgrowths extending in the form of fingers along the valleys of the rivers Seine, Marne and Oise (see Figure 16.3). While 50 per cent of its total land area is used for agriculture, it is one of the first regional bodies to have actively acknowledged the importance of developing the land in a sustainable manner so as to protect agricultural land and ensure the survival of farming enterprises. The most recent sign of this commitment of the regional authorities has been their recognition of, and support to, local initiatives for the conservation of agricultural land in inter-municipal areas under strong urban pressure ('agri-urban programmes'), as well as of the four Regional Nature Parks situated within the rural belt.

The tensions caused by the existence in the same area of antagonistic activities inherent to the multifunctionality of the peri-urban space are many and acute not only because of the scarcity of space but also because of the high diversity of production activities and of the local populations.

16.2.2. Conceptual framework of the analysis of land-use conflicts

Conceptual definition of a land-use conflict
Several publications have examined conflicts and analysed their development and local characteristics (Melé and Rosenberg, 2003; Kirat and Torre, 2005). Most authors have found that the diversity of tensions related to the many uses of land makes them, on the whole, difficult to observe and survey: as they are not always expressed, trying to make an inventory of them would be unrealistic. Focusing exclusively on actual protests (Rucht et al., 1992) would drastically narrow the field of observation, at the risk of missing out on interesting information[1] (Trudelle, 2003). An intermediate option – certainly the most open and operational – is to identify conflict through the observation of the act of opposition of at least one of the protagonists; it is this act, limited in time and space, that indicates a crystallization of the tensions.

Analyses based on game theory use the notion of 'credible engagement' or 'commitment' to conceptualize this action (Caron and Torre, 2005). Engagement

---

[1]   While the term 'conflictual activity' covers all acts or deeds of opposition, the expression 'protest activity' implies collective action and a physical manifestation.

manifests itself in more or less institutional forms (verbal opposition, placards, registered letters, administrative proceedings...), or in more or less radical ways (assault, signs forbidding access, fences...). Defined in this manner, conflict can be identified more easily using direct or indirect information, and this definition is then adapted to a quantitative approach to conflictuality. We define as conflict an *opposition between actors with antagonistic goals, an opposition that leads to the credible engagement of at least one of the parties.*

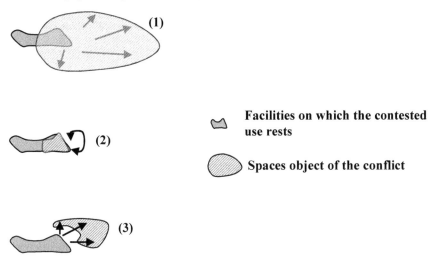

Facilities on which the contested use rests

Spaces object of the conflict

Figure 16.4   The different spaces that are the object of conflict

The spatial dimension of land-use conflicts: between contested activities and protected resources
More than the use itself, it is its location within an area occupied by other users that is contested during conflicts. In these situations, it is more precisely the object or facilities on which the contested activity rests that generates the conflictual reaction of the actors. This reaction is related to the antagonisms which arise from several uses conflicting with one another. These antagonisms can be found within a perimeter that corresponds to the physical characteristics of the contested facilities, but they can also concern a neighbouring area affected by a nuisance caused by the use of these facilities. Therefore, all the areas whose characteristics are altered by the contested use of these facilities will be considered as the spaces that are the object of conflict.
The physical characteristics of the spaces that are the object of conflict vary:
   (1) The resources whose state or conditions of use are constrained by the object of conflict are located within the perimeter of this object. This is the case for some conflicts related to the zoning designated in urban plans, in which some parcels of land are classified as land that cannot be built on (for example, conflict between

people who wish to protect the land from being built on, and those who want to use it for residential purposes). It is also the case when urbanization projects alter the characteristics of rural landscapes. Thus, residences built illegally in agricultural zones are contested not only

 because they are incompatible with conservation goals, as defined in the zoning plans, but also because they modify the rural landscape that the residents value as part of their living environment.

(2) The resources constrained by the contested facilities are located in areas that are adjacent or close to the facilities in question. Thus, wild boar breeding within private estates is not contested, but the damage caused by wild boars to neighbouring farmers' crops lead to protests against the ways in which the estates are managed.

(3) Finally, the parties who engage in conflict use the two arguments: the contested new facilities represent a threat both to the resources on which several users rest, and those located within neighbouring areas. Thus, projects of industrial development are conducive to conflict not only because they are synonymous with the production and emission of noise related or olfactory nuisance that will affect neighbouring residential areas but also because it is suspected that the planned factories will contaminate the soil on which they are built and destroy the natural landscape resources present on the sites.

Preventive and remedial conflicts
Furthermore, a distinction is made (by borrowing two terms used in the medical world) between *preventive* and *remedial* conflicts. In preventive conflicts, one party anticipates the impact of a certain activity or use on space and protests against it before the other party can implement it. The objective of the contesting party is then to protect resources from possible degradation.

In these situations, the ability to determine the spaces that might be used for undesirable activities depends on the accessibility of the information that makes it possible to locate the contested facilities, and on the actors' ability to evaluate the potential spatial extent of the nuisance and related risks. This evaluation – which cannot be based on in-situ measurements – is strongly dependent on the actors' experience of similar conflictual processes; the latter can indeed serve as an experimental reference (see the case of the wind turbines with pro or con arguments). In this regard, networks of people play a determinant role in the exchange of experience and information. Depending on the nature of the contested facilities, on the accessibility of the information concerning its characteristics, and, finally, on the ability of the contesting party to model its impacts on the resources present in the area, the zone under dispute may extend far beyond that of the facilities in question.

Remedial conflicts are triggered when an effective degradation of the resources has already been observed. The objective of the protesting parties is then to obtain either the restoration of the resources in question to their initial state or benefits or compensation for the harm incurred. The determination of the perimeter of

Figure 16.5 Location of the spaces in which preventive conflicts have occurred

Note: GUC: Geographical Unit of Conflict: A conflict that affects several communes is represented by the same number of GUC

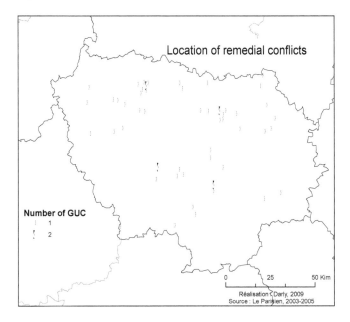

Figure 16.6 Location of the spaces in which remedial conflicts occur

the affected area then strongly depends on the ways in which the nuisance or risks are evaluated by the actors and is performed following two possible types of chronological sequences. In the first type of sequence, one person or a group of people experience a nuisance (by means of odour, noise, or otherwise) within a certain area, which prompts them to look for and identify the source of this nuisance, and possibly to adjust the initial perimeter of use and neighbourhood incompatibility (the case of the pollution of water resources). Inversely, in the second case, it is the identification of the object perceived as a potential source of nuisance that prompts certain parties to search for and identify the neighbouring areas at risk of being affected by the nuisance (see the example of agricultural silos: following a number of silo explosions, silos are now all subjected to risk assessments).

16.2.3. Inventory of the conflicts reported in the press: sources and methods

A first inventory of all the land-use conflicts reported in *Le Parisien* (regional daily newspaper) in 2005 (182 in total), indicated to us that agriculture is seldom the object of conflict and that the actors of the agricultural industry are rarely involved in conflicts. But 30 per cent of the conflicts are related to the non-agricultural use of open pieces of land identified as agricultural (cultivated, fallow, or meant for farming). Furthermore, this first inventory highlighted, firstly, that local elected representatives and associations are involved in the majority of the conflicts (70 per cent), and, secondly, that a large percentage of the conflicts are related not only to uses but also, more specifically, to land-use regulation (40 per cent of the conflicts).

We then extended the inventory of agriculture-related conflicts to cover two additional years (2003 and 2004), which enabled us to build a database containing 90 conflicts of various scopes and intensities, related to the use of agri-urban resources. Compiled in the form of a relational database, the information found in the newspaper articles, once encoded, enabled us to locate the *communes* (i.e. French municipalities) in which one or several conflicts had occurred between 2003 and 2005. Figures 16.5 and 16.6 represent the spatial distribution of these municipalities.

16.3. Results: Geographical Characteristics of Land-use Conflicts: From Objects to Social Processes

Using the information gathered from the daily newspaper *Le Parisien* for the years 2003-2005, we first describe the diversity of the contested objects and the nature of the antagonisms they generate and which cause the actors' reaction. We then present the patterns of interaction between the various actors who oppose these different categories of objects. Finally, we evaluate the influence of the socio-economic situation in the municipalities on the probability of emergence of a conflict.

16.3.1. Origins and spatial extension of conflicts related to the sharing of agri-urban resources

The information we collected enabled us to highlight the diversity of the facilities contested by the actors at the origin of conflicts, as well as the different types of antagonisms that explain their reaction.

Nature and diversity of the contested facilities
Conflicts related to the use of agri-urban resources are, for the most part, caused by the extension and renewal of urbanized areas. These represent 63 per cent of all land-use conflicts and are reported in 70 per cent of the newspaper articles.

This type of struggle involves a contest against certain urban activities, which modify the state of agri-urban resources. The category that comprises the facilities used for the management and processing of waste is the most significant in this regard (it represents almost one-third of the conflicts related to the consequences of urban expansion). However, these facilities are used for activities of different natures, ranging from the burial of solid waste in landfills, the incorporation of sewage treatment sludge waste into cultivated soil to the destruction of this waste through incineration. The other categories of urban facilities at the origin of the reported conflicts are, in order of importance, those related to housing, transport and communication activities, and those related to trade, recreational and public service activities (prisons, caravan parks). The other facilities that are directly involved in urban extension at the expense of natural resources are related to certain primary sector activities, such as wind energy extraction and production (5.5 per cent of the conflicts are related to these two categories). Finally, 8 per cent of the conflicts are caused by urban development regulations authorizing the conversion of open spaces into urbanized or industrial zones.

The other non-agricultural uses (non-commercial and non-planned) of space represent the second source of conflicts after those related to urbanization. They were, between 2003 and 2005, at the origin of 18 per cent of the conflicts inventoried and 17 per cent of those reported in the Press. They are related to the residential use of agricultural land (uncleared, fallow or meadow land) by groups of caravans or vehicles, and also to recreational uses such as hunting or motor sports, which cause damage to crops. Some illegal uses of agricultural land, the objects/equipment for which are not always identified, are part of this category of uses (e.g. theft).

Finally, the conflicts related to agricultural uses of space or to the extension of land for farming purposes represent the smallest percentage of the conflicts reported in the press (the constraints they generate are at the origin of only 16 per cent of the inventoried conflicts and 12 per cent of the press articles). In these conflicts several categories of objects are contested. The first is that of agricultural

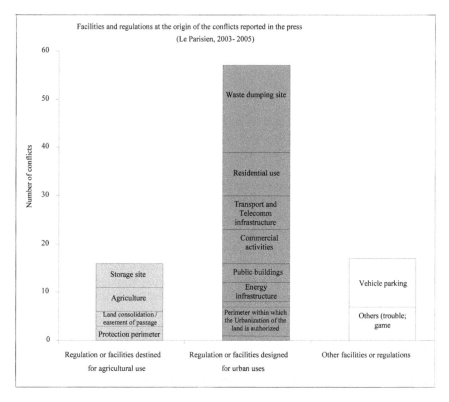

Figure 16.7   Proportion of the different categories of facilities or regulations at the origin of the 90 conflicts – reported in the Press – related to the use of agri-urban resources

Source: Le Parisien (2003 - 2005)

practices/facilities that are considered hazardous or dangerous (the illegal burning of crop residues, the experimental use of GMO seeds, well-drilling for irrigated crops). The second concerns the activities of storage and transformation of agricultural inputs and products, which necessitate the extension, development or functioning of industrial sites regulated as scheduled facilities (crop silos, the noise produced by beet trucks). The other conflicts in which actors protest against facilities developed for the agricultural use of land are directed against the adoption of regulations that restrict the use – urban or agricultural – of natural resources. The objects targeted by these processes of protest are therefore essentially the administrative boundaries that define the territory within which the protection measures (contested by the farmers themselves, who consider that the restrictions are too stringent) must be applied, but also the new parcel plans resulting from land consolidation operations (opposed by environmentalists because of the

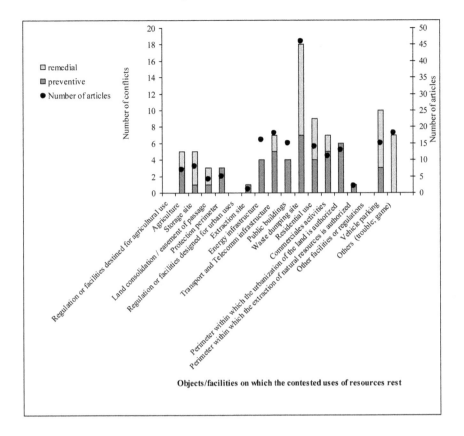

Figure 16.8   Proportion of remedial or preventive conflicts according to the type of facilities/objects contested

Source: Le Parisien, 2003-2005

environmental consequences of the destruction of hedges) or even more local regulations that designate certain rural roads for agricultural use.

Preventive conflicts

The majority of conflicts (57.7 per cent) occur in an attempt to prevent the creation or development of objects or facilities considered to be associated with environmental constraints (the other conflicts are remedial. They are triggered by people who seek to minimize or eliminate a nuisance they are already experiencing).

The conflicts related to facilities or regulations that are considered necessary for urban functioning are mostly preventive, with the exception of some categories such as waste management or residential use (Figure 16.8). Inversely, in almost all the conflicts related to other non-agricultural uses of space, the parties react and protest against objects that do exist and that have already modified the state of the resources. In these situations, the protesters start a process of remedial conflict. The cases of protests against facilities or regulations meant to enable certain parties to make agricultural use of natural resources are not as clear-cut. Half of these cases concern virtual objects and uses (projects of agricultural well-drilling, for example, or of genetically modified crops) whereas the other half are protests against practices, buildings or regulations that already exist (stubble burning, silos, easement of passage).

The resources and interests threatened by the close proximity or juxtaposition of incompatible land-uses

People who protest against the existence or development of the types of facilities we have just mentioned seek, above all, to protect individual or collective interests related to the consumption, exploitation or conservation of territorial resources. In almost half of the conflicts (46 per cent; Table 16.1), the actors fight for the preservation of the agricultural use of certain local resources. The latter are located within open spaces, or in some rare cases, within parcels of land that are meant for agriculture but are 'used' for other activities (4 per cent of the cases). These resources can be immovable natural resources, such as land, or 'mobile' resources that circulate between close urbanized reas and agricultural land (water, air). A large number of these conflicts (1/3 of them) are also cases where actors join forces to fight for the preservation of the landscape resources and that of the agricultural use of natural resources.

In 25 per cent of the conflicts, it is not so much the open spaces or landscapes that the actors seek to preserve, but rather the environmental quality of the atmospheric and water resources that circulate between the different peri-urban territories and are used in residential zones. In these cases, the residents wish these resources to circulate between agricultural, natural and residential spaces rather than between future urbanized or industrial zones and their areas of residence. Finally, in 10 per cent of the conflicts reported in the press, the people who engage in a conflict claim that they wish to protect agricultural land so as to ensure the preservation of the biodiversity resources that it provides.

Table 16.1   Types of disputes leading to conflicts about the use of agri-urban resources and their distribution among all the conflicts reported in the Press

Objects/facilities on which the contested activities rest	Protected agri-urban resources	Geographical proximity of the uses	Geographical proximity of the users	Origin of the reported disputes
• All types of buildings / infrastructures for use by • Sewage sludge application / Waste treatment • Cement exploration zone • Zoning/Permits • Vehicle parking • Outdoor recreational activities	Land destined for agriculture	Multiple uses (juxtaposition)	Users of the same parcel of land	'The facilities developed for urban use consume or modify resources which some wish to reserve for agricultural activities' (72% of the conflicts)
• Transport infras. facilities • Industrial zones (extraction, activity zone, logistics) • Land treatment / Waste • Wind turbines	'Mobile' resources (air, water)	Neighbouring uses	Users of neighbouring parcels of land	
• Developed sites for urban use • Cement exploration zone	Ecological resources	Multiple uses (juxtaposition)	Users of the same parcel of land	
• Landscaping of waste storage sites • Housing, activity zones, zoning maps • Wind turbines	Landscape resources	Multiple uses (juxtaposition)	Users of neighbouring parcels of land	'Urban facilities damage the agricultural landscape' (27% of the conflicts)

Objects/facilities on which the contested activities rest	Protected agri-urban resources	Geographical proximity of the uses	Geographical proximity of the users	Origin of the reported disputes
• Industrial zones where entrant suppliers or agricultural product wholesalers are located • Irrigation well drilling	'Mobile' resources (air, water)	Neighbouring uses	Users of neighbouring parcels of land	'Agricultural facilities or regulations consume or modify resources some wish to reserve for urban activities' (16% of the conflicts)
• Regulations to preserve the agricultural use of land	Land destined for urban use	Multiple uses (juxtaposition)	Users of the same parcel of land	
• *Perimeter within which agricultural land uses are regulated.* • Game damage	Land destined for agriculture	Multiple uses (juxtaposition)	Users of the same parcel of land	'"Nature conservation' uses of resources represent an obstacle to the agricultural exploitation of these resources" (8% of the conflicts)
• GMO crops	Ecological resources	Neighbouring and Multiple uses (juxtaposition)	Users of neighbouring parcels of land	'The facilities or regulations meant for agricultural activities have a negative impact on the biodiversity resources' (1% of the conflicts)

Source: Le Parisien (2003-2005)

16.3.2. Land-use conflicts and interaction between the actors: Differentiating the various patterns of opposition

Even though they are dependent on the nature and arrangement of objects/facilities in space, conflicts are above all social processes that can be described in terms of social interactions between groups of actors.

The interactions between the actors reveal that preventive conflicts are mostly collective actions
A first quantitative synthesis of the information found in the Press concerning actors engaged in conflicts shows that it is less the reaction of the actual users of land (professionals, individuals) than the actions of their representatives (elected representatives, associations, representatives of the public authorities) that are reported in newspapers (Figure 16.9). Among these representatives, municipal elected officials and local or generalist associations are those that initiate most of the actions covered by the Press, whereas the representatives of State authorities, municipal elected officials and professional users are the group of actors who are the most contested.

Among the conflicts triggered by groups opposing the urbanization of agricultural land, three scales of conflicts can be distinguished that correspond to different categories of contested objects and uses. They are the conflicts related to regional development, those related to the management of municipal land, and those related to the consequences of urbanization (Cadene, 1990).

In the first case, the conflictual interactions develop at the level of the sub-region, through alliances between elected officials and associations who oppose representatives of the public authorities accused of supporting private developers, or the managers of regional development and planning (Table 16.2). In the case of conflicts related to the management of municipal land, the conflictual interactions only involve members of the municipality. The municipal council plays an important role here. Finally, the conflicts triggered by actors who protest against the nuisance and constraints generated by agricultural activities develop mostly at the scale of the municipal territories and their neighbouring areas. They involve local environmental associations, and municipal officials who oppose the professional representatives of the agricultural or agribusiness sector.

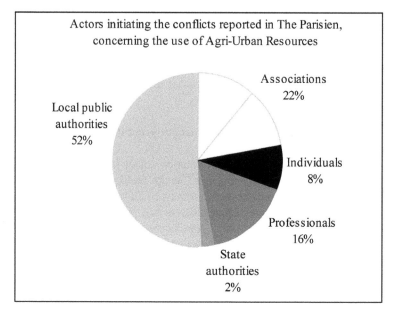

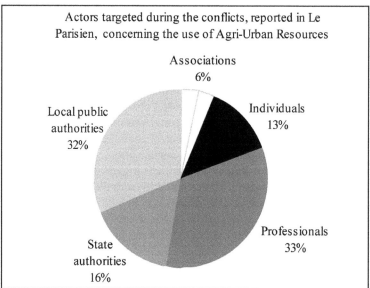

**Figure 16.9   The different groups of actors initiating conflicts and those
                targeted by these processes**

Source: Le Parisien (2003-2005)

Table 16.2   Objects of the conflicts according to the intensity and typology

Type of incompatibility (covered by the Press)	Objects/facilities on which the contested activities rest	Actors initiating engagement in conflict	The actors targeted during the conflict
'The facilities developed for urban use consume or modify resources some wish to reserve for agricultural activities' (72 % of the conflicts) and	• Conflicts related to regional planning • Land treatment/ Waste/ Landfills • Industrial sites(extraction, zone of activities) • Transport infrast. • Cement exploration zone • Public utility infrastructure/ buildings	50% Alliances of municipalities 30% Alliances of local and generalist associations	30% professional groups 30% State authorities 30% local public authorities
'Urban facilities damage the agricultural landscape' (27% of the conflicts)	• Conflicts related to the management of municipal land • Zoning/Permit • Housing, local activity zones • Wind turbines • Relay station	55% Municipalities 33% local associations	50% Municipalities 40% Professional groups
'Agricultural facilities or regulations consume or modify resources some wish to reserve for urban activities' (16% of the conflicts)	• Industrial sites and services of • Irrigation well drilling	Local associations Municipalities	Professional groups (farmers/ industrial branch)
'Nature conservation" uses of resources represent an obstacle to the agricultural exploitation of these resources' (8% of the conflicts)	• *Perimeter within which agricultural land uses are regulated.* • Sports damage	Individuals Professional groups (farming/ agribusiness)	Regional public authorities, State authorities

Type of incompatibility (covered by the Press)	Objects/facilities on which the contested activities rest	Actors initiating engagement in conflict	The actors targeted during the conflict
'The facilities or regulations meant for agricultural activities have a negative impact on the biodiversity resources' (1% of the conflicts)	• GMO crops	Associations Individuals Municipalities	Professional groups

16.3.3. The influence of the socio-economic context on the emergence of conflicts

As mentioned above, whether a conflict emerges or not depends on the ability of certain actors to perceive environmental changes, and to use information that enables them to evaluate the nature of the constraints caused by the close proximity or juxtaposition of certain incompatible land uses and their associated facilities and to initiate consultation with the actors at the origin of the contested uses. From a geographical perspective, one may ask in what social-spatial contexts all three criteria are met.

We have highlighted that there are statistically significant correlations[2] between the social-economic profile of municipalities[3] and the probability that a conflict is located within these municipalities. We have based our calculations, not on the location of the objects/facilities that are causing the conflicts, but on the location of the local actors (residents, professionals, elected representatives, local associations…) that initiated the conflictual process.

The test of influence of this geographic factor on the number of conflicts per municipality (Table 16.3) and the number of conflicts per resident (Table 16. 4) reveals that the municipalities with a " rural centre" profile are those that are the most prone to conflict, if we compare the number of conflicts to the number of municipalities with this profile. These municipalities are the most populated of the peri-urban zone with a rural morphology (5,000 inhab./town), their population growth is reduced and they are characterised by population ageing. They are often principal county towns. This indicator of conflictuality therefore seems strongly related to the population density, which increases the number of actors liable to engage in conflict.

---

2   The spatial correlations are assessed using a Chi-squared test based on contingency tables of the number of conflicts and of the total municipal population, per class of factors.

3   This typology was developed by the Agreste department of agricultural statistics, based on census data collected by the INSEE between 1990 and 1999.

Table 16.3 Influence of the social-economic profile of the municipality on the number of conflicts per municipality (the conflictual intensity corresponds here to the relation between the number of municipalities affected by one or several of the inventoried conflicts and the total number of municipalities with the profile)

	Origin of the actors who initiated the conflict			Preventive conflicts		Remedial conflicts	
	Number of municipalities with the profile	Number of municipalities identified	Conflictual intensity of the municipalities with profile	Number of municipalities identified	Conflictual intensity of the municipalities with the profile	Number of municipalities identified	Conflictual intensity of the municipalities with the profile
• **Geographical sectors**							
• *Paris metropolis*	-	28	-				
• *Urbanized Peri-urban (Outside typology)*	-	15	-				
• **Type of socio-economic profile**							
• Upper-class resid.	202	22	0.11	17	0.08	5	0.02
• Middle-class resid.	292	27	0.09	19	0.06	8	0.03
• Traditional rural	247	13	0.05	9	0.04	4	0.016
• Rural villages	92	9	0.10	5	0.05	4	0.04°
• Rural centres	187	36	**0.19****	27	**0.14****	9	**0.05°**
• Total	1020	107	0.15	77	0.07	30	0.03

** $P < 0.01$; ° $P > 0.1$

When we compare the number of conflicts with the total number of inhabitants in the municipalities with the same socio-economic profile, we find that the residents of municipalities with the 'upper-class resid.' and 'middle-class resid.' profiles are those that present the highest rate of conflictuality.

The municipalities with the 'upper-class resid.' profile are characterized by slow population growth (between 1990 and 1999), a high percentage of retired people and professional people with managerial or executive positions and a high rate of individual houses. It must be noted that agricultural spaces in these municipalities are smaller in terms of area and that forested zones are larger. These municipalities tend to be located on the Eastern side of the region, mainly in the Yvelines *département* but also in the Val d'Oise and Essonne.

The municipalities with the 'middle-class resid.' profile are characterized by a slightly faster population growth (between 1990 and 1999) and a larger percentage of young households. The municipalities with middle class populations in 1999 and whose conflictual rate per inhabitant is the highest are those that are situated on the fringes of the Yvelines and Essonne *départements* (symbolic conflicts related to the implementation of wind turbines) and in the new town of Sénart (conflicts related to the construction of public utility infrastructures, a prison, a camping site for itinerant people, etc). They are the municipalities in which large housing construction programmes were implemented in the 1990s and whose residential function is relatively diffuse.

Thus, even though their numbers are smaller, the 'local' actors (residents, farmers, elected representatives, local associations) of the residential rural zones are proportionally more reactive than those of denser zones. This correlation applies in the case of preventive conflicts, whereas, in that of remedial conflicts, the populations of municipalities with a 'middle-class resid.' and a 'rural village' profiles are those that have the highest rate of conflictuality.

Table 16.4 Influence of the social-economic profile of the municipality on the number of conflicts per municipality (the conflictual intensity of the profile corresponds here to the relation between the number of municipalities affected by one or several of the inventoried conflicts and the total number of residents of the municipalities with that profile)

	Origin of the actors who initiated the conflict			Preventive conflicts		Remedial conflicts	
	Total population of the profile	Number of municipalities identified	Conflictual intensity of the pop. of the profile	Number of municipalities affected by conflict	Conflictual intensity of the pop. of the profile	Number of municipalities identified	Conflictual intensity of the pop. of the profile
Upper-class resid.	214.5	22	0.10**	17	**0.08****	5	0.023
Middle-class resid.	237.5	27	0.11**	19	**0.08****	8	**0.033***
Traditional rural	186.3	13	0.07	9	0.05	4	0.021
Rural villages	107.5	9	0.08	5	0.05	4	**0.037***
Rural centres	993	36	0.04	27	0.03	9	0.009
Total	*1738.8*	*107*	*0.06*	*77*	*0.04*	*30*	*0.017*

** P<0,01 ; * P<0,05

16.4. Conclusion: Conflicts and Regulation of the Use of Agri-urban Resources as Reported by the Press

The information provided by the Press indicates that the uses of agri-urban resources are regulated through social processes, and more particularly through protests against the development of regulations or infrastructures serving urban and non-agricultural activities. A number of these conflicts are related to the implementation of urban waste management facilities and to certain unplanned temporary uses of open spaces (caravan sites, outdoor recreation uses, etc.). Indeed, the urban consumption of agricultural land is regulated, and the degradation of the water and atmospheric resources circulating between the different peri-urban territories is controlled by means of protest against these uses.

Other articles from the Press in our collection reveal, however, that other types of conflicts also play a part in this regulation; these conflicts involve protests against the impact of certain agricultural facilities or practices on the resources destined for urban consumption. The nature of the groups of actors initiating these processes of regulation is determined, on the one hand, by their ability to show the links between the resources under threat and the contested facilities or practices, and, on the other, their ability to approach hierarchical or influence networks so as to be able to take action at the appropriate governance level (i.e. territorial, governmental or economic authorities).

We have also shown that all these conditions were met, in the case of preventive conflicts, within upper- and middle-class residential rural municipalities, and, in the case of remedial conflicts, within middle-class residential rural municipalities, as well as in the newly attractive rural villages. We can deduce from this that though the spatial morphology of municipalities explains the nature of the protected resources and of the contested objects, it is the 'residential rural' profile of the actors that conditions their ability to engage in a conflict that is reported by the Press. Our results confirm the general intuition of Ley and Mercer (1980).

References

Boisson, J.-P. 2005. *La maîtrise foncière, clé du développement rural: pour une nouvelle politique foncière*. Paris: Conseil Economique et Social.

Bruinsma, W., Hertog Leusden, W. (eds.) 2003. Annotated bibliography on urban agriculture. The Netherlands: ETC - Urban Agriculture Programme.

Bryant, C.R. 1992. Agriculture in the city's countryside. Toronto: University of Toronto Press.

Bryant, C.R. 1973a. L'agriculture face à l'urbanization: le cas des exploitations de grande culture expropriées par l'emprise de l'aéroport Paris-Nord. Economie Rurale, 95, 23-35.

Bryant, C.R. 1973b. L'agriculture face à la croissance métropolitaine, le cas des exploitations fruitières de Groslay et Deuil-la-Barre dans la grande banlieue nord de Paris. Economie Rurale, 98, 35-55.

Caron, A. and Torre, A. 2005. Conflits d'usage et de voisinage dans les espaces ruraux, in *Proximités et Changements Socio-Économiques dans les Mondes Ruraux*, coordinated by A. Torre, M. Filippi. Paris: INRA Editions.

IAURIF, 2005. Sensible ralentissement de la consommation d'espaces naturels et agricoles en Ile de France: les derniers résultats du MOS 2003. 387, Paris: IAURIF.

Kirat, T. and Torre, A. (dir) 2006. Conflits d'usage et dynamiques spatiales: les antagonismes dans l'occupation des espaces périurbains et ruraux. Géographie, Economie et Société, 8(3).

Ley, D. and Mercer, J. 1980. Locational conflicts and the politics of consumption. *Economic Geography*, 56(2), 89-109.

Melé, P., Larrue, C. et Rosemberg, M. (coord.) 2003. Conflits et Territoires. Presses Universitaires François Rabelais, collection perspectives «Villes et Territoires», 6.

Melé, P. 2004. Introduction: conflits, territoires et actions publique, in *Conflits et territoires*, coordinated by P. Melé, C. Larrue and M. Rosemberg, Presses Universitaires François Rabelais, collection perspectives «Villes et Territoires», 6, 13-32.

Mormont, M. 2006. Conflit et Territorialisation, *Géographie, Economie et Société*. 8(3), 299-318.

Moustier, P. and Salam Fall A. 2004. Les dynamiques de l'agriculture urbaine: caractéristiques et evaluation, in Développement durable de l'agriculture urbaine en Afrique francophone. Enjeux, concepts et méthodes, editeb by O.B. Smith, P. Moustier, L.J.A. Mougeot and A.S. Fall. CIRAD, CRDI, 23-43.

Owen, L., Howard, W. and Waldron, M. 2000. Conflicts over farming practices in Canada: the role of interactive conflict resolution approaches. *Journal of Rural Studies*, 16, 475-483.

Rucht, D., Koopmans, R. and Neidhardt, F., (eds.) 1992. Act of dissent, New developments in the study of protest. Rowman and Littlefield publishers, 349 p.

Trudelle, C. 2003. Au-delà des mouvements sociaux, pour une typologie relationnelle des conflits sociaux. Cahiers de Géographie du Québec, 47(131), 223-242.

PART V
Conclusion

Chapter 17

Lessons from Successful Small Towns

Teresa de Noronha Vaz, Eveline van Leeuwen and Peter Nijkamp

Human settlement patterns all over the world show a great diversity. But they have one thing in common: they serve people in varied spatial situations, in both urbanized and rural areas. In the literature, there has been a tendency to address the urbanized part of our world, but in many regions we still observe rurality as a common phenomenon. This book aimed to focus attention on the possible contribution of towns to rural development. By acting as a place of knowledge creation and innovation diffusion, towns – even the smallest – can combat processes of structural decline and even act as a catalyst for a geographically-balanced income distribution and sustainable productive structure. How to take advantage of the often hidden potential existing in urban areas in the rural world in order to favour competitiveness and to encourage economic health has been extensively discussed in the 16 preceeding chapters of this volume on "Towns in a Rural World". Clearly, towns have a role to play in less urbanized regions, but their role is not undisputed. As in Gruber and Soci (2010), peripheries also have a functional role in society, and within such areas, small towns agglomerate knowledge, skills and promote networking systems.

Whether or not small towns will survive as strong players in the coming decades strongly depends on their resilience in reorganizing their urban structures, and improving their critical attributes. Most of the success of European small towns relies, in the end, on their ability to devise and monitor development strategies designed to make the best use of their territorial resources, to optimize sectoral policies, and to deal with all crucial dimensions of sustainable development.

In contemporary societies, small and medium-sized towns are an important element of the global settlement system.

In terms of housing the biggest proportions of the world's population, large cities are followed by small and medium-sized towns. Big cities, as well as small and medium-sized towns, have resulted from the specific human atavism: big cities result from the human propensity to live in a group. On the other hand, small towns reflect the human yearning to live in harmony with nature broadly defined (at least to some extent). Nature's rhythm makes individuals and groups pursue their goals in the most effective way possible. Thus small towns acquire a special importance in this respect.

An important characteristic of many rural areas is the still dominant position of the agricultural sector. Not only is the production process of farms different from that of firms, but also the lifestyle of those persons active in the agricultural sector often differs from the rural lifestyle of those who are engaged in other non-farm activities. Nowadays, with the decreasing economic importance of agriculture, new economic activities are possible and needed in rural areas in order to achieve a more appropriate balance between urban and rural areas. What can we learn from the presentation of the various chapters in this volume?

The analysis of 24 European towns in Chapter 2 showed convincingly that towns continue to be important places for local households to shop and to work. In particular in countries like Poland and Portugal, households are still very dependent on the local economy. However, it is also in these countries that economic diversity is relatively low. In particular, the Polish rural areas continue to have a large share of total employment in agriculture. This means that new developments, such as new farming regulations, new technologies, or modernization will have very strong local effects. People who lose their jobs will have few opportunities to find a new one, and thus will have less money to spend in the local economy. Therefore, in particular, towns are very important places from which to start new economic activities and local development projects, and, at the same time, preserve the indispensable ecosystem services. In this sense, they form a bridge between social community capital and ecological cultural heritage, on the one hand, and the new growth and creativity trends, on the other. An important question coming from Chapter 14 is, however, how rural areas can keep their assets and traditions, while exploiting their increasing attractiveness. How can the transformation of rural areas from being depreciated to being appreciated be sustained?

First of all, rural networks and partnerships (rural social capital) appear to be very important. Goods and services can be delivered by governments in a number of different ways. Governments that previously both produced and provided services, now tend to rely increasingly on the market either for inputs to government production and provision or for the direct provision of goods and services. This change has occurred for ideological reasons and to obtain better value for money, i.e. in order to ensure the best use of resources. Public-private partnership (PPP) is part of this trend. Through PPP the government enters into a long-term contract with a private partner to deliver a good or service.

As Chapter 6 describes, there are many examples of an improvement in the provision of public goods by private firms, especially in the telecommunications sector, in countries where people have money to spend. But there are also many examples where privatization of the provision of public goods has had negative effects, from the British railway system to the drinking water supply in Latin-American and African cities. In all cases, deregulation and privatization have reduced the capacity of state institutions to intervene in economic processes.

Although sometimes PPP is seen primarily as a way to privatize public services, PPP implementation could actually prevent excessive pressure from building up within public systems driving them to move towards privatization. We should not forget that PPP is a type of public procurement in the sense that the combination of market efficiency and public interest in satisfying needs of the population is made possible through this model. This combination allows for private production along with guarantees of public regulations and institutions.

In Chapter 3 it is even stated that small and medium-sized towns could act as a laboratory to experiment with new forms of PPP: for example, when deciding where to locate education centres, such as universities, in towns. As Chapter 10 describes, for medium-sized towns with a population of between 50,000 and 200,000 inhabitants, the challenge to engage in the Knowledge Economy can be quite a difficult one, in particular when there is no higher education centre in the local area. However, higher education centres can only be useful for a town when there is a close collaboration between different stakeholders and government levels, and when the needs of the towns are clearly defined.

Cooperation between local stakeholders is also very important when developing the tourism sector in less favoured areas. Chapter 12 discusses how the lack of new models of governance that encourage the implementation of integrated strategies, in order to increase the local critical mass, has had a negative effect on the development of Almeida in Portugal as a modest tourist attraction.

A second important factor in rural development is the transfer of knowledge in rural environments. Chapter 8 showed that the key features that relate to a town's innovative capacity depend on complementarities between internal and external sources of knowledge. It appears that the capacity for technological transfers grows with the presence of an increasing number of entrepreneurs, particularly in the creative industries and knowledge-intensive business services. In addition, from Chapter 4 it may be concluded that the presence of many small firms in different sectors has a positive effect on new firm formation in all sectors. Hence, the more small firms there are, the higher the potential for new firm formation.

Chapter 11 explains how small towns could encourage the innovation process by extending ICT infrastructure, developing the agro-food chain and by cooperating in research and development in specific fields and sectors (Chapter 11). It is no longer possible to foresee future spatial developments without considering the influence of the practicability brought by the use of ICTs. Increasingly more affordable to all, they redefine the productive models based upon the diffusion of information, by means of e-learning, e-commerce and e-production and social-networking. Unlimited possibilities will produce opportunities, precisely because different ideas and creative thinking are the greatest incentives to move forwards.

Nevertheless, chapter 9 warned that, despite some positive effects of information and knowledge systems in rural areas, the implementation of these new systems mau have ambiguous and even detrimental implications for a regions long-term development prospects, and even seems to be destroying the role of production agglomeration economies in small and medium-sized towns.

However, as underlined in chapter 15, the effectiveness of actions that focus on the transfer of knowledge and innovation, through the development of internet technologies, depends on the functional types of these towns (e.g. peripheral, agricultural, tourist or residential/industrial). When these functional types are taken into account, improvement of ICT accessibility may lead to: (i) Orientation of the labour force and local business in the peripheral territories toward opportunities in neighbouring urban centres; (ii) increase of self-employment in tourism-recreational communes, with further development of communication with urban centres; (iii) support of city centres with information on the possibilities offered in the surroundings territories; (iv) increase of access to information in rural communes, both for farmers who are searching for new technologies and markets and for farmers who are willing to up take non-agricultural activities or are searching for seasonal non-agricultural jobs; and (v) support of uptake of home-based work in residential-industrial communes.

Apart from ICT these are other ways for rural areas to keap the benefits of urban agglomeration economies. Chapter 5 introduced the new concept of the Agricultural District to support corporate networks of entrepreneurs in the primary sector. As another solution chapter 7 proposed the formation of clusters of small and medium-sized towns.

A third factor that affects the development of towns in rural areas, also mentioned above, are urban-rural interdependencies. Small and medium-sized towns are an important element of the continuum between rural and urban areas, including the peri-urban areas which, as Chapter 16 demonstrated have their own particular problems of conflicting land uses. At present a feature of this continuum is tolerant complementarity and duality rather than dualism. The most important relationship between towns, hinterlands and regions tends to occur in this particular continuum. The concept of self-organization and related theories (including Christaller's theory) explain, albeit not in an entirely satisfactory way, the power, structure and spatial distribution of these relationships. As is described in Chapter 11, towns, which are smaller urban agglomerations with an administrative function and a lifestyle relatively similar to urban areas, have developed a relationship with rural areas mainly regarding trade, employment opportunities, migration and remittances, exchange of population and services to the rural area. The influence of small towns depends, however, on their economic, social and cultural strengths.

In addition, today peri-urban areas can no longer be considered merely as a stock for future urban expansion. The green belt surrounding the town represents a strong economic and ecological asset to be protected. Small towns may manage such areas even better than other urban structures and can guarantee their protection. For that, the most necessary requirement is to promote the existence of professional actors with conditions to support the survival of a sustainable multifunctional agricultural economy. Another option is the development of new "eco-neighbourhoods". The goal of such locations is to save natural resources, to limit energy consumption, and to decrease travelling, thereby promoting the use of public transportation and the integration of different social classes.

The title of this concluding chapter is 'Lessons from Successful Small Towns', because various changes with impacts on spatial development are expected to take place in the near future, such as climate change and also a decrease of population in the Western (European) countries. Those impacts on daily urban life, on transportation systems, on urban industrial design, and on the existing biodiversity should be investigated and monitored, so as to arrive at transferable lessons for other towns and regions. Planners need to be able to adapt their tools and their practices to face these big challenges, to reduce the impacts of future urban development on natural resources, and to create better living environments, and as advocated in chapter 13, an unproved balance between urban and rural environments.

As town competition will increase, towns will have to attract citizens with increasingly appealing amenities and services. It is very important that municipalities in the rural peripheries be aware of the approaching reality so that appropriate strategies may be prepared in advance. Immaterial interventions are expected in the first place – at least, at the level of the conceptualization of what kind of a small town the planners envisage for the future. In this respect, it is necessary to ensure that the chaotic growth of small towns must no longer occur, because if not properly planned small towns will vanish forever. If, on the other hand, planners want to formulate sound future strategies, then it would be advisable to rely on indicators such as the historical pathways of these towns and their present identities. To build up from such already existing values may save some investments from potential failure, although, at the same time, these small or medium-sized urban structures of the future should also be ready to offer new, quite complex, life-quality products to their residents and visitors.

Today, rural areas are increasingly places that are appreciated by (urban) citizens through the experience of the rural idyll. Although this appreciation of towns and rural areas started with the pursuit of quality of life, today what makes a village attractive depends on its will to be part of the global system, and on the will to be known by outsiders and to accept new developments (novelty). Towns may take advantage of their very precious cultural and architectural heritages. The international reputations of such historical or modern outstanding environments are based on different economic activities, and attract people, as residents or tourists, pulling in further development opportunities such as investments and jobs. Sometimes, labels have to be created to emphasize the cultural attributes of such towns. In other words, the 'idolization' of attractive towns depends not only on their intrinsic visual qualities, but also on their creative capacity and openness to today's network society (Chapter 14).

References

Gruber, S. and Soci, A. 2010. Agglomeration, Agriculture, and the Perspective of the Periphery. *Spatial Economic Analysis*, 5(1), 43-72.

Index